Twin Evils:

Communism & Facisim

By George F. Nafziger, Ph.D.

Cover Art from George Nafziger
Twin Evils: Communism and Fascism by George Nafziger
This edition published in 2026

Published by Winged Hussar Publishing, LLC
Wrong Way Books
1525 Hulse Road, Unit 1
Point Pleasant, NJ 08742

PB ISBN 978-1-969892-02-8
EB ISBN 978-1-969892-03-5

Bibliographical References and Index
1. History. 2. Political. 3. World

Winged Hussar Publishing 2026 All rights reserved

For more information on Winged Hussar Publishing, LLC, visit us at:
https://www.whpsupplyroom

This book is sold subject to the condition that it shall not, by way of trade or otherwise, be lent, resold, hired out, or otherwise circulated without the publisher's prior consent in any form of binding or cover other than that in which it is published and without a similar condition, including this condition, being imposed on the subsequent purchaser.

The scanning, uploading, and distribution of this book via the Internet or via any other means without the permission of the publisher is illegal and punishable by law. Please purchase only authorized electronic editions, and do not participate in or encourage electronic piracy of copyrighted materials. Your support of the author's and publisher's rights is appreciated. Karma, its everywhere.

Acknowledgement

I would like to express my thanks and acknowledge the contributions of John R. Shock to the preparation of this work. John selflessly spent hours reading, critiquing, editing, and contributing to this work. Without his efforts it would not be what you see before you today.

THE EVIL TWINS:
COMMUNISM AND FASCISM

By George F. Nafziger, Ph.D.

TABLE OF CONTENTS

Introduction 2

Chapter 1 Feudalism 5

Chapter 2 The Prelude to Maxism: Babeufism 15

Chapter 3 Marx and Engels 26

Chapter 4 Lenin and Stalin 99

Chapter 5 Mao and Maoism 154

Chapter 6 Global Marxism 215

Chapter 7 What is Fascism, Mussolini's Rise to
          Power and Italian Fascism 239

Chapter 8 Nazism and Hitler 283

Chapter 9 Comparisons of Communism and
          Fascism 302

Chapter 10 The Historical and Pyscological Basis
           of Communism and Fascism 317

Chapter 11 Where We Stand Today 331

Bibliography 361

INTRODUCTION

There is an old saying that the road to hell is paved with good intentions. That road has may forks that lead to the same end, misery and suffering. This is true with Marxism, socialism, communism and fascism. All sang sweet siren songs of relief from suffering, equality, and freedom, and all have lead to the same hellish totalitarianism, where one oppressive system is replaced by another. Marxism, socialism, and communism are purely variations of the same song. Marx described his theories as both socialism and communism. Fascism might seem opposed to it, but its roots are absolutely founded in the socialist idealism.

The origins of both communism and fascism are found can find their origins in the French Revolution even though while communism seems to have sprung fully formed from the mind of Carl Marx. They were both a response to the grinding poverty that had affected most the world's population since the beginning of time.

Prior to the French Revolution there were essentially two three classes of people: the nobility, clerics and the masses. The former had held the latter under control by means of physical force and religion. The nobility had as its allies both in a collection of minor nobility who shared in the best that the world had to offer and provided the muscle to enforce the will of the king. There was also the priestly class who controlled the mines minds of the masses, and which was the second and third sons of the nobility who would not inherit the noble's title and fief.

The first crack in this system occurred when the starving French citizens of Paris rose up against their king and his ally, the Catholic Church. An obscure Frenchman, Gracchus Babeuf, who swam in the sea of revolutionary tumult, had a program of ideas that would was the source of both communism and fascism. He cast his ideas on the fields of revolution, but they did sprout for another 60 years. It is interesting to note that his ideas were far too radical for the Jacobins, who sent him to the guillotine.

The revolutionary politicians who took control of France quickly attacked the infrastructure of the existing system. A national assembly was formed in which the common man had a voice. Because the leaders of the Catholic Church were the second and third sons of the nobility, the Church was seen as part of the problem, so the Church was stripped of its wealth, Christianity was uprooted, and efforts were made to obliterate it. The Paris mob struck back at all who they perceived as being their oppressors. In October 1793, the Christian calendar was replaced by a new calendar starting with the day the Revolution began, its holidays were secular dates celebrating the Revolution. New forms of moral religion emerged, including the deistic Cult of the Supreme Being and the atheistic Cult of Reason.

Marx had described religion as the opiate of the masses. Its function in the pre-French Revolution system had been to convince the masses that God willed them to be poor, to starve, and to suffer, and that they were to accept their condition because it was the will of God - Deus vult. This was, of course, a misinterpretation and a perversion of Christianity that was employed by the men of Medieval Church, its popes, cardinals, and bishops and the various kings and emperors. They used Deus vult to justify their position, their power, the luxury they enjoyed, and to control the masses. They even created the concept of the Divine Right of Kings, which the Church supported.

The French Revolution also brought out framed the concept of nationalism and spread it across Europe. Nationalism is a fundamental element of fascism. The common man began to see himself as French, English, etc., something that was absolutely new. If God willed it, then God had willed the execution of Louis XVI. There was, of course, a counter revolution. However, it was different as the counter revolutionaries were the Kings of England and Prussia, the Holy Roman Emperor, the Republic of the Netherlands, the Czar of Russia, and even the Pope and the various dukes in Italy. They sent armies to invade France and a force of émigré French nobility was part of those armies.

The foundation was destroyed in the minds of men and even though the Bourbons returned to the French throne, all the other European thrones had been undercut and weakened. There were further revolutions. France had revolutions in 1789, 1830 and 1848; between 1810 and 1820 the Spanish colonies in the New World rebelled; in 1820, there were uprisings in Portugal, Spain, Italy, and Greece; in 1848 all of Europe suffered from revolutions; in 1870 a commune was set up in France after the Germans defeated Napoleon III at Sedan and the existing government collapsed. Not all of these revolutions were the result of economic issues, as both the Polish and Greek revolutions were seeking national independence. Even so, those revolutions were based on the concept of nationalism, which is, as mentioned earlier, a fundamental element of fascism. {How does the American Revolution fit into this? It deserves a mention as it contains elements of all the above}

These foundations laid, it was the industrial revolution and the revolution of science that occurred during the 19th century that added fuel to the philosophical foment. The ideas of Gracchus Babeuf and the other French revolutionaries evolved, boiled, and were picked up by others. They then split into two competing theories.

Twin Evils

It is not the intention of this work to examine the causes of those revolutions, but to document the evolution of political thought that produced communism and fascism; to examine their historical roots and their ideologies; to compare and contrast them; and to point out the flaws in their philosophies.

CHAPTER I
FEUDALISM

Why should a system intended to provide the worker an escape from capitalism's oppression result in a return to the feudal system?

To understand, we need to again examine the feudal system's components. In feudalism, the king owned all the land in theory, which at that time was the principal industrial process of 99% of society. Yes, there were some craftsmen who escaped their bondage to the land and by their trades established themselves independent of feudalism's chains. These craftsmen formed the kernel around which the first European cities were formed. By their trades, they slowly created the industries that produce today's economies. They would later become the hated bourgeoises.

There were three types of farmers; the "freeholder", who owned the land he worked and the "serf". There were many variations of this system, but this is its fundamental basis. For the sake of simplicity, I will speak of the system as it existed in France.

In Medieval France, all land belonged to the king with few exceptions, under an "allodial" title. However, he was not the landlord of all land; some pieces were owned by men who were not in a feudal relationship with the king. This relationship meant that those to whom the king granted "fiefs" of land owed him various services, including military service if a war should occur, and they were taxed by the king.

The freehold farmers [*censitaire*] were actually bonded tenant farmers holding a *cens*. These tenants held their land as a loan or *tenure roturière* from a lord. The freeholder had economic ownership of his land and the freeholder did not have personal obligations to his Lord, He was also a free man, i.e. not a serf. He did have obligations, however, that included the following:

- Pay a *seigneurial taille aux quatre cas* to his lord in certain cases;
- Pay a compensation for having the loan *le cens*; or
- Pay a rent for the loan *rente foncière seigneurial;*
- Work for his lord on certain times corvée; [1]
- Was obliged to use manorial facilities *banalités*, i.e., use the

---
[1] Secretan, E., *Essai sur la Féodalité* (Lausanne, Switzerland : Bridel, 1858) p. 68.

noble's mill;
- Pay the *Lods et Vends*

The first of these obligations, the *taille seigneuriale aux quatre cas* [seigneurial tax in all four cases] consisted of chivalry, crusade, ransom, and the marriage of any daughters. However, if another agreement had been made, it could entail up to nine cases. This could mean that a landlord could claim this tax when he bought land or had children. [2]

The chivalry obligation meant that the son of the lord was admitted to the *Ordre du Saint Esprit* [Order of the Holy Spirit]. The second, the crusade or *voyage d'outremer* [overseas voyage] a mandated a pilgrimage to the Holy Land or joining in a crusade, which eventually became irrelevant.

The case of ransom arose when the lord was taken prisoner and held for ransom. This payment occurred when the ransom was due. In the last case, the marriage of daughters was, depending on circumstances applied only to the first marriage of the eldest daughter, or to the first marriage of all the daughters of the lord. This provided a dowry for the daughter. The height of the *taille aux quatre cas* was primarily fixed upon the value of one year's *cens*.

Le cens, a tax imposed on the vassal and owed the lord, involved the transfer of the economic ownership of the land. This had often been made on the condition of *cens*. The annual *cens* and fixed fee attached to the land were held by the tenant or vassal.[3] Most of the *cens* contracts had been instituted in medieval times for a fixed amount of money. By 1700 the height of the *cens* was often unchanged and still something like 1 or 2 *sou* for each *arpent* of land (about 5,000 square meters).

The public and private *cens* often came to merge as a result of the immunities leading to concession of taxes, which were so numerous. Their union in the same hands became the rule, when, following the establishment of the feudal regime, the nobility appropriated both taxes and land.
Hence two species of *cens* which were linked, the first, to the sovereignty of the lord, the second, to his ownership of the land.

The first, recognizing the lordship and representing the old tax, was called *chef cens* (*capitalis cens*), *menu cens*, because of its modesty. It was regulated in a fairly uniform manner at so much per house, so much per acre (*census fonsalis*). The second, rather a rent, was more

---

[2] Ibid. p. 328.
[3] Secretan, E., *Essai sur la Féodalité* (Lausanne, Switzerland: Bridel, 1858) p. 68.
Seignohos, C., *The Feudal Regime* (New York: Hold, 1907) p. 14.

related to income and, for this reason, called *croit de cens* (*incrementum censûs*), *surcens, gros cens* or *cher cens*. We further opposed the first, also called *cens coutumier*, established by virtue of custom, with the second, *cens contractuel,* the result of a contract.

Let's summarize their differences.

The head tax is a tax; it is recognitive of lordship, imprescriptible, indivisible, small, invariable, and finally *querable,* that is to say that, to pay, the debtor waits the agent of the lord, as in the past the taxpayer waited for money from the Roman and later royal *fis*.[4]

The *surcens*, like the *cens,* was an amount of money, or a specified amount of produce, fixed for eternity. Often the lord imposed it in addition to the original *cens* when he owned the loan and gave it to someone new. If given to someone new, further obligations could be imposed.

The second form of land holding was the *rente foncière seigneurial,* which was almost certainly a variation of *cens.* This brought an institute of Roman law into seigneurial relations.

The basic *rente foncière* was a leasehold whereby the economic property was transferred for eternity and for a fixed price (in money or in kind), on the condition that the *rente* was paid.[5] At its base the *rente foncière* was a debt that produced by a piece of land. This *rente foncière* could not be paid off and the obligation to pay was transferred to any party who took possession of the land. It was possible, however, that a redemption could be stipulated for the *rente foncière*. This stipulation therefore, was a provision in the *rente foncière* providing for a transfer of ownership, thus making it a mortgage. Among the cities and towns of France, a *rente foncière* was either a mortgage or was made redeemable by royal decree.

Then there was the the *rente foncière seigneurial* which was variant that bound the land to a lord. It arose when an explicit stipulation of retaining fealty was made. It had some advantages over the ordinary *rente foncière*. It was from fealty that the obligation that the holder of the land was obliged to pay the *lods* and *vents* when he sold it.[6]

The *Champart seigneurial* or *terrage* was the obligation to pay a certain amount of the produce to the landlord. The *champart seugneurial,* which was a variant of the *cens.* This was the case when the *champart* was the only stipulation that had been made for the loan, or if it had been stipulated together with the *cens* in money. *Coutumiers de champart* was

---
[4] Fachan, J.M., *Finances Féodales* (Paris : Félix Alcan et Guillaumin Rénis, 1909) p. 23.
[5] Seignohos, C., *The Feudal Regime* (New York: Hold, 1907) p. 17.
[6] Seignohos, C., *The Feudal Regime* (New York: Hold, 1907) p. 17

applicable only to grains, not to grapes or vegetables *de droit* **écrit**. The *champart* could be applicable to all produce and was generally called the *agrier*. Just like the *cens,* the *champart seigneurial* carried *Lods et Vents* and was not subject to *usucaption.*[7]

The *champart seigneurial* or the *champart* was rarely customary; it usually derived from a bailiff concession.

The duty on grain was generally called *civerttgé* (*eiveragium, civadagcum*) and *mestive* (*mestiva*); however *civerage* designated more particularly the duty on oats, *mestive*, the duty on wheat. The right of *champart* was also called *agrier*, in the North and *agrer* (*agrarium, agrerium*), in the South, where the word *tasque* was still frequently used. In some provinces it was called the *terrage* (*terragium*) the *agriculture*, the *ychide*, and in the Bourbonnais and Auvergne the *parciere* (between the *champart* and the *dîme*.)[8]

The *lods et vends* were payable when the *cens* or *champart* changed hands by sale. These generally amount to a fifth (*quint*) and a fifth again of that (*requint*) of the value of the contract by which it was sold. In Normandy it amounted to a twelfth (8.333%).

Some *coutumes* distinguished *lods* from *vents*. According to the *coutume* of Troyes, the seller owed the sales and the buyer the lods and in half. Article 199 of the *coutume* of Meaux states that the buyer owes half of the *lods* and *vents* and the seller the other half, "if it is not said francs deniers to the seller." On the other hand, in the Contume of Etampes, *lods* and *vents* are one and the same right. This distinction between lodging duties, paid by the buyer, and sales duties, by the seller, disappeared and the two rights merged from the thirteenth century.

Auxerre custom set the amount of *lods* at two sols and that of *vents* at 20 deniers. The rate of *lods* and *vents* was generally set at one twelfth of the value of the goods. It was lower than that of similar duties collected on fiefdoms.[9]

It did not amount to the value of the *cens* and the lord could not demand an estimation. The contractors could simulate a lower price in order to evade the *lods et vents*. [10] The *lods* and *vents* were far more extensive than just these feudal dues and go beyond the scope of this work. These are but a sample.

---

[7] Secretan, E., *Essai sur la Féodalité* (Lausanne, Switzerland : Bridel, 1858) p. 387.
[8] Fachan, J.M., *Finances Féodales* (Paris : Félix Alcan et Guillaumin Rénis, 1909) pp. 27-28.
[9] Fachan, J.M., *Finances Féodales* (Paris : Félix Alcan et Guillaumin Rénis, 1909) pp. 84-84.
[10] Secretan, E., *Essai sur la Féodalité* (Lausanne, Switzerland : Bridel, 1858) p. 68.

As for *corvées* and *banalités* the *corvée* was an obligation to work for the lord for a limited number of days each year.[11] The *corvées* that lasted longer, were often paid off, but were usually replaced by the *corvée royal;* this entailed working on streets, roads, canals, or fortifications. The *banalités* could entail the obligation to use the manorial mill, cellars and ovens for a specific price.

As for the third form, and the largest part of the population, the serfs had an implied servitude and personal obligations to the lord independent of holding the loan. More specifically, the serf or *main-mortable* did not own a right to the land, but only the right to possess it.

The *coutume* of Nivernois was, reputedly, the most difficult. Here the serfs could be taxed by their lord, at will - but within reason - annually. The tax was imposed upon the body of these serfs, their houses, and what they held on condition of servitude. The lord of such a village also had the right to pursue his serfs for these taxes if they left the seigneurie. He could then seize their holdings, and they became his property when the serf was absent for 30 years. If the serf died without immediate heirs, his holding resorted to the landlord.

The serf's obligations to his landlord were as follows:
- Pay the *taille à volonté* [tax at will] that the seigneur could levy from the serfs living on his premises;
- Pay a seigneurial [*taille aux quatre cas*] to his seigneur [landlord] in certain cases; [12]
- Pay a head tax [*chevage*] to his lord on account of his personal obligation to the lord; [13]
- Work for his seigneur on certain times, the *corvée;*
- Obliged to use manorial facilities *banalités;*
- Could not leave the domain without permission [*forfuyance*][14];
- Could not marry freely [*formarriage*][15];
- Could not inherit freely [*main-mortabilité*].

---

[11] Demante, G. *Etude historique sur les Gens de Condition Mainmortable en France au XVIII Siecle* (Paris: Picard, 1804) p. 25.

[12] Secretan, E., *Essai sur la Féodalité* (Lausanne, Switzerland : Bridel, 1858) p. 326.

[13] Secretan, E., *Essai sur la Féodalité* (Lausanne, Switzerland : Bridel, 1858) p. 573. Morel, *La commune de Compiègne 1153-1319* (Compiègne: Lefebvre, 1901) p. 8.

[14] Anonymous, *Memoire pour l'Entirere Abolition de la Servitude en France* (Paris: Chenault, 1765) p.54.

[15] Morel, *La commune de Compiègne 1153-1319* (Compiègne: Lefebvre, 1901) p. 8.

Twin Evils

The *taille à volonté* or *taille a merci*[16] [mercy tax] was a tax as high as the landlord may determine. By 1700 this had been severely limited. At that time, it could only be imposed once a year. It was also subject to *usucaption* when it had not been levied in 40 years. It was, furthermore, possible to make a subscription to this *taille*, the so-called *taille abonnée* [subscribed tax]. It seems that this *taille á volonté* could be levied as a sum payable by all the serfs of the seigneurie as a group. It could either be levied in money or in kind.[17]

Though the *taille à volonté* was limited to once a year the lord could add to it the *taille aux quatre cas*.

The *chevage* or head tax was a tax that had, for some time, been levied upon foreigners and bastards, mainly in Vermandois but also Compeigne. It was abolished by 1700.

The concept of *forfuyance* meant that the serf was not permitted to leave the domain of his lord without permission.[18] The penalty for doing so varied. Originally it could be the loss of all his property and his loan. He was required to pay the seigneurial taxes. The concept of *formarriage* meant that the serf was not permitted to freely marry someone outside his lord's lands. The original basis for this was that the seigneur would lose laborers; the children of such a marriage were legally obligated to the mother's original lord. By 1700 this too was abolished.

For the serf's existence as a class the most important component of his legal position came from the the concept of *mainmorte*.[19] Originally, this meant that the holder of the loan held it with a "dead hand". The "dead hand" could not make a will, could not sell it, and could not give away. At the death of the serf, the lord could give the loan to one or more of his children, or he could give it to anyone else at his discretion. By 1700, this had changed so that a serf could usually leave his estate to those living with him.

Farming as a serf under these conditions may not seem a very desirable way to farm. On the other hand, the serf did have permanent right to the land he farmed. He could not easily be evicted, and his rights were

---

[16] Secretan, E., *Essai sur la Féodalité* (Lausanne, Switzerland : Bridel, 1858) p. 555.

[17] Demante, G. *Ètude historique sur les Gens de Condition Mainmortable en France au XVIII Siècle* (Paris: Picard, 1804) pp. 23-25.

[18] Seignohos, C., *The Feudal Regime* (New York: Hold, 1907) p. 12.
Anonymous, *Memoire pour l'Entirere Abolition de la Servitude en France* (Paris: Chenault, 1765) p. 54.

[19] Secretan, E., Essai sur la Féodalité (Lausanne, Switzerland : Bridel, 1858) p. 204, 435.
Demante, G. *Etude historique sur les Gens de Condition Mainmortable en France au XVIII Siecle* (Paris: Picard, 1804) pp. 15 , 30-31.

inheritable. As a result, his rights were very similar to the ownership that the *censitaire* enjoyed. Compared to some of the farmers described below, he was well off. During medieval times the majority of the rural population were serfs. However, by 1700 serfs were a minority. This resulted from the nobility's self-interest.

As history marched toward the French Revolution, the rights of the nobility's tenants and serfs eroded because of money tampering and inflation. That part of the nobility which was sufficiently affluent or powerful, therefore, tried to replace the feudal rights by more modern instruments that rendered a price that was proportional to the economic value of their land. The first of these was the *bail à rente foncière* which was a freehold where the economic property was transferred for eternity and for a fixed price (in money or in kind), all on condition that the *rente* was paid. The essence of a *rente foncière* was that it was a debt due by a piece of realty. A *rente foncière* was a portion of fruit delivered by the tenant in recognition of the original concession of the fund. It could also derive from capital lent to the holder of the fund, which encumbered its land with the agreed interest; but generally land rent arises from the first of these two origins.[20] If it could not be paid, and the obligation to pay was transferred to any party coming into possession of the land.

Because the vast majority of land was held by lords, getting the "ownership" of a land under a simple *rente foncière*[21] was difficult. If a lord was prepared to close such a deal, he needed permission from his lord, and the buyer became the vassal of that lord. This had nothing to do with the vast majority of the population and involved only members of the nobility. A simple *rente foncière* for a farmer was possible in case of *Franc-aleu*, but because of the scarcity of such land this was not likely either.

The *rente foncière* was something very different from farms or rents; and the difference was the difference between an annuity lease and a rental or farm lease. The latter did not grant to the tenant or farmer any right of inheritance, which is given to him for rent or to farm the property in full residence with the lessor; it only produced personal obligations that the parties reciprocally contracted towards each other: the farms or rents therefore only constituted a pure personal debt of the tenant or farmer who was obliged towards the lessor to pay them to him for the price of the fruits of each year's harvest of the leased property, which the lessor was

---

[20] Thomassin, *Essai sur les rentes foncières* (Strasbourg: Levrault, 1800) p. 3.
[21] Secretan, E., Essai sur la Féodalité (Lausanne, Switzerland : Bridel, 1858) p. 387. 391-2, & 435.

obliged to collect from the farmer or tenant as inheritance. On the contrary, through an annuity lease, the property of the annuity leased inheritance is transferred to the lessee without the burden of the annuity that the lessor retained in this inheritance, this annuity is due mainly by the inheritance and by each party of the inheritance on which it was imposed, although the lessee and his successors were also personally debtors, as long as they possess the inheritance.[22]

As can be seen, feudalism involved the vast majority of the population under obligations to the nobility. The obligations were paid in the form of taxes (money or kind) and services. Though technologically life was very hard, the nobility lived off the fruits of the labor of those tied to the land and farmed for a living. Some of the individual taxes were not very significant, but such taxes as the *banalités,* where the serf was obliged to use the mills, ovens, etc., owned by the lord, who charged them for their use, and the variety of other taxes and impositions placed a huge burden on the serfs the value of which is difficult to determine.[23] That said, it was often oppressive, particularly in times of crop failures, and provoked the serfs to revolt.

To be sure, the vast majority of the population was in an absolutely equal state of poverty, forced labor, and oppression. We have not talked about the right of *primae noctis*[24], which was particularly insulting, but we have addressed how, in some situations, serfs were forbidden from owning mills, ovens, and other tools necessary for life and that they had to use those belonging to the nobility, who charged them for the privilege of using the tools.

The nobility exercised authority over the serfs and imposed their rights by tradition and by force of arms, upon any serf who objected to his situation. It was immaterial if the serfs took up arms or not. They faced an armored opponent who had spent all his life in the training of the use of arms. The difference between the military ability of the serfs and the nobility was so dramatic. that when there were peasant revolts, such as in western Germany in 1524, though the peasants had some initial success and pillaged a few castles, they could not withstand the armed force of the nobles and their mercenary soldiers. Every uprising, until 1789, ended with the peasants being crushed and forced back into servitude to the nobles. The real difference in 1782 was that the nobles had, by that time,

---

[22] Pothier, R.-J. *Traite du contract Bail a Rente* (Paris: Debure, 1764), p.17.
[23] Secretan, E., *Essai sur la Féodalité* (Lausanne, Switzerland : Bridel, 1858) p. 550.
[24] The right of the lord to sleep with a newly married peasant woman on the night of her marriage.

ceased to be fighting men, i.e., handling weapons, and had alternatively used money to procure standing armies that were no longer composed of foreign and domestic mercenaries; they were formed from the people within their kingdom.

But how does this relate to socialism and communism? In both of these two political theories the economic resources of the state are either fully owned or totally controlled by the government. This is identical to the feudal situation where the king owned all the land.

In socialism and communism, there is a hierarchy of politicians replacing the hierarchy of nobles. The king, duke, marquis, count, baron, and knight have been replaced by bureaucrats of various titles operating within a political hierarchy, each reporting to the government organization level above him.

In socialism and communism, the ownership of the means of production - the equivalent of the land in feudal Europe - is held by the state. The bureaucrats, resembling the lords, direct the activity of the workers.

In socialism and communism, the force of arms used by the Medieval nobility to enforce their control of the serfs, is supplemented by the secret police who look for dissidents through the use of spies reporting to the secret police. However, when the oppression becomes too great and the people rise up against their oppressors, the socialist and communist governments resort to the brute force of tanks – e.g., Tiananmen Square in 1989, Czechoslovakia in 1956, and East Germany in 1953. In addition, socialist and communist states have established concentration camps for the housing, isolation, and elimination of dissidents, e.g., the Gulag of the Soviet Union, the Re-education camps of China and of post 1975 Vietnam. They have literally slaughtered anyone within their state that <u>might</u> oppose them, such as Mao's Cultural Revolution and Pol Pot's murder camps in Cambodia.

In these camps there is the equivalent of the *corvée,* or forced labor. The bureaucrats determine, by their control of the educational system, who is trained for a specific job; they are then sent to work in a factory where their education prepares them to support the socialist economy. That said, the children of the bureaucratic elite are afforded access to superior education and taken into the governmental system, inheriting to some degree the positions of their parents, and certainly a position in the socialist/communist society that is above that of the serf/workers.

In the socialist or communist society, the hierarchy lives in a style above that of the common serfs or workers. Their life has everything that the serf or worker does not have. They have cars, do not stand in line for their food, have special stores where they shop, live in the best neighborhoods, have vacation homes/dachas, and have in every aspect formed a new nobility similar to the one the Russians replaced in 1917 with their communist revolution.

Yes, the vast majority of the population in a socialist or communist society is absolutely equal. They receive the same number of crumbs, live in the same tiny apartments, and have no hope for a better or improving their lives. Their situation is very similar to the Medieval serf who watched the lord take the fruits of his labor; the lord lived in comparative luxury eating the best of the fruits of the land, while the serf lived in a thatched hut and ate gruel. Whether it is a tank grinding the worker into the ground for his disobedience to the rules of the state, or the serf being ridden down by an armored knight on his charger, the difference is insignificant.

The worker in the socialist or communist state is tied to his job, a job he did not look for, but which was assigned to him. It is a job he cannot leave. The Medieval serf was born into his lot and as you can see, he could not leave his lord's domain without permission. What is the difference between medieval serfdom and life in a socialist or communist state?

As for the feudal system, it ended on 14 July 1789, with the storming of the Bastille. The revolution occurred because of an accumulation of events. At that time France had been at war for the better part of the previous century. Around the turn of the 18th century Louis XIV had been forced to end one war because there were too many demands on the treasury. A drought had ruined the harvests for a few years, and the peasants were becoming restless. Louis had to choose between prosecuting his war or importing grain to feed the peasants. He chose the latter.

The year 1789 followed several years of drought and once again the peasants were starving. In Paris, every morning carts went through the streets picking up the bodies of those who had starved to death the day before. The French treasury was empty, for a variety of reasons, and could not buy grain as it had under Louis XIV. The nobility continued living well while the peasants starved, hence the statement attributed to Marie Antoinette, "Let them eat cake." It was a minor incident, a scuffle in the streets of Paris that was exacerbated by soldiers who were angry at the behavior of their commanding officer, an arrogant and well-fed noble. The spark fell into a pool of gasoline, and the flames of revolution were lit. Within hours the Bastille was stormed, and the revolution was on.

Chapter 2

The Prelude to Marxism: Babeufism

What is Babeufism? Who was Gracchus Babeuf? His real name was François Noël. He was a French revolutionary born in Saint-Quentin on 23 November 1760 and executed by the guillotine in Vendôme on 27 May 1797. However, before discussing his ideas and theories, let us begin with his place in the history of fascism and communism. To this end, let us look at comments from a French magazine, *Le Pensée:*[25]

Karl Marx and Frederick Engels testified in the 1840s, when shaping their conception of the revolutionary and communist world, they had an extraordinarily keen interest in Buonarroti's book[26] and in the history of Baboufism. Marx studied Buonarroti's book as late as 1843. This is evidenced by the well-known text of *La Sainte-Famille*: '... the French Revolution has brought forth ideas that led beyond the ideas of "the old state of things." The revolutionary movement, that began in 1789 in the *Cercle Social* and had as main representatives Leclerc and Roux, finally succumbed to the conspiracy of Babeuf. It had hatched the "communist" idea that Buonarroti, the friend of Babeuf, reintroduced in France following the revolution of 1830. This idea, developed in all its consequences, constitutes the principle of the modern world.

"In the history library of socialism, that Marx and Engels proposed to publish in the 1840s, was Buonarroti's book in a German translation entrusted to Mr. Hess, who had intended of writing a biography of Babeuf. Marx and Engels made repeated mention of Babeuf's movement in their works during the 1840s. The *Manifesto* of the Communist Party gives an extremely important appreciation of the principle of this movement - its social roots. not literature which, in all the great modern revolutions, formulated the demands of the proletariat (writings of Babeuf, etc.). Moreover, the *Manifesto* also criticizes the primitive, grossly egalitarian character, of

---

[25] Daline, V.M., *L'Histoiregraphe de Babeuf, (La Pense, Revue du Rationalism Moderne* No. 128, August 1966) pp. 68-101.
[26]Buonarroti, P., *Graccus Babeuf et la Conjuration des Ègaux* (Paris : Chevalier, 1869).

Babeufism."²⁷

Daloine adds, "Marx particularly retained and almost literally copied the passages from D'Avenel's book dealing with the influence of the failure of the Babouvistes on the sale of national goods." Speaking of the movement's stakeholders, he notes:

> 'Imagine this crowd, this world of the poor, the expropriated, the reprobate, rolling throughout Paris, and penetrating the stolen houses, and putting an end to the thieves' orgy.' We throw out these dogs as financiers, we take back all that they have taken, and we apply the law of sharing as promised (p.42, *National Goods*).

According to Avenel, the conspiracy was likely to succeed, and it caused confusion, for a moment, among the purchasers of national property. However, the failure of the Babouvist movement revived them. In the words of D'Avenel, recopied by Marx, it was precisely then "…that they threw themselves upon the property of emigrants²⁸ as they had never done." The victories of the Army of Italy and Bonaparte were another favorable turn for them. Marx recopied very carefully in Avenel the history of the introduction of 'territorial mandates' - new monetary units exchanged for the depreciated and suppressed assignats.²⁹ As indicated by Avenel, this

---

[27] Daline, p. 75.

[28] Author : The emigrants being referred to are the nobles who fled France fearing execution. The reference to « national property » is to the personal property of these nobles that was confiscated and sold by the Revolutionary government to fund the operations of the Revolutionary state.

[29] Author: The "assignat" was a form of paper money issued during the French Revolution, between 1789 and 1796. The name comes from the Latin "assignats" for "assigned" and represented land that had been seized by the new French government from the church and nobles and was being used as the basis for the value of the money issued in the form of assignats. The issuance of the assignats was a plan to address the absence of gold and silver coinage, deal with the financial crisis of the French government, and redistribute seized land. Initially they acted as mortgage bonds on these nationalized church lands, and were issued as a result of a motion by Mirabeau, and by the Constituent Assembly on 2 November 1789. Further assignats were issued against confiscated crown lands taken over on 7 October. Assignats were used to pay state creditors and it was assumed that they would exchange those assignats for parcels of national land. If the holder of assignats did not wish to purchase land, then he could simply use them as currency and eventually they would accumulate in the hands of an individual wishing to buy these confiscated properties. When the state was paid in assignats for a parcel of land, the assignats would simply be destroyed.

The first printing was for 400,000,000 assignats in the form of 100-franc notes. A total of 120 million were redeemed in 1791, 100 million in 1792, 80 million in 1793 and 1794 and the surplus in 1795.

The system would have worked well if the numbers of assignats had been limited to what Mirabeau had envisioned. However, as with all irresponsible or desperate governments 'campaign of warrants', the 'financier'... Brought it no less ardently than Bonaparte and his soldiers during their Italian campaign. It took eight months for the rascals to put the assignats in distress; in four months they had exhausted the credit of the new paper, so much that they exported goods at the lowest possible price. In the fourth month it was reduced to one-twentieth of its value. Marx reported in his work Avenel's conclusion: "After such territorial debauchery, despotism was fatal ..." It is very clear that in this analysis, d'Avenel appears the place between the failure of the Baboufist movement, the march of the sale of national goods as "bourgeois debauches of the Directory", and the victory of Bonapartism."[30]

We then find the following:

> "Of extreme importance for the study of the biography of Babeuf was the publication in 1884 of the two-volume study of V. Advielle. If Coët only used the local archives, insufficiently, Advielle, wrote his biography on the basis of an extremely valuable source - the very rich personal archives of Babeuf made available by the famous French collector Pochet-Derqche. Of all the biographers of Babeuf, Advielle was the only one who used these archives; in Jan-

that control printing presses and can print money, Mirabeau's plan was exploited and its viability destroyed by a second issuance of 800 million francs that carried no interest, in contrast to the first issue. Further issues of assignats occurred, raising the total issued to 3,750 million assignats. Inflation occurred and the value of an assignat fell to 20 francs in gold or silver. Rampant speculation resulted in criminal sentences, the first offense bringing six years of imprisonment, the second 20, on 1 August 1793 and eventually increased to death on 10 May 1794. However, Robespierre would eventually eliminate the death penalty for speculation. Despite these legal remedies, speculation continued and the value of the assignat fell to one-sixth of its face value. This resulted in the issuance, on 3 May 1793, of the Law of the Maximum, which required all farmers and wheat dealers to declare the quantity of wheat in their possession and then to sell it only to state-recognized markets. No person was to be allowed to hold more than one month's supply. The maximum price was then fixed, and none were permitted to sell for higher prices.

With prices fixed, the French Government turned up the printing presses and issued a further 8 billion francs in assignats, of which only 2,464 million were returned to the state and destroyed. The Law of the Maximum was extended and economic chaos began to reign. Trade was paralyzed and manufacturing facilities began closing.

The Directory committed further abuses, and in 1796 issued a further 45,500 million francs of assignats, but if this weren't enough rampant counterfeiting further flooded the already saturated market. Repurchases of assignats reduced the outstanding number to 24 billion francs in assignats, but their face value had fallen to 30 to 1 of coin. They were converted, at that value, to *mandats territoriaux* or land warrants, which were to constitute a mortgage on all lands of the Republic, but they were no more successful than the assignats and sold on their day of issue at a discount of 82%. These *mandats* lasted only six months and were eventually repurchased by the state at 1/70th of their face value.

[30] Daline, p. 76.

uary 1883 these archives were auctioned off, and this was only in 1925-1926 - thanks to the then director of the K. Marx Institute and F. Engels, D.-B. Ryazanov that these archives took place in Moscow and that their study became possible again."[31] [32]

Further we find the following:

"Buonarotti's book has a great importance for the history of French socialism, but the plot that he recounts was not properly speaking, a communist plot – Buonarrotti was '…. probably more of a communist that Babeuf himself. In the world of Babeuf the communist ideas did not play and further, the role that one habitually gives them. …… 'In Babeuf's system, there is nothing original…. Babeuf was not always a communist. He adhered to communist very late."

In his first articles devoted to Buonarroti, but particularly in the article published in 1917 on "Babeuf and Robespierre", Mathiez strove to show that Maximilian Robespierre must be considered as the true precursor of French socialism, that it is precisely Babeuf and the Babouvists were attached to him. "The first French socialists who formed a party, the Egaux ... professed for Robespierre a true cult. They gave themselves before contemporaries and posterity for his heirs and his followers. In his article Albert Mathiez meticulously collected all the comments of Babeuf then known about Robespierre, but he gave a unilateral and inaccurate interpretation."[33]

We then find the following:

1.) Lefebvre was particularly interested in the question of the place of communist ideas in the conception of Babeuf's world. He maintained on this question the directly contradictory points of view of those of A. Mathiez. As early as 1935, in his preface to the *Pages choisies de Babeuf*

---
[31] Original footnote in quote: « They are actually conserved in Moscow in the Central Archives of the Cenral Committee of the Communist Party of the Soviet Union."
[32] Daline, p. 79.
[33] Daline, p. 89.

Lefebvre wrote: 'Dommanget has brought to light the documents that prove that communism was at the center of his thought (of Babeuf, V.D.) from before 1789 ... In all the problem being posed, we must find the solution in the evolution of its ideas during the years preceding the Terror ...' But if communist ideas held such a large place in the conception of the world of Babeuf before the Revolution, to what must we attribute their birth? According to Lefebvre, it would be wrong to look for the social roots of Babeuf's ideas only in ideological influences. '... Did Babeuf's communism have its source in philosophy alone? I have said elsewhere that I did not believe it, and I am pleased to note that Mr. Dommanget shares that opinion. Babeuf was Picard, and it was in the midst of the peasants of the plain of Picardy that his mind was formed. This point of view Lefebvre developed in more detail in his report on *Les origines du communisme de Babeuf*, at the IXth International Congress of Historical Sciences in Paris in 1950.[34]

And one final quotation:

2.) The communism of Babeuf, according to Mazauric, would have a purely agrarian character; the nascent capitalist Picardy production, he did not notice it, apparently, not at all; it was not until 1795, after his stay in Paris, that Babeuf 'abruptly' became interested in industry. The economic program of the Baboufists, Claude Mazauric considers it 'absolutely retrograde' with regard to technical progress, to which they nourished 'a deep distrust' which brought them much closer to the 'Malthusian pessimism.

In his detailed review of the studies on the history and ideology of the Baboufist movement, Cl. Mazauric again emphasized the thesis of the 'economically reactionary character' of Babeuf's communism, a character which could be explained by the depressed economic situation of the years 1795-1796. Babeuf's theory remained 'pessimistic' unlike that of the Saint-Simonians, whose views were developed during a period of rising

[34] Daline, p. 92.

upheaval, he never envisages that the offer of employment can be greater than the demand. According to Mazauric, the ideological development of Babeuf was in no way linear, it was made in zigzags. Until the beginning of 1794, he followed Robespierre, and it was only because of the pursuit he suffered for his activity in Picardy and made him 'a disciple of the Hebertists who advocated a *sans-culotte* democracy.[35]

All these quotations have been provided because there is some debate on the true place of Babeuf in the development of communist theology. Yet there is the common threat of accepting that Babeuf does fit into the pantheon of communist forerunners. It is not our desire to say more than he had a position in the development of socialist and communist philosophies and present some of Babeuf's own words in order to allow our readers to determine how Babeuf fits into the pantheon of socialist and communist philosophy.

Babeuf was a radical and looking at the problems he saw in France, he imagined a vast plan of fiscal reform which he vainly presented to the French authorities in 1787, which he later published after the fall of the Bastille under the title *Cadastre perpétual* [*Perpetual Land Registry*].

This was the time of the French Revolution. This great revolution commenced on 4 July 1789 with the fall of the Bastille. There had been troubles for months before this event, however. Several years of bad harvests had created a tremendous shortage of bread and the people of France were literally starving. Men were tasked to roam the streets of Paris in the morning to pick up and carry away the bodies of people who had died of starvation. The uprising that erupted on the morning of the 4th was not just the people but had a core of soldiers from the French infantry regiment, *Gardes français*, whose noble colonel was particularly brutal. The discontent of the soldiers from this regiment merged with the anger of the starving people and the Revolution erupted.

The French system allowed for a parliament, or National Assembly, which had been called by Louis XVI, to deal with various fiscal problems. Being in session, it sent out a call to the provinces for lists of grievances, which were sent in for consideration.

Babeuf contributed to the preparation of the notebook of grievances of the Bailly of Roye This notebook was issued in 1790 and asked for the abolition of most of the taxes imposed on the French people. After several attempts to be elected to various functions in the Somme, entered the General Council of this department in September 1793.

---
[35] Daline, p. 100.

A conflict quickly erupted with his colleagues and was compromised in a legal affair. This resulted in his being sentenced to 20 years in irons. He escaped and hid in Paris. He found work in the commission of substances in the city of Paris. He was later discovered by the Somme authorities and arrested. He then obtained a reversal of his sentence through the assistance of Thibaudeau.Liberated after 9 Thermidor, he was employed by the Conventional Officer Guffroy as the director of the *Journal de la liberté de la presse* [*Newspaper of the Liberty of the Press*]. Soon however, it broke with him and he was arrested for publishing an article against Tallien and was incarcerated in Arras for seven months. He was barely released from prison when he resumed his publishing efforts and simultaneously decided to pass into action in October 1795. On 29 March 1796, the "secret directory of public safety" was constituted which included Babeuf, Antonelle, Félix le Pelletier, and Sylvain Maréchal, who undertook to "revolutionize the people" with flyers and placards. Disturbed, the French Directory, then the group that ruled what remained of Revolutionary France, inserted one of its agents, Captain Grisel, into the plot. designated time, the police arrested Babeuf and approximately 50 other people. The government launched a press campaign to convince the public that by the grace of the diligence of the authorities, France had escaped a very grave danger. Babeuf sent a message to the Directory, declaring himself ready to "negotiate with it" as "one power with another" and proposed using his influence in the "democratic" circles to bring them to power, in exchange the conspiracy "of the equals" would be considered "null and void". No reply is made to this grotesque proposition. The government was determined to end this "agitator" who had already been arrested and sentenced several times. The case is submitted to High Court sitting at Vendôme.

The trial lasted from 27 February to 26 May 1797 and in the end, Babeuf was sentenced to death and was executed on the guillotine. Of his fellow conspirators, Antonelle and Lepelletier were acquitted, Buonarotti was condemned to deportation, but remained in prison in France.[36]

Why do we talk about Babeuf? Because he falls into the pre-history of Marxism by his proposals and philosophies, which we will explore. We must examine what the French Revolution was about. Aside from the fact that there had been several failed harvests and the French people were starving, the issue was feudal rights.

---

[36] Tuilard, Fayarard, and Fierro, *Histoire et dictionnaire de la révolution française 1789-1799* (Pris, Laffont, 1998) pp 553-554.

Twin Evils

Initially feudal rights extended only to rights that derive from a fief contract, or *infeodiation*. However, this term eventually extended to all the rights of any sort that were ordinarily united in the hands of the nobles and of which the whole composed what feudalists call *feudal complexum*. Thus, they included seignorial rents, the rights of *"champart"* [right of the lord to part of the peasant's harvest], *corvée* [forced labor on roads, etc.], *banalité* [the peasant being forced to use the lord's mill and pay for its use], *tailles seigneuriales* [direct taxes]

In breaking down *feudal complexum*, one finds various elements. In the first place a certain number of rights can be representative of the rights of sovereignty. In the Middle Ages sovereignty followed property, and vice versa. The lord was both sovereign and suzerain. His title of proprietor conferred on him all or part of the public power. Reciprocally, the sovereign, the king for example, was at the same time proprietor and sovereign.

It is from this confusion that a multitude of rights arose. Before long, public power was concentrated in the hands of the king. The lords retained only the least public authority. A large number of these rights initially had the character of public contributions, but they were converted into private revenues.

These representative rights of sovereignty were called "rights of justice," and feudal sovereignty was called "justice." Hence this aphorism: justice follows the fief, but without being confused with it. The seigniorial justice not only included the rights of jurisdiction and the courts, but all the pecuniary and other rights which derived from the sovereignty. Seigniorial justice had become abusive, since the authority of the state had replaced feudal authority everywhere. These were the principal ones of these rights: the confiscation of the property of those condemned to death, also called the "fruits of high justice"; the right on the weights and measures; the right of escheat [reversion of property of someone dying without heir to the lord]; the right to salvage of anything washing ashore from a sinking ship and, in general, any lost object; the right of *aubaine* [to tax foreigners traversing the lord's lands]; the right to take possession of the goods of any foreigner dying on his lands; the right to tax grain stocks, which according to some was the repurchase of prohibited sales; right of *affouage* [right to firewood taken from the lord's forests]; the right of coinage; the right to tax drinks sold in cabarets; ownership of non-royal roads and navigable rivers; and, finally, the rights of fishing and hunting.

There was also a second class of rights, improperly called "feudal rights" that included the right of mortmain [right of ownership of land], personal servitude, and all rights representative of servitude. Beside the relations of the vassal and the lord, there was that of the serf and the freeman. Serfdom was barely short of full slavery. Although it had greatly diminished by the time of the Revolution, it still existed when the Revolution erupted. It included certain personal or pecuniary dues.

These rights made life difficult for the commoners who owned land, something that had been increasing before the Revolution. For instance, the right to hunt allowed nobles to ride their horses through the planted fields of the commoners, destroying crops. Closely tied to this were the pigeons kept by the lords that were protected and the killing of which bore heavy penalties. These birds fed on the peasant's fields. The corvée was basically forced labor that tore the peasants away from tending their fields. Many of the other rights were little more than a tax imposed by the lord on the peasants who occupied and farmed his lands.

In a time of bad harvests, as France faced in 1789, bread was scarce and expensive. Bread was so scarce and expensive that in Paris men were charged with daily traveling the streets of Paris to remove the bodies of those who had died of starvation overnight. All these taxes and everything that damaged the crops were seen as a terrible imposition on the starving peasants. Then, as they saw the luxurious lives led by the nobles, their anger grew to a peak and erupted in the Revolution. This was epitomized by the purported statement by Marie Antoinette, "Let them eat cake."

As a result, aside from the abolition of feudalism and all its rights, the issue of property and ownership of the land was a principal issue. By owning the land, the peasants escaped the right of *champart* [taking part of the harvest].

In 1789, France had suffered several years of failed harvests. Food, specifically bread which formed the principal element of the French diet, was not only very scarce, but very expensive. France's economy was almost entirely agrarian. Not only did this agrarian economy produce food, but it also produced other crops that were used in industry, e.g., the perfume industry. When harvests were bad, not only was there little food, but unemployment also exploded because the raw materials for French industry were scarce; therefore, industry slowed. Being an agrarian society, not an industrial society, sets France in this historic period apart from Marx's conception of a revolution by the "workers". The industrialization that Marx knew in Germany, when he wrote *Das Kapital*, did not yet exist.

Twin Evils

This puts Babeuf in an agrarian society. As Dommanget said above in quote no. 1, he is looking at people starving while the nobility lacked for nothing and where the nobility, living under the rules of feudalism, controlled everything.

The 15 points of Babeuf's theories in his own words.

ANALYSIS OF THE BABEUF DOCTRINE
AS PROSCRIBED BY THE EXECUTIVE DIRECTORY [37]

1. Nature has given to each man a right equal to the enjoyment of all the goods.
2. The object of society is to defend this equality, often attacked by the strong and the wicked in the state of nature, and to increase, by the concurrence of all, the common enjoyment [of those goods].
3. Nature has imposed on everyone the obligation to work. No one could, without [committing a] crime, evade work.
4. Work and enjoyments must be common to all.
5. There is oppression when one is exhausted by work and lacks everything, while the other swims in abundance without doing anything.
6. No one has been able without [committing a] crime to appropriate exclusively the ownership of the land or industry.
7. In a true society, there must be neither rich nor poor.
8. The rich who do not want to give up their surplus in favor of the poor are the enemies of the people.
9. No one can, by the accumulation of all means, deprive another of the instruction [i.e., education] necessary for his happiness; education must be common.
10. The goal of revolution is to destroy inequality and restore the happiness of all.
11. The revolution is not over, because the rich absorb all goods and command [those goods] exclusively, while the poor work as slaves, languish in misery and are nothing in the state.
12. The Constitution of 1793 is the true law of the French: because the people have solemnly accepted it; because the Convention did not have the right to change it; because, in order to succeed, we

---

[37] Buonarroti, P., *Graccus Babeuf et la Conjuration des Ègaux* (Paris : Chevalier, 1869). Pp. 181-182

must shoot the people who demanded its execution; because they hunted and slaughtered the deputies who did their duty by defending it; because the terror against the people and the influence of the emigrants presided over the drafting and the supposed acceptance of the Constitution of 1795, which did not have not even the fourth part of the suffrages that it had obtained from that of 1793; because the Constitution of 1793 had enshrined the inalienable rights of every citizen to consent to the laws, to exercise political rights, to assemble, to claim what he thinks useful, to educate himself, not to die of hunger; rights that the counterrevolutionary act of 1795 openly and completely violated.

13. Every citizen is bound to restore and defend, in the Constitution of 1793, the will and happiness of the people.

14. All the powers emanating from the so-called Constitution of 1795 are illegal and counter-revolutionary.

15. Those who laid hands on the Constitution of 1793 are guilty of *lèse-majesté populaire*.

Articles 12-15 are particular to the situation in France after 1794. They are irrelevant to the question of whether Babeuf was an early communist and what is compatible with communist ideology.

If you look at the others, it is clear that Babeuf believed that all property, be it land or manufactured goods, housing, etc., should be held in common by everyone. He believed in absolute equality. This even extended to education, which in 1789, was also limited to the select people.

CHAPTER 3
Marx and Engels

In looking at Marx's life one sees several interesting points that surely influenced his later political philosophies. He was of Jewish ancestry. The Jews in Europe had been despised and persecuted for several reasons. The first was the Catholic Church's condemnation of the Jews the murderers of Christ. The second was that the Jews were prohibited from owning land and found themselves pushed into various trades and businesses, the most notorious of all being money lending.

The loaning of money for interest was also condemned by the Catholic Church, but it was a necessary function as there were always emperors, kings, and merchants looking to borrow money. The Jews filled this need and, as a result, attracted further hatred. Education was also another path to success taken by the Jews.

Marx's father, though born into Judaism, converted to Lutheranism prior to Marx's birth. It is probable that, like all converts, Karl's father was a fervent and very religious Lutheran. He was also a very successful lawyer and saw success coming from education, so he pushed Karl hard to be successful academically. Politically he was a conservative and, according to Spargo, Karl Marx's biographer, possibly "even a reactionary."[38] He hoped that Karl would follow him in the practice of the law, but Marx wanted to be a great philosopher and a great poet.[39] Following his family's tradition Marx entered the University of Bonn and soon failed. This was most certainly a disappointment to his father, which, according to Spargo, was surprising as Marx was purportedly a very competent student. Indeed, he says that Marx paid little attention to his studies and preferred drinking with his friends and incurred significant debts. Debt would be a significant element of Marx's life. As for his academic performance, a comment by Spargo is quite interesting: "Like many another genius, he [Marx] found the greatest difficulty in passing examinations which men of less ability could pass with ease."

In reading *Karl Marx: His Life and Work*, there is no indication why Marx became a raging anti-Semite, but if one were to read *Das Kapi-*

---
[38] Spargo, J. *Karl Marx: His Life and Work* (New York: Huebsch, 1912). p. 18. As an observation, in his biographical account of Marx's life, Spargo appears to be very neutral, but in the last chapter it becomes apparent that Spargo was a Marxist as he argues some points of Marx's theories against his opponents.

[39] Spargo, p. 32-3

tal and *The Communist Manifesto*, one will find constant derogatory references to Jews and money lenders. Throughout *Das Kapital* there are references to "usurers" and "Mr. Moneybags." But the most striking comment is "The capitalist knows that all commodities, however scurvy they may look, or how badly they may smell, are in faith and truth money, inwardly circumcised Jews, and what is more, a wonderful means whereby out of money to make more money."[40]

In speaking of Marx vis-à-vis the Jews, Spargo says, "The rule of the Jew over the small landowners developed into an economic tyranny of the most odious and oppressive type, constantly provoking wild outbursts of anti-Semitism. (This is odd as the Jews in Europe were generally forbidden to own land in some countries.) Wonderful indeed was the wisdom of the young Karl Marx when, in his study of the Hebrew question, he declared that the emancipation of the Jew, and of society from the Jew, required the emancipation of the Jew from himself, from this 'practical Judaism' – from money and business."[41] Spargo adds, "There was a financial crisis in the early [eighteen] twenties which brought many Gentiles, especially among the landowning class, to grief and compelled them to endure the repressive rule of Jewish money lenders. This ancient cause of anti-Semitism gave rise to a great deal of ill-will against the money lenders. Provoked by the usurious extortion of them, it naturally and inevitably extended to many of the race who were not money lenders at all and had nothing in common with them….. there was a vigorous campaign in 1826 to exclude the Jews from citizenship altogether."[42]

That said, Marx's personal life was financially catastrophic. He attempted and failed miserably at making a living by writing and working for newspapers. He was frequently destitute, with his family near starvation[43] and reduced to eating bread and nothing else. He was evicted at least once for non-payment of rent. The only time his family was on sound financial ground was when he or his wife received an inheritance, which was soon spent. He frequently resorted to using usurers of unknown ethnicity and borrowed to keep his family afloat financially at rates of from 30% to 50%.[44] This clearly explains his hatred of people who made a living by loaning money and is probably part of the source of his theory that labor was the only true source of wealth, that providing capital to support the

---

[40] Marx, *Capital (Das Kapital)*, (USA: Fingerprint Classics, 2020) pg. 95.
[41] Spargo, p. 21.
[42] Spargo, p. 25.
[43] Spargo, p. 27.
[44] Spargo, p. 208.

economy did not merit compensation.

Coming from the upper class of society and his early successes, Marx developed a narcissistic personality that he displayed in his writing. It also produced a complete rejection of everything his father stood for and represented. This too surely led to his development of his economic theories and political opinions.

In reading both the *Communist Manifesto* and *Das Kapital*, one finds that Marx had romanticized Medieval Europe. His study of French history apparently produced this fascination. He speaks longingly of the joy the Medieval artisan took in his craft, but he completely misses the miserly and harshness of the Medieval life, where weather and ravaging armies frequently left the peasants to starve; where crop failures were common; where disease, such as the Black Death (bubonic plague) and small pox carried off thousands every year; where the means of production were crude and inefficient at best and required that even the youngest child be sent to the fields to wrest a living from the soil. This acceptance of child labor in the Middle Ages is in complete juxtaposition to his position about child labor in *The Poverty of Philosophy.* Yes, there were "common" lands shared by all the peasants of the village. He does not recognize that life was short and miserable for the vast majority who were dominated by a rapacious nobility instead of an industrial bourgeoisie.

In *Das Kapital* he also speaks of primitive East Indian village life where everyone made everything they needed to live. They wove their own cloth and made their own tools. The land was held in common, and all of the villagers worked communally in the fields, sharing equally the harvest of those fields. He ignores the fact that these Indians suffered from the same calamities and misery as the Medieval European peasant.

Marx's idealization the Medieval period in Europe and ancient India is much like a young man I once encountered at a Native American arts and crafts festival. He arrived in an old car, whose trunk was wallpapered with liberal bumper stickers. One particular bumper sticker struck my eye. It expressed his longing for the glories of the primitive lifestyle espoused by Marx. Then the young man climbed out of his car, opened the back door, pulled out a wheelchair and rolled down the asphalt path to the festival.

As I pondered this it dawned that the young man thought the primitive life meant frolicking joyously in the woods with the bears and bees. He had an idealized view of the primitive life of the Native Americans. What he did not realize was that, given the chance, the bear would eat him.

He also did not consider that not only would there be no asphalt paths on which to roll his wheelchair, there would be no steel or plastic with which to make his wheelchair. He also didn't seem to know that the first person to die in the primitive world was the cripple who could not provide for his own sustenance and was a burden on the able bodied.

So too, Marx ignored the realities of his idealized era and saw it as a model for the modern world. This attitude is pervasive in *Das Kapital*. His idealism and his blindness to reality led him to write a massive economic study that is based on selected and limited economic theories, that even he could not support, though he promised to do in Volume 3 of *Das Kapital*. His theories had a foundation in the sand of historical idealism.

Marx's main objection to capitalism is that it is immoral for money to earn interest. Again, this is a repudiation of his Jewish ancestry and its history of money lending, not to mention Marx's history of debt problems. In this rejection of the accumulation and loaning of capital he condemns those who embrace his theories, to the misery of the feudal society of the Middle Ages. Consider this: the accumulation of capital allows entrepreneurs to build factories, which they could never have been built, had they been limited to what they could produce with their hands. Primitive man had only one tool, his hands. He then discovered the hammer (a rock). With the rock he discovered the sharp edge he could make with flint. From flint he moved to the wheel and on and on to more and more tools. However, eventually, his tools, his means of production became larger and required substantial investments in time, effort, and materials; more than a single man could produce in several lifetimes.

Marx talks at length about how early capitalists in England oppressed and dehumanized their workers, giving them minimal wages and exploiting them. Unfortunately, he forgets that those same workers had a choice to work or not to work in the factories. Labor is mobile and can move to places where wages and working conditions are better. Those same workers had a clear choice to remain in the factory or to withhold their labor as they did in the multitude of labor strikes that occurred throughout Europe in the mid-19th century, even though such strikes were occasionally outlawed. Sadly, returning to the farm in the 18th century in England was not an option, but elsewhere it was. Those workers obviously decided that life was better in the "horrible" factory that supposedly "exploited" them than it would be back on the farm. If they hadn't come to that conclusion then would they not have returned to the farm? They also chose the path of strikes against their employers to both improve work conditions and to increase their wages. That said, anyone who has read Upton Sinclair's *The Jungle* will be very familiar with the abuses of the factory workers. Yes, absolutely there was a problem and, fortunately, it has been resolved, though it took time, effort, and legislation.

Marx rambles endlessly attempting to analyze and explore the nature of labor, work, and capital. However, all his theorization is limited because industry was in its very early stages of development. He does recognize that the workers being organized into a factory took away the self-actualization of making the whole finished good by causing them to become specialized in one specific step of the spectrum of steps necessary to create that good. However, Marx saw this as dehumanizing. Maybe so, but if you look at Maslow's motivational theory the basic motivation is food, shelter and clothing. The peak, the gratification of the artisan or craftsman making the entire product, which Maslow calls "self-actualization" does not need to be realized in the daily labor necessary to address those basic motivations of food, shelter, etc.

Regarding the transition from the artisan to the factory worker, Marx says "The division of labor reduces the worker to a degrading function; to this degrading function corresponds a depraved mind; with the depravity of the mind goes a constant reduction of wages. In order to prove that this reduction of wages is adapted to a depraved mind, M. Proudhon says, to absolve his own conscience, that it is the universal conscience which wills it thus. It is the soul of M. Proudhon counted in the universal conscience?"[45]

Though Marx's feet probably never stepped onto the factory floor, I have spent thousands of hours on them, as an hourly worker, as a supervisor, as an industrial auditor, and as a quality engineer. I have frequently observed that where the workers were in proximity of each other and performing an operation over and over again the task itself became automatic and the workers would carry on a lively conversation with each other. Psychologists call it dual tasking. Even when working in environments where this was not possible, once away from the job, there was no sign of depravity of the mind. In addition, particularly since these were all unionized facilities, there was only a steady increase in wages as each new contract was negotiated.

In addition, despite what Marx says, the specialization of tasks allows for more efficient production of goods that flood the market and produce a better life for all. The faster and more efficiently a factory can make

---

[45] Marx, K., *The Poverty of Philosophy*, p. 144.

its products the more goods it can put on the market, as the law of supply and demand says, drive down the price of those goods, thereby making them cheaper. Please note the historical example of Henry Ford's institution of the assembly line. Before he instituted the assembly line, were the individual worker performs only one task, i.e. putting fenders on the right rear of the car, a car was a luxury that could be purchased only by the very rich. After Ford introduced the assembly line, the cost of the Model T was such that his assembly line workers could actually afford to buy one. Marx, of course, was unaware of this technological innovation and its economic ramifications as it came about 50 years after he'd died. And that ignorance, plus the passage of time and the innovations that occurred, clearly shows the fallacy of Marx's thoughts on this issue, i.e. he assumed there was no option to escape the "evils" of capitalism in his day except revolution.

Let me once again revert to a personal story that relates to this directly and shows the fallacy of the Marx's rejection of capitalism and the idea of "from each according to his ability, to each according to his need." I was once working out of the U.S. Embassy in Monrovia, Liberia. In traveling around Liberia I'd noticed where several slabs for the foundations of houses had been poured and a few rows of concrete blocks laid as the owner started building a house. Let me give some background. There were three classes of dwellings for the common folks: 1.) dob and waddle walls (web of sticks covered with mud) with thatched roofs (most common in the countryside and jungle), 2.) dob and waddle walls with tin roofs, and 3.) the best was a cement floor with cement block walls and a tin roof (the cities). Somewhere in between were tin shacks with tin roofs and it does not include the more sumptuous houses where the ruling class lived.

With that said, back to these modest beginnings that were overgrown with grass and brush. I saw numerous such building sites. I inquired in the embassy and was told this story: There was a U.S. Marine embassy guard who had dated a female Liberian who also worked as an embassy guard. When he rotated out, because he cared for the woman, he built her a two-unit house, cement block walls and tin roof, where she could live and rent the other half so as to earn some income. A family member of the woman rented the other half of the house and paid the rent for a while but eventually stopped. When confronted, the family member told the woman that she had two houses, that he was family, that he needed a house, and because it was the custom in Liberia, that if a family member needed something the others had extra, they were obliged to give it to them. The lazy family member essentially robbed this woman of her means of income and moved from mud hut to one of the finest homes for the common folk in Liberia.

As for those partially built houses, when the individuals who were building them had accumulated some money, but before some lazy family member discovered that they had some extra money and could ask for it, they spent it on a few cement blocks. This is the purest form of Communism, from each according to his ability to each according to his need. The lazy and incompetent stripped the hard working and successful of the fruits of their labor. As a result, capital could not be accumulated and the money necessary to build the smallest workshop was consumed. Without the first step, the building of that small workshop, nobody could ever have built the great factories of today. It took hundreds of people making sacrifices, delaying consumption of the fruits of their labor or completely sacrificing them to allow the accumulation of the capital necessary to lay the first brick of a small workshop. Not only do those who made those sacrifices deserve compensation for those sacrifices, the progress made as a result of that accumulated capital being loaned to an entrepreneur who built the factory could never have built it.

All progress of mankind has depended on the willingness of individuals to sacrifice present or future consumption, i.e. delayed gratification, so the great industries of today could be built. And with those great industries we have an abundance of food that starvation is almost unheard of in the United States. In fact, instead of hunger we have a problem with obesity. Not only do we have drugs, medications, and vaccines to wipe out the diseases that ravaged Medieval Europe, but the life expectancy of the average person has doubled since then. So, it becomes obvious that the progress we have realized in our modern society is the direct result of capital being accumulated and loaned for interest. Yes, some people took out loans and failed, as Marx himself repeatedly failed, losing everything. But a critical number of borrowers succeeded and progress was made for the benefit of all humanity.

Before we turn to actual Marxist philosophy, let me indulge in another personal experience. While working in Mali, one of my co-workers showed a magazine article in which a poor American Black woman, who probably weighed 300 lbs., was complaining how she didn't have enough money in her welfare check. The African's response was, "She's not poor, poor people starve to death!" As this story clearly shows, we see that poverty is a relative thing. Indeed, in Africa, a fat wife is actually a status symbol. It means her husband can afford to feed her. The point of this story

is that poverty is a relative thing, and today has nothing to very little to do with the actual need to survive.
and today has nothing to very little to do with the actual need to survive.

Let's look at the flood of immigrants over the southern US border. If you look at the videos of them you will see many are on the "plump" side. They are well enough dressed and lots of them have cell phones. If they can afford a cell phone and phone service, they can't exactly be starving. By African standards they are rich, then again 80% of Africans, according to the US Department of State earn $2 or less a day. Yet those crossing the US southern border are "poor people" seeking a better life, even though they are paying up to $10,000 to the drug cartels to smuggle them across our border. That's more than 80% of Africans will earn in 13.7 years.

Marxism and Observations on It.

Rather than give Marx's theories and rebut them in a separate chapter, which would require restating them, it seemed preferable to simply state his theories and then comment on them. Some of his theories have already been discussed, as they came up logically when talking about his background and history, but now it becomes necessary to plunge into those theories and ideas and present observations on them.

Louis Boudin, in *The Theoretical System of Karl Marx*,[46] says "To criticize any of its [Marxist theory] parts as if it were a complete structure in itself is, therefore, a mistake which must necessarily lead to all sorts of fallacious conclusions, as many of the latter-day critics do, simply betrays ignorance of the parts which are accepted and rejected alike. The Marxian theoretical system must be examined as a whole and accepted or rejected in its entirety, at least as far as its structural parts are concerned."

In essence he says that one must study and accept the whole house and not attack the elemental parts of its structure, even though the foundation may be cracked, the basement flooded, the windows broken, and there is a ten-foot wide hole in the roof.

So, let's start with the foundation. Marx says: "A use value, or useful article, therefore has value only because human labour in the abstract has been embodied or materialized in it. However, then, is the magnitude of this value to be measured? Plainly, by the quantity of the value-creating substance, the labour contained in the article. The quantity of labour,

---
[46] Louis Boudin, L.B., *The Theoretical System of Karl Marx* (Chicago, Kerr, 1907), p. 9.

however, is measured by its duration and labour time in its turn finds its standard in weeks, days, and hours." [47]

At no time does Marx mention the quality of that labor. He speaks only of the number of hours some pair of hands spent in creating the commodity that carries the "value." So, according to Marx, an hour of time expended by a high school dropout flipping hamburgers has the exact same value as an hour of a PhD's time in a university teaching Marxist theory.

Now subsequent authors espousing Marxist theory found this unacceptable and sought a way to escape their prophet's statement of truth by stealing a concept from the capitalists and modified this concept by stating that "ability" was a factor of the creation of wealth. Now they speak of people of genius creating devices or systems that expand the productive capacity of the worker or of people whose managerial skills allow an increase in that same productive capacity. In essence, they cut a loophole to explain what George Orwell so clearly stated in *Animal Farm*, that "All animals are created equal, but some animals are more equal than others."

Now, in defense of those who rush through this loophole, Marx clearly felt that some were more equal than others. If you recall from earlier in this chapter, he preferred letting his wife and children subsist on bread alone instead of taking any menial job that would at least bring some income into his household. He obviously felt he was too good to demean himself by working with his hands. After all he had a doctorate and was a published author. Instead, he applied for a clerical job with the railroad, but was rejected because his handwriting was too sloppy. As a result, while his wife and children starved, he wrote articles for newspapers as a correspondent that paid only pennies. So modern Marxist theoreticians and exponents are safe in their hypocrisy, as they are following in the ideological footsteps of their master.

The very foundation of Marx's theory is cracked and settling as his fundamental concept on which he builds his entire philosophy is ignored in his own personal lifestyle and that of his strongest adherents. What is good for the gander is not good enough for the goose if they have a PhD.

On Marxist Philosophy

Marxism originally consisted of three related ideas: a theory of history, a philosophical anthropology, and an economic and political program. This is different from Marxism as it was understood and practiced by the

---
[47] *Capital*, pp. 18-19.

numerous socialist movements prior to 1914. There is also a third form, which was developed by Vladimir Lenin and, subsequently, modified by Joseph Stalin. This form has since become known as "Marxism-Leninism" and was the doctrine of the communist party set up in the wake of the Russian Revolution. As this period boiled with political tumult Leon Trotsky evolved an anti-Stalinist form of Marxism, which cost him his life when Stalin had him murdered in Mexico so as to eliminate him as a rival. Then there is the Maoist form of Marxism, Mao often talking about Marxist-Leninism as his concept of this political system, but which he modified Marxism to fit the circumstances in China, and his own desires and objectives. The problem for Mao was that Marx anticipated his revolution to occur in an industrialized world and China was a non-industrialized, agricultural society. In post-World War II other forms of Marxism arose by borrowing from other philosophies, principally those of Edmund Husserl and Martin Heidegger but also from Sigmund Freud and others.

Poor person walking the streets of Thies, Senegal. (Author's collection)

Communism as Presented by Marx

Sadly, unlike Hitler and Mussolini, who clearly laid out their philosophy in their works and speeches, Marx's works cannot be summarized as a simple philosophy or even a simple system. He attacks philosophy, particularly Hegel's idealist system and the theories of the post-Hegelians, both right and left. Marx was an idealist, as was discussed earlier in this chapter, and declared that philosophy must become reality. He focused on transforming the world and the human consciousness of the world. Marx argued that all knowledge involves a critique of ideas. This criticism process flows throughout most forms of communism and frequently involves self-criticism.

Twin Evils

Marx's theories are filled with concepts (appropriation, alienation, praxis, creative labor, value, and so on) taken from earlier philosophers and economists, including Kant, Hegel, Adam Smith Johann Fichte, David Ricardo, and others. Marx, however, recasts those ideas by making abstract affirmations about a whole group of problems such as human nature, knowledge, and matter. In his works he attempts to examine each of these problems in a dynamic relation to the others and then attempts to relate them to historical, social, political, and economic realities.

On Historical Materialism

In 1859, in the preface to his *Zur Kritik der politischen Ökonomie* [*Contribution to the Critique of Political Economy*], Marx briefly formulated the hypothesis that had served him as the basis for his analysis of society follows:

Marx declared his hypotheses as historical law and called it "historical materialism." He then, in *The Communist Manifesto, Das Kapital*, and other writings, applied it to capitalist societies. He pondered and meditated on this for many years, but never presented it a very exact manner. He used different expressions for identical realities and if one takes his writings literally, social reality is structured as follows:

1. An economic structure is the real basis of society. This structure includes (a) the "material forces of production," which is both labor and the means of production, and (b) the overall "relations of production," by which he meant the social and political arrangements that regulate production and distribution. He claims that there is an interchange between the "material forces" of production and the indispensable "relations" of production. He does not define and explain these relations, and his thoughts on the nature of these interchanges has produced a multitude of interpretations among his acolytes. In other words Marx was so unclear and imprecise in what he described that nobody knew exactly what he meant.

2. This economic structure lies under a cap consisting of legal and political "forms of social consciousness" corresponding to the economic structure. Once again, he says nothing about the elements and nature of this correspondence between ideology and economics, except individuals become aware of the conflict within their economic system and the material forces of production and the relations of production expressed in property ownership. Speaking of this he says that "The sum total of the forces of production accessible to men determines the condition of society" and is

the base of society. Marx says: "The social structure and the state issue continually forms the life processes of definite individuals . . . as they are in reality, that is acting and materially producing." He further says that the political relations between individuals are dependent both on material production and legal relations. His claim that the economic elements of society are supported on a foundation of the social. This concept is found in *Das Kapital* and in *Die deutsche Ideologie* [*The German Ideology*] and the **Ökonomisch-philosophische** *Manuskripte aus dem Jahre 1844* [*Economic and Philosophic Manuscripts of 1844*].

Marx on the Nature of Society

The principal point of Marx's work is found in his program for humanity. This is certainly important if one is to understand Marx when reading *The Communist Manifesto* and *Das Kapital*. Marx contended that human nature begins with human need. "Man," he wrote in the *Economic and Philosophic Manuscripts of 1844,* "is first of all a natural being. As a natural being and a living natural being, he is endowed on the one hand with natural powers, vital powers…; these powers exist in him as aptitudes and instincts. On the other hand, as an objective, natural, physical, sensitive being, he is a suffering, dependent and limited being…, that is, the objects of his instincts exist outside him, independent of him, but are the objects of his need, indispensable and essential for the realization and confirmation of his substantial powers."

Marx contends that human history begins with living humans who should satisfy their fundamental needs. "The first historical fact is the production of the means to satisfy these needs." The satisfaction of these needs creates new needs. Again, we are addressing Maslow's first motivational need, food, clothing, shelter, and defense. Humans struggle with nature to satisfy those needs. This produces the development of human powers, and that leads to the development of the human intellectual and artistic abilities. This brings out the productive nature of humans and through their labor they satisfy those needs. Humans, in this process, impose humanity on nature and nature imposes itself on them. By employing human labor and creativity, they master nature and achieve free consciousness. [He contends that by opposing nature they become by]; that the awareness of their struggle against nature, they separate themselves from it and achieve conditions that fulfil them and produces a realization of their true stature. Marx says that this struggle is inseparable from the drawing of consciousness. This leads to the realization, according to Marx. that "all that is called history is nothing else than the process of creating man through human labor, the becoming of nature for man. Man has thus evident and irrefutable proof of his own creation by himself." In turn this leads to the idea that "for man, man is the supreme being." Following on, it is obvious as man has come to the point where he is nominally, with a few exceptions, the complete master of his environment. No other living creature on earth has achieved such a position and operate on a completely instinctive basis, lacking any reasoning ability or desire to master their environment. They adapt to it instead of adapting it to their needs. Fully naturalized, humans are sufficient unto themselves: they have recaptured the fullness of humanity in its full liberty.

    Marx believed that if one lived in a capitalist society, one was not truly free. Then again, is anyone anywhere in any society completely free? Someone is always in charge and some actions are always prohibited, be it by the ruler, the ruling class, or society in general. Marx felt that the capitalist society alienated the individual, a concept he drew from Hegel and Feuerbach. This influence can be found in his earliest writings and flows through *Das Kapital*. In examining *Economic and Philosophic Manuscripts* he claims that the more the worker produces the less he has to consume and that in creating more value, he diminishes his own value, because his product and his labor is taken from him. This idea is particularly and repeatedly expressed in *Das Kapital*. Marx claims that the worker's life depends on what he has created, but that does not belong to him, so that instead of establishing his rightful existence through his labor, it is lost in products that are external to him. He claims that money, the wage, denies the worker of a concrete and fulling sense of his own humanity or as Maslow would say, his self-actualizing. Marx writes: "The generic being of man, nature as well as his intellectual faculties, is transformed into a being which is alien to him, [and] into a means of his individual existence." He implies that man's body, his spiritual existence are alienated from him by means of not being an artisan making a product through every step of production from beginning to end. This alienation, he claims, is extended to the point where private property becomes "the product of alienated labor…the means by which labor alienates itself (and) the realization of this alienation."

    This issue of alienation is repeatedly emphasized in *Das Kapital*. It springs, Marx claims, from the division of labor into specialized activities in the factory environment and the division of society into classes that compete with each other. As for the products that the worker makes, Marx goes into convoluted formulas that he claims the part of the value of the goods produced by the worker is taken from the worker and transformed into "surplus value," which the capitalist then steals from the worker.[48] Here Marx misunderstands the nature of the exchange between the employer and the worker. The employer is buying the worker's time. The product of his time at no time belongs to the worker as the employer provides the machines, the raw material, and everything else necessary to produce the end product.

Marx also makes the fallacious assumption that everyone is capable of being an artisan and making whatever tool they may want or require.

According to Marx the pay the worker receives, is not suitable compensation for that labor. This is a judgment call and hails back to Marx's idea that specialization of a worker focused on one step in the production of a product is bad and that the worker should make the entire product himself and then sell that product himself. But then since Marx and most particularly Engels, thought that money was evil, how can an artisan sell the product of his hands without reverting to barter and where would our society be if it depended on barter as a means of exchange?

Marx also ignores the fact that in this situation the worker, making the complete product, provides all machinery and materials necessary to produce that product. In an environment of specialized workers, each individual worker is ignorant of the whole process, both individually and socially. He contends that this causes the goods to lose their quality as human products, that the products of the worker's labors become fetishes, or alien and oppressive realities where one individual possesses them privately and to which the individual who is deprived of them submits themselves. Marx continues that in a market economy, this submission to things is lost in the process of exchanging goods for money, which obscures the alienation.

On the other hand, if money is so evil, it should be considered how constricted the economy would be if man's economic system was reduced to a barter system. Could the assembly line worker exchange so many twists of his wrench for a box of cereal? Money lifted man from an economy of exchanging simple products to one where science and industry has produced cell phones, space travel, and the internet, because the labor used in creating those things is converted into a universally acceptable commodity, money, which can then be exchanged for anything.

---

[48] von Böhm-Bawerk, Eugen, Translated by Macdonald, A.M., *Karl Marx and the Close of His System* (New York: MacMillan, 1898), p. 6.

Twin Evils

Marx says that along with economic alienation comes secondary political and ideological alienations, which distort the representation and offer an illusory justification of a world where the relations between individuals is distorted. Workers become closely tied with their material activity and material relationships. Marx says: "The act of making representations, of thinking, the spiritual intercourse of men, seem to be the direct emanation of their material relations." This is basically an attack on materialism and ignores the quality-of-life issues that have come from the wide spectrum of goods that become available at low prices, directly influencing the quality of life of the workers. It seems that Marx believed that this moves man away from morality, law, and religion. Strange that Marx should worry about moving man away from religion, when Marxism itself drives man away from religion. This is obviously another flaw in Marxist ideology.

Marx believed that in a capitalist society individuals are divided into political and economic actors. He labels this political alienation, which is intensified in a bourgeois state. Unfortunately, he based this on his evaluation of the world enduring a massive industrial evolution in its earliest stages and came to the conclusion that it was through this that the propertied class used the state to dominate the other classes. Marx sought to break this domination of one class by another, but in Marxist societies, as they have been established, it is the leadership of the State that dominates all classes. Human nature being what it is, some groups always dominates the rest of society.

In speaking of ideological alienation, Marx saw different forms appearing in his economic, philosophical and legal theories. In *Das Kapital*, he undertakes a tedious critique of this and repeats it in *The German Ideology*. However, Marx finds the greatest expression of ideological alienation in religion. Marx considered it to be a product of human consciousness and that it was a reflection of a person who has "either .. not conquered himself or has already lost himself again" in the world of private property. Of course, he notably declared it the "opium for the people." Marx believed (or hoped) that religion would disappear as a result of changes in society.

In fact, religion has not diminished because of the changes Marx envisioned. There is a correlation between the quality of life of the members of society and their engaging in religious activities. That is to say, the harder life is and the more suffering in society, people tend to turn to religion for the hope it offers, while when the economy is good, life is easy, and there is little suffering, people are inclined to move away from religion.

This easy life has resulted from the plenty produced by the Capitalist system. By contrast, if one looks at modern China or North Korea, where life is not so easy, Christianity and other religions are expanding because life is filled with hardship and suffering.

Marx on the Factory

Marx had great emotional problems with factories and the division of labor into small, repetitive tasks. He then expanded that concern to society as a whole. In the *Philosophy of Poverty*, he says:[49]

"Let us now examine, from the historical and economic point of view, and see if really the workshop or the machine has introduced the principal of authority into society subsequent to the division of labor; if it has on one hand rehabilitated the worker, while on the other subjecting him to authority; if the machine is the re-composition of divided labor, the synthesis of labor opposed to its analysis.

"Society as a whole has this in common with the interior of a factory, that it also has its division of labor. If the divisions of labor in a modern factory, were taken as a model to be applied to an entire society, the society the best organized for the production of wealth would be incontestably that which had but one single master to distribute the work, according to a regulation arranged beforehand, to the various members of the community. But it is not so. While in the interior of the modern factory the division of labor is minutely regulated by the authority of the capitalist, modern society has no other regulation, no other authority, to arrange the distribution of labor, than free competition. shit

"Under the patriarchal régime, under the régime of castes, under the feudal and corporative régime, there was division of labor in the whole of society according to fixed regulations. <u>Were these regulations established by a legislature?</u> No. Originally born of the conditions of material production, it was not till much later that they were established as laws. It was thus that these various forms of the division of labor became to such an extent the bases of social organization. As to the division of labor in the facto-

---

[49] Marx, K., *Philosophy of Poverty,* p. 147.

ry, it was very little developed in all these forms of society.

<u>"It might even be set up as a general rule, that the less authority presides over the division of labor in the interior of society, the more will be the division of labor be developed inside the factory and the more absolutely will it there be subject to the authority of a single individual.</u> Thus the authority in the factory and that in society, in relation to the division of labor, are in inverse ratio the one to the other."

To examine this, one must first look at the two elements: 1.) the machine, and 2.) society. It is not impossible that Marx was looking at a machine that operated in a continuous fashion and the worker was obliged to scramble to keep up with the machine, so it directed his activity as if a supervisor, and forced him to keep up. It may also be that Marx was looking at the fact that there was surely a foreman on the factory floor who directed the worker's activities.

In the second paragraph, Marx shifts to society. If his society "best organized for the production of wealth" is the authority, and he says that such society is under the control of a single individual, then is he advocating for a dictatorship?

In the third paragraph Marx asks if there was a legislature that made these decisions, the operation of the factory decisions. His answer, "no," is obviously correct, but they why should the decisions be made in a factory by a vote of legislators? Once again Marx jumps to society in his conversation, but here he is talking about how he believes that society was always and had been historically built around the system in use at that time for the production of commodities, be it food in antiquity or automobiles in modern society.

Marx seems to be suggesting that the factory or the method of production is the source of the model that mankind has used to develop society and is advocating for a democratic process rather than an authoritative system. In considering this, it should be recognized that Marx lived at a time when universal suffrage did not exist in Europe and in Russia it was the czar that ruled absolutely. In that light, Marx is probably talking about a purely democratic system where every one stops work, gathers, votes, and then goes back to work.

In the next paragraph Marx says: "<u>Under the patriarchal *régime*, under the *régime* of castes, under the feudal [*régime*]……</u>" These were all authoritative regimes and there were no machines in the modern sense during those regimes. At most there may have been water or wind mills in the feudal period, so where is it that Marx finds the *principal of authority* being introduced by the machine?

Marx's training was in philosophy, not psychology, and he has totally missed the fact that no matter what the situation, man has historically gravitated towards systems where human activity that is directed by a single individual, be the authority, established by force, birth, or elections. If, for example, a village of 100 people had a major decision to make and there were 100 different ideas of what to do, there would be chaos and nothing would be accomplished. Humans innately recognized this and chose systems where a small group or a single individual took the decision on what to do.

The utopian societies of the 18th and 19th centuries proved the truth of this once again. When the charismatic leader died, utopia turned into chaos and fell apart. Even in all the various communist nations of today there is a single leader who quickly turns his leadership into a lifetime service in the position of the nation's leader and leadership passes through a small group of senior party leadership as has occurred in Russia, China, Cuba, and Venezuela, or, as in the case of North Korea, it has literally been turned into a hereditary position along the lines of the kings of Europe and the emperors of China. The practical application of Marxism in the 20th and 21st centuries has made the legislatures Marx address here simply rubber stamps and elections are meaningless when the political machine establishes its authority.

If we look at Chapter III of Mallock's *A Critical Examination of Socialism*[50], we find the idea of "ability", which I mentioned earlier in this chapter. In a capitalist society those with proven ability have created something new that expands productivity, e.g.. Ford's assembly line, or those whose managerial or engineering skills have made improvements in productivity rise to the top and control production.

However, in communist societies, as they have actually been established, those with "ability" are not selected because they created something to improve production, or have shown managerial skill, they are chosen for other reasons, generally for political reliability and commitment.

Communists claim that nobody "created" anything, but that what they did develop was based on the line of inventions and improvements made over the centuries of man's development. As a result, they should

---

[50] Mallock, W.H., *A Critical Examination of Socialism* (New York: Harper & Brother, 1907)

not profit from that development or invention that they created. This was exactly what President Obama meant when he said, "Somebody helped to create this unbelievable American system that we have that allowed you to thrive. Somebody invested in roads and bridges. If you've got a business, you didn't build that."

Have you ever worked in a government bureaucracy? If you had you will find that they are not driven by the goal of efficiency or improvement, they are driven by fear. Fear you ask? Yes, fear, they are afraid that if they do not follow the prescribed rules and regulations laid down for them in regards to how they do their jobs, they will be fired or prosecuted under law. It does not matter how unrelated to the given situation or how outdated the rule may be. Failure to comply means punishment.

I once oversaw the production of explosive detonators in a governmental facility. One program was coming to an end and there was a single lot of about 1,000 units, valued at about $2,000 apiece, to be produced to finish the program. The governmental auditor insisted that I implement Deming's systematic control processes on the last lot. This would have required that I destroy at least 1,000 units in order to gather the necessary data to prove that the welding process involved in making this detonator was "in control." This was despite that over 20,000 units had been produced and the required tests had proven that these welds had exceeded the standard. I didn't know of a single failure. The government auditor was calling for the spending of well over a million dollars simply to prove what we already knew were good products because he was following orders. But then from the bureaucrat's perspective *"Befehl ist befehl!"* [Orders are orders!] Thought and reasoning does not enter into the process.

As for the worker, he has no choice in the communist society, the machine he is assigned, in which factory he works, what profession in which he might engage, what education he might seek or even where he will live. All of that has been dictated to him by the State. As to wishing to take the step of being an independent entrepreneur, control in the former Soviet Union was so strict that the best one could do was to have a small garden plot. In a strange and ironic twist, these private garden plots were the source of a huge percentage of the foodstuff produced by the former Soviet Union, as the system that the government was so inefficient that it could not meet the needs of the people. During the 1970's the US sold thousands of tons of wheat to the USSR to prevent the starvation of its people.

George Nafziger

The Soviet system of agriculture, i.e. "collectivization", was such a failure that in 1932-33 Stalin confiscated all the grain in the Ukraine to feed the starving inhabitants of the major Russian cities. In doing this Stalin also forced the collectivization of the small Ukrainian landholders' farms. The immediate result of this process was the starvation of 4 to 5 million Ukrainians.

By contrast, in the capitalist society, the worker can quit his job and get another. He can even seek to further education and obtain a better job solely at his discretion. In that new job he will fall under the authority of a new plant manager or corporate CEO, or "master" as Marx might call him, but corporations are independent of each other. Coordination between them in capitalist states is, in some circumstances, expressly prohibited by law. Marx himself railed against monopolies, yet today the only monopolies that are allowed to exist in a communist state is the party, which has centralized control of all economic activities. The problem with this is that the state now becomes the monopoly and, in the practical application of this monopoly, the Marxist state has never looked out for the workers, but only for the upper levels of the party establishment.

The second underlined passage: "modern society has no regulation, no other authority, to arrange the distribution of labor, other than free competition." To what "modern society" is Marx referring? Is it the society of the 19th century or is it of his idealized communist society? Again, looking at the centralized control of the former Soviet Union there was no freedom, yet Marx seems to be calling for the worker to escape the dehumanizing nature of the centralized control of the factory or the machine on which he works. Marx contrasts the factory with this "modern society." He seems to be praising "free competition," but his system, as instituted, removes all free competition through the bureaucracy of centralized control.

The third underlined passage: "Were these regulations established by a legislature?" It seems strange that Marx should advocate legislation to determine where and how the individual worker works. It would seem that he is advocating that the government, i.e. the legislature, make those decisions. Again, in the former Soviet Union, which was run by a dictator throughout its history, like every other communist nation, the idea of a freely elected legislature is a joke, as there were no opposition parties allowed to run for office or any legislature that was more than a rubber stamp whose sole purpose was to give a façade of freedom and democracy.

The same observations can be made of the fourth underlined passage "that the less authority presides over the division of labor in the interior of society, the more will the division of labor be developed inside the factory and the more absolutely will it there be subject to the authority of a single individual." As established, the communist system completely contradicts this. Centralized control of all the means of production, of all economic activity, is driven by the whim of the "single individual", be he Vladimir Lenin, Joseph Stalin, Nikita Khrushchev, Leonid Brezhnev, Yuri Andropov, Konstantin Chernenko, or Mikhail Gorbachev.

Analysis of the Economy

Marx analyzed the market economy system in *Das Kapital* using most of the categories of the English economists Smith and Ricardo but adapts them and introduces new concepts such as surplus value. In *Das Kapital* Marx studied the economy as a whole and not in any of its individual elements. His analysis is based on the concept that humans are productive beings and that all economic value comes from human labor and as it existed in 19th century England. This system rose from private economic activities and competition between mercantile houses that began in the 16th century resulting from international trade and colonial expansion. The growth of this system was facilitated by technical developments in the methods of production and factories that replaced the guilds, the adoption of mechanization, and various technological developments, such as the steam engine and water and wind driven mills. These developments produced and required the accumulation of wealth that was invested in factories that grew larger and larger, and employed more and more workers. This produced an "enormous accumulation of commodities." It is from this point that Marx begins with the study of this accumulation, analyzing the unequal exchanges that take place in the market. By unequal exchanges, Marx looks only at the number of hours of labor used to make any individual produce and totally ignores the quality of labor and the capital investment by the "capitalist" in the means of production that allows workers to be more productive. As I said earlier, he considers an hour of one worker to be the equivalent of that of another, assuming that an hour of labor by an engineer is as valuable as the hour of work by a high school dropout. This is equal in value to the professor teaching Marxist theory.

Marx is correct when he says that if a capitalist lends funds to buy a raw material and then produces a finished good, which he then sells at a profit, he is able to invest that profit in additional production capacity. "Not only is the value advance kept in circulation, but it changes in its magnitude, adds a plus to itself, makes itself worth more, and it is this movement that transforms it into capital." This transformation, according to Marx, is only possible because the capitalist has "appropriated the means of production, including the labor power" of the workers. Because of this, he contends that labor power produces more than what it is paid as a wage. Marx continues to say that the value of labor power is established by the quantity of labor necessary for its reproduction, i.e. the amount required by the worker to subsist and provide for his children. He then says that in the hands of the capitalist and in his factory, this labor power produces more than the value of the sustenance required by the worker and his family. Again, Marx is focused on subsistence existence and gives no consideration to how modern capitalism has raised the standard of living in the U.S. to a point where it is flooded annually by immigrants seeking to improve their economic status. Marx claims that this difference, or profit if you prefer, is appropriated by the capitalist, who obtains it through the market where the finished goods are sold. Marx does not consider that in capitalist society there are sources of surplus value other than the exploitation of human labor. He focuses solely on the element of the labor involved in the process.

In Marx's terminology, surplus value is produced by the employment of labor power. Capital buys the labor power (the worker's time and effort at his job) and pays labor's wages. Marx believed that by means of his work, the laborer produces a new value, which does not belong to him, but to the capitalist, who paid the worker a wage to work in the factory and thus produce that value. The worker works for a period of time to produce the equivalent value of his wages. Somehow Marx believed that the worker should receive all the value of his work and no profit be accrued to the capitalist. He seems to have forgotten the concept of a willing seller and a willing buyer of the labor power. He also ignores the concept that labor is a commodity that is both mobile and can be sold on the open market to the highest bidder. Instead, Marx believed that when the worker had created a value X, the value of his labor, he continues to work further hours and that this new value that he produces, beyond the value of his wages, is "surplus value." This may be, but the worker has sold his time, in the form of hours of labor in a factory for a given sum of money and if the capitalist provides him with the tools and mechanisms to produce this surplus value, that workers deserve some compensation for the capital investment he has made in the factory and the risk and delayed gratification the capitalist has incurred or made to accumulate the wealth necessary to create those circumstances, i.e. factory, tools, machines, that allow the production of surplus value.

In *Das Kapital,* Marx argues that the development of capitalism is accompanied by increasing contradictions, but he does not explain what he means by "contradiction." For example, the introduction of new technology is profitable to a given capitalist because it enables him to produce more goods at a lower cost, his new technology is quickly adopted by his competitors, and the expenditure for new technology grows faster than the increase in wages. He goes on saying that since only labor can produce the surplus value from which profit is derived, the capitalist's rate of profit on his total outlay tends to decline. He then contends that with a declining rate of profit, unemployment increases. Marx ignores the fact that technological development is not static, but that in the quest for a technological advantage over competing companies produces continuous technological development and the obsolescence of older technologies. The result of this constant change actually produces new jobs that frequently require new skills; that it results in the production of more goods per labor hour, which increases the goods that the worker can buy, i.e. as Henry Ford did with his production line where he changed automobiles from the toys of the rich to something the factory worker could afford.

Marx claims that the equilibrium of the system is unstable and subject to change, which it is. He claims that periodic crises shake the system and will lead to a general crisis that will destroy the system. This instability, he claims, is increased by the formation of a "reserve army of workers," be they factory workers or peasants, which are steadily driven into poverty. "Capitalist production develops the technique and the combination of the process of social production only by exhausting at the same time the two sources from which all wealth springs: the earth and the worker." Marx says that these fundamental contradictions can only be resolved by a change from capitalism to a new system. Of course, he was writing in the mid-19th century and though there has been nearly two centuries of technological development and evolution, no such systemic collapse has occurred. The per-capita, adjusted for inflation, income in capitalist America is far greater than the rest of the world and most particularly the various socialist and communist countries.

There is another issue. If one looks at the world today it is in the undeveloped countries where poverty is highest, and by poverty, I mean actual starvation. By contrast, it is in the most industrialized nations where poverty is least common. Of course, there are always individuals who, through no fault of their own, fall into poverty. However, if one looks at the systems in the United States and in other developed, western nations. There are systems established to feed people, e.g. food stamps, EBT cards, so nobody should be hungry. If they are hungry, it is by the bad life style decisions, e.g. drugs, that they have made or mental illness which precludes them from availing themselves from these programs.

Class struggle

It was from the utopian socialism and the theories of Henri de Saint-Simon that Marx drew his ideas of class and class struggle. Saint-Simon had in turn drawn these ideas from the writings of French historians such as Adolphe Thiers and François Guizot who were well-aware of the ideas of Gracius Babeuf. Unlike these individuals, Marx made class struggle the centerpiece of a social evolution. From this Marx says, "The history of all hitherto existing human society is the history of class struggles."

In Marx's view, history is a record of class struggle. Originally the class struggle occurred between the nobles and the peasants, but with capitalism, it assumed acute form. Once again, Marx ignores history. The medieval peasant was a serf, in essence a slave, who was tied to the land and had few rights. Everything belonged to his noble lord. Marx also believed that there are other lesser classes that group around these two basic classes that confront each other in the capitalistic system. The two principal groups are the bourgeoisie, who own the means of production, and the workers or proletariat. In this instance, however, the proletariat is not a slave and can do as he wishes. Marx, in the *Communist Manifesto*, stated that the fall of the bourgeoisie and the victory of the proletariat was inevitable. He talks about the process of social production, whose last contradictory form is the bourgeois relations of production. He says that this is not an individual contradiction, but something that springs from the conditions of the social existence of individuals. He believed that the forces of production that had developed in the midst of the bourgeois society would simultaneously create the conditions necessary to resolve this contradiction. Sadly, however, Marx does not provide a clear definition of what he means by contradiction.

Marx perceived that there are two views of revolution. One is that of a final conflagration, "a violent suppression of the old conditions of production," which occurs when the opposition between bourgeoisie and proletariat has been carried to its extreme point. This conception is set forth in a manner inspired by the Hegelian dialectic of the master and the slave, in *Die heilige Familie* (1845; *The Holy Family*). The other conception is that of a permanent revolution involving a provisional coalition between the proletariat and the petty bourgeoisie rebelling against a capitalism that is only superficially united. Once a majority is won to the coalition, an unofficial proletarian authority constitutes itself alongside the revolutionary bourgeois authority. Its mission is the political and revolutionary education of the proletariat, gradually assuring the transfer of legal power from the revolutionary bourgeoisie to the revolutionary proletariat.

If one reads *The Communist Manifesto* carefully one discovers inconsistencies that indicate that Marx did not reconcile the concepts of catastrophic and of permanent revolution. Moreover, Marx never analyzed classes as specific groups of people opposing other groups of people. Depending on the writings and the periods, the number of classes varies; and unfortunately the pen fell from Marx's hand at the moment when, in *Das Kapital* (vol. 3), he was about to take up the question. Reading *Das Kapital*, one is left with an ambiguous impression about the destruction of capitalism: will it be the result of the "general crisis" that Marx expected, or the action of the conscious proletariat, or of both simultaneously?

Marx was correct about the source of the revolution being a "general crisis." In Russia the collapse of the Russian transportation system, which was overwhelmed by the demands of the war effort in 1916-17, preventing adequate food supplies from being moved to the cities and even to the armies fighting the Germans. The subsequent starvation produced riots in the cities and mass desertions in the army. Czarist Russia literally collapsed. Then began the political struggle, the mutiny of the Russian fleet, the Russian Civil War, and the eventual establishment of the Soviet regime.

In China the Kuomintang Government was already struggling with a communist revolution, but that was one of many internal struggles following the collapse of the Imperial government, when the Japanese invaded. The Japanese invasion nearly destroyed the Communist Party, but it recovered and when the Japanese were finally defeated, the weakened Kuomintang Government was unable to deal with the communists.

The same destabilization process was produced by the Japanese invasion of Vietnam. In this instance the Viet Min had been fighting to liberate Vietnam from French colonialism. This opened the door for the Vietnamese communist party to eventually take control. The short-lived communist regime of Pol Pot in Cambodia started in crisis but collapsed and failed before it could become strongly established.

As almost an exception to this, the communization of Poland, Hungary, Czechoslovakia, Bulgaria, and Rumania were produced by the destruction of the German armies that were fighting the USSR and allowed the Soviets to occupy and impose communist governments on those states. Only Yugoslavia had a strong communist guerilla force under Tito that was able to impose communism on Yugoslavia.

Cuba had no crisis as such. It had a revolution led by Castro against the corrupt Batista regime, but it was funded and supported by the USSR. The only truly non-crisis establishment of a communist government occurred in Venezuela through a free election process that a communist regime was established.

Engels and Communism

Unlike Marx, Engels actually had experience with factories, which resulted from his managing a Manchester factory belonging to his father's cotton firm. He was born in Germany in 1820, educated at the "Realschule" at Barmen, Germany, and the Gymnasium at Dilberfeld for a commercial career. He also studied the classics.[51] In 1842, Engels joined his father's firm, but he became a communist. In 1844, the year he and Marx began their long friendship, Engels working on *Umrisse zu einer Kritik der Nationalökonomie* [*Outline of a Critique of Political Economy*] - a critique of Smith, Ricardo, and others. This work contained the critique that Marx intended to make of the bourgeois political economy in *Das Kapital*. Engel's work *Die Lage der arbeitenden Klassen in England* [*The Condition of the Working Class in England*] was based on his observations of the life of the workers in Manchester, England. It was an analysis of the evolution of industrial capitalism and its social consequences. In addition, because of his close friendship with Marx, he worked on other works: *The Holy Family, The German Ideology,* and *The Communist Manifesto.* Apparently, Engels provided Marx with both technical and economic data on the industrial world and reviewed the early drafts of *Das Kapital*. Marx died before he completed *Das Kapital*, and Engels picked up that task, working from Marx's notes, and completed Volumes 2 and 3 of *Das Kapital*.

---

[51] Spargo, p. 73.

Twin Evils

Observations and Critique of *Das Kapital*

Advocates of Marxism proclaim *Das Kapital* as a literary masterpiece. Having read it, I support the opinion of Eugen von Böhm-Bawerk in *Karl Marx and the Close of His System*.[52] Von Böhm-Bawerk says the following:

> As an author Karl Marx was enviably fortunate. No one will affirm that his work can be classified among the books which are easy to read or easy to understand. Most other books would have found their way to popularity hopelessly barred if they had labored under an even lighter ballast of hard dialectic and wearisome mathematical deduction. But Marx, in spite of all this, has become the apostle of wide circles of readers, including many who are not as a rule given to reading difficult books. Moreover, the force and clearness of his reasoning were not such as to compel assent. On the contrary, men who are classed among the most earnest and most valued thinkers of our science, like Karl Knies, have contended from the first, by argument that it was impossible to ignore, that Marxian teaching was charged from top to bottom with every kind of contradiction both of logic and of fact. It could easily have happened, therefore, that Marx's work might have found no favor with any part of the public – not with the general public because it could not understand his difficult dialectic, and not with the specialists because they understood it and its weaknesses only too well. As a matter of fact, however, it has happened otherwise.
>
> Nor has the fact that Marx's work remained a torso during the lifetime of its author been prejudicial to its influence. We are usually and rightly, apt to mistrust such isolated first volumes of new systems. General principals can be very prettily put forward in 'General Sections' of a book, but whether they really possess the convincing power ascribed to them by the author, can only be ascertained when in the construction of the system they are brought face to face with all the facts in detail. And in the history of science it has not seldom happened that a promising and imposing first

---

[52] von Böhm-Bawerk, Eugen, Translated by Macdonald, A.M., *Karl Marx and the Close of His System* (New York: MacMillan, 1898, pp. 21-25.

volume has never been followed by a second, just because, under the author's own more searching scrutiny, the new principals had not been able to stand that test of concrete facts. But the work of Karl Marx has not suffered in this way. The great mass of his followers, on the strength of his first volume, had abounded faith in the yet unwritten volumes.

The faith was, moreover, in one case put to an unusually severe test. Marx had taught in his first volume that the whole value of commodities was based on the labour embodied in them[53], and that by virtue of this 'law of value' they must exchange in proportion to the quantity of labour which they contain; that, further, the profit or surplus value falling to the capitalist was the fruit of extortion practiced on the worker; that, nevertheless, the amount of surplus value was not in proportion to the whole amount of the capital employed by the capitalist, but only to the amount of the 'variable' part – that is, to that part of capital paid in wages – while the 'constant capital,' the capital employed in the purchase of the means of production, added no surplus value. In daily life, however, the profit of capital is in proportion to the *total* capital invested; and, largely on this account, the commodities do not as a fact exchange in proportion to the amount of work incorporated in them. Here, therefore, there was a contradiction between system and fact which hardly seemed to admit of a satisfactory explanation. Nor did the obvious contradiction escape Marx himself. He says with reference to it, 'This law' (the law namely that surplus value is in proportion only to the variable part of capital), 'clearly contradicts all *'prima facie'* experience.' But at the same time he declares the contradiction to be only a seeming one, the solution of which requires many missing links, and will be postponed to later volumes of his work. Expert criticism thought it might venture to prophesy with certainty that Marx should never redeem this promise, because, as it sought elaborately to prove, the contradiction insoluble. Its reasoning, however, made no impression at all on the mass of

---

[53] The actual quotation reads: "First, that the value of each commodity is only and solely determined by the quantity of labor exacted by its production; ...." Marx, K. *The Poverty of Philosophy*, (Chicago: Kerr, 1820). p. 11.

Marx's followers. His simple promise outweighed all logical refutations.

The suspense grew more trying when it was seen that in the second volume of Marx's work, which appeared after the master's death, no attempt had been made towards the announced solution (which , according to the plan of this whole work, was reserved for the third volume), nor even was the slightest intimation given of the direction in which Marx proposed to seek for the solution. But the preface of the editor, Friedrich Engels, not only contained the reiterated positive assertion that the solution was given in the manuscript left by Marx, but contained also an open challenge, directed chiefly to the followers of Rodbertus, that, in the interval before the appearance of the third volume, they should from their own resources attempt to solve the problem 'how, not only without contradicting the law of value, but even by virtue of it, an equal average rate of profit can and must be created.'

I consider it one of the most striking tributes which could have been paid to Marx as a thinker that this challenge was taken up by so many people, and in circles much wider than the one to which it was chiefly directed. Not only followers of Rodbertus, but men from Marx's own camp, and even economists who did not give their adherence to either of these heads of the socialist school, but who would probably have been called by Marx 'vulgar economists,' vied with each other in the attempt to penetrate into the probable nexus of Marx's lines of thought, which were still shrouded in mystery. There grew up between 1885, the year when the second volume of Marx's *Capital* appeared, and in 1894 when the third volume came out, a regular prize essay competition on the 'average rate of profit,' and its relations to the 'law of value.' According to the view of Friedrich Engels – now, like Marx, no longer living – as stated in his criticism of these prize essays in the preface of the third volume, no one succeeded in carrying off the prize."

This passage covers much ground. Let me start with the first issue, Marx's literary style. It was the practice of educated Germans and the German nobility to speak in long, convoluted sentences heavily punctuated with colons and semi-colons, breaking up what might otherwise be considered as run-on sentences, and three paragraphs later ending in a solitary and lonely period. This was done as a method of distinguishing the speaker as being of the higher social classes when considered vis-à-vis the language of the common man.

In a strange contrast to Marx, Engels, who finished *Das Kapital*, usually wrote in a much clearer and less stilted style. Sometimes, however he chose to continue Marx's style, or, in using Marx's notes, he translated instead of rewriting those notes, when he completed *Das Kapital*.

Adding to this Marx never defines any of his terminology, leaving it to the reader to guess what Marx is talking about. Then again, Marx had a degree in philosophy, *ipso facto* it was *de rigueur* for him to speak thus. And I demonstrate my point by writing the previous sentence as he would.

To the second point: "Marx had taught in his first volume that the whole value of commodities was based on the labour embodied in them, and that by virtue of this 'law of value' they must exchange in proportion to the quantity of labour (not is quality) which they contain; that, further, the profit or surplus value falling to the capitalist was the fruit of extortion practiced on the worker...."

To deal with this point we need to explore more of Marx's life and his writings. Marx was very much a man of his time and, the little the history of the industrial world that had preceded him and existed around him, greatly influenced him and limited the applicability of his theories.

In reading *The Poverty of Philosophy* industrial history becomes very apparent. He says, "But labor time serving as means of value, does it at least give rise to the proportional variety of commodities, which so charms M. Proudhon?

"On the contrary, monopoly in all its dreary monotony, follows in its train and invades the world of commodities, as, in the sight and to the knowledge of everybody, monopoly invades the world of the instruments of productions. It appertains only to certain branches of industry to make very rapid progress, as for instance the cotton industry."[54]

Marx is complaining about how the linen industry was overwhelmed by the cotton industry, which is a secondary issue, but one of importance. He is, however, complaining about monopolies and their predatory and oppressive nature. Marx did not live long enough to see the Sherman Anti-Trust Act, which outlaws monopolies. Sadly, it is now liberal and "progressive" politicians, the same people who promote

---

[54] Marx, K., *The Poverty of Philosophy* (Chicago: Kerr & Co., 1920) p.71.

socialism, who are protecting Facebook, Google, Twitter, etc., in their monopoly of the communication system. Then again, those monopolies are the "progressive's" monopolies, ergo they are good.

Then Marx says, "Cotton, potatoes, and spirits are the object of the commonest use. Potatoes have engendered scrofula[55]; cotton has largely driven linen[56] and wool out of the market, although wool and linen are in many cases of much greater utility, if only from consideration of hygiene; spirits, again have largely replaced beer and wine, although spirits, used as food, are generally recognized to be poison. For a whole century Governments vainly struggled against European opinion; economies prevailed, they dictated workers to consumption.

"Why, then, are cotton, potatoes, and spirits the pivots of bourgeois society? Because the least amount of labor is necessary for their production and they are in consequence at the lowest price. Why does the minimum price decide the maximum consumption? Can it by any chance because of the absolute utility of these objects, of their intrinsic utility, of their utility in so far as they correspond in the most useful manner to meet the needs of the worker, as man, and not of the man as worker? No, it is because in a society based upon poverty, the poorest products have the fatal prerogative the poorest products have the fatal prerogative of serving the use of the greatest number."

At this juncture Marx is making the assumption that cheap prices necessarily mean poor quality. Marx came from an upper-class family, and it is clearly apparent that his upbringing greatly influenced his tastes. He drank wine and beer, not whiskey or other spirits; he slept on linen sheets and wore linen underwear and shirts; and Heaven forbid that a potato should cross his lips. If he ~~basis~~ bases his economic theories on these issues, then he not only missed the boat, he was on a mountain peak when the boat sailed.

Talking 150 years after he wrote *The Poverty of Philosophy* it is easy for me to use hindsight to pick at his theories, but the law of supply and demand worked back in his day just as it does today. Take the potato and let's look at Europe. The War of the Bavarian Succession was fought

---

[55] Scrofula is a condition in which the bacteria that causes tuberculosis causes symptoms outside the lungs. This usually takes the form of inflamed and irritated lymph nodes in the neck. Doctors also call scrofula "cervical tuberculous lymphadenitis." Let's be polite and say that Marx didn't study medicine and his grasp on medical issues is about as good as his grasp on economics.

[56] Linen was a major German industry and employed many Germans. Marx's anger against cotton stems from the unemployment the English cotton mills produced in Germany and would appear to be another indication of his nationalism.

from 3 July 1778 – 21 May 1779. It is sometimes called the "Kartoffeln Krieg" or "Potato War." It got this name because the soldiers supplemented their diet by scrounging potatoes from the fields to supplement their diet, which consisted of mostly bread, with some wine or beer, a bit of meat, and sometimes dried vegetables. As for this "bread" it was called "caisson bread" and was basically a rock-hard biscuit that didn't mold very quickly and had to be soaked in wine or water before it could be eaten. Furthermore, the weevils in it were considered another source of protein. So, the potatoes were a luxury to the soldiers. As for the general population, the potatoes had already become a staple in the diet of the peasants. Look at our diet in the United States today. Potatoes are everywhere. But in Europe at Marx's time, they were still fairly new and something looked down on by the upper classes.

The greatest impact, however, of the lowly potato was in Ireland where starvation was commonplace. The introduction of the potato into Irish agriculture literally caused an explosion in the Irish population because there was enough food and children were surviving childhood. Who would argue that children not starving to death was a bad thing? Now, there was a downside to this, which occurred during Marx's lifetime. The potato crop in Ireland and elsewhere were struck by a blight. The famine, also called the "Great Hunger," began in 1845 when a fungus-like organism called *Phytophthora infestans* spread rapidly throughout Ireland. Roughly half the potato crop was wiped out and over a 1,000,000 Irish died of starvation. Sadly, industry hadn't developed the fungicides and pest resistant strains of potatoes or anything else that we have today, all of which are the products of capitalism.

Now, one shouldn't think that grain - barley, oats, and wheat - was exempt from this kind of problem, which leads to beer. Beer had been developed in Mesopotamia as a way of preserving grain, which if stored for long times rotted, developed molds (ergot among others), and was eaten and soiled by rodents. There is nothing quite like rat turds in your bread. Beer was a way of preserving the grain such that those issues were eliminated. In addition, the alcohol in the beer made it safe to drink when compared to water, which often had a pretty nasty mix of bacteria and parasites in it. Beer was literally developed as a food.

So too was whiskey. In particular, in 18th century Kentucky, when farmers had bumper harvests of corn and tried to store it, corn suffered the same issues as grain in Mesopotamia. In addition, whiskey was easier to transport to market and preserved the value of the corn for the farmers, so

Twin Evils

they could sell their harvest to distant markets. No doubt the same thing was done in Europe and that included potatoes, which were turned into schnapps and vodka.

Now, back to Marx: "Why does the minimum of price decide the maximum of consumption? Can it by any chance because of the absolute utility of these objects, of their intrinsic utility, of their utility corresponding to the needs of the worker, as man, and not of the man as worker? No, it is because in a society based upon poverty, the poorest products have the fatal prerogative of serving the use of the greatest number."

First, Marx, looking through his upper-class glasses, is assuming that these are "poor" products and unsatisfactory substitutes for what had existed in the European diet. That is simply a matter of his personal bias. Bread is good, but so too are potatoes and not only are they easier to grow and take less processing than grains; grain produces celiac disease, but if there is any sort of allergic reaction to potatoes, I'm unaware of it.

Grain and potatoes are both preserved for easier and safer storage by a brewing or fermentation process. Both are preserved, therefore, as food. And, once transformed into a beverage they allow the farmer to not only preserve his harvest in a sanitary manner, they allow him an easier and more efficient way to sell his surplus.

So, we have Marx, who rants about the evil bourgeoisie and upper classes, from which he came, is criticizing a food stuff that actually improved the lives of the proletariat.

As for cotton replacing linen, I let history speak to that issue. Linen is very scarce today and cotton is in everything. Obviously, it was not a poor substitute for linen, it was a superior substitute.

That cotton was cheaper (as were potatoes) it has proven to be a benefit, not a harm for the average person. Not only could the workers' wages go further and provide them with more than the more expensive linen, but cheap potatoes also provided a superior nourishment.

Now, you are probably wondering why I went through this analysis. Let me again reiterate that Marx lived in a time of transition and that he was very myopic and culturally biased. He saw what he knew and liked, but was incapable of seeing the real impact of these three new products: cotton, potatoes, and spirits (whiskey, etc.) on his theories. His reaction was arrogant and based on the upper-class upbringing that he'd had as a child. He was incapable of seeing the advantages accrued to the common man. If his biases and arrogance caused him to miss this simple issue, what else did he miss?

Let's return to his concepts of value. In *The Poverty of Philosophy* and *Das Kapital*, he engages in long diatribes and philosophical discussions of value. However, Marx completely misses a major part of value. Marx claims that the value of a product is only in the labor expended by the worker to produce that good or service. He also equates the utility of that good with the labor put into it, confounding the two issues. Let us recall that in this Marx equates the value of the labor of the high school drop out flipping burgers with the university professor teaching Marxist theory. Labor is labor and its quality is irrelevant in Marx's ideology.

Von Böhm-Bawerk also takes issue with Marx on this point. He says the following:

> The fundamental proposition which Marx puts before his readers is that the exchange value of commodities - for his analysis is directed only to this, not to value in use [i.e. utility] - finds its origin and its measure in the quantity of labour incorporated in the commodities.
> Now it is certain that the exchange values, that is to say the prices of the commodities as well as the quantities of labour which are necessary for their reproduction, are real, external quantities, which on the whole is quite possible to determine empirically. Obviously, therefore, Marx ought to have turned to experience for the proof of a proposition the correctness or incorrectness of which must be manifested in the facts of experience; or in other words, he should have given a purely empirical proof in support of a proposition adapted to a purely empirical proof. This, however, Marx does not do. And one cannot even say that he heedlessly passes by this possible and certainly proper source of knowledge and conviction. The reasoning of the third volume proves that he was quite aware of the nature of the empirical facts, and that they were opposed to his proposition. He knew that the prices of commodities were not in proportion to the amount of incorporated labour, but to the total cost of production, which comprise other elements besides. He did not therefore accidentally overlook this the most natural proof of his proposition, but turned away from it with the full consciousness that upon this road no issue favourable to his theory could be obtained.

Twin Evils

I would go further and argue that utility is unassociated with the labor necessary to produce a good; and I would also argue that there is an emotional element in value - desirability, and that there is also an element of risk that is a cost worthy of recovery by the seller. So, I would argue that these four elements labor, utility, desirability, and risk, may or may not be related to the scarcity of the good. First, let's look at labor and its relation to utility examining a simple cutting device - the stone knife. Flint, because of its physical nature, produces conchoidal fractures and with a few well-aimed blows of a stone on a piece of flint a sharp edge can be produced. Life without the ability to cut things would be pretty miserable; imagine gnawing on a whole deer instead of just a piece of it.

Flint, however, is not found everywhere and it was widely traded by primitive humans. Obsidian, a volcanic mineral with the qualities of flint, can be found in Indian burial mounds in the Eastern United States. It is a beautiful jet black that glistens. It also can be turned into long flakes that have the sharpness of a surgical scalpel. It is both beautiful and highly useful and it only comes from the Pacific coast or Central Mexico. It was traded and transported all over North America, because it can be found in Indian burials in the Eastern United States. It wasn't transported as a finished good, it was moved around simply as a chunk of stone so the end user could make of it what he would. The only labor was picking it up and carrying it, yet the utility was tremendous. No one knows what was traded for pieces of obsidian 1,000 years ago, but if it moved hundreds of miles and was so treasured as to be a burial offering, it obviously had a tremendous value, far above flint, chert, or other similar silicates. This "desirability", in addition to its superior utility, obviously added to the price of the product, which caused it to be carried hundreds of miles where the desirability value was highest.

Another instance is rap music. Rap musicians earn millions of dollars a year because some people like that kind of music, but there are others you couldn't pay to listen to it. Again, "desirability." Yet Marx does not take this into consideration at any time in his analysis of value. If he misses that element of value, then how valid are his observations on the whole issue of value?

A similar contradiction to his claim that value is only created by the labor of man can be found in gold and silver. Gold is commonly found in nature in the native, or near pure form. There are some impurities in it, but gold chemically bonds with almost nothing. It is best described as inert.

Thus, the only labor involved in the production of gold is melting it out of the ore. If one wants to take it to 99.999999% pure there is a chemical process, but that methodology was developed after Marx died.

In contrast silver is rarely found in a native form. It is generally found in chemical compounds, i.e. various mineral ores, which must be processed by various means, before it reaches anything near the purity of native gold.

If one takes Marx's theory that value is only created by the human hand, both gold and silver ore must be gathered so there is equal value imparted. Gold is frequently found in the beds of streams and is easily gathered. As a side note, the story of the golden fleece arises from the practice in ancient Greece of placing a sheep's pelt in the bottom of a stream and let the gold flakes accumulate in the fleece by filtration. Silver, even in the native form, is rarely found and must be mined. Then the silver must be refined into a relatively pure form.

It follows that there is far more human labor in producing a pound of silver than there is in producing a pound of gold. By Marx's theory, silver should be far more valuable because it takes more labor to produce in anything like a pure form, while nearly pure gold can be simply gathered by leaving a sheep pelt on the bottom of a stream. So, if any reader of this work, who claims to be a true believer in Marxism, wants to show is commitment to Marxist theory of value wishes to trade me gold for my silver on an equal weight basis, I will gladly do so. Sarcasm aside, Marx's theory clearly does not apply to gold and silver. There is obviously another form of value that exists intrinsically in gold that is greater than the intrinsic value of silver. It also follows that if Marx's theory is invalid in this situation, or at least only addresses part of the issue of value. Does it miss that same type of value in everything else that he examined? This is the inexplicable contradiction that Böhm-Bawerk mentions, and all those followers of Marx could not resolve within the context of Marx's theory. Obviously, Marx's theory is unsupportable by any facts, and it follows that there are inherent flaws in all the rest of his theories that are based on his flawed theory.

Let's look at another example. Look at the following are two paintings. One, when it last changed hands, the owner was given nothing for it. The other, when it last changed hands, when sold went for about $500,000 at the time it was sold. One was painted by an artist renowned for his talent and the other was painted by an untrained novice whose art was unknown to the world a year before it changed hands. Do you know which is which?

 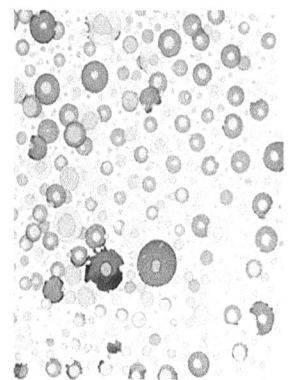

      The Mona Lisa is the work that last changed hands for nothing. Yet it is deemed to be invaluable. The story is that in 1796 the French robbed Northern Italy while the governmental bureaucrats followed Napoleon's victorious army across Northern Italy taking everything of value. The other work, the work of an untrained artist who was the son of a very important politician, sold for $500,000. This shows the juxtaposition of desirability and desirability where the acquisition of some undefined utility is perceived. It also clearly shows that the "skill" of the worker may or may not have any relation to the value created; indeed, there may be some form of "utility" involved in this situation.

      Now let's examine the issue of risk. A 18th century merchant sailing to China to pick up merchandise ran risks to bring those goods back to Europe. First, there were storms and all the other dangers of navigation before weather could be predicted and avoided, and navigational charts were poor at best. Running aground was a serious risk. Second there were pirates and raiders sailing under *lettres de marque*, which made them warships and allowed them to prey on enemy merchant vessels without being treated as pirates. Third, there were enemy warships quick to snap up a rich Indiaman. Today one can buy insurance to address the issues that can result in the loss of a ship and its contents and there is a premium paid for that insurance. In the 18th century the merchants were self-insuring, and they deserved compensation for running the risks of a long sea voyage. The compensation for that risk incurred is the equivalent of the insurance premium paid; insurance is a cost that must be considered when determining the selling price. If the selling price is acceptable to the buyer, we have the concept of a willing seller meeting a willing buyer.

Today manufacturers incur risks as well. Today there is a different type of pirate, the lawyer. Anyone can sue anyone for anything, and large companies are frequently subject to lawsuits. My comment is not intended to say that no company is ever guilty of negligence, but that there are multitude of lawyers who will take any case on contingency and, thus, impose the risk of frivolous lawsuits. This is a cost or a potential cost that the manufacturer must consider when determining the price of that commodity.

Then there is this argument found in *Karl Marx: His Life and Works*:[57] "Professor Jevons himself recognizes that the two theories were not mutually exclusive.[58] He says in one passage of his celebrated work that his theory of final utility leads 'directly to the well-known law, as stated in the ordinary language of economists, that value is proportional to the cost of production.'"[59] It will be remembered, too, that he rests his whole logical structure ultimately upon labor, making in the final determination of value. The relation of labor to value Jevons expresses in tabular form as follows:

"Cost of production determines supply;
Supply determines final degree of utility;
Final degree of utility determines value.

"Could anything be clearer than that according to this reasoning, labor and not utility, is the final determination of value?"

I sincerely wish that all these economists and Marxist philosophers would take a cost accounting class, or maybe spend some time with a factory controller and ask him to explain how he develops the cost of producing a commodity and its ultimate selling price. Having spent time in a factory making commodities let me present a partial list of the expenses, including, beyond pure labor, that goes into making any commodity and explain how the selling price of a commodity is developed:

1.) Direct labor - The actual wages paid to the factory workers expended to make the commodity.
2.) Indirect labor - The wages paid to those who work in

---
[57] Spargo, pp. 344-45.
[58] The two theories are Marx's which says that the value of a commodity is the labor put into it and Ricardo's theory where the value is the labor necessary to the production of a commodity that determines its value. The difference is only one that a philosopher would car about.
[59] "*Theory of Political Economy*, by W.S. Jevons, Third edition, page 186."

quality control, maintenance, warehousing, the accounting staff, janitors, security, human resources, etc.

3.) Direct material - The material that became part of the commodity. This includes wastage and spoilage

4.) Indirect material - The grease, etc., used to maintain the machines the worker uses to make the commodity, safety equipment, maintenance parts of every nature, pens and pencils used in the office, gasoline or other fuel for vehicles, toilet paper, etc.

5.) Electricity & gas - To run the machines that make the product, air conditioning, lighting, etc., etc.

6.) Water - Cooling for machines that make the product, sanitation, drinking fountains, etc.

7.) Depreciation - Every machine used directly or indirectly to make the commodity, including, but not limited to the furniture in the factory, the maintenance tools, the warehouse equipment, i.e. forklifts, computers, carpeting, the parking lot, the factory's sign, any other vehicles. It also includes the factory and any other structures. The purpose of depreciation is to recover the costs so as to be able to replace any of this equipment when it wears out.

8.) Transportation - A potential incidental cost.

9.) Warehousing - As necessary.

10.) Waste disposal - This can include government imposed environmental costs.

11.) Other expenses - Advertisement to hire employees, advertising to sell the commodity, cost of travel by management and staff, training, and lawyers to deal with frivolous lawsuits, etc.

All the costs other than direct labor and direct material are added up and a ratio is developed of indirect costs to each dollar of direct labor. This is called the overhead rate. Then using the standard established for each commodity that is based on the direct labor costs and the direct material costs to make one unit, the accountants take the overhead rate and multiply it by the number of direct labor hours and add to that number the direct materials costs to make one unit. To this, to determine the selling price, a profit margin is added.

The overhead rate can vary widely. In an artisan's shop where there are only simple hand tools, the overhead can be tiny. On the other hand, in a highly complex industrial complex with numerically controlled machine tools, robots, high tech environmental controls, etc., the overhead rate can be very high, because the costs of buying high tech machines and systems can be tremendous and their life expectancy may be very short.

Though the modern accounting system does link the value of the final commodity to the direct labor hours, which Marx saw as the only source of value, modern accountants recognize a wide variety of other costs without which the high-tech commodities of today could never be produced.

Regarding wages paid for direct labor, within modern contracting there is the concept of an economic exchange. This occurs when a willing buyer meets a willing seller. It is a simple concept in the factory environment; the capitalist offers an hourly wage to the potential worker who has the option to "willingly" accept it or reject it. If he accepts that wage for his time, the contract is signed, and the worker goes to work in the factory.

The Communist Manifesto

The *Communist Manifesto* begins with a history of human society and calling it a history of class struggles. It begins: "Freeman and slave, patrician and plebeian, lord and serf, guild-master and journeyman, in a word, oppressor and oppressed, stood in constant opposition to one another, carried on an uninterrupted, now hidden, now open, fight, a fight that each time ended either in a revolutionary reconstruction of society at large, or in the common ruin of the contending classes.

"In the earlier epochs of history, we find almost everywhere a complicated arrangement of society into various orders, a manifold gradation of social rank. In ancient Rome we have the patricians, knights, plebeians, slaves; in the Middle Ages, feudal lords, vassals, guild-masters, journeymen, apprentices, and serfs; in almost all of these classes, again, subordinate gradations.

"The modern bourgeois society that has sprouted from the ruins of feudal society, has not done away with class antagonisms. It has but established new classes, new conditions of oppression, new forms of struggle in pace of the old ones.

Twin Evils

"Our epoch, the epoch of the bourgeoisie, possesses, however, the distinctive feature: it has simplified the class antagonisms. Society as a whole is more and more splitting up into two great hostile camps, into two great classes directly facing each other: Bourgeoisie and Proletariat."[60]

It is with this declaration that Marx and Engels begin a discussion of the evolution of capitalism and how an exploitive class struggle arose from it. They point out that political revolutions, i.e. the French Revolution of 1789, etc., overthrew feudalism, that system was replaced by a new class struggle between those who owned the means of production, the bourgeoisie, and the wage workers, the proletariat). They further explain: "The modern bourgeois society that has sprouted from the ruins of feudal society has not done away with class antagonisms. It has but established new classes, new conditions of oppression, new forms of struggle in place of the old ones."

It is accurate to say that the bourgeoisie achieved state power after those revolutions and that they established a new political system. And Marx and Engels accurately state that this new system focused on the views and interests of the wealthy, a powerful minority, and not the interests of the proletariat, who make up the majority of society. They also accurately state that the class antagonisms of the feudal era remained. This society was rocked by the revolutions, those of 1789, of 1848 and again by the establishment of the Commune in Paris in 1871. However, this is, above all, a cry of "Victimhood," declaring to their followers that you have been oppressed, you have been cheated, and your oppressors have lived off of your labor. Historically, from pre-historic times until the early 20th century, this may have been the case, but is it true today? That is the question that the modern reader must answer and again do so in the light that poverty is a relative condition, not an absolute condition.

From there Marx and Engels speak of the exploitive situation where workers compete with each other and sell their labor to the owners of capital, i.e. the bourgeoisie. They neglect, however, to recognize that the workers are mobile and can sell their labor where they wish. They assume a conspiratorial monopoly that they seem to believe existed among the factory owners and do not recognize that there is such a thing as competition for labor where the factory owners may face labor shortages and compete for competent or skilled labor to work in their factories. The situation they discuss may not have existed at the time of the writing of the *Manifesto*,

---

[60] Marx, K. and Engels, F., *The Communist Manifesto and Other Writings*, (New York: Barnes & Noble Classics, 2005. p. 7. Spargo, pp. 108-9

but as time passed, the competition for labor has resulted in the growth of wages. Indeed, in September 2022 in America, despite rising wages, there were 16,000,000 jobs that were open, and employers were desperately looking to rehire the workers that had had before the Covid pandemic. Marx and Engels believed that the social ties used to bind people together were removed and that workers became expendable and replaceable. This concept is known as the "cash nexus." Of course, 2022 proved this wrong.

Marx and Engels believed that as the capitalist system grew and expanded, ownership became increasingly centralized. In this they were accurate, as can be seen by the "Robber Barons of Industry", i.e. J.P. Morgan, Henry Ford, Andrew Carnegie, Cornelius Vanderbilt, and John D. Rockefeller, who rose to prominence at the turn of the 19th-20th centuries, and today exemplified by Jeff Bezos (Amazon), Mark Zuckerberg (Facebook), and Tim Cook (Apple) to mention a few. They go on to predict that the capitalist system is doomed to failure because as this concentration of power and wealth continues, the exploitation of the proletariat will, over time, sow the seeds of revolution. At the time they wrote the *Manifesto*, this was indeed happening, that is the seeds of revolt had been sown, but neither Marx nor Engels showed a direct connection between the concentration of wealth and the revolts that occurred. They end this section of the *Manifesto*, by saying: "What the bourgeoisie therefore produces, above all, are its own gravediggers. Its fall and the victory of the proletariat are equally inevitable."

In Part 2, "Proletariats and Communists", they begin by saying: "In place of the old bourgeois society, with its classes and class antagonisms, we shall have an association, in which the free development of each is the condition for the free development of all." In this section Marx and Engels describe what the Communist Party wants for its ideal society. They claim that it will represent the interests of the proletariat as a whole.

Marx and Engels claimed that capitalism depended on wage-labor and that wage-labor, in turn, depended on competition among the workers. They conceived the iron law of wages, which needed this competition for its operation. They believed that competition belonged to production on a small scale, to the comparative isolation of the workers, that small-scale, competitive industry involved. The development of large production, massing great bodies of workers would inevitably lead to produce a sense of solidarity of interests, of mutual interdependence among the workers. This would sooner or later lead to their forming unions, which did occur, and that this forming of unions would allow for improved conditions, again, which it did. They maintained that though there might be victories in the workplace concerning work conditions and pay, the more important issue was their forming a union. "The real fruit of their victory lies, not in the immediate result, but in the ever-expanding union of the workers." And that the necessary conditions for these unions were provided by the development of capitalist production, massing the workers together, bringing the workers of various localities together, and thus centralizing the numerous local struggles of small groups into a national class struggle.[61]

Marx and Engels then say that the organized workers should become a political force that, to achieve its purposes, that elements of the bourgeoisie would appeal to the proletariat to secure its own interests. By drawing them into the political arena political education and training would begin. Subsequently the proletariat would eventually fight the bourgeoisie, turning the bourgeoisie into its own "grave diggers."

When they said that unions should become a political force, they believed it would produce an inevitable struggle, and the communists openly declared that their aim was to produce a social revolution. However, by "revolution" they meant the result, not the method of attaining it, not the method of bringing about the transformation of society, but the result, regardless of the methods by which it was attained. The revolution was, to them, the transformation of the social forces of production from capitalist property to social property, i.e. private property becomes communal property.

However, Marx said: "The trades unions should never be affiliated with or made dependent upon a political society if they are to fulfil the object for which they were formed. If this happens, it means their death blow. The trades unions are the school for Socialism, the workers there are educated in Socialism by means of the incessant struggle against capitalism which is being carried on before their eyes. All political parties, be they what they may, can hold sway over the masses of the workers for only a time; the trade unions, on the other hand, capture them permanently; only the trades unions are thus able to represent a real working class party, and to form a bulwark against the power of capital. The greater mass of the workers conceive the necessity of bettering their material position whatever political party they may belong to. Once the material position of the worker has improved, he can then devote himself to the improved education of his children; his wife and children need not go to the factory, and he himself can pay some attention to his own mental education. He can

---
[61] Spargo, p. 116.

see to his physique. He becomes a socialist without knowing it."[62] Marx also went so far as to regard trade unions as "schools for Socialism."[63]

In a seeming contradiction to this warning about unions becoming involved with political parties, Marx and Engels stated that the goal of the Communist Party was to turn the proletariat into a cohesive class with clear and unified class interests, to overthrow the rule of the bourgeoisie, and to seize and redistribute political power; that the transformation of social forces of production from capitalist property to social property was the revolution. The key to doing this, Marx and Engels said, was the abolition of private property. They claimed that this confiscation of property had already been done by the capitalists and that nine-tenths of the population had been stripped of their private property. Aside from being a grand eloquent statement, it is a phenomenal exaggeration of facts.

Marx and Engels claimed that private property only benefited the bourgeoisie in a capitalist society, which produced suffering amongst the proletariat, hence their advocation for a "social" revolution that included the confiscation of private property. They went on to say that "Capital is, therefore, not a personal, it is a social power.

"When, therefore, capital is converted into common property, into the property of all the members of society, personal property is not therefore transformed into social property, it is only the social character of the property that is changed. It loses its class character."

Continuing, they said: "Communism deprives no man of the power to appropriate the products of society; all that it does is to deprive him of the power to subjugate the labour of others by means of such appropriation."[64]

Their first step in the revolution was to raise the proletariat to the position of being the ruling class. It would then use its political supremacy to wrest all the capital from the bourgeoisie, centralize all instruments of production and place them in the hands of the state, and increase the total productive forces as rapidly as possible.

At this point Marx and Engels lay out a ten-point agenda, which is as follows:

1. Abolition of private property in land and application of all rents of land to public purpose.
2. A heavy progressive (graduated) income tax.

---

[62] Spargo, p. 248.
[63] Spargo, p. 253.
[64] Sparge, p. 124-5.

3. Abolition of all rights of inheritance.
4. Confiscation of the property of all those who emigrate and rebels.
5. Centralization of credit in the hands of the state, by means of a national bank with state capital and an exclusive monopoly.
6. Centralization of the means of communication and transportation in the hands of the state.
7. Extension of factories and instruments of production owned by the state; the bringing into cultivation of waste lands, and the improvement of the soil generally in accordance with a common plan.
8. Equal obligation of all to work. Establishment of industrial armies, especially for agriculture.
9. Combination of agriculture with manufacturing industries; gradual abolition of the distinction between town and country by a more equable distribution of the population over the country.
10. Free education for all children in government schools. Abolition of children's factory labor in its present form. Combination of education with industrial production, etc. etc.

    The first four points and the seventh point are focused on the confiscation of all personal property, particularly land and factories, i.e. the sources of wealth, but extending to dwellings and all other forms of wealth. The fifth point places all the levers of the economy in the hands of the state and makes it impossible for any individual to act in an entrepreneurial manner. However, if the state controls all credit and all the means of production, who will need credit? Furthermore, as there is no privately held land, nobody will be borrowing money to buy property of any sort, so controlling credit is in essence the elimination of credit and state control of all economic activity.
    The sixth point, the control of communications and transportation by the State, is controlling the masses by filtering and manipulating all information by the State. Another element of this is the elimination of privately owned conveyances, i.e. automobiles. In the early 21st century there has been a movement to eliminate fossil fuels and replacing gasoline propelled vehicles by electric vehicles. This is a clear attempt at the implementation of state control of transportation. The excuse may be to save the environment, but in fact it is intended to stop the ability of people to freely move about at their will and subject them to state controlled means of transportation. The limited range and expense of electric vehicles is

part of this as it will push people to public, i.e. government-controlled transportation. Even those who are sufficiently wealthy to buy an electric vehicle will be constrained by their limited range.

The eighth point, an equal obligation to work, is aimed at those people who made a living by lending money, which Marx saw as having no value. It implies that those who refused to work would be forced to work.

The ninth point is a strange concept of de-urbanization, i.e. spreading the population "equitably …… over the country." This redistribution springs from Marx's love of primitive Medieval societies. Indeed, this suggests an equalization of the quality of life on a massive scale, either the raising up of the masses to a higher level, or more likely their reduction to an equal level of misery as found in the primitive life of Medieval Europe or India.

Finally, the tenth point may sound like a resolution of the illiteracy that Marx and Engels saw in the general public. The last sentence exposes the most evil intentions, i.e. the state determining the education of individuals to fit into a master plan of production.

In the third part of the *Manifesto* Marx and Engels give three critiques against the bourgeoisie that include reactionary socialism, conservative or bourgeois socialism, and critical-utopian socialism or communism. They claimed that the first part, reactionary socialism, sought to return to feudalism, which was in direct opposition to communism.

The second, conservative or bourgeois socialism, comes from members of the bourgeoisie that recognized that one must address some of the grievances of the proletariat and that they do this through philanthropists, humanitarians, those who run charities, and many other "do-gooder" organizations that espouse and produce this particular ideology. Marx and Engels argue that this group makes only minor adjustments to the system, retaining its overall control, but giving a few crumbs to the proletariat to satisfy it for a while. Conservative or bourgeois socialist certainly exists and to name a few we have George Soros, Jeff Bezos, Mark Zuckerberg, Jack Dorsey, Tim Cook, and others of their ilk. These men spout socialist rhetoric, donate millions to socialist causes and politicians, who they have literally bought, in order to maintain their economic dominance of the American economy and in the hopes of surviving any revolution that might occur.

In contrast to these two groups, Marx and Engels claim that critical-utopian socialism or communism offers real critiques of the class and social structure and that they would bring about this utopia by means of their ten-point program.

In the last part of the *Manifesto*, which addresses the various opposition parties, Marx and Engels state that the Communist party supports all revolutionary movements that challenge the existing social and political order. It then ends with a call for the proletariat to unite. They take the words from the statement made in 1874 when the International announced its dissolution: "Proletariats of all countries, Unite!"

Issues with Marxist Theory

In the terms of the 19th century Marxism is a scientific theory of economics. There are many theories about various part of our economic world: the Keynesian Theory, Modern Monetary Theory, Classical economics, Malthusian economics, Laissez-faire capitalism, Market socialism, and Monetarism to name a few.

There are a wide variety of theories on a multitude of subjects: Evolution, Creationism, Intelligent Design, Relativity, there are seven theories of psychology, five theories of development, and five theories of education.

Each possesses some element of truth. However, at the "inspiration" of its creator they wander off into a philosophical or scientific world that springs from their imagination. When there are several theories on a given subject they will have some elements in common and areas of disagreement. However, one characteristic is true; if there are two or more theories on the same subject, all but one are certainly wrong and even that one may be wrong.

Let us look at the word theory, as defined in the Merriam Webster Dictionary[65]:

> "1: A plausible or scientifically acceptable general principle or body of principles offered to explain phenomena the wave theory of light.
> "2a: A belief, policy, or procedure proposed or followed as the basis of action, i.e. her method is based on the theory that all children want to learn.
> "2b: An ideal or hypothetical set of facts, principles, or circumstances —often used in the phrase in theory, we have always advocated freedom for all.

---
65 https://www.merriam-webster.com/dictionary/theory.

"3a: A hypothesis assumed for the sake of argument or investigation.
"3b: An unproved assumption : CONJECTURE.
"3c: A body of theorems presenting a concise systematic view of a subject, i.e. theory of equations.
"4: The general or abstract principles of a body of fact, a science, or an art, i.e. music theory.
"5: Abstract thought: SPECULATION.
"6: The analysis of a set of facts in their relation to one another."

The reader should notice that none of these definitions use the word fact, proven, etc., but they all use terms like "plausible, conjecture, speculation." In sum, theories are not proven fact.

So, as Marx himself described his ideas as a theory as Engels and the Marxist defenders did through the 19th and early 20th century, thus we have to accept the fact that Marxism is an effort to describe how the economics of production, value, and exchange work, but that it is not proven fact.

Other Issues: Marx and Engels on the Nuclear Family

Communism, as it exists today, seeks to destroy the nuclear family. Marx, however, did not address this. His only commentary on marriage concerns the practice of families giving their daughters in marriage to other families without the daughter's consent. At no time does Marx address taking children away from their parents. According to his biographer, Spargo, he loved children and would frequently play with them, letting them play as they would.

Marx did not explain why he opposed girls being given away in marriage without their consent. It is, however, quite possible that, since he married the daughter of the Baron von Westphalen, that Fraulein Von Westphalen may have been placed "on the market" for marriage by her father. Marx "saved" her from an arranged marriage. It was not the proletariat who arranged marriages for their children; it was the extreme rich who arranged marriages to control family wealth.

Frederick Engels, however, in his dissertation *The Origin of the Family, Private Property, and the State,* addresses giving women away in marriage as a business arrangement, either to consolidate power, or to gather wealth.

In *The Origin of the Family, Private Property and the State,* Engels

Twin Evils

examines a multitude of lifestyles vis-à-vis sexual relationships - from monogamy to polygamy, to polyandry and group marriages among a wide variety of primitive cultures and civilizations. One point to consider is that Engels selectively chooses his cultures to support his theories while totally ignoring others. For example, Engles ignores the Muslim marriage practices and furthermore does not address marriage practices in the Chinese or other oriental cultures.

Engels addresses primitive forms of group marriage where males and females sexually mixed without restriction. The result was that all children were considered the children of every man. While children belonged to the mother, the fathers were unidentifiable Engels eventually claims that this paradise was ruined by technical progress which permitted the production of sufficient food stuffs that could be accumulated thus creating wealth. It is Engel's theory that the accumulation of this wealth produced monogamy allowing the father to pass to his biological children, who were clearly identifiable because of monogamy and virgin marriage. He suggests that monogamy and virgin marriage are the beginning of capitalism, and is, therefore, evil.

Because monogamy, by his analysis, was evil, the group marriage relationship was preferable. It was coupled with an absolutely pure communal lifestyle where few material possessions existed, and all procured food was equally shared. He uses the term "communistic" in discussing this situation. He curses the technological progress that fostered greater food production than necessary for survival. Technological progress permitted the accumulation of food. Food could then be sold for other goods and stimulated the accumulation of wealth that could be passed on to a man's heirs. This suggests, Engels thought, that having only enough food to survive was ideal, because having a surplus of food was the accumulation of wealth. This to Engles, by definition, was evil.

Associated with Engel's theory about technology and food production was the manufacture of various manufactured goods and the concept of possession. Engels continues asserting that the objects of production, together with the excess goods, resulted in greed and the desire to pass on those goods to the man's children. Both Marx and Engle believed that the means of production drove social organization. Male-female relations were, therefore, drawn into their economic theories.

Sadly, Engels ignores two major issues regarding the nature of the "free love" system of the most primitive tribes, particularly among the North American Indians, and possibly the other groups he mentions.

First, one should consider the danger of hunting in the wild when the most powerful weapon was the bow and arrow. Hunters frequently became prey and never returned to the tribe. From the grizzly bear's perspective, a bow and arrow are an annoyance, and the Indian was a tasty snack. Therefore, if the tribe's children were identifiable as the child of one specific individual man, why would another male Indian waste risk his life hunting, while feeding the children of another man, when food was always scarce and starvation was near? Does not Darwin discuss survival of the fittest as being a fact of life in the wild and that successful reproduction, i.e. bringing children to adulthood, the second objective of life? From the Darwinian perspective, the woman's choice of making her child's father questionable, incentivized every male Indian to assure the survival of all the children. The woman was, therefore, completing Darwin's objective of her successful reproduction.

Second, the desirability of such a situation, where there is no accumulation of wealth and the people lived on subsistence farming and hunting, one only needs to consider that it was not an uncommon practice among North American Indians to engage in cannibalism.[66] Ritual cannibalism, or simply cannibalism, is difficult to justify even in the most extreme situations. Therefore, the life among the primitive North American Indian societies must have been very hard. In a civilized society it is morally unacceptable. Marx and Engels, however, clearly ignore this as they attempt to recreate these primitive, non-capitalistic societies. Addressing monogamy, Engels says the following:[67]

> "Monogamy was the first form of family not founded on natural, but on economic conditions, the victory of private property over primitive and natural collectivism."

---

[66] Casgrain, Abbé H.R. *Guerre du Canada – 1756-1760 – Montcalm et Lévis* (Tours : Alfred Mame, 1899). p. 98. "There followed an orgy and nameless cruelties inflicted on the prisoners, three of whom were boiled and eaten." In citing the account of Father Roubaud on page 99 : "The Father approached and recoiled in horror when he saw one of the Indians holding a human head which he was devouring……" We then find on page: 100 "….Sakis, Iowas from the far west, Mascoutins, [who were] man-eaters……"; on page 101: "For lack of fresh meat or English prisoners to eat, they invaded a park where a herd of cattle was kept in reserve……."; and on page 123: "They [the Indians] had thus arrived in Montreal, laden with booty, gorged with blood and human flesh, exalted by a series of successes that surpassed anything they had imagined."

[67] Engels, F., *The Origin of the Family, Private Property, and the State* (Chicago: Kerr, 1902) pp. 79-80.

Twin Evils

Does this mean that all the birds (e.g. cardinals) that are monogamous and mate for life are capitalists? Engels apparently missed this class lesson in biology.

Engels believed that the supremacy of the male in the family and generation of children composing his offspring alone, were destined to be the heirs of his wealth. He states that this was openly avowed by the Greeks to be the sole objects of monogamy. For the rest, it was a burden, a duty to the gods, the state, and their own ancestors, a duty to be fulfilled and no more. In Athens the law enforced not only the marriage, but also the fulfillment of a minimum of so-called "matrimonial duties" on the man's part. Engles writes the following:

> Monogamy, then, does by no means enter history as a reconciliation of man and wife and still less the highest form of marriage. On the contrary, it enters as subjugation of one sex by the other as the proclamation of an antagonism between the sexes unknown in all preceding history. In an old unpublished manuscript written by Marx and myself, in 1846, I find the following passage: 'The first division of labor is that of man and wife in breeding children.' And today I may add: The first-class antagonism appearing in history coincides with the development of the antagonism of man and wife in monogamy, and the first-class oppression with that of the female by the male sex. Monogamy was a great historical societal advance. But by the side of slavery and private property it marks at the same time epoch which, reaching down to our days, takes with all progress also a step backwards, relatively speaking, and develops the welfare and advancement of one by the woe and submission of the other. It is the cellular form of civilized society which enables us to study the nature of its now and fully developed contrasts and contradictions.

It is strange that monogamy is oppressive to women, but polygamy, in Marx's eyes, was not. This is one of Marx's contradictions. Engels further states:[68]

> We have, then, three main forms of the family

---
[68] Ibid. pp. 90-92.

corresponding in general to the three main stages of human development. For savagery group marriage, for barbarism the pairing family, for civilization monogamy supplemented by adultery and prostitution. Between the pairing family and monogamy in the higher stage of barbarism, the rule of men over female slaves and polygamy is inserted.

As we provided by our whole argument, the progress visible in this chain of phenomena is connected with the peculiarity of more and more curtailing the sexual freedom of the group marriage for women, but not for men. And group marriage is actually practiced by men to this day. What is considered a crime for women and entails grave legal and social consequences for them is considered honorable for men or in the worst case a slight moral blemish born with pleasure. But the more traditional hetaerism is changed in our day by capitalistic production and conforms to it, the more hetaerism is transformed into undisguised prostitution, the more demoralizing are its effects. And it demoralizes men far more than women. Prostitution does not degrade the whole female sex, but only the luckless women that become its victims and even those not to the extent generally assumed. But it degrades the character of the entire male world. Especially a long engagement is in nine cases out of ten a perfect training school of adultery.

We are now approaching a social revolution, in which the old economic foundations of monogamy will disappear just as surely as those of its complement prostitution. Monogamy arose through the concentration of considerable wealth in one hand – a man's hand – and from the endeavor to bequeath this wealth to the children of this man to the exclusion of all others. This necessitated monogamy on the woman's part, but not on the man's part. Hence this monogamy of women in no way hindered open or secret polygamy of men. Now, the impending social revolution will reduce this whole care of in heritance to a minimum by changing at least the overwhelming part of permanent and inheritable wealth – the means of production - into social property. Since monogamy was caused by economic conditions, will it disappear when these causes are abolished?

One might reply, not without reason: not only will it not disappear, but it will be perfectly realized. For with the transformation of the means of production into collective property, wage labor will also disappear, and with it the proletariat and the necessity for a certain, statistically ascertainable number of women to surrender for money. Prostitution disappears and monogamy, instead of going out of existence, at least becomes a reality – for men also.

In all events, the situation will be very much changed for men. But also, that of women, and of all women, will be considerably altered. With the transformation of the means of production into collective property, the monogamous property ceases to be the economic unit of society. The private household changes to a social industry. The care and education of children becomes a public matter. Society cares equally well for all children, legal or illegal. This requires the care about the "consequences" which now forms the essential society factor – moral and economic – hindering a girl to surrender unconditionally to the beloved man. Will not this be sufficient cause for a gradual rise of a more unconventional intercourse of the sexes and a more lenient public opinion regarding virgin honor and female shame? And finally, did we not see that in the modern world monogamy and prostitution, though antitheses, are inseparable and poles of the same social condition? Can prostitution disappear without engulfing at the same time monogamy?

Thus, we have Engels speaking of the end of monogamy when no man can clearly identify which children are his; this will result from the collective ownership of the means of production. He declared it evil that a man might plan to pass on to his children the wealth he had acquired by the time of his death. This allowed the accumulation of wealth. He wanted a situation where nobody could accumulate generational wealth. This is strange belief for a man like Engels who came from a wealthy family.

Addressing separating children from their family, Engels is very clear when he says, "The care and education of children becomes a public matter. Society cares equally well for all children, legal or illegal." If the man cannot identify which child is his, he has no interest in who possesses his property after his death, and the "nirvana" of the communist society can be achieved. Society taking care of the children may well be part of the source of the "free education" plank of the *Manifesto*. There is no discussion of the details of this in the *Manifesto*. Therefore, it is possible that this is an expansion of an originally reasonable concept of educating everyone. It is transformed into a means of controlling the masses; the education system, by indoctrinating children, would produce a brain washed mass supported by a system of informers within every family who will report to communist authorities any anti-communist thoughts that might be expressed by their parents or others in their presence. This process was established in every communist society and, in conjunction with the means of communication, it was a method for control.

In light of this, one might examine Hillary Clinton's book *It Takes a Village*. This book emphasizes the shared responsibility that society has for successfully raising children. This contention is quite Marxian. Though Mrs. Clinton does give some responsibility to the parents and grandparents, she emphasizes that neighbors, teachers, ministers, doctors, employers, politicians, nonprofits, faith communities, businesses, and international governmental groups have the responsibility to contribute to the raising and development of children. Does this include politicians, nonprofit organizations, and international groups? Yes. Therein lies the rub.

Beyond Hillary's thoughts, there is the issue of destroying the nuclear family and doing so by any means. This includes indoctrinating children in ideas that fundamentally attack the nuclear family, e.g. encouraging sexualization of children at an early age, not only in traditional sex, but in homosexuality and transsexualism. These practices tear at the base of the nuclear family by preaching to and indoctrinating children in alternative lifestyles.

There is an interesting discussion of this to be found in some North Korean documentation.[69] When it is read one should examine the perspective of one socialist/communist speaking about another socialist/communist's methodology aimed at destroying the capitalist system.

> .... In the quest for gender equality, these leftists have simply expanded the potential workforce for the capitalists

---
[69] *Essential Juche Works* (Red Flame Press) pp, 175-177 Comrade Max Juche 109 "The Impotence of the Left.

to women, a second half of the population which, relatively recently, has been liberated from the prisons as housewives. Another example of this counterproductive "progressive" agenda only proving to service the aims of the bourgeoisie is the phenomena of transgenderism. With the inception of "trans rights", the demand for hormone therapy drugs and surgeries has seen more attention. A new purpose for these already existing drugs has opened a new revenue stream for big pharma by effectively adding a new purpose for these drugs. For example, the popular anti-androgen, spironolactone, used to be mainly used as a diuretic, and similarly, a medication primarily used for menopause, estradiol has been repurposed as an estrogen supplement for trans women.

The systematic castration of the left that I have talked about previously has been perpetrated by the ruling class themselves, and this is observable by looking at the current political climate, with Corbyn's recent campaign in the UK and Sanders's campaign in the US. The ruling class, consciously or not, is reigning in this previously disenfranchised and angry portion of the population and directing their anger into electoral politics instead of at the establishment itself, in a roundabout and deceitful manner, revitalizes the hopes of the left in reform and in the notion that the system can be changed by using the system itself. This is the flaw of ideology. The complex web of policies, values, and rivalries that encompasses ideology is counterproductive when it comes to actually dismantling the system that perpetuates the conditions that led to the inception of these ideologies in the first place. An alternative to this convoluted method of praxis is at first glance, retarded, but when actually considering the way that history is going, is the only plausible way that ANYTHING will change. This alternative would be the anthesis of this intellectual and academic approach. Instead of pontificating and ruminating on historical injustices and debating and debunking nobodies on the internet, one should find in themselves the state of mind in which the sole enemy is the system itself, and one's approach should be to instigate violence and opposition to system politics.

Other issues: Religion versus Atheism.

There is no doubt that Karl Marx was an atheist. However, Spargo directly addresses this issue and clearly says that Marx was tolerant of the religious beliefs of others. Atheism was common among socialists. As the International and other socialist groups struggled for dominance in the late 19th century, there were some very radical groups that pushed for the eradication of religion. This was nothing new. When the French Revolution first took control of Paris and subsequently all of France, there was great anger among the peasantry against the leadership of the Catholic Church. It needs to be understood that at that time the first son of a nobleman received the title and the lands as an inheritance, the second and other sons were expected to go into the Church or the military. Those that went into the Church often lived extravagant lives. They were not generally parish priests, but were immediately made bishops, archbishops, and even cardinals where they lived an opulent life at the expense of the peasants. There are numerous lists of the complaints of French peasants against the church to be found in reading the history of the French Revolution. The churches were land lords who took advantage of the peasants who worked their lands. It was those lands and properties that were expropriated by the Revolutionary Government and sold to the citizenry. They also required the *dime*, or the 1/10th tithe, be paid by everyone to the church. To the peasants, this was just another tax.

In reaction to clerical extravagance, atheism arose. The Catholic Church was driven out of much of French life. Robespierre founded the Cult of the Supreme Being, which was a form of deism. The Cult of Reason, its rival, was founded by Jacques Hébert and it rejected any form of deity. The aim of this Cult of Reason was to seek the Revolutionary goals of Truth and Liberty through the exercise of Reason. Though the Catholic Church was re-established under Napoleon's rule, they constituted the first rebellion against organized religion. Like Gracius Babeuf on socialism, they had their impact on the growth of atheism.

So, from where did the phrase "Religion is the opiate of the masses" derive? Well, despite his moderation in his atheism, it did indeed come from Marx. He wrote it in 1843 as a passing remark in the introduction to a book of philosophical criticism. The book was never published, but in

1844 the phrase appeared in an article he had published in a radical journal that had a print run of 1,000 copies. It was not until the 1930s, when Marxism became stylish, that the maxim entered the popular lexicon. So, here we have a case where Marx's atheism has been misinterpreted and that misinterpretation has been expanded into a dictum.

That said, there is another quote attributed to Marx, which is, "The idea of God must be destroyed. It is the keystone of a perverted civilization. The true root of liberty, of equality, of culture, is Atheism."[70] According to Spargo, this is a quote from Wilhelm Marr, taken from his work *Das junge Deutschland in der Schweize.*

Engels, however, clearly discusses how both Lutheranism and particularly Calvin's doctrine of pre-destination were used to justify holding or condemning people as peasants and the ruled masses. In this he also attacks the idea of "the divine right of Kings", which established and maintained a strict separation of classes - royalty, nobility, bourgeois (city dwellers) and peasants/serfs. Because of these issues, it appears that Engels held religion responsible and supportive of the class system; therefore, religion was the enemy of his communist paradise.

Religion is one of the glues that holds capitalistic society together and its destruction is, therefore, by Marxist theory, something that must be eliminated so that the great Marxist society can be built. In order to achieve the communist society, everything that comes from religion must be destroyed, including the family as presented in various religious doctrines in order that Marx's ideal society may become reality. To this end, today we experience the attack on religious prohibitions against homosexuality and other forms of non-heterosexual behavior. This is also an attack, as advocated by Engels, upon monogamy. By establishing a variety of other sexual options, the traditions that allowed capitalism to exist are subverted, the ties between family members broken, and state control of all human interaction more easily established. Communism is based on the concept of the group, not the individual, so the social bonds that obstruct the formation of greater groups, i.e. the family, must be destroyed together with the encouragement of prohibited sexual practices. This is the way modern Marxism has chosen to achieve that goal.

Furthermore, if one looks at the elements of government control of the masses found in the *Communist Manifesto*, it is easy to see where a communist government could not tolerate any rival to its control over the masses and would, therefore, act to outlaw it. A good example of this

---
[70] Spargo, p. 237.

can be found in modern China where the religion of Falun Gong is being brutally suppressed, and where owning a *Bible* is prohibited. The US State Department's 2016 report on international religious freedom describes the repression of religious freedom in Tibet as "severe." It records "reports of extrajudicial killings, prolonged detention without trial, torture, and arrests of individuals due to their religious practices". One might even look on the extermination of the Muslim Uyghurs as another attack on organized religion. However, though religion may be part of the story of the Uyghurs, it is probable that this is more a matter of resettling Han Chinese in Uyghur territories, along with the forced marriage of Uyghur women to Han Chinese men. This solidifies Chinese control of those areas. This use of Uyghur women may also enable the Communist Chinese program of one child per family that existed in China for many years and subsequently produced a shortage of women in today's China. A similar process of resettling Han Chinese into Tibet has existed for years - to establish a majority Han Chinese population in China making it impossible for Tibet to ever recover its independence. Stalin took similar steps distributing ethnic Russians into ethnic areas and members of the various ethnic groups throughout the Soviet Union.

Other Issues: Marx on Revolution

Marx's name has become synonymous with the concept of revolution. This must have been a later development in his ideas. Spargo says the following:

> During his stay in Paris in 1843-1844, Marx had discussed with the leading spirits of the movement there the desirability of such a reorganization, and ever since that time he and Engels had been urging it by newspaper articles, speeches, and correspondence. Marx had therefore made his position perfectly plain: he wanted a strong proletarian political movement with a definite revolutionary aim and policy, that involved abandoning the creation of a Utopian paradise beyond the seas, and secret conspiracies and violent insurrection. Thus, the suggestion of Moll was not unwelcome. It was, in fact, exactly what Marx and Engels had been wishing.[71]

Moll's suggestion was the domination of the socialist movement by Marx

---
[71] Spargo, p. 95.

and Engels. **See page 3 on revolution and blend.**

Other Issues; Marx on Free Trade

Marx was apparently in favor of free trade and addressed it in his *Discourse upon Free Trade*. In *Discourse upon Free Trade,* Marx states the following:

While recognizing that protection may still, under certain circumstances, for instance, in the Germany of 1847, be of advantage to the manufacturing capitalist; while proving that free trade was not the panacea for all the evils under which the working classes suffered, and might even aggravate them; he pronounces, ultimately, and on principal, in favor of free trade. To him, free trade is the normal condition of modern capitalist production. Only under free trade could the immense productive powers of steam, of electricity, of machinery, be fully developed; and the more rapid the pace of this development, the sooner and more fully will be realized its inevitable results: society splits up into two classes, capitalists here, wage laborers there; hereditary wealth on one side, hereditary poverty on the other; supply outstripping demand, the markets being unable to absorb the ever-growing mass of the productions of industry; an ever-recurring cycle of prosperity, glut, crisis, panic, chronic depression, and gradual revival of trade, the harbinger, not of permanent improvement, but of renewed over-production and crisis; in short, productive forces expanding to such a degree that they rebel, as against unbearable fetters, against the social institutions under which they have been put in motion; the only possible solution: a social revolution, freeing the social productive forces from the fetter s of an antiquated social order, and the actual producers, the great mass of the people, from wage-slavery. And because free trade is the natural, and the normal atmosphere for this historical evolution, the economic medium in which the conditions for the inevitable social revolution will be the soonest created - for this reason, and *for this alone*, did Marx declare in favor of free trade.[72]

If one harkens back to the story of my co-worker and the Malian about a Black American complaining about her poverty and the conclusion that poverty is relative, one will clearly see that Marx totally underestimated modern society's ability to consume. Though there are economic cycles, recessions and even depressions, followed by boom, they have not produced the social revolution that Marx predicted. It is possible that

---
[72] Ibid, p. 105.

the contrast between the consumption of various groups within a society may produce class related strife. This strife will not be the result of abject poverty and starvation as Marx had witnessed in the 19th century, but the result of greed on the part of one element of society for the possessions of another part of society; and political propaganda stating that the lower consumption of various groups is the result of racism, unfair practices, and special treatment of one group over others by corrupt governments.

Errors in Marx's Economic Theories

In *The Poverty of Philosophy* Marx makes the following statement:

> In English society, the day of labor had thus acquired in seventy years a surplus of 2,700 per cent of productivity, that is to say, that in 1840 it produced twenty-seven times as much as in 1770. According to M. Proudhon it is necessary to put the following question: 'Why is the English workman of 1840 not twenty-seven times richer than the workman of 1770?' In putting such a question one would naturally suppose that the English had been able to produce these riches without the historical conditions in which they were produced – such as: the private accumulation of capital; the modern division of labor; the automatic workshop; anarchic competition; the wage-system, and, in fine, all that which is based upon the antagonism of classes – having to exist. But these were precisely the necessary conditions for the development of the productive forces of the surplus of labor. Thus, it was necessary, in order to obtain this development of the productive forces, and this surplus of labor, that there should be some classes which derive and others which persist.

In looking at Marx's figure of 2,700% I attempted to make some similar calculations so to analyze it vis-à-vis today's economies. I found it impossible, even with the assistance of the internet, to gather the necessary data. I have to wonder where Marx obtained this figure. Also, if the "surplus" was 2,700% where was it? Surely the bourgeoise, which Marx contends was 10% of the population, did not have 2,700% more shoes, coats, etc., etc., than they had at the beginning of those 70 years. There aren't enough palaces to house all that stuff. One must, therefore, suspect that this figure was purely a figment of Marx's imagination.

A later paragraph further on in this commentary Marx says the following:

> If then, in theory, it suffices to interpret as M. Proudhon does, the formula of the surplus of labor in the sense of equality without taking account of the actual conditions of production, it must suffice, in practice, to make among the workers an equal distribution without changing anything in the actual conditions of production. This distribution would not assure a great degree of comfort to each of the participates.
> But M. Proudhon is not so pessimistic as one might believe him to be. As proportion is everything for him, it is indeed necessary that he should see in his fully endowed Prometheus, that is to say, in actual society, a commencement of the realization of his favorite idea.
> But everywhere also the progress of riches, that is to say *the proportion of values,* is the dominant law; and when the economists oppose to the complaints of the social party of the progressive growth of the public wealth and the amelioration effected in the condition of even the most unfortunate classes, they proclaim, without suspecting it, a truth which is the condemnation of their theories.

Marx then asks the following, in continuing this discussion of Proudhon's thoughts:

> What, in effect are collective riches, public wealth? They are the wealth of the bourgeoisie and not that of each individual bourgeois. Well, the economists have simply demonstrated how, in the relations of production as they exist, the wealth of the bourgeoisie has developed and must still grow. As to the working classes, it is still a much debated question whether their condition has been ameliorated at all as a result of the growth of the so-called public wealth. If the economists cite to us, in support of

their optimism, the example of the worker engaged in the English cotton industry, they only notice their position in the rare moments of commercial prosperity. These moments of property are to the epochs of crisis and stagnation in the 'exact proportion' of three to ten. But also, in speaking of amelioration, the economists may have wished to refer to the millions of workers condemned to perish, in the east Indies, in order to procure for the million and a half of workpeople employed in England in the same industry, three years of prosperity out of ten.

As to the temporary participation of the public wealth, that is different. The fact of the temporary participation is explained by the theory of economists. It is the confirmation of that theory and not the 'condemnation' as M. Proudhon says. If there was anything to condemn it would certainly be the system of M. Proudhon, which, as we have demonstrated, would reduce the worker to the minimum wage, in spite of the growth of riches. It is only by reducing the worker to the minimum wage that he could make an application of the "exact proportion" of values, of "value constituted" – by labor time. It is because wages, in consequence of competition, *oscillate above and below the price of the necessities of life essential to the sustenance of the worker* that he can not only participate, to however small a degree in the development of collective wealth, but also that he can perish of want. There is a whole theory of economists, which sets up no illusion.[73]

First, let's address the issue of "oscillate above and below the price of the necessities of life essential to the sustenance of the worker." What are the necessities that are essential? Food? Clothing? Shelter? How about cell phones? How about internet service? How about designer purses or fancy sneakers? Is anyone in the USA today unable to get food assistance if they need it? And if you can find one, is it because they can't work, or because they won't work? Food stamps or ADT cards are available to anyone who is hungry, but there are people who are hungry. Why is that? Well, ADT card fraud is rampant, and they sell their cards to get cash so they can buy something other than food. Yes, there are homeless, but 80% of

---

[73] *The Poverty of Philosophy* pp. 108-111.

them are reported to be addicted to various drugs and a substantial number of them have mental illnesses. A compassionate country would take those with mental issues and house them, but years ago the ACLU took a lawsuit and it was decided that putting them in asylums, where they were clothed, fed, housed, and given treatment for their mental issues violated their civil rights. This a self-inflicted wound, not the fault of the capitalist system.

The minimum wage is another issue. It was not established as a "living wage." It was intended to be an entry wage where young people could get experience and either find a trade or obtain further education that would allow them to increase their wages. A living wage flipping hamburgers is not what Maslow had in mind when addressing self-actualization.

The problem here is that our educational system has collapsed and in many major cities 80% or more of the minority students that leave high school are functionally illiterate. The system, run by the government and elected officials, not capitalists, have deprived those children the education that would have allowed them to escape poverty and become productive members of society. This may not be what Marx envisioned in point #10 of the *Communist Manifesto*, but it is certainly the result of it.

The worst part of the minimum wage is that once it rises, capitalists pass that increase on to their customers because they are in business to make a living from the profits of their business and if they do not make a profit that minimum wage job will vanish as the business goes bankrupt. Moving from there, raise the minimum wage, the increased costs of labor are passed on and soon the system readjusts itself to the point where the increase in the quality of living of the minimum wage earner is gradually, steadily, and inevitably lost as all costs readjust upwards and the relative position of the minimum wage earner has, as Marx says, "oscillated" back to a subsistence level.

It would be desirable at this point to make a comparison between the growth in the average wage during the days of the Soviet Union, to the growth of the average wage in the U.S. over the period of the Soviet Union's existence. However, that is not possible. There are too many variables ranging from inflation to exchange rates, and the issue of health care, which was free in the Soviet Union. In the United States, however, health care was generally available only through one's employer or self-purchased medical insurance programs where it was arguably a part of the worker's wages or were purchased directly by the individual. In addition, there is the question of the quality of that health care. Only a few points of comparison can be made. It is, however, noteworthy to observe that numerous leaders of Third World countries came to the US for medical treatment and few if any went to the Soviet Union.

As for the quality of life, (food, clothing, and shelter), it is interesting to note that blue jeans were a highly desired item and highly desired in the Soviet Union in the 1970's through 1990's. Though clothing was certainly available, one cannot determine how many changes of clothing the average person in the Soviet Union had in comparison to the average working class American. One can, however, point to the constant existence of lines of people waiting to purchase scarce commodities and rationing, be it clothing or other such goods, or even food in the Soviet Union. In speaking of the collapse of the Imperial Russian railroad system in 1915-17, I mentioned the inability of the Russian system to provide food to the cities, which provoked riots. This problem continued into the 1930s when the Russians collectivized the Ukrainian farms and confiscated their stocks of grain.

During the siege of Leningrad in WWII, being cut off from the rest of Russia and besieged, food was very scarce in Leningrad. Elena Skrjabina, a citizen of the Soviet Union, lived in Leningrad in 1941 when the Germans invaded. She describes life in Leningrad after it was blockaded and food, which had been rationed before the war began, became so scarce that people starved to death. After several pages describing daily rations falling to 250 grams of bread per person per day (about a slice of bread) and the eating of cats, dogs, and rats, she writes the following in *Siege and Survival*:[74]

> Dima [her 14-year old son] has finally been placed in the hospital. My husband did everything possible and with great difficulty got Dima a place in an infirmary for wounded soldiers. Since there are no more sources of transportation, I had to take the boy to the Petrograd side on foot. The trip was a horrible nightmare. Dima could barely move his swollen feet and leaned heavily on me. He looks so bad that even our citizens, who are used to all sights, stared at us. Dima's face is blue-black and swollen; his eyes are dull [from starvation]. We walked for three whole hours. Of course, at the hospital there were all sorts of complications. There was no vacant cot, so Dima was

---

[74] Skrjabina, E., *Siege and Survival: The Odyssey of a Leningrader* (Carbondale & Edwardsville, IL: Southern Illinois University Press, 1971) pp. 53-54.

placed in the hall. Besides this, I had to fill out a great many forms. I am very afraid that Dima won't get better. I stopped by the room of the head of the hospital – Eshkelev. His son lives with him, a healthy, rosy-cheeked boy [note the description of Dima above for contrast], who, despite the late hour, was still in bed and munched ham and cheese sandwiches. I couldn't believe my eyes, but it was so. We had already forgotten what ham and cheese looked like. Seeing my incredulity, his father put together a story that the boy had nearly died after losing his ration card. Afraid to confess it, he supposedly had not eaten anything for nearly two weeks. I thought about all the unfortunate wounded and sick who were lying in the hospital halls, about the people from whom this official, by <u>*utilizing his position, was taking food to feed his own healthy son*</u>.

<u>*"But this is going on all around us. Everyone who has power or is in a position to deal with foodstuffs, uses his privileged place to the utmost*</u>.[75] It makes no difference to them that people die like flies. And I am a good one, too – expressing my sympathies for the son, because Dima's life depends on this 'father-official.' [The life of her son depended on the good will of this corrupt official, so she did what was necessary.]

Skrjabina's book is filled with numerous paragraphs recounting where officials, with power and control over the masses, took advantage of their situation to feed and provide for themselves at the expense of those masses. Plump and healthy, they ignored the suffering of the starving masses, just as the French nobility ignored the starvation in France prior to the French Revolution. Remember Queen Antoinette who supposedly said "Let them eat cake" when they cried for bread.

Though Marx and Engels complained about how the workers were oppressed by the capitalists who lived on the fat of the land while the workers received starvation wages, it would appear that the same problem existed in the communist utopia that was set up on Marx's principals. The only difference was that the Romanovs and Russian nobility had been replaced by the Leninists and the Stalinists.

It is worth mentioning again that the collectivization of agriculture

---

[75] Underline and italics added.

proposed by Marx was a miserable failure. The production of food was so inadequate that in the 1970's the Soviet Union had to import millions of tons of American grain to feed their population. In 1980 the USSR imported 34 million tons of grain. In 1981, the Soviets imported 46 million tons of grain. In 1982, President Reagan authorized the sale of an additional 23 million tons of grain to the Soviet Union.

The failure of the Soviet centralized planning system, which was organized under the principals of the *Communist Manifesto,* principals 7 and 9, was a disastrous failure. In the 1980's in Russia there was a joke: "A boy asks his mother, 'Mama, where is papa?' She responds by saying that 'he is standing in the line to get coupons for the coupons.' "

Until the mid-1990s Russia distribution system of goods and even food was based on a system of coupons, or, if you prefer, ration cards. Originally, the ration coupons were given as a motivation system. An exceptional employee would be given a coupon entitling him to receive a TV, a pair of shoes or other goods. Without those coupons it was very difficult to buy almost anything. Later, a similar system was implemented for food items that were not readily available in the shops. From 1983, the USSR started experiencing a shortage of food supply and food items were rationed for approximately a decade.[76]

The centralized planning system established quotes for numbers of completed factory goods, be it tractors, tanks, or fighter aircraft. This led to an interesting phenomenon. When Soviet equipment was given to Third World countries, they received tractors but they did not receive any spare parts; there were none. There were no quotas on spare parts, only finished goods. Even Soviet operations had the same problem. Broken down equipment littered Africa and slowly rusted away for lack of spare parts. Another failure of centralized planning.

There is a story about an American church group that brought Soviet citizens into the U.S. on an exchange program between the Russian Orthodox Church and various American churches. One of those Soviet citizens, a woman, was taken into a Walmart a day or two after her arrival and she fell to her knees and cried. She later explained that she had never seen so many goods for sale. Bare shelves were common in Soviet shops.

Other Issues: Marx on Nationalism

---

[76] *Russia Beyond,* https://www.rbth.com/society/2013/10/16/a_look_at_the_old_ration_system_in_russia_30163.

Twin Evils

Communism is generally considered not a nationalistic philosophy. Instead, it is an internationalist philosophy, calling for the workers of the world to unite. Nationalism is a characteristic of Fascism. That said, according to Spargo, "Without being in any way a jingo, Marx was, as we know, a German of the Germans, and as ardent an advocate of German unity as Bismarck himself."[77]

Other Issues: Marx on Slavery

Marx said the following:

> Slavery is an economic category as well as any other. That then has, that also, its two sides. Let us leave the bad side and speak of the beautiful side of slavery; being understood that it is only a question of direct slavery; of the slavery of the blacks in the East, in Brazil, in the Southern States of North America.[78]
>
> Direct slavery is the pivot of bourgeois industry as well as machinery, credit, &c. Without slavery you have no cotton, without cotton you cannot have modern industry. It is slavery which has given their value to the colonies, it is the colonies which have created the commerce of the world, it is the commerce of the world which is the essential condition of the great industry. Thus, slavery is an economic category of the highest importance.
>
> Without slavery, North America, the most progressive country, would have been transformed into a patriarchal country. Efface North America from the map of the world and you would have the anarchy, the complete decadence of modern commerce and civilization. Cause slavery to disappear, and you will have effaced America from the map of the nations.
>
> Thus slavery, because it is an economic category, has always existed in the institutions of the nations. Modern nations have known how to disguise slavery in their own lands alone, they have imposed it without disguise in the New World.

---

[77] Spargo, p. 291.
[78] Marx, K. *The Poverty of Philosophy*. Pp. 121-122.

What will M. Proudhon do to save slavery? He puts the problem: Conserve the good side of this economic category, eliminate the bad.

In his comment about slavery being disguised in modern nations, Marx is equating working a factory with slavery.

In *The Origin of the Family, Private Property, and the State,* Engels repeatedly addresses slavery. He calls monogamy slavery of the woman, as it stripped women of their position of the principal grower of crops in the post hunter-gatherer system and gives examples of this by discussing various societies among the Iroquois and other North American tribes. He condemns monogamy as being a form of slavery. As he discusses slavery through the ages, he does say that it was an integral and important part of various societies; but, unlike Marx, he never finds any good side of slavery.

Novosti Press Agency

Marx's ideas were criticized by a socialist named Eugen Dühring. Engels, defending his friend, wrote several articles that were published in 1878 under the title *Herr Eugen Dührings Umwälzung der Wissenschaft* [*Mr. Eugen Dühring's Revolution in Science,* better known as *Anti-Dühring*]*,* and an unfinished work, *Dialektik und Natur* [*Dialectics of Nature*]. His rebuttal of Dühring is quite unprofessional, riddled with name calling and the use of childish derogatory adjectives when describing or rebutting Dühring's ideas.

Much of this work is two philosophers arguing over interpretations of various issues. Engels also, in discussing the use of force, addresses a superficial discussion of the evolution of warfare. He does demonstrate, however, some knowledge of the minuscule details of warfare. However, he selectively chooses his facts and ignores facts that would argue against his suppositions. Facts are awkward things.

These articles led to the further development of Marxism. This can be seen from Lenin's observation that Engels "developed, in a clear and often polemical style, the most general scientific questions and the different phenomena of the past and present according to the materialist understanding of history and the economic theory of Karl Marx." However, Engels goal in simplifying the problems was the establishment of a dogma. Taking a major, and perhaps unjustified leap, he systematized Marx's theories as if the fundamental questions and contradictions were settled fact. His merger of some of Marx's governing ideas and scientific ideas of the late 19th century gave rise to the idea that Marxism was a complete philosophy; but in doing so he completely ignored a number of unresolved issues. He either wished or assumed them away. This contributed greatly to the transition of Marxism from a "critique of daily life" to an integrated doctrine that united into a single system where philosophy, history, and the sciences were fused.

Engels outlined what the socialist society will be like, "a society in which the notion of value had no longer anything to do with the distribution of the goods produced because all labor becomes at once and directly social labor, and the amount of social labor that every product contains no longer needs to be ascertained by 'a detour.'" A production plan, which in the Soviet Union were called 5-Year Plans, were to coordinate the economy. Engels contended that the division of labor and the separation of town and country would disappear with the "suppression of the capitalist character of modern industry." With these economic plans, industry was to be relocated throughout the country in the interest of the collective, which would eliminate the opposition between town and country and as a result both industry and agriculture would profit. Finally, after the liberation of humanity from the condition of servitude imposed by the capitalist mode of production, the state will also be abolished, and religion will disappear by "natural death."

We also need to address his comment about making the "separation of town and country" disappear. Did he envision the mass exile of city dwellers to the country? Is he looking to re-establish the primitive village lifestyle of Marx's Medieval Indian peasants? He cannot be envisioning maintaining an industrial culture, because in order to operate modern industries it requires the concentration of labor within commuting range of the factories. As a result, if one considers this in light of Marx's hatred of work specialization in modern industry, one can only believe that the goal of this process was to de-industrialize the world and return civilization to Medieval India.

In addition, one of the unusual features of *Anti-Dühring* is the insistence with which Engels refuses to base socialism on absolute values. He admits only relative values, linked to historical, economic, and social conditions. Socialism cannot possibly be based on ethical principles; each epoch can successfully carry out only that of which it is capable. Marx had written this in his preface of 1859 edition.

Summary

The foundation on which Marxism stands is Marx's theory that the only source of value is labor, i.e. the number of hours, put into a product by the hand of the worker, without differentiation of the skill of the worker. This was so obviously wrong that even Marxist theoreticians came up with the idea of "ability" to justify why, as George Orwell said in *Animal Farm*, "Some animals are more equal than others."

In addition, no Marxist has yet accepted exchange of silver for gold on a per pound basis. Even the true believers do not believe this part of Marx's economic theory.

The second major point of Marx's economic theory was that capitalists stole the excess labor from their workers. As I pointed out there is much more than the direct labor of the workers that goes into making any product, but then Marx never studied economics, let alone cost accounting. The second problem with his theory on this point, of capitalists stealing the labor of the workers, is that the workers are not slaves. That they can freely move about and sell their labor where they can get the maximum for it; that the market for labor today is competitive, where both the quantity and the varying skill levels of the workers are exchanged in an open market for jobs in various businesses. How can anything be stolen when the workers of their own wills can accept or reject the working situation that the capitalists offer them? And then there is the issue of the modern unions which negotiate to sell the labor of their membership to the capitalist every few years when their contracts expire and are renegotiated. Apparently, Marx never heard of the concept that a sale occurs when a willing buyer meets a willing seller.

Marx said, "The trades unions are the school for Socialism....." the workers may easily be called slaves of the unions. In that in many states they have no choice, but to join the union and pay dues to it for the privilege of belonging to the union; that the union leadership uses union dues to support politicians of the union leaders' choice, not the choice of the workers; and unions demand that seniority, and not skill, be the key to promotions and job choices in unionized plants. In a union, the worker does the right vote, but if he wants to leave the union and keep his job, or refuses to pay his dues, the union will have him fired. Where is Marx's legislature making these decisions? It doesn't exist.

Twin Evils

It is true, however, that the modern situation and relationship between the worker and his employer is different from what it was in the 19th century. It is clear that Marx's theory did not survive the 19th century if it was ever valid.

Another part of Marx's economic theory was that charging interest for the loaning of money was evil and should be prohibited. This is a strange conflict with point No. 5 of the *Communist Manifesto,* which read "Centralization of credit in the hands of the state, by means of a national bank with state capital and an exclusive monopoly." How can it be evil on one hand and good in the hands of the government?

Marx was blind to the fact that money is nothing but the means by which man stores his labor for use at a later date. Let me explain this concept. When I work and either sell my labor or create the product that I then sell, my wage or my sales are the fruit of my labor. They represent the maximum of what society thinks my labor is worth. I then have a choice to buy something I want with the money I have earned or I can save it. In either case, it represents my labor and has converted it into a means of universal exchange. In essence, it allows us to escape the barter society. So, the $100 in my checking account represents 5 hours of my time at a wage of $20 per hour. It is a storage of my labor, which I can then exchange at a later date for something I want.

So, why can I not then loan, or better, rent out that store of my labor, my hours of labor as represented by those $100 and put them to work somewhere else. After all, they represent my labor and are a store of that labor. The problem for Marx here is that an hour of one's time at $20 per hour is worth more than an hour of a high school drop out working at the minimum wage. This reflects upon the problem that later Marxists theorists attempted to solve by talking about ability. If the modern Marxists believe that ability influences the value of labor, why then can I not store that labor in the form of money in my bank account and then lend that substitute labor to someone else to let it work for him? Why can I not charge the borrower interest when I lend him my money? After all, it's my labor and I should be able to use it, i.e. work, wherever I wish. Marx did want the workers to vote on how they worked in the factory; so why should they not have a vote on how it works elsewhere? Again, Marx missed the fundamental point that money is a store of labor that is used to escape the shackles of a barter economy.

Beyond Marx's economic theories, there were the prejudices and idealized systems of Marx and Engels. For instance, they both believed that the societies of Medieval Europe and India were ideal societies because everyone worked together in the fields and then shared everything equally. This is also patently absurd because life was miserably short in those days and no one, except the Marxists, wants to go back to the situation where humans lived hand-to-mouth on the edge of starvation.

Marx idealized the craftsman and saw Barefoot Bob in his hut crafting his own tools from start to finish as ideal. Let's examine that. If Barefoot Bob wanted an iron shovel, he would need an iron mine, source of heat, and a black smithy. Iron and steel were produced on a small scale during the Middle Ages; but as society developed the need for steel expanded and became a massive industry in support of modern society's demand for steel. Every other product in our society today is also supported by a massive industrial base with huge financial investments and a web of other industries that feed into each industry and support it.

The process for making steel is not a short one or a simple one. It takes massive investments in mines for both coal and iron ore. Steel also requires coke ovens, blast furnaces, oxygen furnaces, steel refining facilities, and then a variety of mechanical systems for making sheet, bar, tube, and other forms of final steel. Barefoot Bob in his hut or blacksmith could not produce the steel needed to support the demands of our society. Who wants to live in a world without computers, cell phones, air planes, and the other trappings of our economy?

Marxist idealists also ignore several things that are necessary for the quality of life that we have today, which include, but are not limited to:

1.) Capital investments to build the machines that go into the factories that make the machines that produce the chemicals and metal components that make today's society.
2.) That in order to create that capital there must be incentives to cause the investors to forego immediate consumption of their wealth so it can be loaned to the entrepreneur/capitalist.
3.) That it takes people with specialized skills doing specialized work, not doing the whole process themselves, but as part of a chain of people working towards a final goal. It is not Barefoot Bob self-actualizing in his hut.
4.) That all people are not capable of doing all those specialized tasks, because they do not have the mental ability to learn the skills necessary to produce those goods, i.e. "the ability."
5.) That to operate efficiently it is human nature for one person

to be in charge; legislatures determining what to be done is the least efficient method of managing any human activity. Because of this, all societies tend towards one or a few people controlling all societies and human activities.

Marx and Engels either reject as evil or ignore all of these pillars upon which our modern life style stands. If one were to establish Marx and Engel's ideal society, we would be living a "hand-to-mouth" subsistence existence, barely beyond the hunter-gather society.

Chapter 4
Lenin and Stalin

Marx and Engels participated in many conferences on socialism where they argued their position and won and lost followers. After both died, the arguments surrounding socialism continued with many notable socialists arguing fine points of Marx's theories; but since Marx was gone, there was no definitive answer, just factions arguing that the other was wrong. These arguments were as much concerned with the interpretation of Marx as they were a struggle for power. It doesn't matter which interpretation won the discussion of how to implement socialism, as Marx had presented. However, what is important is that the most fanatical and strident, Lenin, became the predominant path to a socialized world under the title "communism." Where some wanted to walk down the path of Socialism, Lenin chose to charge down that path and implement socialism, which he renamed communism, in its most extreme form.

What follows is a discussion of several of the leading socialists; however, it focuses on Lenin and not only his actions. It also focuses on his motives - what he called for, what he introduced, and how it continued under Stalin.

The Work of Kautsky and Bernstein

The theoretical leadership after Engels was assumed by Karl Kautsky, editor of the official organ of the German Social Democratic Party, *Die Neue Zeit*. He wrote *Karl Marx' ökonomische Lehren* (1887; *The Economic Doctrines of Karl Marx*), in which the work of Marx is presented as essentially an economic theory. Kautsky reduced the ideas of Marx and Marxist historical dialectic to a kind of evolutionism. He stressed the increasing working-class pauperization and the increasing capitalist concentration. While opposing all compromise with the bourgeois state, he accepted the contention that the socialist movement should support laws benefiting the workers provided that they did not reinforce the power of the state. He rejected the idea of an alliance between the working class and the peasantry and believed that the overthrow of the capitalist state and the acquisition of political power by the working class could be realized in a peaceful way, without upsetting the existing structures. This is the opposite of Lenin, who believed only in a violent overthrow. As an internationalist Kautsky supported peace, rejecting war and violence. For him, war was a product of capitalism. Such were the main features of "orthodox" German Marxism at the time when the "revisionist" theories of Eduard Bernstein appeared.

Bernstein created a great controversy with articles that he wrote in 1896 for newspaper Die *Neue Zeit*. He argued that Marxism needed to be revised. His divergence widened with the publication in 1899 of *Die Voraussetzungen des Sozialismus und die Aufgaben der Sozialdemokratie* (Evolutionary Socialism), to which rejoinders were made by Kautsky in *Bernstein und das Sozialdemokratische Programm: Eine Antikritik* (1899; "*Bernstein and the Social Democratic Program*"). The Polish-born Marxist Rosa Luxemburg in *Sozialreform oder Revolution* (Reform or Revolution), both in 1899.

Bernstein's focus was on the labor theory of value, i.e., Marx's belief that man's labor was the only source of value. Along with the economists of his time he considered it outdated, both in the form expounded by British classical economists and as set forth in *Das Kapital*. He believed that class struggle was becoming less rather than more intense, because concentration of wealth was not accelerating in industry, as Marx had forecast. In agriculture it was not increasing at all. Bernstein demonstrated this on the basis of German, Dutch, and English statistical data. He also argued that cartels and business syndicates were slowing the evolution of capitalism. These facts cast doubt on the validity of Marx's theory of capitalistic crises. Arguing that quite a few of Marx's theories were not scientifically based, Bernstein blamed the Hegelian and Ricardian structure of Marx's work for his failure to take sufficient account of observable reality.

These two men are important because they were the Marxists who Lenin argued against when explaining his form of Marxism.

The Radicals

One of the most divisive questions was that of war and peace. This was brought to the fore at the outbreak of World War I, when Social Democratic deputies in the German Reichstag voted for the financing of the war. Among German Marxists who opposed the war were Karl Liebknecht and Luxemburg. Liebknecht was imprisoned in 1916 for agitating against the war. On his release in 1918 he took the leadership of the Spartacus League, which was later to become the Communist Party of

Germany. Luxemburg had also been arrested for her antimilitary activities. In addition to her articles, signed Junius, she debated with Lenin on the subject of World War I and the attitude of the Marxists toward it (published in 1916 as *Die Krise der Sozialdemokratie* [The Crisis in the German Social-Democracy]. She is known for her book *Die Akkumulation des Kapitals* [The Accumulation of Capital]. In this work she returned to Marx's economic analysis of capitalism, in particular the accumulation of capital as expounded in Volume 2 of *Das Kapital*. There she found a contradiction in Marx that had until then been unnoticed: Marx's scheme seems to imply that the development of capitalism can be indefinite, though elsewhere he saw the contradictions of the system as bringing about increasingly violent economic crises that would inevitably sweep capitalism away. Luxemburg concluded that Marx's scheme was an oversimplification and assumed a universe made up entirely of capitalists and workers. However, if increases in productivity were taken into account, she asserted, balance between the two sectors would become impossible. In order to keep expanding, capitalists must find new markets in non-capitalist spheres, either among peasants and artisans or in colonies and underdeveloped countries. She postulated that capitalism would collapse only when exploitation of the world outside it (the peasantry, colonies, and so on) had reached a limit. This conclusion was the subject of passionate controversies.

The German Socialists

The Social Democratic Party (SPD) sprang from the merger of the General German Workers' Association, founded in 1863, and the Social Democratic Workers' Party, which founded six years later. They merged in 1875 and formed the Socialist Workers' Party of Germany (*Sozialistische Arbeiterpartei Deutschlands*). It immediately ran afoul of the anti-socialist laws signed by the Kaiser which banned, from 1878 to 1890, any group that looked to spread socialist principles. Despite this, the party still gained support in elections. In 1890, when the ban was lifted, the party adopted the name SPD. By 1890 the SPD was the largest Marxist party in Europe.

Prior to World War I the SPD continued to adhere to radical principals, but practiced moderation, speaking of democracy and calling themselves social democrats. This drew the ire of Lenin, who believed they were not true Marxists. In the 1912 federal election, the SPD became the largest party in the Reichstag, but with only 110 seats, it had no part in running the country.

Twin Evils

The members of the SPD participated in the Second International Congress and supported its agreement to oppose militarism. However, when WWI erupted the SPD supported the German war effort and adopted a policy of refraining from calling for strikes or criticizing the government. Lenin considered this as the SPD's second sin; Lenin maintained that the war was part of the Imperialist phase of capitalism and a nationalistic action, therefore running afoul of his internationalist philosophy.

That said, there was an anti-war element of the SPD. They were expelled in 1916 and 1917, leading to the formation of the Independent Social Democratic Party of Germany (USPD).

When the war ended and the Kaiser had fled to Holland, the SPD played a key role in the German Revolution of 1918–1919. On November 9, 1918, Chancellor Friedrich Ebert, a member of the SPD, proclaimed Germany a republic. The government introduced a large number of reforms in the following months, introducing various civil liberties and labor rights. The SPD government, which was committed to parliamentary liberal democracy, and despite being a Marxist party, it used military force against more radical communist groups. This led to a permanent split between the SPD and the USPD (later the Communist Party of Germany, KPD), which was more closely aligned, philosophically, with the Russian communist party.

Russian and Soviet Marxism

Das Kapital was translated into Russian in 1872. Marx maintained steady relations with the Russian socialists and took an interest in the economic and social conditions of the tsarist Empire. The person who originally introduced Marxism into Russia was Georgy Plekhanov, but the person who adapted Marxism to Russian conditions was Lenin.

Lenin

Before talking about Lenin, it is necessary to examine Russia. The ideas of the French revolution had not penetrated into Russia during Napoleon's invasion of Russia in 1812. During the French Revolution, the idea of *Liberty, Equality, and Fraternity* were spread by the French armies through-out Western Europe. The French began eroding the idea of absolute monarchies. As an institution, serfdom had long vanished in the West, but in Russia it still existed until 1861. Under the idea of serfdom, the Russian peasants were little more than slaves that were tied to the land and could actually be sold as if they were slaves.

Even though serfdom had been ended in Russia, the peasants were tied to the land and acted more or less as share croppers, paying for the use of the land with a portion of their harvest with the lord of the manor. As an improvement in the lives of the peasants, it was only a minor difference.

During the 19th century there was a movement of the peasants to the cities where they were attracted by the prospect of work in the various factories that began appearing. Their lives there, however, were only a little better than back on the farm. Discontent grew in the ranks of the peasants and the factory workers. To this was added the ideas of the French Revolution and socialism.

On March 13, 1881, after several failed attempts, Czar Alexander II was assassinated in Saint Petersburg, Russia. The assassination was planned by the Executive Committee of *Narodnaya Volya* ("People's Will"), an extremist revolutionary group. The attack against the Czar was made by two assassins. One assassin, Nikolai Rysakov, threw a bomb which damaged the carriage, prompting the Tsar to disembark. At this point a second assassin, Ignacy Hryniewiecki, threw a bomb that fatally wounded Alexander II.

The objective of the People's Will was to overthrow the autocratic system and stop the government reforms of Russian Tsar Alexander II. The organization declared itself to be a populist movement that succeeded the *Narodniks*, who were a politically conscious movement of the Russian intelligentsia in the 1860's and 1870's. Some members became involved in revolutionary agitation against tsarism.

"The People's Will" was primarily composed of young revolutionary socialist intellectuals believing in the efficacy of terrorism. "The People's Will" emerged in Autumn 1879 as a result of a split in an earlier revolutionary organization called *Zemlya i Volya* ("Land and Liberty").

Then came the revolution of 1905. The Russian Revolution of 1905, erupted on January 22, 1905, and was a wave of mass political and social unrest that spread through vast areas of the Russian Empire. The mass unrest was directed against the Tsar, the nobility, and landowners. It included worker strikes, peasant unrest, and military mutinies. In response Tsar Nicholas II enacted some constitutional reforms, which included the October Manifesto. This document established a State Duma, the multi-party system, and the Russian Constitution of 1906. Despite popular participation in the Duma, the parliament was unable to make law, and frequently came into conflict with Nicholas. Its power was limited and Nicholas remained an autocrat. Furthermore, he could dissolve the Duma, which he often did.

The primary cause of this revolution was the international humiliation resulting from Russia's defeat by the Japanese in the Russo-Japanese War pf 1905. Calls for revolution grew as various sectors of Russian society recognized the need for reform. Politicians, such as Sergei Witte, had succeeded in partially industrializing Russia but failed to reform and modernize Russia socially. Despite this revolution, Nicholas II and the monarchy survived the Revolution of 1905, but would not survive World War I.

At first the Russian armies were successful and defeated the Austrians repeatedly. Their first setback occurred at German hands at the battle of Tannenberg fought from 26 to 30 August, 1914. The war soon settled into trench warfare and a grist mill that would kill millions. On the Russian front, however, life for the solders in the trenches became exceptionally miserable. Bad officers, defeats, and most particularly starvation destroyed the morale of the Russian troops.

The mobilization of 1914 had seriously disrupted life in general in Russia and most particularly the economy. The heaviest burden of mobilization fell on the long-suffering peasantry. Almost half of the peasant men were called to the colors by the end of 1916. The 1917 census showed that in most of the Russian provinces one-third to two-thirds of the peasant households had lost their male workers. The demands of war also drastically reduced the number of draft animals on the land and most plants responsible for producing agricultural machinery were turned over to war production. Starvation was the result.

The effects of mobilization were less than in the countryside, as many worked in industries necessary for the war effort and were exempted from service. Though there were strikes among these factory workers for better wages, they were negated by wartime inflation. The prices of necessities rose from 100% to 500%. Much economic inflation, however, was not the result of government spending, but because the Russian railroad system was a single-track system; they did not have pairs of tracks so trains could run uninterrupted in both directions. This single-track system, forced trains to go onto sidings to allow a train moving in the opposite direction, to pass. Additionally, there was a shortage of locomotives and freight cars. This system worked in peacetime; however, with the necessity of supplying both the armies in the field and the city populations, shortages of everything arose. Starvation and grumbling began to appear in both the urban centers and in the trenches.

The Germans were well aware of these logistic problems and resulting discontent. A novel approach, therefore, was taken in an effort to knock Russia out of the war. They decided to send Vladimir Ilyich Ulyanov, better known as Vladimir Lenin to St. Petersburg. A known revolutionary exiled to Switzerland; he was placed in a sealed train. On April 16, 1917, this train rolled into St. Petersburg. In doing this, the Germans threw a "lit match" into a pool of revolutionary gasoline.

Though the Russian army held the line, its spirit was broken and the morale of the Russian people was no better. The Russian people were exhausted with the war, which Russia had undertaken without being prepared for it. Order No. 1, issued on March 1 (March 14, New Style) by the Petrograd Soviet, destroyed discipline among the troops by prescribing that committees of soldiers or sailors be formed in all military and naval units and that those committees should, in essence, mutiny against their officers, seizing control of arms and munitions in the name of the soviet. The Provisional Government, by its weakness, permitted an uncontrollable to pass out into the hands of the Soviets. The corps of officers, which had deteriorated during the war, was powerless to act. A pivotal event was the mutiny of the Russian fleet at Kronstadt.

Lenin

There are two easily obtained biographies of Lenin: Trotsky's *On Lenin*, and Lars Lih's *Lenin*. Trotsky's biography is interesting. In its Trotsky shows a writing talent, unlike Marx, who is turgid and tedious, or Lenin, whose writing boils with anger and argument.

Vladimir Ilich Ulyanov, or Lenin, was born in 1870 at Simbirsk (now Ulyanovsk). Ethnically, and going back to his great-grandparents, Lenin's family contained Russian, German, Swedish, Jewish and reportedly some distant Kalmyk blood. Like Marx, he came from an affluent, middle-class family. His father's family had risen from serfdom to become a middle-class family. Lenin's father served as Director of Primary Schools in the Simbirsk and provided the family with a comfortable lifestyle. He was so successful that the Czarist government recognized him by bestowing upon him a hereditary title of nobility. Therefore, Lenin was literally a nobleman.

Twin Evils

Lenin's early life was scarred by the execution of his older brother for his participation in an attempted assassination of Czar Alexander II. This produced a great hatred in him for the Russian government, which is reflected in his writings and behavior during and after the 1917 Revolution. Indeed, his brother's treatment at the hands of the police surely provoked his particular hatred of the police, which appears in several of his works. His father died shortly after his older brother was executed, which seems to be the cause of his atheism.

With his father gone, Lenin's mother acquired a small property with a garden and orchard. Lenin never lived the life of a peasant, nor did he work in the fields. His only understanding of the lives of the peasants came from his observations of them in his home town and his tending the family garden. Therefore, Lenin's understanding of a peasant's life is vicarious at best. Like Marx, there is no record of Lenin ever having set foot in a factory to observe the life of the proletariat.

As a student, according to the obsequious Trotsky, Lenin was brilliant, graduating first in his high school class. When he applied to attend Kazan University and study law, but after participating in some student demonstrations he was expelled and exiled to his family's Kokushkino estate. In May 1890, his mother, who retained societal influence as the widow of a nobleman, persuaded the authorities to allow Lenin to take his exams externally at the University of St Petersburg. Despite this handicap, according to Trotsky, he graduated first in his law class.

It was during Lenin's formal education that he found and read Marx's works. According to Trotsky, Lenin became infatuated with Marxist ideology and adopted the concepts of the confiscation of all means of production and land from the rich and its collective ownership by the masses. This position was clearly stated in Lenin's *April Theses*, published in 1917, where in Point Six of April Theses, he states:

- In the agrarian program, the emphasis must be shifted to the Soviets of Agriculture Laborer's Deputies.
- Confiscation of private lands.
- Nationalization of all lands in the country, and management of such lands by the local Soviets of Agriculture Laborers' and Peasants' deputies.
- A separate organization of Soviets of Deputies of the poorest peasants.

- Creation of model agriculture establishments out of large estates.

Lenin practiced law for a short period in his home town; however, making a living defending peasants did not produce an income worthy of his skills. Therefore in 1893, he settled in St. Petersburg, joined a law firm, and became actively involved with the revolutionary workers. The condition of Russia and the Russian revolutionary movement at the end of the 19th century and the beginning of the 20th century led Lenin to diverge, in the course of his development and his analyses, from the positions both of "orthodox Marxism" and of "revisionism." He returned to the original concepts of Marx by a careful study of his works, in particular *Das Kapital* and *The Holy Family*. He saw Marxism a practical affair and tried to go beyond the accepted formulas to plan political action that would come to grips with the surrounding world.

In his pamphlet *What Is to Be Done?* Lenin specified the theoretical principles and organization of his view of an ideal Marxist party. This is a strange work. Looking at it from the perspective as expressed in the title, *What is to be Done?* It suggests beginning with a statement defining the problem and conclude with a program for correcting those issues. However, it does nothing of the sort. Instead, it is an angry screed in which he denounces one socialist after another for failing to believe in the same exact interpretation of Marx as he did. Much of his writings follow this path and can be summarized in the phrase "It's my way or the highway." Lenin made no attempt to compromise or listen to anyone who disagreed with him. Lenin referred to those who disagreed with him as "philistinism" and railed against it frequently with a "visceral hatred."[79] This hatred of those who disagreed with him can be found in many of his works. It became a basic tenant of Leninism that only Leninism represented the authentic interpretation of Marxism. This was the source of the antagonism between Leninism and all other variations of Marxism or socialism.[80] As a result, this led to Lenin's belief that he was the only one who could anticipate the real will of the masses and act in their behalf.

As early as 1894, in his populist study *What the "Friends of the People" Are, and How They Fight the Social-Democrats*, Lenin addressed Marx's distinction between "material social relations" and "ideological social relations." To him the importance of *Das Kapital* was that "while

---

[79] Lih, L. T., *Lenin* ((London: Reaktion Books, 2011) p. 33
[80] Harding, N., *Leninism* (Durham, N.C.: Duke University Press, 1996) p. 13.

explaining the structure and the development of the social formation seen exclusively in terms of its relations of production, (Marx) has nevertheless everywhere and always analyzed the superstructure which corresponded to these relations of production." In *The Development of Capitalism in Russia*, Lenin sought to apply Marx's analysis by showing the growing role of capital, in particular commercial capital, in the exploitation of the workers in the factories and addressed the large-scale exploitation of the peasants, as Russia was far from being as industrialized as Western Europe. Marx had written about factory workers, not peasants. In *The Development of Capitalism,* Lenin gives the means to apply to Russia the models developed by Marx for western Europe. At the same time, he did not lose sight of the importance of the peasant in Russian society. Although a disciple of Marx, he did not believe that he had only to repeat Marx's conclusions. He wrote:

> *We do not consider the theory of Marx to be a complete, immutable whole. We think on the contrary that this theory has only laid the cornerstone of the science, a science which socialists must further develop in all directions if they do not want to let themselves be overtaken by life. We think that, for the Russian socialists, an independent elaboration of the theory is particularly necessary.*

Lenin took part in the Second Congress of the Russian Social-Democratic Workers' Party, which was held in Brussels and London (1903), and induced the majority of the Congress members to adopt his views, thereby establishing himself as a leader of the movement. Two factions formed at this Congress: the Bolsheviks (from the Russian word for "larger") with Lenin as its leader and the Mensheviks (from the Russian word for "smaller") with L. Martov at its head. The former wanted a restricted party of militants and advocated the dictatorship of the proletariat. The latter wanted a wide-open proletarian party, collaboration with the liberals, and a democratic constitution for Russia. Lenin saw this as compromising with pure Marxism and rejected the Menscheviks completely calling them "philistines."

In his pamphlet *One Step Forward, Two Steps Back*, Lenin compared the organizational principles of the Bolsheviks to those of the Mensheviks. After the failure of the Russian Revolution of 1905, he drew positive lessons for the future in *Two Tactics of Social Democracy in the Democratic Revolution.* He then violently attacked the influence of Kantian philosophy on German and Russian Marxism in *Materialism and Empirio-Criticism.* In 1912 at the Prague Conference the ideological battle lines were drawn and a division of the party occurred when Bolsheviks constituted themselves as an independent party.

During much of this period Lenin lived in exile - Finland, Paris, and finally Switzerland. In Switzerland he studied Hegel's *Science of Logic* and the development of capitalism. He engaged in debates with Marxists, like Luxemburg, on the meaning of the war and the right of nations to self-determination. In 1915 at Zimmerwald, and in 1916 at Kiental, he organized two international socialist conferences to fight against the war. Immediately after the February 1917 revolution he returned to Russia. In October 1917, the Bolshevik coup brought him to power.

During the period prior to the outbreak of WWI that Lenin developed his concept that capitalism was a logical and necessary transition in world economics from Feudalism to Socialism. It was published in 1916 as *Imperialism, the Highest State of Capitalism.* In it Lenin believed that capitalism had to become monopolistic and parasitic. He believed that it could only survive through the ruthless exploitation of colonies and given the finite territory of the world and the infinite desire of capitalism. He asserted that war was inevitable as each capitalistic nation sought to expand its colonial empire at the expense of the other. He believed that militarism and war were an intrinsic part of the survival capitalism in its Imperial phase. Lenin also believed that the bourgeois state and politics were similarly premised on extraordinary wartime conditions, which would produce the suppression of civil rights; draconian legislation to limit the worker's rights, and the taking over of the capitalistic state into the management and direction of both the economy and society. He advocated the necessity of censorship and enforced unanimity in the face of the foreign threats. Lenin presented all this as being typical characteristics of the contemporary capitalist system in general at that time

The Imperialist Capitalism's occupation of colonies is where the internationalist aspect of Leninism concentrated. Lenin believed that it was necessary, once a communist state was established, to continue the communist's state's efforts to destroy capitalism wherever it was found. This meant that it had to provide support to liberation movements in the various colonies, as they too were part of the oppressed and exploited masses.

Twin Evils

Lenin also considered this process as the necessary precursor to the Dictatorship of the Prolitariat, which would precede his idealized socialist world. What Lenin and Marx expected would eventually occur is that after a period of the Dictatorship of the Proletariat, all forms of government would wither away. One must ask, however, what is the result of "wither away?" If there is no government, there are no laws and their enforcement. Without laws and its enforcement, the worst of humanity rises to the top. The role of government is to protect the rights of the people that established that government; but if there is no government there are no police to arrest criminals and the strong preying on the poor. One cannot believe that even Lenin wanted this. But when his Dictatorship of the Proletariat ended with the rise of Stalin, the withering of government ceased and the Dictatorship of the Party began. As the reader will see, Lenin recognized the reality of his situation. In order to deal with various issues, the rule of law, even a communist rule of law, was necessary. Enemies of the state, who opposed Lenin's proposed path to paradise, needed control. Lenin recognized that peasants, right off the farm, did not possess the education necessary to run steel mills. Therefore, it was necessary to make use of bourgeoisie experts in order for the Russian economy to work, design and operate factories, maintain the financial records, run the centralized banking system, etc.

One cannot accurately determine, Lenin's motives 100 years following his death. It can clearly be said that he hated repressive governments, which for him was the Czarist government. It is probable that if his hatred for the Czarist government was not just hatred for the Czar, but a hatred for despotic and repressive governments of every kind. The fact is that as Lenin's communist government great and expanded it became Stalin's government, which made the Czar's government look like an enlightened government in comparison.

The *April Theses*

The *April Theses*, published in 1917, is an interesting document. Parts of it are discussed elsewhere; however, one part of it needs to be discussed separately and that is Point 7. This point reads as follows:

> *Immediate merger of all banks in the country into one general national bank, over which the Soviet of Workers' Deputies should have control.*

Lenin's earlier analysis of monopolies and finance capital, saw the role of the banks as a fundamental element of capitalism. In his view they had largely displaced stock exchanges as the place where the decisions concerning financial resource allocation were made. Banks, therefore, controlled much of the decisions made by the monopolies. Today the role played by banks in 1917 is in the hands of such brokerages as Black Rock; however, this type of organization did not exist in 1917.

Lenin's theory of banks and their role in capitalism was that after they controlled industry, their influence on governmental affairs expanded to a direct control of government by the banks. Lenin sought to end this, but he also looked to use it as a system for State control. Lenin said:

> "Capitalism has created an accounting apparatus in the shape of the bans, syndicates, postal service, consumers' societies, and other employees' unions. *Without big banks socialism would be impossible.....* The big banks are the 'state apparatus' which we need to bring about socialism, and which we take ready-made from the capitalists, our task here is merely to lop off what the capitalistically mutilates this excellent apparatus, to make it even bigger, even more democratic, even more comprehensive. Quantity will be transformed into quality. A single State Bank, the biggest of the big, with branches in every rural district, in every factory, will constitute as much as nine-tenths of the socialist apparatus. This will be country-wide book-keeping goods, this will be, so to speak, something in the nature of the skeleton of socialist society....... We can 'lay hold of' and 'set in motion' this 'state apparatus' (which is not fully with state apparatus under capitalism, but which will be so with us, under socialism in one stroke, by a single decree, because the actual work of bookkeeping, control, registering, accounting, and counting is performed by employees, the majority of whom themselves lead a proletarian or semi-proletarian existence."[81]

This is a strange divergence from Engels who held that money was the source of all evil and is a recognition that in a modern society

---

[81] Harding, N., *Leninism* (Durham, N.C.: Duke University Press, 1996) pp. 145-146, which cites Collected Works, 26, 106

money is a necessary evil. Therefore, instead of eliminating money it needed to be absolutely controlled by the government, be it Soviets of Workers' Deputies, or more precisely the Soviet Central Committee as things evolved in the USSR. How better to control the peasants than to control their money. This centralization of finance is a fundamental element of Socialism and Communism. If one looks at how the 2022 trucker's protests in Canada against the COVID vaccination requirement was suppressed by the Canadian government one can see the truth of this. Trudeau's Canadian government froze the bank accounts of the protesters and literally financially starved them into submission. Controlling the people's money is a method of controlling the people.

Lenin's Work *State and Revolution*

State and Revolution was written in August-September 1917. It is focused on Marx's theory of the evolution of government from Feudalism to Socialism, i.e., Communism in Lenin's terminology. The vast majority of this work is focused on the idea that there was a natural, historical process by which government would evolve from Feudalism, XXX, capitalism, dominant capitalism, monopolistic capitalism, imperialism, and finally into socialism. Lenin devotes most of his time to arguing this Marxist theory and how the ultimate end of the historical process is the socialistic system Marx conceived. It is basically an argumentative document in which Lenin contends that he is the only person capable of seeing the true interpretation of Marx. In this work he repeatedly calls for violent revolution.

> "On the other hand, the "Kautskyist" distortion of Marx is far more subtle. 'Theoretically,' there is no denying that the state is the organ of class domination, or that class antagonisms are irreconcilable. But what is forgotten or glossed over is this: if the state is the product of the irreconcilable character of state antagonisms, if it is a force standing *above* society and increasingly separating itself from it, then it is clear that the liberation of the oppressed class is impossible not only without a violent revolution, *and also without* the destruction of the apparatus of state power, which was created by the ruling class and in which this 'separation" is embodied. Lenin further states, 'Engels

develops the conception of that "power' which is termed the state – a power arising from society, but placing itself above it and becoming more and more separated from it. What does this power mainly consist of? It consists of special bodies of armed men who have at their disposal, prisons, etc.

We are justified in speaking of special bodies of armed men, because the public power particular in every state is not 'absolutely identical' with the armed population, with its 'self-acting armed organization.'

Like all the great revolutionary thinkers, Engels tries to draw the attention of the class-conscious workers to that very fact which to prevailing philistinism appears least of all worthy of attention, most common and sanctified by solid, indeed, one might say, petrified prejudices. Standing army and police are the chief instruments of state power. But can this be otherwise?"[82]

Later, Lenin speaks of the police and army as maintaining the oppression of the masses. This is important when you look at the contemporary situation in 2023, how a revolution might be imposed on the modern state. First, as the army and the police are the "chief instruments of state power" and one wishes to begin a revolution, those two institutions must be attacked and destroyed, or to use Lenin's words, "crushed." This cannot be done by a direct attack, as both institutions are heavily armed and trained. Armed peasants attacking either would meet with disaster, so the approach must be subtle and indirect.

In his *April Theses*, Point Five, Lenin calls for "Abolition of the police, the army, the bureaucracy."

The situation in Russia in 1917 was ripe for a revolution because the morale of the Russian Army had been destroyed; without the army the police were not sufficiently strong to resist the revolutionaries. Three years in the trenches, with all their horrors, were exacerbated by the incompetence of the Russian generals who were outclassed by the Germans and that the railroad system had completely collapsed and was unable to supply the army and the civilians in the cities. Starving, the Russian soldiers mutinied and deserted. Their ability to defend the state was gone.

In their effort to destroy the state by breaking the army, one

---

[82] Lenin, V.I., *State and Revolution* (Mansfield Center, CT: Martino Publishing, 2011) p. 10.

objective of their attack is to destroy the military's heritage, i.e., by renaming bases that are named after leaders of the "oppressors." The heritage of the armed forces is a source of pride, speaking of skill, tenacity, and aggressiveness on the battlefield, all skills that are necessary for an army to be effective. When that history is attacked, by calling historical military leaders oppressors and evil, the pride soldiers have of being members of various units or serving on various bases is attacked. This directly attacks the morale of the soldiers. What is the importance of morale in the military? Napoleon put it succinctly when he said, "The moral is to the physical as three to one."

The second approach is to sow discouragement and discontent into its ranks by introducing inequities into the ranks where some classes of individuals are treated more favorably than other classes. Strangely, one of the major gifts of the French Revolution, the first great socialist revolution, was the concept of competence and skill, i.e., meritocracy, not birth (or class) being the key to success.

This is not what you imagine. The military was historically a masculine organization. Yes, women have historically served in the military, but in very limited roles, i.e., clerical, nursing, etc. In 1917 the Russian army established women combat units (The Battalions of Death), but thy were withdrawn by 1918. In WWII the Soviet Union had women manning artillery and serving as snipers. Even the Israeli Defense Force contains women. In both instances women were engaged because of a lack of manpower. However, subsequently, women have been removed from the combat arms in the Russian army, but they exist in nearly all female units in the Israeli Defense Force. There is no indication that the requirements for Israeli women are any different than those for the Israeli men.

In the United States Army and the other services, things are different. First, the physical fitness requirements for men ages 17 to 21 requires that they are able to perform least 35 push-ups and 47 sit-ups, as well as running two miles in no more than 16 minutes and 36 seconds. Male recruits ages 22 to 26 have to complete a minimum of 31 push-ups, 43 sit-ups and a two-mile run in 17 minutes and 30 seconds or less. On the other hand, female recruits ages 17 to 21 must be able to perform 13 push-ups (less than half the number of men) and 47 sit-ups, and post a time of no more than 19 minutes and 42 seconds for the two-mile run. Female recruits ages 22 to 26 have to perform 11 push-ups, 43 sit-ups and a two-mile run of 20 minutes and 36 seconds or less.

You will note that the requirements for a female are significantly lower than those for men of the same ages.

The maximum allowable percentage of body fat for men ranges from 18% to 26% depending on service and age, while for women it ranges from 26% to 34%. Again, the requirements for women are less stringent than those for men.

Inequality of requirements and pressure from politicians to promote individuals who have lower requirements is a direct assault upon morale. Indeed, it is also dangerous, as a weaker 125-pound female soldiers simply cannot compete on the battlefield against a 240-pound male in a bayonet fight. She does not have the endurance of a male. This inequity attacks the morale of the male soldiers, who are the backbone of the Army and places the lives of the women at risk, by placing them into situations where an enemy male soldier has a decided advantage.

Then there are the standards for various prestigious training and duties, e.g., flight school and elite units such as the Rangers. The standards are purportedly maintained; but a blind eye is often turned towards the inability of females to meet those standards so that politicians can speak of the "First Female Fighter Pilot", "the "First Female Ranger," "the First Female General" etc., where if a male failed to meet those standards, he would be immediately expelled from that program. This also attacks the morale of the soldiers, because it is blatant political favoritism.

Sadly, when a female meets the standards applied to males and moves up the ladder, there is always the nagging thought that the politically preferred individuals only succeeded because they were a member of a favored class.

Then there is the political indoctrination imposed by politicians on the armed forces. For example, Critical Race Theory (CRT), a communist theory, is taught and Caucasian service men and women are told that they are oppressors and that the country they love is evil because there was once slavery in the United States. Love of country is one of the primary drivers for enlistment in the all-volunteer military service and this process subverts and attacks it, driving away those potential enlistees. Added to this is the introduction of openly homosexual service men and now transvestites into the service.

First the heterosexual males are subjected to performing various bodily functions in the presence of individuals who are sexually attracted to them. Furthermore, there is the possibility of higher-grade homosexuals

Twin Evils

making sexual demands on their juniors. This already happens with women in the service. It is foolish to say that it will not occur among the homosexual community. Either situation is considered absolutely unacceptable in the case of a heterosexual male and a female soldier, yet the socialist politicians advocate and support policies that directly create and foster these situations in the name of equity.

Of course, this same problem exists with units of mixed men and women, but so far, they are placed in segregated berthing situations. Homosexuals and transvestites are not segregated, but mixed into the general population as far as berthing, etc., are concerned

Again, the fairness issue will be introduced where men claiming to be female are measured against the female body fat and physical fitness requirements, while a heterosexual male must pass the stricter physical requirements.

All this inequity slowly and steadily erodes morale and the ability of the military to function declines.

Now let's look at the issue of the police, the second pillar of the state. Once again, the approach is to attack its morale. One must remember that Lenin talked about these two forces being the agencies that "repress the subjugated masses." Recall the constant drum beat that various minorities are imprisoned disproportionately to their percentage of the population, irrespective of their actual statistical levels of criminal activity.

The destruction of police morale is done by placing individuals who oppose the police in offices that interface with the police. First, the state governments pass laws that decriminalize clearly criminal activity, i.e., making the theft of less than $1,000 a non-prosecutable crime or eliminating cash bail. These laws place criminals back on the streets before the police officers have completed all the documentation related to the criminal's arrest. This greatly frustrates the police and their morale subsequently declines.

Second, by putting individuals in the prosecuting attorney's offices who refuse to prosecute various crimes or instead of charging the criminal with the maximum crime they have committed, they reduce felonies to misdemeanors, and third they approve paroles for individuals who should never be released from prison. The direct result is that the police begin to wonder why they went to the effort to arrest those individuals when the system will not prosecute them. Police conclude, they are risking their lives to arrest these criminals, yet nothing is being done, no prosecution and no subsequent judicial action, as a result of criminal activity.

Then there is the more direct attack against the police - the demand that they be defunded. Again, here socialist politicians proceed, as Lenin has urged, to destroy the police force by literally reducing their manpower by cutting their budget.

The objective of both of these processes, the attacks on the military and the attacks on the police is to remove them as supports of the state and thereby make the state vulnerable to the violent revolution that Lenin advocated.

The Dictatorship of the Proletariat

Lenin also put much emphasis on the leading role of the party. As early as 1902 he was concerned with the need for a cohesive party with a correct doctrine, adapted to the exigencies of the period, which would be a motivation among the masses, aiding the masses to become aware of their real situation. In *What Is To Be Done?* he called for a party of professional revolutionaries, disciplined and directed, capable of defeating the police; its aim should be to establish the dictatorship of the proletariat. In order to do this, he wrote in *Two Tactics of Social-Democracy in the Democratic Revolution*, it was necessary "to subject the insurrection of the proletarian and non-proletarian masses to our influence, to our direction, to use it in our best interests." But this was not possible without a doctrine: "Without revolutionary theory, no revolutionary movement." On the eve of the revolution of October 1917, in *The State and Revolution*, Lenin defined conditions for the Dictatorship of the Proletariat and the suppression of the capitalist state. Indeed, in this work, he devotes much time to the "withering away" of capitalism as postulated by Marx and Engels and explained how it would logically be followed by the dictatorship of the proletariat. Sadly, he does not describe how this dictatorship would function given his desire to eliminate all the capitalist state structures including the police and military who supported that state.

According to Marxist theory, the Dictatorship of the Proletariat is the intermediate stage between a capitalist economy and a communist economy. During this phase the post-revolutionary state seizes the means of production, compels the implementation of direct elections on behalf of and within the confines of the ruling proletarian state party, and institutes elected delegates into representative workers' councils who nationalize the means of production from private to collective ownership. During this phase, the administrative organizational structure of the party is to be largely determined by the need for it to govern firmly and wield state power to prevent a counterrevolution and to facilitate the transition to a lasting communist society.

Lenin assigned major importance to the peasantry in formulating his program. It would be a serious error, he maintained, for the Russian revolutionary workers' movement to neglect the peasants. Though the industrial proletariat constituted the vanguard of the revolution, Lenin wanted the discontent of the peasantry to be directed to supporting the revolution by placing among the goals of the party the seizure of all privately owned land. To this end, in 1903, at the third congress of the party, Lenin secured a resolution to this effect. Thereafter, the Dictatorship of the Proletariat became the "Dictatorship of the Proletariat and the peasantry." In 1917 he encouraged the peasants to seize land long before the approval of agrarian reform by the Constituent Assembly.

On October 26, 1917, Lenin declared himself chairman of a new government, the Council of People's Commissars. His dictatorship of Russia began on that date.

Among Lenin's legacies to Soviet Marxism was one that proved to be injurious to the party. This was the decision taken at his behest by the 10th Congress of the party in the spring of 1921. While the sailors were rebelling at Kronstadt and the peasants were growing restless in the countryside, Lenin forbid within the party all factions, all factional activity, and all opposition political platforms. The theory was "if you are not with us you are against us." This was typical of Lenin's attitude towards "philistines." He then turned to violently crushing the sailors at Kronstadt, who were only demanding what earlier had been promised to them.

Contradiction in Lenin's Politics

There is a fundamental contradiction in Lenin's political philosophy. Beginning with Marx, we are presented the concept that the only source of wealth is the labor of the worker (as discussed in the chapter on Marx).

Shortly before the Russian Revolution of 1917, land was redistributed to peasants. It was far from a total taking of land from the wealthy landowners that Lenin later implemented. It permitted peasants to put their individual hard effort into their own land and succeed or fail depending on how hard or efficiently they worked. Smart and hard-working peasants grew abundant crops, more than enough to feed themselves and their families, while the lazy and drunken peasants failed miserably and mortgaged their property to the successful peasants, who because the incompetent or lazy peasant failed again, took possession of the lazy or incompetent peasant's land. It was this successful peasant that Engels had decried when he discussed the successful farmer creating a surplus that he was then able to bank as wealth and pass on to his heirs. This created the rich, who became oppressors. These hard-working peasants were called *kulacks,* and Lenin had no love for them either and saw them as exploiters.

Lenin constantly speaks of two things: (1) the need to expand productivity so as to feed the starving masses of Russians; and (2) exploiters, i.e., the evil people who sell their goods to others and make a profit in that process. In his speech *"The tasks of the Youth Leagues"* delivered at the Third All-Russian Congress of the Russian Young Communist League[83] we find the following quote: "The old society was based on the principle; rob or be robbed, work for others or make others work for you, be a slave-owner or a slave. Naturally, people brought up in such a society imbibe with their mother's milk, so to speak, the psychology, the habit, and the concept that you are either (1) a slave owner or a slave, or (2) a small owner, (3) a small employee, (4) a small official, or (5) an intellectual - in summary a man who thinks only of himself and does not "give a hang for anybody else."

And on the previous page we find "If the peasant is settled on his separate plot of land and appropriates superfluous grain, that is grain that he does not need for himself or for his cattle, while the rest of the people have to go without bread, then the peasant becomes an exploiter."

The contradiction is that the successful small, landowning peasant has worked hard for his success, raising and harvesting a bountiful harvest beyond his needs; although he created this wealth, he is an exploiter because he does not give away the sweat of his brow, the wealth he created, to other people, who for whatever reason, were not as productive.

This is the conflict between equality and equity. Everyone in this situation had the equal opportunity to work hard and produce. Some succeeded and some failed. And because of the concept of equity the successful peasant is forced to give up the wealth he created to those who failed. The hard-working peasant created that wealth and he is then stripped of it.

Aside from the fact that this is grossly unfair to the hard-working

---

[83] Lenin, V.I. *On Utopia and Scientific Socialism, Articles and Speeches* (Amsterdam, the Netherlands: Fredonia Books, 2002) p. 199. His speech given at the Third All-Russian Congress of the Young Communist League, October 3 ,1820.

peasant, human psychology kicks in. After a few times of being stripped of the fruits of his extra hours of work the productive farmer will realize that there is no point in working hard, as there is no incentive beyond the altruism that Lenin never speaks of per se, but definitely believed was needed for Communism to succeed. With no incentive, the productivity of society declines to the level of productivity of the least productive worker. The attitude quickly becomes "Why work harder, as I won't get anything more than lazy Joe."

Lenin constantly harped on the need to be more productive, to electrify Russia to improve productivity, and to feed the "starving peasants" that seemed to be everywhere in his mind. Yet, his policy of not rewarding hard work produced a quite contrary result, therefore the contradiction. The program he advocated and instituted could never attain the goal he established for it.

In a strange contradiction,[84] Lenin wrote: "In this peasant country it was the peasantry as a whole who were the first to gain, who gained most, and gained immediately from the dictatorship of the proletariat. The peasant in Russia starved under the landowners and capitalists. Throughout the long centuries of our history, the peasant never had an opportunity to work for himself; he starved while handing over hundreds of millions of *poods* of grain to the capitalists, for the cities and for export. Under the Dictatorship of the Proletariat the peasant for the first time has been working for himself, and feeding better than the city dweller. *For the first time the peasant has seen real freedom* – freedom to eat his bread, freedom from starvation. In the distribution of the lad, as we know, the maximum equality has been established; in the majority of cases the peasants are dividing the land according to the number of 'mouths to feed."

So, on one hand, as in the earlier quote, the successful peasant who worked hard and fed his family and also had the temerity to produce more than a level of simple subsistence, is considered evil. He is an exploiter because he does not give away that excess production. Communism is seen by Lenin as countering this evil. Yet another contradiction coming from the mouth of Lenin.

Here are some personal examples and observations of how this destruction of the self-motivated workers works in the real world and not in the mind of the idealistic socialists and communists. I once worked in

---

[84] Lenin, V.I. *On Utopia and Scientific Socialism, Articles and Speeches* (Amsterdam, the Netherlands: Fredonia Books, 2002) p. 174. *Economics and Politics in the Era of the Dictatorship of the Proletariat*, Published in Pravda NO. 250 and Izvestia No. 250, November 7, 1919.

a factory as a foreman. There were several production lines adjacent to each other and personnel were allocated to those lines based on the worn necessary to operate them. At the end of the lines there were rollers on which loaded trays of goods rolled to a point where a worker unloaded them, placed them on a pallet, and bound up the pallet of finished goods for removal to the warehouse.

In one situation there were three lines where two men handled this process of palletizing the goods. They would let the line fill up with full trays, then work frantically, clear the lines, then sit down and have a smoke. They repeated this over and over rushing hard for 10 minutes, then taking a 10-minute break. A woman saw this and wanted to be able to sit down and smoke. So, she bid into the job; she was moved there because of seniority, she then discovered that she couldn't handle the 10-minute rush of work to get the 10-minute break. She complained and management was forced to put one worker on each of the three lines instead of the two that had previously handled the three lines with ease. This was an increase of 50% of the labor needed to handle the job two men had previously been able to handle with ease. This increase in labor needed for the job resulted in a decrease in productivity. This is exactly what happens when there is no reward for working hard in a climate of equity. All productivity is reduced to the level of the poorest workers. As a result, there are fewer goods and services, there are shortages, there can even be famine in the worst cases. Why work hard when there is no reward for the effort?

To reinforce this, I heard a story of a retired postal worker who returned for the Christmas rush. At a break he commented to a fellow worker that he still "had it." That he could sort 500 pieces of mail in an hour. The other worker was aghast and said, "We only do 250 pieces an hour here. You don't want to make Joe look bad do you?"

In another such situation I once did an audit in a rubber factory where there were piece-part quotas and bonuses on various machines. The controller told me on the first day that this was a license to steal. As I explored the system it became obvious that the workers were claiming on their work sheets that the machines were down for varying periods of time, when the machines were actually fully functional. They worked the machine making product during that time when the machine was purportedly non-functional and then claimed greater production over a shorter period of time qualifying for bonuses. Again, the lazy look to cheat the system and claim productivity rewards when there is no increase in productivity.

Twin Evils

These examples are not unique. If you talk to anyone who has worked in a factory environment you will hear hundreds of such stories. People work for rewards for themselves, not to give to others who refuse to work or can't work. Obviously, Lenin's taking from the hard workers to give to the non-productive directly undercut his demands for greater productivity. In order to create abundance and improve the condition of society it is absolutely necessary to motivate those who are willing to work and create that abundance by rewarding their efforts.

Collectivization

Lenin advocated collectivization and believed that the workers and peasants working together in collectives was the ideal way to structure a society and industry, including agriculture. Where Lenin's concepts are deficient. He had focused, as had Marx, all his attention to the city dwelling factory workers - the proletariat. He may have understood the proletariat, but he did not understand, or perhaps he disdainfully ignored the fact that the peasant population of Russia was of an entirely different mindset. At the time of the revolution only 3% of Russians population were city dwelling proletariat, while 85% were peasants.[85] Lenin also failed to recognize that the peasants had a very different culture from the city dwellers, even though he had grown up in a small provincial city.

The communist party had always advocated large-scale farming. Early on it declared that large-scale operations had a competitive advantage over small-scale operations. However, it was very conscious of the popularity among the peasants of subdividing the great estates and allocating plots of land to every peasant. As a result, during its struggle for power early in the revolution, in order to gain the support of the peasants, it gave "lip service" to the idea of land distribution. They even went so far to permit the formulation of the first agricultural policy and prepare the first agrarian law, on February 19, 1918.

This law focused on the equalization in the use of the land. It declared that all ownership in land ws abolished and that the land was transferred, for use, to all the working people; that all land was to be distributed on the principles of equalized land possession; and that every citizen, in principle, acquired the right to use the land. It embraced both the confiscation of estates and the land of the peasants. It declared that "socialization" was to level all the existing inequalities of land possession.

---

[85] Viola, L., *Peasant Rebels Under Stalin* (New York: Oxford University Press: 1996) p. 15.

In their revolutionary activity, the peasants did not completely conform to the principle of a a thorough equalization of land, but preferred the leveling of land holdings within narrower boundaries. Large estates were subdivided, including buildings, inventories, livestock, etc. The "surplus" lands of wealthier peasants were also appropriated and subdivided. All existing large-scale and even middle-sized farms vanished. Not more than 2-3% of the arable land remained in the hands of the Soviet government. Instead, it went into the hands of the local population. Despite the subdivision of the large estates, the average size of peasant holdings did not significantly increase. This new land was given to landless peasants, householders, and even city workers returning to the country. The peasantry desired nothing more than the right to be left alone; to prosper as farmers and consume or sell the fruits of their labors as they saw fit. There may have been sone peasants that looked favorably on the socialist aims of the proletariat, but most were totally opposed to the principles of socialist collectivism.

During the war the grain trade had broken down completely as inflation roared and the logistical systems of supply and distribution collapsed. The communist party was, in order to feed the cities, forced to resort to requisitioning of grain to feed the cities and the army. The Communist Party sought to collect grain through committees of the village poor, the *kombeday*. These committees worked with the urban requisitioning detachments to find and seize grain. In return, the *kombeday*, received a small portion of the grain seized. These groups encountered a united peasantry prepared to resist these requisitions with violence, when necessary, and stubbornly defied the party's requisitioning efforts.

Lenin recognized that grain was the central and most divisive issue in the alliance of the workers and peasants. He declared that any of the "owners of grain who possess surplus grain" and do not surrender it, regardless of social status, "will be declared enemies of the people." All peasants were now lumped together under the term *kulak*, defined as a class enemy and a counter revolutionary. Lenin declared a "ruthless and terrorist struggle and war against peasant or other bourgeois elements who retain surplus grain for themselves."[86] In essence, all peasants could be enemies of the people if they acted contrary to the policies of the party. The party that was the mirror of Lenin's will and philosophy. Again, this was Lenin's arrogance personified by the belief that he knew the only truth and no opposition to his will would be tolerated.

---

[86] Viola, L., *Peasant Rebels Under Stalin*, p. 16.

Twin Evils

Lenin addressed his apparent contradiction of class by refereeing to a "kulak mood" that prevailed among the peasants. He called the kulaks "demonic and subhuman," "avaricious," "bloated," "bestial," "the most brutal, callous and savage exploiters," "spiders," "leeches," and "vampires." The kulaks were the party's implacable foe.[87] Lenin believed that the peasant's attitude needed to be changed to be consistent with his socialist agenda. Once this was done "any peasant who is a little bit developed and has emerged from his primordial muzhik darkness will agree that there is no other way [but to turn over his grain to the Soviet state.]"[88] If he failed to do so, he was declared an enemy of the people and there would be repercussions.

This was the state of affairs in early 1919 when the Soviet government separated from the left wing of the socialist-revolutionary party. An agriculture policy was then formulated that was more in accordance with communist principles.

The Decree of February 14, 1919, declared the principals of "socialistic organization or agricultural production" where all land was proclaimed a "single state fund", that "all forms of individual land possession" were declared to be "dying out", that "big soviet farms, communes, communal land cultivation, and other forms of associated farming" were declared to be the "best means towards organizing a farming system on socialist lines." It declared that the land reserves were to be used in the first place, for satisfying the needs of the soviet arms and communes and then for satisfying the needs of artels, associations, and other collective farm units. The peasants who sought land as a means of their subsistence occupied the third priority.

Thus, the state's preference for state run farms and collective farms was proclaimed. However, it could not yet be implemented, as the Soviet government held only 2-3% of the arable and pasture land. The "communes" or collective farms, were organized on land that provisionally belonged to the great estate. The peasants, who had long wanted their own plots of land, were unwilling to surrender the lands they had taken from large estates or organize them into collective style farms.

Simultaneously, the government attempted to retain 10,000,00 to 12,000,000 acres of land taken from large estates. These lands were associated with sugar factories that had already been nationalized, and use

---
[87] Ibid. p. 16.
[88] Ibid. p. 17.

them for the production of sugar beets. This policy failed miserably. The government was only able to retain 1,000,000 to 2,000,000 acres, as the rest was occupied by peasants who had divided it into small lots.

The first attempt to organize large scale farming in the form of collective farms had failed. Only a small portion of the agricultural land, not more than 2% of the total tillable land, was held by state farms and communes. These farms too failed. The 4,000 to 5,000 state farms that contained about 5,000,000 acres and were spread across all of Soviet Russia were unable to produce sufficient food for their own staffs and their livestock. They found themselves obliged to rent more than half of their land to peasants.[89]

In 1921 the New Economic Policy (NEP) was introduced, many of these state farms were abandoned because of a lack of financial assistance. The collective farms were no more successful than the state farms although they had obtained their buildings and part of their livestock and inventories by confiscating them from the large estates. In May 1921, there were about 14,000 collective farms and their agricultural land had decreased rather than increased.

There were no state funds invested to financially support the collective farms. The state expected them to be self-supporting. The NEP was a retreat and a concession to the peasantry. It eliminated grain requisitions and replaced them with a tax in kind. This later became a money tax. The NEP also legalized private trade and traders, and denationalized all but the most important industries and foreign trade. The NEP eventually took the form of a mixed economy, a market socialism. Reality had momentarily forced the Communist Party to accept the reality of non-Marxist economics.

During the NEP the expansion of the grain trade was expected to provide the revenues necessary to finance the state's massive industrial expansion. It was also hoped that by granting a degree of peasant prosperity, the peasants would turn into consumers of the industrial output. However, in order to produce a profit for industry, it was necessary to shift the balance of trade terms away from the peasants and to industry. This meant that the prices paid for grain were artificially reduced so there would be a net profit for industry. This produced a crisis of excess production during the 1923-24 period. This was paralleled by an unwillingness of the peasants to sell their grain. Once again, the immutable laws of the market forced the party

---

[89] Swidersky, A.T., Agricultural policy over a period of 10 years. "Puti Sieskogo Khozislstva," official periodical of the Commissariat of Agriculture, 1927, N 10, pp. 18-40.

to lower industrial prices by introducing a series of reforms in industry. By 1927 the Soviet Union entered into a shortage of manufactured goods, seriously impeding trade between the cities and the countryside.

The party had a choice. It could allow the peasants to enjoy the free market and accumulate wealth and a prosperous agriculture that would produce the revenues for industrialization, or it could heavily tax the peasantry, maintain low agricultural prices, expand grain exports, and thus accumulate the funds necessary for capital industrialization. The idea of the latter path was that once industrialization was completed, the revenues could then be redirected back to agriculture. E.A. Preobrazhensky, the spokesman for the Left Opposition supported the latter course and he dubbed this process "primitive socialist accumulation," in a cynical perversion of Marx's detested "primitive capitalist accumulation." On the other hand, Nikolai Bukharin, the party's leading socialist theoretician, warned that "primitive socialist accumulation" would produce massive discontent among the peasants, once again driving them out of the market as had occurred during the Russian Civil War. Starvation would once again strike at the cities and threaten the stability of the Soviet state.

Lenin on Morality.

Again, turning to Lenin's speech, *"The Tasks of the Youth Leagues"* delivered at the Third All-Russian Congress of the Russian Young Communist League[90] we find the following quote:[91]

> *In what sense do we repudiate ethics and morality?*
> *In the sense in which it is preached by the bourgeoisie, who derived ethics from God's commandments. We, of course, say that we do not believe in God, and that we know perfectly well that the clergy, the landowners, and the bourgeoisie spoke in the name of God in pursuit of their own interests as exploiters. Or instead of delivering ethics from the commandments of morality, from the commandments of God, they derived it from idealistic or semi-idealistic phrases, which always amounted to something very similar to God's commandments.*
> *We repudiate all morality drawn from outside*

---

[90] Lenin, V.I. *On Utopia and Scientific Socialism, Articles and Speeches* (Amsterdam, the Netherlands: Fredonia Books, 2002) p. 199. His speech given at the Third All-Russian Congress of the Young Communist League, October 3, 1820.
[91] Lenin, V.I. *Ibid.* p. 197.

human society and classes. We say that it is a deception, a fraud, a befogging of the minds of the workers and peasants in the interests of the landowners and capitalists.

We say that our morality is entirely subordinated to the interests of the class struggle of the proletariat. Our morality is derived from the interests of the class struggle of the proletariat."

What are "the interests of the proletariat?" This seems to be summarized in the following passage:

That is why we say that to us there is no such thing as a morality that stands outside human society; that is a fraud. To us morality is subordinated to the interests of the proletariat's class struggle.

What does that class struggle consist in? It consists in overthrowing the Tsar, overthrowing the capitalists, and abolishing the capitalist class.[92]

It is a few paragraphs later that we finally find this:

Communist morality is that which serves this struggle and unites the working people against all exploitation, against all petty private property; for petty property puts into the hands of one person that which has been created by the labor of the whole society. In our country the land is common property.

According to Lenin, what is communist morality? It is that the end justifies the means. There is no morality beyond taking, by any means necessary, what the communist ideology claims is due to the proletariat. But who is it that defines what is due? It is obviously the communist party, which at this time was directed by Lenin and later by Stalin and his successors. Morality is what was defined at the moment by the leadership. Who was the leadership? It was Lenin in 1917. Here is what Trotsky said about how the leadership, Lenin, operated:

..... But all the time and everywhere <u>Lenin ruled by decisions, decrees, and orders in the name of the government.</u> It

---

[92] Lenin, Collected Works, Vol. 31, "*The Tasks of the Youth Leagues*" first published Pravda Nos. 221, 222, and 223, October 5, 6, and 7, 1920.

Twin Evils

goes without saying that Lenin less than anybody else was inclined to be impressed by the magic of formality. He was acutely conscious of the fact that our strength lay in this new government apparatus, which was organizing itself from below, from the Petersburg districts.[93]

In Trotsky's biography of Lenin we find the following passage, which clearly reinforces this perception: "'In the morale make up of Vladimir Illych (Lenin)," Vodovozov continues, "one was at once struck by a certain amoralism." In my opinion, it was an inborn trait of his character." This amoralism, it turns out, consisted in recognizing that any means was admissible if it led to the desired end. Yes, Ulyanov (Lenin) was no admirer of clerical or Kantian morals, which are allegedly supposed to regulate our lives from celestial heights. His purposes were so great and so far above personal considerations that he openly subordinated his moral criteria to them. He regarded with an ironic indifference, if not with disgust, those cowards and hypocrites who concealed the pettiness of their goals or the shabbiness of their methods behind high principals, which, though absolute in theory, are quite flexible in practice."[94]

Lenin on the Use of Terror

Given Lenin's contention that the ends justified the means, it is necessary to examine the thoughts of various authors, and even Lenin himself, concerning the means that Lenin believed were justified to achieve the end - establishing the communist state.

"Led by the urban workers, the masses had effectively wielded a purely proletarian reason: the mass political strike, on a scale unprecedented even in the most developed countries. They had set up new authoritative institutions; the myriad soviets, peasant committees, and other organizations that had spontaneously sprung up during the revolution. These new institutions were distinguished by extreme democratism: 'a public authority (*vlast*) open to all, one that carried out all its functions before the eyes of the masses, that was accessible to the masses, springing directly from the masses and a direct and immediate instrument of the mass of the *narod* of its will: Lenin did regret the anarchic violence of the masses, not because it was violent, but because it was anarchic. As Lenin expressed it

---

[93] Lih, L. T. *Lenin* (Great Britain: Reaktion Books, 2011) p 289.
[94] Ibid. p. 186.

a year or so later, a revolutionary Social Democrat should never indulge in "hackneyed, philistine, petty bourgeois moralizing about violence." The proper response was rather to transform "attitudes, senseless, sporadic acts of violence into purposeful mass violence."[95]

Lenin apparently came by this honestly. He executed older brother, Alexander Ulyanov, is quoted by Trotsky as saying "I do not believe in terror," said Alexander Ulyanov, who considered himself the adherent of a People's Will of a new type; "I believe in systematic terror."[96]

In talking about Lenin's college years, Trotsky says: ".... The fact that, despite his revolutionary attitudes, amply manifested both in his (Lenin's) choice of acquaintances and in the direction taken by his intellectual interests, he did not join any political group in those years shows unmistakably that he did not yet have a political credo, not even a youthful credo, but was still only searching for one. Nevertheless, the search began on the basis of the Populist tradition, a fact that left a marked imprint on the course of his (Lenin's) future development. Even after he had become a militant Marxist, Vladimir continued for several years to sympathize with individual terrorism, an attitude that set him distinctly apart from other young Social Democrats and was unquestionably a vestigial remnant from the period when Marxist ideas were still intermingled in his mind with Populist sympathies."[97]

Trotsky provides us with this passage: "'Nonsense,' he (Lenin) kept on repeating, 'How can one make a revolution without firing squads? Do you think you will be able to deal with all your enemies by laying down your arms? What other means of repression do you have? Imprisonment? To this no on attaches any importance during a civil war when each side hopes to win.'"[98]

Continuing with Trotsky, we find: "'On the contrary!' exclaimed Lenin, 'exactly in this resides the genuine revolutionary 'dramatic effect,' (He pronounced the words 'dramatic effect' with an ironic twist.) 'Do you really think that we shall come out victorious without any revolutionary terror?'

"This was the time when Lenin at every suitable opportunity stressed the inevitability of terror. Any signs of sentimentality, of easy-going cordiality, of softness-and there was a great surplus of all this-angered him not by themselves, but because he saw in them proof that even the elite of

---

[95] Ibid. p. 94, which cites Lenin *PSS* 12:322;; *CW* 10/248 (1908)
[96] Trotsky, *On Lenin* (Chicago, Haymarket Books, 2017). p. 64.
[97] Lih, L. T. *Lenin*, pp. 172-173.
[98] Ibid. p. 288.

the working class was not fully aware of the extraordinarily difficult tasks which could be accomplished by means of white extraordinary energy."[99]

Harding provides us with the following:

> *The history of the Russian revolutionary movement has been combed assiduously to produce precursors' such as Zaichnevsky, Nechaev, and Tkachev, who, it is maintained provided Lenin with the model of how to transform society. The historical process could, they argued, be transformed by the purposive intervention of a dedicated, disciplined <u>and ruthless minority resorting, when necessary, to terror, to accomplish their aims</u>. Some warrant for this view could, in the eyes of some commentators, be extrapolated from the fiery writings of Marx himself in the heady period of European revolution and reaction during 1848-51. It was the 'voluntarist' Marx, a reflecting on the desperate measures needed to put down the anti-democratic reaction in Europe – a Marx desperate to unleash socialist revolution in backward Germany that Leninism allegedly appropriated.*[100]

According to Harding, "All states were, however, class states. In the contemporary epoch, as we have seen, they became, in Lenin's analysis, class dictatorships. The Dictatorship of the Proletariat was, therefore, "*won and maintained by the use of violence against the bourgeoisie.*' In these terms, it was obvious that any arbitrary action of the party/state would be justified, for the regime itself was the sole judge of who it was that constituted the ill-defined 'bourgeoisie' that was so easily read as a synonym for all the regime's opponents. In the dialectic logic of Leninism, after all, those who are not with us are against us; they form, objectively the camp of the enemy. In this oppressive logic it is, as we have remarked, particularly the moderates, the conciliators, the consensus men who are, in fact, the most dangerous of antagonists. They are of the type of the reformists socialists and labor aristocracy who pose as socialists, but are objectively '*the real agents of the bourgeoisie in the working-class movement,* the labor lieutenants of the capitalist class...'[101]

---

[99] Ibid. p. 290.
[100] Harding, N., *Leninism* (Durham, N.C.: Duke University Press, 1996) p. 6.
[101] Ibid, pp. 162-163., which cites Lenin, *Collected Works,* Vol. 22, p. 194.

Armed with this, Lenin actively encouraged the growth of the new secret political police, the Cheka, which was used to root out the bourgeoisie dissidents. They now included all opponents of the decrees of the communist regime. This now included liberals, social democrats, peasants who withheld grain, speculators, hooligans, idlers and drunken workers. The punishment varied from time to time and varied by the group concerned. It could vary from deprivation of a ration card to compulsory labor, from imprisonment to summary execution.[102]

The Fruits of Leninism

Lenin criticized contemporary capitalism and promised a redress of the suffering of the exploited masses. He offered an explanation for their suffering and an organization to motivate them to seek redress of those grievances. He promised an end to wage slavery among the workers; to the poor peasants he offered an end to landlordism; to the oppressed nations, the colonies of the Imperialist powers he offered a brotherly hand in the common struggle against international imperialism. He offered a route to the elimination of injustice. To those who sought a better world it offered an end to war and national antagonism. "The gap between promise and performance was, of course, to grow wider as the century progressed, to the extent that Leninism in power fell prey to the accusation that it had in fact created the inverse of what it professed. But it was precisely in terms of its own protestations that it was judged and found wanting. It was finally rejected because not only could it not realize the aspirations it had itself promoted, it could no longer maintain, even to itself, that it was making progress towards their fulfilment."[103]

Lenin had anticipated that the end of WWI would produce economic collapse of the European powers and as they demobilized their armies there would be massive political unrest that would allow his brand of socialism, i.e., communism, to spread throughout Europe. Fortunately, this did not come to pass, despite the actual Soviet invasion of Poland from 1919 to 1921.[104] In addition, instead of having a free hand he was obliged

---

[102] Ibid, p. 163.
[103] Harding, N., *Leninism*, p. 8.
[104] Poland had been destroyed as a state in 1795 when it was occupied by and its territories shared between Russia, Austria, and Prussia. There is a long history of the Russian taking Polish territory, far too long to cover in a footnote. Let it suffice to say that once Kiev was a Polish city. The death thralls of Poland began in 1772 when the "1st Partitioning" occurred. The 2nd Partition

to fight a long civil war that received support from, including military contingents from the Americans, the French, British, Japanese, and the famous Czech Legion.

The numerical strength of the communists was such that they had no hope of remaining in power if they allowed free elections or by democratizing the actual business of public administration through a revitalization of the soviets. Either option would have swept the communists from power and that was unacceptable.

Russia was not yet completely controlled by the communists. Russia found itself surrounded within by an unsubdued peasantry and externally by the imperialist powers. In order to justify this Lenin resorted to political relativism that was compatible with orthodox Marxism, but which was based on arguments that were harsh, cynical, and deeply apolitical, which Lenin used to justify the sole power of the communists. He decided that the only way to maintain his regime was to militarize it, to centralize it, and to make it a dictatorship, with him as its dictator. As discussed earlier, the end justified the means. But in this case, Lenin's attitude was "I know what is best for the peasants, they will adopt it and they will enjoy it." Lenin's earlier disdain for the "philistines" who would dare to argue with his interpretation of Marxism expanded into a similar attitude towards anyone who would not submit to his will.

The result was the basis for the Soviet state. The Soviet state replaced the authoritarianism of Czarism with an even more brutal authoritarianism. The only differences were that the Winter Palace in St. Petersburg had a new occupant and the Okhrana, the Czarist secret police, were replaced by the Cheka, the Soviet secret police (1917-1922), and its following successors: GPU (1922–1923), the OGPU (1923–1934), the NKVD (1934–1946), the NKGB (February–July 1941/1943–1946), and the MGB (1946–1953). Siberia remained a place for the exile of political dissidents, but by comparison the Czarist exiles lived in relative freedom, under Stalin they became barbed wire enclosed death camps where dissidents were worked to death known as the "Gulag".[105]

---

occurred in 1792 when Russia and Prussia seized large portions of its territory and the last occurred in 1795. As a result, when the Treaty of Versailles recreated Poland the new Polish state had claims on much of what had become Russian 123 years before. The Poles occupied those territories and the Russians, ignoring historical claims and Russian territorial crimes against Poland, reacted militarily and were crushingly defeated.

[105] For those who doubt this, I recommend that they read *One Day in the Life of Ivan Denisovich*, by Alexander Solzhenitsyn. Though it is a novel, it is what Solzhenitsyn experienced during his incarceration in the Soviet Gulag. For a much longer discussion of the Soviet gulags, I recommend Solzhenitsyn's *Gulag Archipelago*.

Stalin

Stalin was born on December 18, 1878 and baptized on December 29th. His birth name was Ioseb Besarionis dze Jughashvili. He was the son of an impoverished family, his father being a cobbler employed by another man. His father was apparently a brutal man and a drunk, who beat Stalin frequently. Life was hard, but he was taken into a church school where he excelled.

In 1894, Stalin enrolled in the Orthodox Spiritual Seminary in Tiflis, enabled by a scholarship that allowed him to study at a reduced rate. He joined the trainee priests and, apparently, was academically successful earning high grades. He wrote poetry that, according to Stalin's biographer Simon Sebag Montefiore, they became "minor Georgian classics."

Later Stalin lost interest in priestly studies, his grades dropped, and he was repeatedly confined to a cell for his rebellious behavior. The seminary's journal noted that he declared himself an atheist, stalked out of prayers and refused to doff his hat to monks. His rebelliousness led him to read Marx's *Das Kapital* and other proscribed socialist material and he became a confirmed Marxist.

In 1899, Stalin began work as a meteorologist at the Tiflis observatory. The light workload gave him time for his revolutionary activity. Soon, he attracted a group of supporters through classes he taught on socialist theory. He then co-organized a secret workers' mass meeting for May Day 1900. In this meeting he provoked some of the workers to start a strike. This attracted the attention of the Czarist police, and they attempted to arrest him, but he fled and went into hiding. He planned yet another mass demonstration in 1901 that clashed with authorities. In 1901 Stalin was elected to the Tiflis Committee of the Russian Social Democratic Labor Party (RSDLP), a Marxist party founded in 1898.

Stalin continued organizing strikes and demonstrations and finally in 1902 he was arrested. Initially he was held in Batumi Prison and then Kutaisi Prison. By mid-1903 he was sentenced to three years of exile in Eastern Siberia. When released he returned to his activities and in November 1905, the Georgian Bolsheviks elected him as one of their delegates to a Bolshevik conference in Saint Petersburg.

By 1907 Stalin had established himself as "Georgia's leading Bolshevik." After returning to Tiflis, Stalin organized the robbing of a large delivery of money to the Imperial Bank in June 1907. His gang ambushed the armed convoy in Erivan Square with gunfire and home-made bombs.

Around 40 people were killed, but all of his gang escaped alive. After the heist, Stalin moved to Baku where the Mensheviks confronted him about the robbery and voted to expel him from the RSDLP, but he took no notice of them.

While in Baku he had reassembled his gang, "the Outfit." This criminal gang continued its criminal activities by running protection rackets, counterfeiting currency, and performing robberies. They also kidnapped the children of several wealthy individuals, who they then ransomed. In early 1908, Stalin travelled to the Swiss city of Geneva to meet Lenin. Their long relationship began.

In the following years he was repeatedly arrested and prosecuted, but he continued his activities and was eventually placed on the Communist Central Committee and became editor of *Pravda*, the Communist Party newspaper.

He was again arrested. This time he was exiled to Siberia. Stalin was called up for conscription into the Russian Army; however, he was rejected because of his crippled arm resulting from being struck by a carriage as a child.

Stalin rose through the ranks of Lenin's Communist Party and eventually became one of the principal players in it. He had his eye set on the leadership, of succeeding Lenin, but knew that there was no way to push him out of office and replace him. Stalin, therefore, built alliances and played the role of the crown prince.

When Lenin died, there were two conflicting schools of thought regarding the future of the Soviet Union. The left-wing communists or Trotskyites believed that the world revolution was essential for the survival of socialism in the new born Soviet Union. Trotsky, the leader of this faction, called for the support of a worldwide perpetual revolution. Domestically the Trotskyites pushed for rapid development of the economy and the creation of a socialist society. The right wing, or militant communists, recognized that the world was not likely to disintegrate into revolution in the near future and favored the gradual development of the Soviet Union through NEP programs. A major theoretician of the right, Bukharin, believed that in order for socialism to triumph it must receive assistance from more economically advanced socialist countries.

Amid these issues, the leading figures of the All-Union Communist Party (Bolsheviks) – the new name of the Russian Communist Party, which was led by the troika of Kamenev-Zinov'ev-Stalin, supported the militant international program and maneuvered against Trotsky. They succeeded in having Trotsky removed in 1925 from the post of Commissar of War. Meanwhile, Stalin worked on expanding his personal political strength and when sufficiently strong, he broke with Kamenev and Zinov'ev. Kamenev and Zinov'ev realized the depth of their error in trusting Stalin, made amends with Trotsky and together they struggled against Stalin for control of the state. Stalin countered with his formulation of the theory of "socialism in one country," which called for the construction of a socialist society in the Soviet Union regardless of the international situation. This theory's implementation distanced Stalin from the left and gained for him the support of Bukharin and the party's right wing. Thus strengthened, Stalin ousted the leaders of the left from their positions in the party from 1925 to 1927 and forced Trotsky into exile. At this point, free debate of ideology within the party became progressively restricted as Stalin gradually eliminated any opposition to his idea of socialism and his dictatorship.

During the 1920's the Soviet Union gradually moved away from the revolutionary path to socialism and adopted a less ideological approach in its relations with the rest of Europe. Lenin, being practical, had become convinced that socialist revolutions would not occur in other nations in the near future and recognized that the Soviet Union, if it was to grow, needed to normalize its relations with Western Europe. This was not easy, because of lingering distrust and debts owed to the West by Czarist government. In April 1922 a break through occurred when Germany, signed the Treaty of Rapallo with the Soviet Union and normalized relations and trade between the two countries. This treaty also had a secret clause that allowed Germany to cooperate with the Soviets in military developments. The ice broken, soon the other European nations and America soon opened diplomatic and trade relations with the Soviet Union.

By 1932 it was clear, even to Stalin, that the economy and society were overstained. Industry failed to meet its targets and agriculture lost ground when compared to 1928 yields. Stalin, unwilling to admit failure, declared that the first 5-Year Plan had met its goals in four years. The truth was officially concealed, but apparent to everyone. A second 5-Year Plan was then issued (1933-1937) and it focused on consumer goods, with factories built during the first plan helping the industrial output in general.

Then came the third 5-Year Plan, which produced poorer results, because of Stalin's perception that war was on the horizon and industrial output shifted from consumer goods to armaments.

Stalin's Economy

Twin Evils

    In Marxist ideology, there is no basis for the Soviet Union's economy as it existed under Stalin. Stalin's economy was a planned economy. It had been a centralized economy under Lenin during the early years of communism. This planned economy provided a legitimate precedence for Stalin's use and the planned economy's further development. Between 1927 and 1929 the Soviet State Planning Commission drew up Stalin's first 5-Year Plan. This 5-year Plan focused upon intensive economic growth. Stalin's "Revolution from Above," a paradoxical slogan for a dictatorial decree, in 1928, called for the rapid industrialization of the Soviet economy and focused on heavy industry. Under it small-scale industries and services were nationalized and labor unions were converted into aggressive supervisory organizations that focused on increasing labor's productivity. The plan rested purely and simply on quotas of finished goods set by the party. These quotes were unrealistic. However, Stalin did not care and did not have the industrial experience to understand trivial technicality. As a result, the serious problems rapidly appeared. The greatest share of investment went into heavy industry. Widespread shortages of consumer goods and inflation ultimately resulted.

    At the beginning of 1927 official statistics estimated that there were from 14,000 to 15,000 collective farms holding from 5,000,000 to 6,000,000 acres of land, but only about 1,700,000 was under active cultivation. The total of land capable of supporting crops for the entire nation came to 280,000,000 acres, but the land under cultivation by collective farms came to little more than 1% of the total crop producing land of the country. Collective farming and state farms were a complete failure, so the government found itself obliged to confiscate all the food necessary to feed the cities from the small peasant farmers, the kulaks.

    Both Lenin and Stalin hated the *kulaks* and called them exploiters. Stalin desired to replace them with collective farms. Lenin repeatedly called them exploiters. Stalin simply saw them as capitalists in peasant clothing.

    In 1921 a new policy was proclaimed and it included a new agricultural policy. The government abandoned an immediate socialist organization of agriculture. Instead, it left more freedom to the peasants. The policy of confiscating all surpluses of agricultural products was replaced by a fixed taxation of the peasants in kind. The market for agricultural surpluses was reopened. The purpose of this was to stimulate the production of small scale and medium scale peasant farms, to increase their production beyond their needs for consumption, and to solve the food problems in the cities.

The Code of 1922 abandoned the principle of land nationalization of land and the abolition of private rights to land and replaced them with a practically unlimited tenure, in time, for the agricultural use of the current holders of that land. It did not impose new forms of land tenancy; it did, however, recognize the equality of all previous existing forms – the community of land, the individual buildings in open fields, and the holdings in closed fields. It also abolished all private rights to land and prohibited land purchase, sale or mortgaging. The prohibition of peasant land purchase pre-dated the revolution. It did permit, however, the leasing of agricultural lands with restrictions. It also permitted the use of hired labor in agriculture, which had been excluded by previous Soviet laws. It is interesting how "wage slavery" crept back into the socialist tool box.

In 1925 even more freedom was allowed for the lease of agricultural land. Leases of agricultural land were permitted for 12 years and longer. It also permitted rented land to be worked by hired labor. The use of hired labor in agriculture was further facilitated by temporary regulations issued in 1925 concerning hired labor on peasant farms. These revisions to Soviet policy actually proved to be moderately successful. From 1922 to 1926 the Russian peasantry made great efforts to equal the pre-war and pre-revolution food production.

Unfortunately, this conciliatory program directed towards the peasants did not last long. Though it was obvious that the *kulaks*, the well-to-do peasants, produced the surplus of goods that the Soviet government needed, ideology and crop failures soon intervened

In spite of a good harvest in 1927, grain supplies dropped markedly. The war scare had caused the peasants to hoard grain. This compounded an existing problem that the peasants were consuming much of their production. During the 1920s, when the peasants were confronted with the option of selling at an artificially low price, chose consumption over giving their grain away at an unacceptable price. By 1927 a "goods famine" had removed much of the incentive for the peasants to seek cash, as there were no goods to buy. This resulted in disastrous grain supply shortages.

In the cities food prices skyrocketed. Lines formed at stores and rationing reappeared. The city dwellers, remembering the famine of the civil war, added to the panic of the war scare. The Stalinists interpreted the peasants' behavior as a "kulak grain strike." Stalinists believed it was a conscious and intentional sabotage of Stalin's industrialization program, and sabotage of the national defense.

In 1928 the party implemented what it called "extraordinary measures" in grain procurement. Thousands of communists and factory workers left the cities and towns and moved into the countryside to take the grain they needed. To do this they overrode local officials who had accepted the NEP. Markets were closed, roadblocks were established to apprehend private traders. Article 107 of the Criminal Code was widely used to stop speculation and hoarding. These two activities were interpreted very broadly by the grain procurement brigades, which seized any and all reserves of grain they could find. Peasants looked upon these "extraordinary measures" as a return to the forced grain requisitioning of the civil war. Violence became an everyday feature of rural life as the grain procurement campaign destroyed the uneasy truce the NEP had produced with the peasantry. Stalin assumed the role of chief advocate of these extraordinary measures. During his trip to Siberia in early 1928, Stalin lashed out against the local communists claiming they were not seriously concerned about the hunger threatening the cities and the Red Army. He accused them of being afraid to use Article 107. This behavior was not universally accepted and Bukharin and Rykov argued that these measures threatened the very survival of Soviet power. There was, so it appears, a temporary compromise between them. Stalin reduced extraordinary measures after the April 1928 plenum of the Party's Central Committee. Unfortunately, in early 1929 the communists returned to those extraordinary measures when the grain supply once again stalled.

The Right Opposition, Bukharin and Rykov, argued that these steps would cause the loss of peasant support in the *smychka*[106]. Stalin maintained that the leading role of the working class in the *smychka* was paramount. He believed that the working class held a leading role and that the peasants would necessarily be subordinate to them. He defined the aims of the *smychka* as strengthening the position of the working class in order to guarantee the leadership of the working class within the union. To Stalin, the break-up of the *smychka* meant a disruption of the flow of grain into the cities. The disruption of the food supplies and grain exports threatened both his industrialization program and the support of the working class. This would also jeopardize the ability of the state to defend itself. He

---

[106] The *Smychka* was a popular political term in Soviet Russia and Soviet Union. It can be roughly translated as "collaboration in society" "union", "alliance", "joining the ranks".

believed that raising grain prices would hurt the working class in the cities and he wanted to merge the peasantry with the working class and prepare the conditions for the destruction of all classes, that is to create the desired classless society that was necessary for the socialist world.

Stalin later stated that the *smychka* was only useful when aimed against capitalist elements and exploited as a tool to strengthen the dictatorship of the proletariat. In essence the peasantry was a useful ally only when and to the extent that it served the interests of the dictatorship of the proletariat. The grain crises of the 1920s made it clear to Stalin that the peasants were no longer suitable partners in the *smychka* and that he had to find a final solution for the peasant problem.[107]

From 1927 on Stalin turned to the idea of collective farms as the solution for the grain problem. He argued that the peasants had to pay a tribute for the industrialization program and to feed the cities and the army. The collective farm, he believed, was the best way to address this problem.

At the April 1929 plenum of the Central Committee, Stalin was challenged by an individual who said that such tribute should not come from the "middle peasants." To this Stalin responded "Do you think that the middle peasant is closer to the party than the working class? Well, you are a sham Marxist."[108] He went on to declare that the kulak stratum was growing in size, that the class struggle was worsening in the countryside, and that the peasantry was divided into poor peasants, middle peasants, and kulaks. He stated that it was the kulaks who were "wrecking" and "intriguing" against the Soviet economic policy.

The following quote is from Stalin's address to the Conference of Marxist Students of the Agrarian Question, in December 1929:

> The characteristic feature of our work during the past year is: (a) that we, the party and the Soviet government, have developed an offensive on the whole front against the capitalist elements in the countryside; and (b) that this offensive, as you know, has brought about and is bringing about very palpable, positive results.
>
> What does this mean? It means that we have passed from a policy of restricting the exploiting proclivities of the kulaks to the policy of eliminating the kulaks as a class. This means that we have made, and are still making, one of

---

[107] Viola, L., *Peasant Rebels Under Stalin* (New York: Oxford University Press: 1996) p. 22.
[108] Ibid, p. 23.

the most decisive turns in our whole policy.

..... Could we have undertaken such an offensive against the kulaks five years or three years ago? Could we then have counted on success in such an offensive? No, we could not. That would have been the most dangerous adventurism! That would have been playing a very dangerous game at offensive. We would certainly have come to grief and, since we had come to grief, we would have strengthened the position of the kulaks. Why? Because we did not yet have a stronghold in the rural districts in the shape of a wide network of state farms and collective farms upon which to relay in a determined offensive against the kulaks. Because at that time we were not yet able to substitute for the capitalist production of the kulaks socialist production in the shape of the collective farms and state farms.

But today? What is the position? Today, we have an adequate material base which enables us to strike at the kulaks, to break their resistance, to eliminate them as a class, and to substitute for their output the output of the collective farms and state farms....

Now, as you see, we have the material base, which enables us to substitute for kulak output the output of the collective farms and state farms. That is why our offensive against the kulaks is now meeting with undeniable success. That is how the offensive against the kulaks must be carried on, if we mean a real offensive and not futile declamations against the kulans.

That is why we have actually passed from the policy of restricting the exploiting proclivities of the kulaks to the policy of eliminating the kulaks as a class..... Now we are able to carry on a determined offensive against the kulaks, to break their resistance, to eliminate them as a class, and substitute for their output the put put of the collective farms and state farms. Now, the kulaks are being expropriated by the masses of poor and middle peasants themselves, but the masses who ware putting solid collectivization into practice. Now the expropriation of the kulaks in the regions of solid collectivism is no longer just an administrative measure. Now the expropriation of the kulaks is an integral part of the formation and the development of the collective farms....[109]

Why is this speech important? It is important because the kulak class of farms were the largest producer of grain and other foodstuffs in the Soviet Union. Food had become a serious problem. Stalin's 5-Year Plan called for the collectivizing of farming. Collectivized farms became a method to for government control of the kulaks and peasants. Collectivization resulted in the peasants' land being consolidated into large farms and their animals were taken and placed into those collective farms. The distress of the peasants had, since the earliest days of civilization had been the issue of holding land and owning domestic animals. The Soviet government, which had based its appeal to the peasants on land redistribution, now became the appropriator of all their land and animals. Stalin focused on the liquidation of the wealthiest peasants, the kulaks, as expressed in the foregoing passage. In fact, these "exploiters", the kulaks were only marginally better than the lowest level of the peasantry. Despite this, Lenin had called them expropriators because they created surpluses of grain, etc., which they then sold for profit.

The process of collectivization produced a sharp reaction by the peasants. They slaughtered their cows and pigs rather than surrender them to the collective farms, which meant that livestock resources fell below the 1929 levels. In response, the state turned to the forced collectivization, deporting kulaks and peasants who refused to cooperate. They were sent to the gulags in Siberia or internal exile. Meanwhile, back in the workers' paradise of the Soviet Union starvation began to appear in the big cities. It was starvation on a scale that had not been seen during WWI. Stalin rightly feared a counter revolution. Therefore, he turned to Ukraine.

The Holodomor or Great Famine was the direct result of Stalin's policies and was a man-made famine in Soviet Ukraine that lasted from 1932 to 1933. It resulted in the deaths of millions of Ukrainians. Because the Ukraine was a major grain producing area, Stalin imposed higher than usual quotas on it. When they were not met, he reacted violently. A statement by the United Nations, issued in 2003, says that from 7,000,000 to 10,000,000 Ukrainians died as a result.

---

[109] *Stalin, J., Works, Vol. 12, April 1929-June 1930,* (Moscow: Foreign Languages Publishing House, 1954) pp. 147-178

Twin Evils

The Soviets were only able to obtain 4.3 million tons of grain from the 1932 harvest compared with 7.2 million tons obtained from the 1931 harvest. Rations in towns were drastically reduced. In winter 1932–1933 and spring 1933, people in many urban areas suffered great shortages, yet rations were cut still further. By spring 1933, urban residents faced starvation. To deal with this the workers were shown agitprop movies depicting peasants as counterrevolutionaries that were deliberately hiding food at a time when workers, who were constructing the "bright future" of socialism, were starving. The goal was to direct the urban population's hatred away from the party and against the kulaks.

Mass starvation and deaths by starvation began to appear. The problem spread and epidemics of typhus and malaria appeared. Cannibalism was even reported.

To address the problem a blacklist system was established in 1932 by the Decree of November 20, 1932, "The Struggle against Kurkul Influence in Collective Farms." Blacklisting was synonymous with a board of infamy and was one of the elements of agitation-propaganda in the Soviet Union. A blacklisted collective farm, village, or district had its monetary loans and grain advances called in, stores closed, and supplies of grain, livestock, and food confiscated as a penalty. The farm was cut off from trade. Its communist party and collective farm committees were purged and subject to arrest, and their territory was forcibly cordoned off by the OGPU secret police.

Though this process generally targeted collective farms that failed to meet grain quotas and independent farmers with outstanding tax-in-kind debts, in practice the punishment was applied to all residents of affected villages and districts. This included teachers, tradespeople, and children. In the end, 37 out of 392 districts along with at least 400 collective farms were put on the "black board" in Ukraine. This process extended through all the districts. Some blacklisted areas in Kharkiv had death rates exceeding 40%.[110]

A passport system in the Soviet Union (identity cards) was introduced on December 27, 1932 to deal with the exodus of peasants from the countryside. Individuals not having such a document could not leave their homes on pain of administrative penalties, such as internment in labor camps (the Gulag). In January 1933, Stalin signed a decree entitled

---

[110] U.S. Commission on the Ukraine Famine (1988). Mace, James Earnest; Samilenko, Olga; Pechenuk, Walter (eds.). *Investigation of the Ukrainian Famine 1932–1933* Vol.1: Report to Congress. Vol. 1 of 3. Washington, D.C.: United States Government Printing Office. p. 67. Archived from the original on 7 January 2007. Retrieved 27 July 2012. P. 67.

"Preventing the Mass Exodus of Peasants who are Starving". It restricted travel by peasants after requests for bread began in the Kuban and Ukraine. As usual, Soviet authorities, either blind to their own culpability or unwilling to accept that their political ideology was a complete failure, blamed this exodus of peasants on anti-Soviet elements, saying that "like the outflow from Ukraine last year, was organized by the enemies of Soviet power."

This was followed by the requirement that passports be used if one wished to travel between republics and totally banned travel by rail. In March 1933, the GPU reported that 219,460 people were either intercepted and escorted back or arrested at its checkpoints meant to prevent movement of peasants between districts.[111] There are estimates of 150,000 excess deaths resulting from this policy. Of course, "scholars" dispute the nature and quantity of these deaths.

The Communists then turned to using "Red Trains", which took the first harvest of the season's crop to the government depots. During the Holodomor, these brigades were part of the Soviet Government's policy of confiscating food from the peasants. This was followed by a relentless pillaging of the kulak farms by Soviet officials. Soviet officials took all the food stuffs and anything else that they fancied. Stalin implicitly approved of this pillaging in a telegraph dated January 1, 1933, addressed to the Ukrainian government. His telegraph explicitly reiterated the severe penalties to be inflicted upon farmers who did not surrender all the grain that they may be hiding.

In order to compensate for unfulfilled grain procurement quotas in the Ukraine, reserves of grain were confiscated from three sources. The three sources were (1) grain set aside for seed for the next growing season; (2) a grain fund for emergencies; and, (3) grain issued to collective farmers for previously completed work, which had to be returned if the collective farm did not fulfill its quota.[112]

Aside from what some consider a deliberate effort to destroy the small farmers, the kulak class of the Ukraine, and forced collectivization, there were political repercussions. The Ukrainian Communist party officials were purged at all levels. It is estimated that 390 "anti-Soviet, counter-revolutionary insurgent and chauvinist" groups were eliminated resulting in 37,797 arrests, producing 719 executions, 8,003 people

---

[111] Werth, N., Courtois, S., Panne, J.-L., Pzkowski, A., Bartosek, K, Margolin, J.-L. (Kramer, M, Ed) (1999). *The Black Book of Communism, Crimes, Terror, Repression* (Cambridge, Massachusetts: Harvard University Press, 1999) p. 164.

[112] Wolowyna, Oleh (2 October 2021). "A Demographic Framework for the 1932–1934 Famine in the Soviet Union". *Journal of Genocide Research*. 23 (4): pp. 501–526.

that were sent to Gulag camps, and 2,728 subjected to internal exile.[113] 120,000 Ukrainians were reviewed in the first 10 months of 1933 in an aggressive purge of the Communist party. This resulted in 23% of Ukrainians being eliminated as perceived class hostile elements.[114]

By the end of 1933, 60% of the heads of village councils and district committees in Ukraine were replaced. An additional 40,000 lower-tier workers were purged.[115] Purges were also extensive in the Ukrainian populated territories of the Kuban and North Caucasus. Three hundred and fifty eight of 716 party secretaries in Kuban were removed, along with 43% of the 25,000 party members residing there; in total, 40% of the 115,000 to 120,000 rural party members in the North Caucasus were removed.[116] It had been determined by the Soviet authorities that the party officials were responsible for the failure of grain procurement. They paid the price.

Unwilling to admit the failure to the world, the Soviet government refused to ask for foreign aid and concealed the famine's existence. In response to the famine Stalin callously quoted Vladimir Lenin during the famine declaring: "He who does not work, neither shall he eat."

Under Stalin, not only were industry and agriculture regimented and collectivized, society underwent a similar change. All individual effort was absorbed into the collective. In addition to abolishing private farms and businesses, it collectivized scientific and literary endeavors. The experimentation of the cultural and social life was replaced with conservative norms.

Order, discipline, and conformity dominated social policy and became instruments of the modernization effort. Strict labor codes were issued. These codes required punctuality and discipline. Labor unions became a mere extension of the state charged with enforcing these codes. However, productive workers and labor brigades were granted higher pay and privileges. Marx and Lenin must have been spinning in their graves that anyone was paid more than anyone else, as equality of pay for all was one of their principle demands. In addition, the Soviet state looked to strengthen the family by restricting divorce and prohibiting abortion.

The arts and literature, since the 1930s, had been restricted to

---

[113] Ibid.
[114] Ibid.
[115] Ibid.
[116] Gorbunova, Viktoriia; Klymchuk, Vitalii (2020). "The Psychological Consequences of the Holodomor in Ukraine". East/West: Journal of Ukrainian Studies. 7 (2): 33–68.

members of the unions of writers, musicians, and other artists. Union membership was mandatory. These unions-imposed adherence to established standards. All creative works had to express the socialistic spirit. Socialist realism, the officially sanctioned doctrine, was applied to all fields of artistic endeavor. Of course, the state repressed works that were stylistically innovative or lacked the appropriate content. Though in Czarist Russia works thought to be subversive, such as those of Marx and Engels were banned, it never reached the degree of censorship that existed under Stalin.

In the world of science many soft sciences had to be based on the party's understanding of the Marxist dialectic. Of course, with all the short comings of Marxist theory, this stifled many disciplines. From the 1920's. the party directed that the writing of history, in particular, conform to the subsequent modifications of orthodox Marxist theory. In particular, writing of history must incorporate and emphasize nationalistic themes. In addition, the writing of history must focus on the great leaders of Russia's past. This particular requirement was to enhance Stalin's dictatorship,

The Lunacharskii experimental educational system of the 1920s was discarded. Admission to higher education was now based on academic performance. Class and race no longer played a role, in a clear admission that past performance was the only clear predictor of future performance; that performance was unrelated to class or race and that equity would not produce the success that Stalin's Five-Year Programs demanded.

Stalin's Purges

Though Stalin had established his political domination of the Soviet Union, the economic situation of the 1920s introduced elements that could threaten Stalin's absolutism. As a result, he began a purge of the party ranks of those individuals whose absolute loyalty was questionable. To this end Stalin began a reign of terror that exceeded that of the French Revolution. No one was safe. No class was exempt. The policy was "Swear absolute fealty, or be purged."

The purges began in December 1934, as the famine was reaching its peak. Sergei Kirov was a popular Leningrad party leader advocated a moderate policy towards the peasants. He was assassinated. The culprit is unknown; but it is generally assumed that it was done at Stalin's order.

Twin Evils

Then came a purge of the Leningrad party. Thousands were deported to the Siberian gulags. Zinov'ev and Kamenev, who had previously been strong supporters of Stalin, were sent to prison for their claimed involvement in Kirov's murder.

According to Nikita Khrushchev, Stalin's successor, in a speech he made to a closed session of the 20th Party Congress on February 25, 1956, Stalin had coined the phrase of "enemy of the people"; this automatically rendered it unnecessary that the ideological errors of the accused be proven. This term made it possible to use the cruelest repression, violating all the norms of revolutionary legality. Simply being suspected of hostile intent, or anyone possessing a bad reputation, were sufficient to condemn anyone. Confessions, the only evidence needed, were extracted by torture.

Meanwhile, the NKVD, the new secret police, began an increased surveillance using agents and informers to expose anti-Soviet conspiracies among the long-term party members. There were three heavily publicized show trials in Moscow between 1936 and 1938, where dozens of old Bolsheviks, including Zinov'ev, Kamenev, and Bukharin, were prosecuted for anti-state activities. The last three had confessions forced from them and were subsequently executed. Trotsky, Stalin's bitter enemy, who had fled the Soviet Union, was tracked down and murdered in 1940. In addition to the show trials, purges swept through the rank and file of younger leaders in the party government, industrial management, and cultural affairs. The purges in the non-Russian republics were especially severe.

Nikolai Ezhov, the head of the NKVD, was sent to deal with the army. Stalin feared the possibility of a military coup. Stalwart veterans of the party, men who had risen through the ranks of the Red Army and fought in the Russian Civil War for the Marxist ideals, were ruthlessly taken into custody and executed. Approximately half of the officers of the Red Army were purged, executed or incarcerated. The NKVD also turned its attention to the general public. Thousands, if not millions, were punished for spurious crimes against the state. When the purges subsided, millions of Soviet leaders, officials, and simple citizens had been executed, imprisoned, or exiled.

Certainly, the famine threatened Stalin's hold on power, but it is probable that he wished to completely suppress the population with these purges. He believed he needed to use terror to further his planned modernization program. Sadly, brutal paranoia cannot be ruled out. It should be remembered that Stalin had learned the power of brutality at the hands of his drunkard father.

At this point Stalin issued a new constitution for the Soviet Union replacing the 1924 constitution. Though it was called "the most democratic constitution in the world," stipulating free and secret elections based on universal suffrage and supposedly guaranteeing the citizenry a range of civil and economic rights, all those rights were cleverly annulled by other elements of the constitution; it stated that the basic structure of Soviet society could not be changed and that the party retained all political power.

All power in the Soviet Union was, therefore, concentrated in the hands of Stalin and his handpicked obsequious sycophants. This could be called the first "cult of personality." Marx had presumed that with the establishment of his socialist state, that state power would gradually "wither away," but under Stalin's iron hand it did the exact opposite. The Soviet state became more oppressive than the Czar had ever been. Stalin was now a deity with everything except a declared "divine right of kings" since he was an atheist.

Stalin's Gulag System

The Gulags were an agency of the Soviet government that replaced deportations to Siberia under the Czarist government. The Gulags were a system of forced labor camps. Lenin ordered its organization and it reached its peak under Stalin from the 1930's to the 1950s. It was an expansion of the Solovki prison camp system formed in 1918 and was formally established by a decree, "On the creation of the forced-labor camps", on April 15, 1919. The purpose of these camps was both punishment and re-education with the additional benefit of obtaining free, forced labor for the Soviet system. It served to remove petty criminals and political enemies of the people from Soviet society. Those sent into the system frequently endured extrajudicial courts administered by the Cheka. As discussed earlier, these courts evolved into the NKVD (1934-1945) and the Ministry of Internal Affairs (MVD) (1945-1960). Indeed, the system, because of the extra-judicial processes that could send Soviet citizens into the Gulag, simply telling a joke about the government or criticizing a government official could get one administratively sent into the slave labor system. The system regularly worked outside the Soviet legal system.

Though the Gulag did not use gas chambers and crematoriums, it closely resembled the Nazi concentration camps. By the 1920s it contained and estimated 100,000 prisoners; by 1940, it grew to over 1,500,000.[117]

---

[117] Ellman, M. Soviet Repression Statistics: Some Comments. *Europe-Asia Studies,* Vol. 54, No.

Another 4,000,000 prisoners passed through the Gulag colonies from 1930 to 1953. Conditions were harsh at best and it is estimated, based on the accounts of its victims, that from 1,500,000 to 1,700,000 died while in its camps.

In March 1940, there were 53 Gulag camp directorates (generally called "camps") and 423 labor colonies in the Soviet Union.[118]

Stalin's paranoia was such that when captured Soviet soldiers returned to the USSR at the end of WWII, they were sent to the Gulags for not having fought to the death. In addition, the system contained foreign civilian detainees and prisoners of war. Among the latter, the vast majority were worked to death. The most famous of the Gulag's prisoners was Alexander Solzhenitsyn, who claimed that it was a process of deliberately working people to death.

When Stalin died the process of dismantling began and a general amnesty was granted to non-political prisoners and political prisoners who had been sentenced to a maximum of five years in prison. On January 25, 1960, the Gulag system was officially abolished. However, the practice of sentencing convicts to penal labor was not completely abolished and continues to exist in Putin's Russian Federation,

Marxism as Seen by Stalin

Under the name of Marxism-Leninism, Stalin codified the body of ideas that became the official doctrine of the Soviet communist party. By practicing Marxism, he assimilated it and time simplified it. Stalin's Marxism-Leninism rested on the dialectic of Hegel and on a materialism that can be considered roughly identical to that of Feuerbach. His work *Problems of Leninism* sets forth an ideology of power and activism that rides roughshod over the more nuanced approach of Lenin.

Soviet dialectical materialism can be reduced to four laws.: First, history is a dialectical development. It proceeds by successive phases that replace each earlier phase. These phases are not separate and form a continuum. Though it is true that phase B, by its existence, negates phase A, it contended that the roots of phase B were already contained in phase A and was initiated by it. The dialectic does not regard nature as an accidental string of isolated and independent events; it believes nature as a unified,

7 (Nov. 2002), pp. 1151–1172

[118] Getty, J.H.; Rittersporn, G.; Zemskov, V., (October 1993). "Victims of the Soviet penal system in the pre-war years: a first approach on the basis of archival evidence." American Historical Review. 98. 1017–1049.

coherent whole. It contends that nature is perpetually in movement, in a state of unceasing renewal and evolution, where something is always being born and developing, while something else is disintegrating and disappearing. Second, evolution takes place within limits and is not gradual. Third, contradictions must be made manifest and all phenomena contain contradictory elements. These dialectic views objects and natural phenomenon possessing internal contradictions; they all have a positive and a negative side. These contradictory elements are a "yin" and "yang" in perpetual struggle. it is, according to Stalin, a struggle that is the "internal content of the process of development." Fourth, the law of this human development is economic. All other contradictions are rooted in the basic economic relationships between people. A given epoch is entirely determined by the relations of production. They are social relations; relations of collaboration or mutual aid, relations of domination or submission; and finally, they are social transitory relations that characterize a period of passage from one system to another. "The history of the development of society is, above all, the history of the development of production, the history of the modes of production which succeed one another through the centuries." This, in particular, is very Marxian.

From these principles comes the recognition that it is essential to penetrate the workings of Marxist-Leninist thought and its application. No natural phenomenon, no historical or social situation, no political fact of the human condition, can be considered independent of the other facts or phenomena that surround it; it is set within a whole. Since movement is constant and an essential fact, one must distinguish between what is beginning to decay and what has been brought into existence and is developing. Since the process of development takes place in surges, one passes quickly from a succession of slow quantitative changes to substantial qualitative changes in man's condition. In the social or political realm, these sudden qualitative changes are revolutions launched by the oppressed classes. Thus, it is necessary to purse proletarian-class policy that exposes the contradictions of the capitalist system. It declared that a reformist policy was pointless. Consequently (1) nothing can be judged from the point of view of "eternal justice" or any other preconceived notion and (2) no social system is immutable. To be effective, one must not base one's action on social strata that are no longer developing, even if they represent, for the moment, the dominant force, for even that is evolving.

Stalin's materialist and historical dialectic differs sharply from that of Karl Marx. In *The Communist Manifesto* Marx applied the materialist dialectic to the social and political life of his time. In the chapter entitled "Bourgeois and Proletarians," he examined the process of the growth of the revolutionary bourgeoisie within feudal society, then the genesis and the growth of the proletariat within capitalism, then he emphasized the struggle between the classes. He then connected social evolution with the development of the forces of production. Marx focused not only on the struggle, but the birth of consciousness among the proletariat. "As to the final victory of the propositions put forth in the *Manifesto*, Marx expected it to come primarily from the intellectual development of the working class, which necessarily was the result of common action and discussion." [119]

The result of Stalin's dialectic, however, was what he called "revolution from above," a dictatorial policy he used to increase industrialization and collectivize agriculture using ruthless repression and a strong centralization of power. For Stalin, the immediate goal was all important; this was the basis of his Five-year plans. This was a shift from a dialectic that emphasized both the objective and the subjective, to one purely objective, or objectivist. Human actions were to be judged by ignoring the intentions of the actor and their place in a given historical moment, but only in terms of what they signify objectively at the end of the period considered.

Trotskyism

Alongside Marxism-Leninism as expounded in the former Soviet Union, there arose another point of view expressed by Stalin's opponent Leon Trotsky and his followers that was called Trotskyism. Trotsky had played a leading role in both the Russian Revolution of 1905 and that of 1917. He had also commanded the Red armies during the Civil War. After Lenin's death he fell out with Stalin. Their conflict turned largely upon questions of policy, both domestic and foreign. In the realm of ideas, Trotsky held that a revolution in a backward, rural country could be carried out only by the proletariat. Once in power the proletariat must carry out agrarian reform and undertake the accelerated development of the economy. The revolution must be a socialist one, that focused on the abolition of the private ownership of the means of production, advocated by Marx, or else it will fail. He believed that the revolution could not be carried out in isolation, as Stalin maintained. Trotsky held that capitalist countries would try to destroy it, but that if it was to succeed, the revolution

---
[119] Engels, preface to the republication of *The Communist Manifesto*, May 1, 1890.

must draw upon the industrial techniques of the developed countries. This means that Lenin's idea that the revolution must be worldwide and permanent and directed against the liberal and nationalist bourgeoisie of all countries utilizing local victories to advance the international struggle.

Trotsky emphasized the necessity of finding or creating a revolutionary situation, of educating the working class in order to revolutionize it, to assure that the party remained open to the various revolutionary tendencies and avoided becoming bureaucratized. Finally, when the time for insurrection comes, it should be organizing in accordance with a detailed plan.

By contrast Stalin looked inward. He felt that at that stage, attempting to spread the revolution would weaken the Soviet Union with external distractions and, as discussed earlier, he firmly believed that a bureaucracy, that was totally under his personal control, was superior, if not for the Soviet Union, the at least for Stalin's grasp on power.

Collapse of the Soviet Union

The problems that appeared under Stalin with food supplies continued through the remainder of the life of the Soviet Union. One might argue if it was because the system was flawed and others might argue that it was unfortunate weather circumstances. It is most likely a combination of the two issues.

In 1972 the Soviets secretly bought 18,000,000 tons of wheat and corn. In 1973 there were massive crop failures in the USSR and President Nixon was approached to see if the US would sell grain to the USSR. Of course, this was an admission of the failure of the Soviet system, but it was necessary if the communists were to remain in power. This sale allowed 10,000,000 tons of grain to be sold to the Soviets.

In 1979 another arrangement was made and the Soviets were allowed to buy up to 25,000,000 tons of grain.

In 1980 President Carter ended these sales in retaliation for the Soviet invasion of Afghanistan. Under President Reagan another treaty was signed that allowed the Soviets to buy 9,000,000 tons of US grain every year.

These sales clearly show that the Soviet collectivized farming system was fragile and best and broken at worst. Clearly collectivization did not work. In addition, the Soviet economy was struggling. As a result, Mikhail Gorbachev attempted to reform the Soviet political and economic situation produced by political stalemate, economic backsliding and ethnic separatism.

The first republic to leave was Lithuania. It declared full independence on March 11, 1990. Lithuania was followed by Latvia, Estonia, and Georgia.

Gorbechev's changes, called "Perestroika", were political, social, mental, behavioral, psychological, and economic revolution that reintroduced some elements of capitalism and private property. Gorbachev envisaged a socialist revolution combining Leninism with democracy and a market economy. But the Soviet authorities badly underestimated their ability to control the revolution that was boiling up.

Gorbachev had three goals: (1) preserve socialism, (2) preserve the Soviet Union, and (3) remain in control. Though the Baltic states had left the USSR, he attempted to salvage the USSR by organizing a confederation with nine remaining republics. The treaty for this was signed on August 20, 1991, but it was not soon enough to stop an attempted coup d'état by Soviet hardliners.

The coup, coupled with the heavy casualties suffered by the Soviet Army in Afghanistan produced massive demonstrations in the streets of the USSR and on December 25, 1991. The Soviet Union ceased to exist.

With its collapse, the Warsaw Pact countries broke away from the USSR and threw out their communist leaders, though some held on for a while.

Having inherited a country plagued by economic stagnation, Gorbachev began economic reform. It was inconsistent in its implementation and the cost of that reform had skyrocketed. The authorities failed to bring prices down or start privatization, while the very idea of unemployment was anathema. The citizens were so shaken by such unaccustomed issues, inflation and unemployment, that Gorbachev's popularity collapsed. All his programs came to nothing. The country accumulated debt and the savings of the people became worthless.

Perestroika instituted a period of freedom and the emancipation of society from the state since the country of Russia was formed. People could talk openly about their political opinions, criticize their leadership, and undertake personal enterprise.

Sadly, the Soviet bureaucracy continued in place and slowly and inexorably many of the freedoms that came under Perestroika were eaten away. Though nominally not a Marxist-Leninist state any longer, Russia is once again ruled by a former KGB officer, Vladimir Putin. Opposition parties and leaders are forbidden unofficially, but officially they are sent to prison for whatever reason can be devised. Putin is actively dreaming of re-establishing the Russian or, if you prefer, Soviet Empire. *Plus ça change, plus ça reste même.*

CHAPTER 5
Mao and Maoism

Mao has much in common from his youth with both Stalin and Lenin. Mao's father was a landed peasant and a grain dealer. He was, what Lenin would have called, a "kulak" a middle-class entrepreneur. Despite that side note, his father was in the top 2.5% of Chinese society. He was able to read and insisted that his son also be educated. In this, like Lenin, Mao was very successful and always in the top of his class, if not first. His father insisted that he learn Confucius' morality and other traditional Chinese classics. Like Stalin, his father brutalized him, though there is no indication that his father was a drunk.

Unlike Lenin or Stalin, Mao worked on the family farm when a youth. As he grew and studied, he became exposed to many period writings by men who advocated that China throw off its Emperor and the yoke of the various imperialist powers that occupied parts of China. His attitude towards Japan was mixed, as in 1905 Japan had defeated the Russians, so he took pride in the fact that an Asian country had come to age and that it was becoming a modern industrial society. On the other hand, at the end of WWI, Japan had occupied the German colonies in China and a long struggle began between the two powers.

It was not until the 1920 that Mao began to embrace the tenants of Communism. Like Lenin, Mao wrote numerous articles. His writing efforts were very successful and one of the articles he published, "The Great Union of the Popular Masses" won him national recognition.[120] In his articles he urged the masses to unite so that they could engage the aristocrats and capitalists to combat the oppression of the people and he further proposed that trade unions be formed to protect the interests of the poor. Since 390,000,000 of the total population of China, 400,000,000, were the poor and landless peasants, they greatly outnumbered the aristocrats and capitalists. He believed that if they united they could easily overwhelm their oppressors.

The man Mao idolized, Chen Duxiu was courted by the Comintern to establish an alliance with the Soviet Union as part of the road to a worldwide communist revolution. This most likely spurred Mao to explore

---

[120] Anonymous, *Mao Zedong* (Internet: Captivatinghistory.com/ebook, 2018) p. 21.

the ideas of communism. In pursuing this, he and some of his friends started a bookstore which carried related literature including Darwin, Plato, Marist texts, and some of Mao's personal favorite works. The bookstore proved a major success. Several branches were opened, and it continued spreading the ideas of communism.

After the bookstore proved successful Mao founded the Russian Studies Society, with the idea of organizing the collective study of the Soviet Union. In addition to this, its objective was to publish research and reviews of the nation and its ideology. It went so far as to fund a Russian language class for those who wished to travel to Moscow for further studies. Mao himself even studied Russian with the idea of traveling to Moscow.
In July 1920, Chen Duixu was leading a communist cell in Shanghai. In August the Shanghai Socialist Youth League was formed and such organizations began appearing in other cities. The first Chinese communists, however, were not workers or peasants. As in Russia, they were students, journalists, and intellectuals and their goal was to provoke a revolution in China like that which had occurred in Russia.

It was thought that in China a proletariat revolution would rise against several forces: 1.) the feudal-militarist forces, 2.) the new and emerging capitalist bourgeoisie, and 3.) the imperialist foreign powers that dominated China economically and held great sway over it.[121]

In January 1921 the *Renovation of the People Study Society* met to decide their political and ideological orientation and debated the merits of social policies, moderate, communism, anarchism, radicalism, and social democracy. In the end, they chose to model themselves on the Soviet system of socialism, understanding that a dictatorship, which was historically the style of Chinese government, would be the easiest for the relatively apathetic population to accept and would be the most efficient way to force the necessary changes.

In June 1921, Mao attended the congress of the Chinese Communist Party (CCP). Sun Yat-Sen was, at that time President of the Chinese Republic, which indicated a movement towards democracy in China and the looked to take advantage of this, even though there were only 53 members in it. They appointed Mao as the party secretary, giving him the major role. During this congress the CCP established its core principles:

    1.) The proletariat would stage a revolution to unseat the capitalist class, forming a new nation devoid of class

---
[121] Ibid. p. 25.

distinctions.
2.) The dictatorship of the proletariat was to be formed to achieve the final stage of the class struggle.
3.) All private ownership of capital and the productive means of society (machines, factories, land, buildings, etc.,) were to be replaced by social ownership.
4.) As a communist nation, China would unite with the Third International (also known as The Communist International), the international communist organization that advocated for world communism. [122]

Although small in numbers, the majority of the Chinese communists were opposed to cooperation with the Kuomintang (KMT), which paralleled Lenin's opposition to participating in the Russian parliament and led to the October Revolution.

After the congress closed Mao returned to Changsha where he founded the Hunan branch of the All-China Workers' Secretariat. The goal of this organization was to establish a worker's movement under the direction of the CCP. In April this group organized a 2,000-worker strike in a cotton mill and after that Mao persuaded two leaders of the Hunan Labor Association of the importance of class consciousness. They soon joined Mao's *Socialist Youth League*, but they were soon murdered by thugs working for the Governor of Hunan. This allowed Mao to take over the leadership of the workers' movement in that province.

Though there were only three large industrial operations in Hunan, Mao pushed to provoke a worker-led revolution. Though it may seem a stretch, Mao considered the coolies, rickshaw pullers, and seasonal laborers to be "workers" in the same sense that Marx did the factory workers of England. This was an example of Mao's stretching Marxism to fit the circumstances then prevailing in China.

Mao then became a labor organizer and by 1923 he and his comrades had organized 22 trade unions that covered miners, railroad workers, typographers, rickshaw pullers, barbers, municipal service workers, and other groups. This done, there began a series of strikes with the usual demands, increases in wages, reduced working hours from 12 to 8 hours per day, and improved working conditions. The success of many of these strikes elevated Mao's stature and gave him much support among

---
[122]Ibid. p. 28.

the workers.

On November 5, 1922, Mao founded the *Human Federation of Trade Unions* and Mao became its general secretary. This allowed him to pressure the governor, Zhao Hengti the right of the workers to organize and strike. Mao was now beginning to monopolize the power of the underground Bolshevik movement and allowed him massive influence over the newly recruited communists and socialists in Hunan.

In early 1922 some delegates from the First CCP Congress went to Moscow and Petrograd, attending at the invitation of the Bolshevik leadership, the First Congress of the Peoples of the Far East. The goal of the Soviets was to persuade the CCP members to cooperate with the nationalist revolutionaries in their opposition to the imperialists and militarists. Though this violated their earlier sentiments regarding cooperating with the KMT, they were eventually persuaded and resolved to form a temporary alliance with them. Much of this resulted from the CCP's dependence on Soviet financial support. With Sun Yat-Sen's approval, the proletariat, the peasants, and the national bourgeoisie were united in their opposition to foreign imperialism and the corrupt Peking government. Though the CCP cooperated with the KMT, they did not join it and maintained their independence.

Sun Yat-Sen and the leadership of the CCP held meetings in which Sun's Three Great Principles of the People were reformatted as nationalism (self-definition for the Chinese people), socialism (the people's livelihood) and democracy (the rights of the people). In these meetings Sun agreed that the KMT would copy the CCP's alignment with Soviet Union.

It was also in 1922 that the militarist Wu Peifu retaliated against a railroad worker strike resulting in 32 workers killed, 200 wounded, and many workers' clubs and trade unions were threatened. Mao reacted by organizing a general strike on the Changsha-Wuchang railroad. Twenty thousand workers and students attended the memorial for the dead workers. Further strikes occurred and then Mao organized, as the head of the Special Xiang District Committee, a strike where over 60,000 marched through the streets of Changsha, demanding that Japan surrender the Chinese territory it controlled. In retaliation to this, Governor Zhao Hengti issued an arrest warrant against Mao and the union leaders, which forced Mao to flee.

During the Third Congress of the Communist Party from June 12-20, 1923, Mao agreed the majority of the Congress that the CCP should help the KMT to expand its base outside of Canton. This was because the working class was relatively small and the CCP could not become a mass organization in the near future. Among other things, at this time Mao was elected as a member of the Central Executive Committee for the first time and became head of the Organizational Department and Secretary of the Central Executive Committee.

In early 1926 Chaing Kai-shek led an anti-leftist coup in order to eliminate the growing influence of the CCP and the Comintern. Chaing declared martial law, had several communists arrested, and mobilized his troops to guard the houses of many Soviet military advisors. The coup was peaceful, but it firmly established Chaing in power. Once this was done, he had himself appointed as chairman of the *Standing Committee of the Guomindang Central Executive Committee* (CEC), head of the *National Government's Military Council*, head of the KMT CEC's *Department of Military Cadres*, and Commander-in-Chief of the National Revolutionary Army. Despite this, because Stalin wanted the CCP to remain within the KMT and wait for an appropriate moment, the CCP accepted their diminished position.

Mao was obliged to resign from his post in the KMT CEC. He turned his attention to organizing the Chinese peasantry from his new position of Director of the Sixth Session of the Peasant Movement Training Institute. He had, among the KMT leaders, gained the reputation as the foremost expert in involving the peasants in the revolution. Through this he advocated that peasants, sharecroppers, farm laborers and vagrants' revolt against the entire landlord class, who he declared were as bad as the imperialists, the militarists, and the bureaucrats.

Shortly after this Chaing completed his preparations for his Northern Expedition, which had the goal of eliminating the militarists and unifying all of China. More than 100,000 officers from the National Revolutionary Army (NRA) were sent north to fight the three groups of militarists that opposed Chaing. Despite being outnumbered Chaing's campaign was successful.

In 1926 the National Revolutionary Army assumed control of Wuhan and the National Government was then relocated there from Canton. This was followed, on January 1, 1927, by Wuhan being declared as the capital of Kuomintang (KTM) China. The NRA continued advancing and occupied many provinces, which caused many peasants to act according to their class consciousness. Membership in various peasant organizations grew from 400,000 to 1,300,000 and they attacked and destroyed the homes of the rich landowners as they sought revenge for the years of humiliation and exploitation they had suffered. These attacks were not focused just on the very wealthy but included any individual who was deemed to be a member of the gentry. Their destructive vengeance extended to the destruction or theft of anything of value or beauty.

The situation of the CCP was not good and Mao concluded that it would be necessary for it, if it was to secure power in China, have its own military force. This is where his famous statement, "We must know that political power is obtained from the barrel of the gun." With this in mind, he raised the "Workers' and Peasants' Red Army of China" and engaged the KMT soldiers but was soundly defeated everywhere. Mao and the remnants of his army fled into the Hinggang Mountains in Jiangxi.

With about 1,000 men, Mao organized the *Assembly of Workers, Peasants, and Soldier's Deputies* as a legislative body and the *People's Assembly* as its executive organ. He then formed alliances with the outlaws in the region and solidified power in that region. The communists only held power in the countryside as the KMT focused on destroying them in the urban areas.

It was at this point that the Communist Central Committee expelled Mao from his seat for his "military opportunism" and all his other positions in the party. He was reduced to the post of Commander of the First Division. Mao was effectively removed from all involvement in political and military questions, but his position as Secretary of the Hunan-Jiangxi Special Border Area Committee did allow him to monopolize power in that region.

In Jiaggang Mao commanded 18,000 soldiers and he focused on turning them into trained soldiers. Logistics always being a problem for armies, Mao took the unusual step of land redistribution. He confiscated all the land belonging to the great and poor and then redistributed it to the rural villagers who supported the communist regime. Those who were given land were forced to work on it.

Mao's logistical situation once again forced action on him and having consumed all the provisions in Jiaggang, he was obliged to move his army. His soldiers had been so aggressive in their collection of the provisions they needed that the local industries were destroyed as the people fled Mao's militarized version of communism. His army, however, suffered too and was now reduced to 6,000.

Mao moved to Jiangxi, which is on the Jiangxi-Fujian border. He was now far from the urban centers controlled by the KMT and among a population that was sympathetic to his cause. Nonetheless, the KMT army continued their pursuit, which forced Mao to adopt new tactics. To support that, however, they continued to make exploitative demands on the rich peasants and merchants.

Meanwhile, in order to defend himself against the KMT soldiers, Mao moved to and began perfecting guerilla tactics. In this manner Mao was able to resist the KMT while he implemented his land distribution policy in Jiangxi, as he had in Jinggang. Supporting this, Mao had his soldiers destroy tax offices and kill tax collectors, along with the local gentry, any and all government officials, KMT members, priests, missionaries and militarists. By the end of October 1929, his soldiers had killed over 1,000 Jiangxi communists. This process of selective assassinations of the "enemies of the people" i.e. supporters of the existing government, by his guerilla forces would become the hall mark of all revolutionary guerillas that followed Mao in the 20th century.

Mao's guerilla tactics proved very successful and are summarized in his statement "the enemy advances, we retreat, the enemy camps, we harass; the enemy tires, we attack; the enemy retreats, we pursue."[123] They were so successful that they compelled Chaing Kai-shek to personally come and take over the war against the communists.

At this point the Japanese intervened in Chinese politics and occupied Mukden, the largest city in Manchuria, on September 18, 1931. Being far superior in their military force and discipline, the Japanese soon overran all of Manchuria and controlled 30,000 Chinese by the end of the year.

While the Japanese advanced, Mao solidified his power and whipped up anti-Japanese fervor, which he then directed against Chaing. Despite that, Mao now found himself opposed by elements within the communist party, the Chinese who opposed communism, and comrades who disagreed with him. Not having enough enemies, but perhaps in an effort to draw support, Mao and his Soviet Government of China declared war on the Japanese. This move was successful in that it gave the Chinese communists the image of being the genuine nationalists, which gave the Red Army increased popularity and mass support. Mao was soon able to exercise control over a population of 3,000,000. This allowed Mao to then pursued his land reform program, organized education al programs, and began recruiting women to join the CCP.

---

[123] Ibid. p. 42.

George Nafziger

The Long March

Chaing Kai-shek had, in 1930, come to the conclusion that the communists were more of a threat to China than the Japanese. Between 1930 and 1934 Chaing organized five different campaigns designed to eradicate the communists. In his fifth he managed to deliver a devastating blow to the communists with a force of 700,000 KMT soldiers and forming a series of fortifications around the communists' positions.

Meanwhile, the CCP Central Committee had revoked Mao's leadership, which forced the Red Army to abandon his preferred system of guerilla warfare. Incapable of facing a force of trained and experienced KMT soldiers, the Red Army was crushed and forced to flee. This was the beginning of the famous Long March. The 86,000 communist soldiers in Jiangxi broke through the weakest point in the encirclement and marched west.

Mao, at the time of the communists' departure, was not in control of events; Zhu De was the commander of the army, and Zhou Enlai was the political commissar of the party. The first three months of the march were disastrous for the communists: subjected to constant bombardment from Chiang's air force and repeated attacks from his ground troops, they lost more than half of their army. Morale was low when they arrived in Zunyi, in the southwestern province of Guizhou, but at a conference there in January 1935 Mao was able to gather enough support to establish his domination of the party.

The Red Army marched into northwestern China, near the safety of the Soviet border and near the territory occupied by the Japanese. In June 1935 it was joined by the forces under Zhang Guotao, a longtime communist leader and soon a power struggle ensued between Mao and Zhang. Zhang abandoned Mao and marched towards the extreme southwestern part of China, while Mao and the main body marched towards northern Shaanxi, where the communist leaders Gao Gang and Liu Zhidan had built up another base. When Mao reached them, his forces had been reduced to 8,000 starving soldiers. Not all had died as some communists had left the march to mobilize the peasantry, but the vast majority had died in battle, or from disease and starvation.

Mao's troops joined the local Red Army contingent of 7,000 men and by late 1936 Mao had about 30,000 troops. For the rest of the Sino-Japanese war the Red Army stayed in the district of Yan'an in Shaanxi. The Long March had established Mao's leadership of the Chinese Communist

Party and had saved the Red Army from the superior forces of the Nationalists. From their base at Yan'an, the communists grew in strength and eventually defeated the Nationalists in the struggle to control mainland China.

Mao claimed his army had marched 12,500 kilometers, but British historians have argued it was only 6,000 km. The march crossed some of the worst trails on earth, crossing 18 mountain ranges and 24 rivers, while they constantly were fighting the KMT forces.

The CCP capitalized on this march proclaiming it an act of extreme heroism. This march inspired m any Chinese to enlist in Mao's army, swelling its ranks to the point that when the Japanese withdrew in late 1945, which put it in a position to engage the KMT.

The Communist Take Control of China

When the Chinese communists took power on October 1, 1949, when Mao proclaimed the People's Republic of China. The Chinese brought with them a new kind of Marxism that came to be called Maoism after their leader Mao Zedong. The thought of Mao must always be seen against the changing revolutionary reality of China from 1930 onward. His thought was complex, a Marxist type of analysis combined with the permanent fundamentals of Chinese thought and culture.

One of its central elements relates to the nature and the role of contradictions in socialist society. For Mao, every society, including socialist (communist) society, contained "two different types of contradictions." These were 1.) antagonistic contradictions, which were the contradictions between the people and the Chinese bourgeoisie (the enemies of the CCP), between the imperialist camp and the socialist camp, and so forth - which have to be resolved by revolution, and 2.) non-antagonistic contradictions - between the government and the people under a socialist regime, between two groups within the Communist Party, between one section of the people and another under a communist regime, and so forth - which are resolved by vigorous fraternal criticism and self-criticism.

This concept of contradiction is specific to Mao's thought and differs from the conceptions of Marx or Lenin. Mao saw these contradictions as both universal and particular. In their universality, one must seek and discover what constitutes their particularity: every contradiction displays a particular character, depending on the nature of things and phenomena. Contradictions have alternating aspects - sometimes strongly marked, sometimes blurred. Some of these aspects are primary, others secondary. It is important to define them well, because if one fails to do so, the analysis of the social reality and the actions that follow from it will be mistaken. This differs significantly from Stalinism and purest Marxism-Leninism.

Another essential element of Mao's thought, which must be seen in the context of revolutionary China, is the notion of permanent revolution. It appears in the writings of Marx, Lenin, and Trotsky in various contexts, Lenin, and Trotsky but Mao looked on then with international dimension espoused by his predecessors.

Mao's concept of permanent revolution rested upon the existence of non-antagonistic contradictions in the China of the present and of the future. The people had to be mobilized into a permanent movement in order to continue the revolution and to prevent the ruling group from turning bourgeois. It is necessary to shape among the masses a new vision of the world by inspiring them to leave their passivity and their century-old habits. This process was the source of the Cultural Revolution that began in 1966, that followed a series of smaller such campaigns in Communist Chinese society.

In October 1950 the Chinese Red Army invaded North Korea and struck the UN forces that had pushed north through most of North Korea and were near the Chinese border. Mao used the "Resist America, Aid Korea" campaign to stir up patriotism in China and fed into the earlier anti-colonialism/anti-imperialism that had existed in China prior to the end of WWII.

At the same time China sent troops into Tibet when the Tibetans rebelled against the consolidation of Chinese rule over Tibet. That process was part of the reunification of China with all the territories that had ever belonged to the Chinese Empire at any time during its history. The CCP authorized a police action against its political adversaries, anti-communists, bandits, and groups of people who opposed the CCP's political domination. As mentioned earlier Mao had undertaken land reform in Jianggang and Jianxi. In 1950 he began to implement it throughout China with his Agrarian Reform Law of 1950. This law destroyed the feudal and semi-feudal classes in China by confiscating their land and redistributing it to the peasants. Foreign owned land was also confiscated, which greatly diminished the power of many private industrialists. Despite this, the CCP did increase economic growth by reducing urban inflation, disciplining the labor force and gaining the confidence of the capitalists who had begun to see communist rule as working in their interests. The CCP increased its moral authority, at this time, by issuing a marriage law and a trade union law.

The capitalists were also attacked and subjected to the Five-Antis Campaign, which compelled them to be subservient to the CCP by charging them with bribery, theft of state property and dishonestly in their contractual obligations with the government. University professors were also sought out and purged. Though Mao had himself benefited from the Western liberal educational tradition, but he had determined that the Chinese youth would only be exposed to Soviet philosophy.

The Three Antis

The Three-Antis Campaign (1951) and Five-Antis Campaign (1952) were reform movements undertaken by Mao Zedong to rid Chinese cities of corruption and enemies of the state. It became a series of campaigns that consolidated Mao's power base by targeting his political opponents and capitalists, especially wealthy capitalists. The campaigns negatively impacted the economy of big cities such as Shanghai, Tianjin and Chongqing, forcing many businessmen to commit suicide.[124] In Shanghai alone, from January 25 to April 1, 1952, at least 876 people committed suicide

The Three-Antis Campaign was launched in Manchuria at the end of 1951. It was aimed at members within the Chinese Communist Party who were perceived as fraternizing with Chinese capitalists, former Kuomintang members and bureaucratic officials who were not party members, the heads of various secret societies, all religious groups and religious authorities.

The Three-Antis imposed were: corruption, waste, and bureaucracy. This campaign decimated the communists who were perceived as fraternizing too closely with the few capitalists that remained in China.[125] The Five-Antis Campaign was launched in January 1952. It targeted capitalist class that still existed in China. The CCP set a very vague guideline of who could be charged, and it became an all-out war against the bourgeoisie in China.

The Five-Antis crimes were: bribery, theft of state property, tax evasion, cheating on government contracts, stealing state economic data.

---

[124] Chen, Theodore Hsi-En; Chen, Wen-Hui C. (March 1953). "The 'Three-Anti' and 'Five-Anti' Movements in Communist China". *Pacific Affairs*. 26: pp. 3–23.
[125] Anonymous, *Mao Zedong* (Internet: Captivatinghistory.com/ebook, 2018) p. 47.

An estimated 20,000 cadres and 6,000 trained workers began spying on the business affairs of fellow citizens. Approximately 15,000 trained propagandists were working in Shanghai by late 1951. By February 1952, anti-capitalist activists went door-to-door to visit business and intimidate leaders. Letters denouncing capitalists were called for from any employees and thousands of such letters were received. Confessions were forced from business owners and big companies voluntarily made 1,000 confessions a day to try to protect themselves from the government.

The Five-Anti campaign gave the CCP total control of the Chinese banking system and obliged the few capitalists remaining in China to cooperate with the government if they wished to continue their business.[126] The Antis Campaigns' victims were generally just terrified and humiliated, but some were executed, and others were sent to labor camps. Mao evaluated the situation, saying that "we must probably execute 10,000 to several tens of thousands of embezzlers nationwide before we can solve the problem."[127] And all found guilty of their confessed or unconfessed crimes were made to pay fines to the government. Another result of these campaigns were hundreds of thousands of suicides, not all of which were voluntary.

As these campaigns progressed it became clear that Chinese private businesses and Chinese capitalists would no longer be tolerated and that they would receive the same treatment as foreigners.

In 1953 Mao instituted his First Five-Year Plan, which was intended to promote the rapid industrialization of China. It focused on increasing heavy industry and stimulating the economy. It was based on Stalin's five-year plans and the CCP drew financial assistance and technical experience from the Soviets on how to undertake such a plan and remain true to Stalin's economic priorities. To support China, the Soviet Union provided a loan of $300 million and, more importantly, the services of several thousand engineers, scientists, technicians and planners.

The focus of the industrialization was to increase production of coal, steel, petrochemicals, to develop the automobile industry and there were some major civil engineering projects, such as the road and railroad bridge across the Yangzi at Nanjing.

In the countryside a voluntary form of collectivization was encouraged. Small collective farms were formed that contained from

---

[126] Anonymous, *Mao Zedong* (Internet: Captivatinghistory.com/ebook, 2018) p. 48.
[127] Changyu, Li., Mao's "Killing Quotas" https://web.archive.org/web/20090729194758/http://www.hrichina.org/public/PDFs/CRF.4.2005/CRF-2005-4_Quota.pdf

20 to 30 households. Of course, all efforts of collectivization always produced problems with the land-owning peasants when they were forced to surrender their land. Insult was added to injury after they were stripped of their land. They were also to surrender their surplus produce to feed the cities and, thereby, pay for the investments in capital equipment.[128]

Mao's plan had results similar to those of Stalin's first 5-year plan. It increased industry and stimulated the economy, but it had a negative impact on the rural population, which had serious implications for the society as a whole.

The state monopoly on grain and the impact of collectivization caused, as it had in the Soviet Union, disruptions in the rural areas. Grain output struggled to keep up with the rapid population growth and there were questions about if the countryside could produce enough grain to prevent starvation in the urban areas.

Part of the 5-year plan was the organization of workplaces on the socialist model. Housing and medical care was subsidized by the state for urban and industrial workers. In addition, education was expanded beyond its historical limits. Meanwhile, the urban population grew from 57,000,000 to 100,000,000 between 1949 and 1957, life expectancy rose from 36 to 57 years, while the average income rose by 40%. This surely reflected credit on Mao and increased his popularity. In 1957, in response to these achievements, Mao said: "If China becomes prosperous, just like the standard of living in the Western world then [the people] will not want revolution." A counter revolution was always a concern for Mao, be it from the remnants of the capitalist class or the remnants of the KMT.

In order to assure tranquility, the CCP expanded its control over the citizenry. Life was closely regimented by the work units, which provided the basic structure or labor and control every element of daily life, including accommodation, education, social services, marriages, having children, or travel.

One of the major results of this plan was that state control became very centralized. Private ownership of any industrial operation became almost impossible and by 1956 two-thirds of the Chinese industry was fully state owned and operated, and the remaining third were joint state-private operations.

The centralized planning had its drawbacks, as local needs were generally neglected, particularly in the countryside. A total of 88% of all

---

[128] Anonymous, *Mao Zedong* (Internet: Captivatinghistory.com/ebook, 2018) p. 48.

investment was made in heavy industry, which was located in the urban areas.

As mentioned earlier, the narrow focus of the plan produced food shortages in some areas. Chinese arrogance caused them to ignore the new farming techniques adopted elsewhere in Asia. Collectivization of farming expanded through 1955-1956, all land became state owned, and the farming equipment was taken over by the state. High targets were established, but the collectivization process made these targets difficult to achieve. The targets were often not based on realistically achievable goals, so in order to avoid punishment the party officials responsible for these various projects often falsified the results. Much the same had happened in Stalin's various 5-year plans.

The process of collectivization was not well received and there were physical attacks on officials. In addition, in order to escape the situation in the countryside, tens of millions fled to the relative safety of the cities, placing further strain on collectives to feed bulging urban populations.

By the end of the First Five Year Plan about 93.5% of the farm households had been collectivized, which, according to Mao Zedong, that would solve all the problems of the rural world.

Indeed, even though the first five-year plan was undeniably a success, it is clear that many officials manipulated production figures in order to avoid the fate of the more honest officials in Liaoning who were purged for failure to make their unrealistic targets.

The Hundred Flowers Campaign

By 1956 Mao felt himself in a strong political position and launched the Hundred Flowers Campaign. The name came from a speech in which he proclaimed, "Let one hundred flowers bloom, let a hundred schools of thought contend." In this speech he encouraged constructive criticism, which he perceived might bring about improvements. In theory, he hoped that it would boost the economic success of his first 5-year plan, and he also hoped that he could avoid the type of criticism that Stalin had received after Khruschev had taken control of the Soviet Union. Though Mao hoped that the masses would respond, instead it was the intellectuals. As there are always unexpected results from the best laid plans, Mao found himself being criticized for the excessive control of the CCP over intellectuals, for the harshness of the various campaigns against counterrevolutionaries, the low standard of living in China, the banning of foreign literature, the mindless adherence to the Soviet models, economic corruption among the party leaders and particularly the double standard where members of the party enjoyed that set them above the masses. What was most biting were observations that there was more freedom of speech under Chaing Kai-shek.

Mao, as the typical absolute ruler, took these criticisms as attacks on his person and altered the nature of the Hundred Flowers Campaign and declared that the only criticism that was acceptable was that which contributed to strengthening the socialist government. A harsh backlash of propaganda was then directed against those intellectuals who had spoken out. There are many theories about why this campaign was launched, but the most likely is that Mao was looking to bring his enemies out into the open so that they could be purged.

The Anti-Rightest Campaign, Mao's response to this criticism, was launched in June 1957. Mao labeled all those who had spoken out under the Hundred Flowers Campaign were "rightists." A documentary film by the American Public Broadcasting Service contains a scene where a professor from the People's University of Beijing, named Ge Peiqi, spent 20 years at hard labor as punishment for having criticized the system. He was one of among between 500,000 and 750,000 Chinese who were rounded up. Witness accounts describe torture, death, starvation and suicide in these camps. It was a purge that cemented Mao's control over China and set an example for what would happen to anyone who did not conform. This also started the Chinese equivalent of the Soviet Gulag.

The Second Five-Year Plan or The Great Leap Forward

The Second Five-Year Plan, also known as the Great Leap Forward, was to run from 1958 to 1963, but it ended in 1961. Based on the experience of the First Five-Year Plan it was decided that this plan would push a parallel, rapid development of both industry and agriculture. China had a massive supply of cheap labor, and it was thought this could be fruitfully employed in pushing the industrialization of China and avoid the importation of heavy machinery. In looking at the Soviet experience, it thought to avoid technical bottlenecks using political rather than technical means. Mao hoped that by this means China would demonstrate to the Soviet Union that it was capable of even greater economic development that them. In particular it looked to avoid the mass starvation that had occurred in the USSR during its second 5-year plan.

At the same time the CCP began experimental farming communes. Each commune contained approximately 5,000 families. The state provided and retained ownership of the land, tools, and livestock. The farming was managed by the commune, which also provided its members with food, schools nurseries, healthcare, entertainment, and homes for the elderly who could no longer work. Soldiers assisted in working the fields and CCP part members oversaw all decisions to ensure they complied with the party's ideology. By the end of 1958 7,000,000 people were placed in 26,578 communes.[129]

In fact, the Chinese experience replicated that of the Soviets. The subsequent "Great Famine" lasted between 1958 and 1962, scholars debating on the exact period, but it lasted for three years. The famine resulted from several factors: inefficient distribution of food, the use of poor agricultural techniques, the "Four Pests Campaign," the over reporting of production, and the forcing of farmers to abandon farming and turn to making iron and steel. All these changes coincided with floods and droughts. Another contributing factor to the famine was the forced shifting of farmers from farming to the production of steel in backyard furnaces and the objective was to increase steel production.[130]

The result of this was that the harvest was down by 15% in 1959 compared to 1958, and by 1960, it was at 70% of its 1958 level.[131] Specifically, according to China's governmental data, crop production decreased from 200 million tons 1958 to 170 million tons in 1959, and to 143.5 million tons in 1960.

The impact of famine is subject to considerable dispute. Those who are pro- and con- the communist system take opposite positions and each claims the other's experts over or underestimate it based on their ideology, so the numbers vary from 15,000,000 and 55,000,000 deaths. Irrespective, the number of Chinese who died from this ill-considered policy greatly exceeds the 4,000,000-5,000,000 dead in the Ukraine under Stalin.

Mao saw grain and steel production as the key pillars of economic development. He forecast that within 15 years of the start of the Great Leap, China's industrial output would surpass that of the United Kingdom. The goal established in 1958 was to double steel production within a year.

---

[129] Anonymous, *Mao Zedong* (Internet: Captivatinghistory.com/ebook, 2018) p. 50.
[130] Chan, A.L., *Mao's Crusade: Politics and Policy Implementation in China's Great Leap Forward.* (UK: Oxford University Press, 2001). pp. 71–74.
[131] Lin, J. Y.; Yang, D.. "Food Availability, Entitlements and the Chinese Famine of 1959-61". *The Economic Journal.* 110 (2000): pp. 136–158

Part of this process was the backyard steel furnaces.[132] To Mao, who had no technical education, these backyard furnaces seemed a good idea, but the product of these furnaces was of a very inferior quality and was little better than low-grade pig iron. This iron was used in construction and did not last long. It was, in essence, a sad waste of time and labor.

"What is even more unfortunate is that this diversion of the work force to small-scale industrial production meant that there was an insufficient surplus of food to make up for the food shortage caused by the three years of natural disasters. The estimates for the exact number of Chinese citizens who died because of the disastrous The Great Leap Forward vary, but a 2010 estimate based on recently declassified documents placed the total death count to a staggering 45,000,000 people."[133]

Among those dead were between 2,000,000 and 3,000,000 who died because they ran afoul their CCP overseers when they claimed that their goals were unreasonable. In return they were labeled "bourgeois reactionaries" and imprisoned. Even peasants, who were suspected of being ideologically opposed to the plan or who were deemed to not be working hard enough, were beaten, hung, or thrown into ponds. Other punishments included being forced to east feces or being mutilated.[134]

Because of the starvation in the cities, the CCP officials seized as much of a third of the available grain, leaving the rural workers in a far worse condition.

Recrimination flowed as a result of the failure of the Great Leap Forward. Some believed that it was bad implementation resulting from bureaucratic failures and mismanagement, while others claimed the failure to place higher priority on technical expertise and material incentives to spur productivity.

The Third Five-Year Plan

The problems resulting from the failure of the Second Five-Year Plan delayed the start of Third Plan, which was originally due early in 1963 and work on developing it did not begin until early 1964. It was laid out and approved in September 1965 and was to run from 1966 to 1970.
The Tentative Plan, approved in September 1965, established the following

---

[132] Kung, J.K., Ma, D.; von Glahn, R. (eds.), "The Political Economy of China's Great Leap Famine", *The Cambridge Economic History of China: 1800 to the Present* (UK, Cambridge University Press, 2002). pp. 642–684.
[133] Anonymous, *Mao Zedong* (Internet: Captivatinghistory.com/ebook, 2018) p. 51.
[134] Ibid. p. 52.

basic tasks:[135]

• To spare no efforts to develop agriculture, solve widespread problems concerning people's food, clothing and other basic needs;
•To strengthen national defense, and endeavor to make breakthroughs in technology;
• In order to support agriculture and strengthen national defense, to enhance infrastructure, continue to improve production quality, increase production variety and quantity, to build an economy of self-reliance, and to develop transportation, commerce, culture, education and scientific research.

The Plan also gave priority to national defense in the light of a possible war that might result from the Vietnam War. It called for the preparation for any possible conflicts and speeding up construction in three key areas; national defense, science and technology, industry and transport infrastructure.

The Cultural Revolution

The Cultural Revolution began early in the Third Five-Year Plan. Apparently, Mao felt his position was threatened by internal forces and it is now generally thought to have started so that he could cement his control over the CCP. It appears that after the failure of the Great Leap Forward there was a significant amount of dissent in the party and on the streets of China

The Cultural Revolution began in May 1966 when official party newspapers called for a mobilization that would inject new life into the socialist cause. Mao saw it as a way of reinvigorating the communist revolution by strengthening ideology and weeding out opponents. It is interesting to note that Mao apparently never felt completely secure in his control over China as there were several campaigns for "weeding out" of his opponents. To make his hold on power more secure, there began a nation-wide purge of all "bourgeoisie" and "reactionary" elements. They were labeled "class enemies" and traitors to the communist ideals.

"In 1965, Wu Han's play was investigated, publicly denounced, and banned for its 'reactionary' political nature. This would establish a precedent for the radicalization of all art forms under the Cultural Revolution, effectively censoring all forms of expression – music, cinema,

[135]http://www.china.org.cn/english/MATERIAL/157608.htm

plays, fiction, nonfiction – and replacing them with pro-Mao propaganda. Mao formally detailed his concerns about "bourgeois' infiltrators in a CCP Central Committee document on May 16, 1966. In August that year, the Cultural Revolution was launched across the nation at the Eleventh Plenum of the Eight Central Committee."[136]

It may have put new life into Mao's idea of the socialist cause, but it crippled the Chinese economy, ruined and killed millions of lives and produced 10 years of chaos, bloodshed, hunger, and economic stagnation. It set China's development back many years was described as the "most severe setback and heaviest losses suffered by the party, the country, and the people since the founding of the People's Republic (1949) in the official governmental accounts."

The Party chiefs in Beijing issued the "May 16 Notification," which warned that the party had been infiltrated by counterrevolutionaries that were looking to overthrow the dictatorship of the proletariat and replace it with a bourgeoisie dictatorship.

Two weeks later, the CCP's official newspaper urged the masses to "clear away the evil habits of the old society" and launch an all-out assault on "monsters and demons."

University students flocked to Mao's standard, setting up Red Guard divisions across the country. August 1966, which came to be known as "Red August" chaos was everywhere as the Red Guards looked to destroy the "four olds" - old ideas, old customs, old habits and old culture.

Gangs of Red Guards, wielding Mao's *Little Red Book*, roamed the streets changing the names of streets to new revolutionary names. They attacked people who wore "bourgeois cloths" in public. Churches, shrines, libraries, shops and private homes ransacked or destroyed as the assault on "feudal" traditions began. This destruction of "feudal" traditions resulted in the destruction of numerous works of ancient Chinese art, historical manuscripts, and much of the documentation of China's ancient culture. The homes of the wealthy were ransacked and anything that represented the ancient Chinese culture was destroyed.

In November 1966 the Confucius cemetery was vandalized and throughout the early stages of the Cultural Revolution examples of Chinese architecture were destroyed. Fortunately, the government intervened and fortunately the Mawangdui, the Leshan Giant Buddha and the Terracotta Army were preserved.[137]

---

[136] Anonymous, *Mao Zedong* (Internet: Captivatinghistory.com/ebook, 2018) pp. 54-55.

[137] Gao, Mobo. *The Battle for China's Past: Mao and the Cultural Revolution.* (London: Pluto

Members of the CCP, be they officials, teachers or intellectuals, were targeted and publicly humiliated and beaten. There were cases of outright murder, and some were driven to suicide. Between August and September 1966, nearly 2,000 people died as a result of these activities in Beijing alone.

By 1968 it became apparent that the Cultural Revolution had become more destructive than it was productive, so Mao issued orders for millions of urban youths to be sent into the countryside for "re-education." The army was ordered to re-establish order and China arguably became a military dictatorship until 1971.

Looking back on the period 1965-1971, it is difficult to evaluate the impact of famines and the Cultural Revolution. Accurate data would be difficult to gather under the best of circumstances, but as the CCP would not allow itself to be embarrassed by the number of deaths that resulted, only educated guesses remain.

"While most scholars are reluctant to estimate a total number of "unnatural deaths" in China under Mao, evidence shows he was in some way responsible for at least 40 million deaths and perhaps 80 million or more. This includes deaths he was directly responsible for and deaths resulting from disastrous policies he refused to change.

"One government document that has been internally circulated and seen by a former Communist Party official now at Princeton University says that 80 million died unnatural deaths - most of them in the famine following the Great Leap Forward. This figure comes from the *Tigaisuo*, or the *System Reform Institute*, which was led by Zhao Ziyang, the deposed Communist Party chief, in the 1980s to study how to reform Chinese society."[138]

The Cultural Revolution ended with Mao's death on September 9, 1976. Despite all the propaganda that flowed out of the party's various organs, many Chinese had become very disillusioned with Mao and the leadership of the party. They saw the Cultural Revolution as it was, a play for absolute power within the party.

The ramifications went beyond the destruction of China's cultural heritage and the lives of millions of innocents. It also impacted important members of the CCP and that may have an impact on the future behavior of China.

Press, 2008) pp. 21–22.
[138] Strauss, V., & Southeri, D., Washington Post "How Many Died? New Evidence Suggests Far Higher Numbers for the Victims of Mao Zedong's Era" July 17, 1994.

Twin Evils

"The lives of some of the Communist party's most powerful figures were upended by the turbulence, including future leader Deng Xiaoping, who was purged in 1967, and Xi Zhongxun, the father of China's current president, Xi Jinping, who was publicly humiliated, beaten and sent into exile.

"President Xi's half-sister, Xi Heping, is said to have taken her own life after being persecuted."[139]

Maoism

The distinguishing characteristic of Maoism is that it is purely a peasant-based form of Marxism. He deviated from Marx's idea of an urban worker's revolution. In Mao's China 90% of the population were peasants, so it naturally had a rural flavor and the history of the CCP, particularly the Long March and that period, give it a distinctly military slant. Mao based his socialist ideas on Marxist-Leninist philosophy, he greatly modified it to address the situation in China, specifically the warlords and the unique Chinese bureaucracy. He was greatly influenced by Lenin's concept of internationalism, and his guerilla style of warfare flowed down that path as Maoism spread throughout the world. His speeches and literary style were particularly influenced by classical Chinese thought, not only by its concepts, i.e. the Hundred Flowers Campaign, but also his references to Chinese literature and history.

Mao was a very pragmatic leader, and he brought that into his version of Marxism. He had no qualms about short term alliances with groups that he saw as his enemy, to take advantage of their support against a common enemy, i.e. the KMT to fight the more powerful Japanese armies in China. And once that fight was over, he had no qualms about turning on his erstwhile ally.

To summarize Maoism, it is opportunism and duplicity, wrapped in flowery words of equality and democracy. Its sole objective was to consolidate power in Mao's hands. This can clearly be seen by The Hundred Flowers Campaign and the Cultural Revolution. Mao set himself up as a new Chinese emperor. During the famine, look at his pictures. He never missed seconds in any meal. Furthermore, not only did he have 50 personal estates, but he was also "constantly *entertained* [emphasis added]

---

[139]Phillips, T., The Guardian, https://www.theguardian.com/world/2016/may/11/the-cultural-revolution-50-years-on-all-you-need-to-know-about-chinas-political-convulsion

by young girls and courtesans."[140]

Some other examples can be found in Mao's report *On Coalition Government*, dated April 24, 1945, where he says:

"Some people suspect that the Chinese Communists are opposed to the development of individual initiative, the growth of private capital and the protection of private property, but they are mistaken. It is foreign oppression and feudal oppression that cruelly fetter the development of the individual initiative of the Chinese people, hamper the growth of private capital, and destroy the property of the people. It is the very task of the New Democracy to advocate the removal of these fetters and stop this destruction, to guarantee that the people can freely develop their individuality within the framework of society and freely develop such private capitalist economy as will benefit and not 'dominate the livelihood of the people,' and to protect all appropriate forms of private property."

After the CCP took over complete control of China there was a short period of flirtation with privately held capital, but as can be seen in the foregoing history, it was eventually eradicated in favor of collectivization and state-run industry.

Then there is: "Some people fail to understand why, so far from fearing capitalism, Communists should advocate its development in certain given conditions."

And a few paragraphs later: ".... From our knowledge of the Marxist laws of social development, we Communists clearly understand that under the state system of New Democracy in China it will be necessary in the interests of social progress to facilitate the development of the private capitalist sector of the economy (provided it does not dominate the livelihood of the people) besides the development of the state sector and of the individual and co-operative sectors run by the laboring people. We Communists will not let empty talk or deceitful tricks befuddle us."

In the portion of this report entitled "Our Specific Program" Mao gives a long list of programs, some of which are:

"Abolish the Kuomintang one-party dictatorship and establish a democratic coalition government and a joint supreme command [the CCP is the only legal party in China];

"....Liquidate the reactionary secret service and all its repressive activities and abolish the concentration camps. [See footnote][141]

---

[140] Anonymous, *Mao Zedong* (Internet: Captivatinghistory.com/ebook, 2018) pp. 59.
[141] The Ministry of Public Security (MPS) is a government ministry of the People's Republic of China responsible for public and political security. It oversees more than 1,900,000 of the country's law enforcement officers and as such the vast majority of the People's Police. The MPS is

"Revoke all reactionary laws and decrees aimed at suppressing the people's freedom of speech, press, assembly, association, political conviction, and religious belief and freedom of the person and guarantee full civil rights to the people; [See footnote][142]

"Recognize the legal status of all democratic parties and groups; [There are no other political parties allowed in modern China.]

"Release all political prisoners;

"....Give the Chinese people democratic rights;[143]

"....Abolish the present policy of economic controls;

"....Assist private industry and provide it with the facilities for obtaining loans, purchasing raw materials, and marketing its products..."[144]

Of course there are carefully crafted caveats in these statements, but that is why I say "duplicity." There was no intention to ever allow any of the freedoms listed in the foregoing list.

China Post Mao

In order to discuss post-Mao China, it is necessary to first lay out the sequence of leaders of the CCP as some are more important than others. They are:

Hua Guofeng   CCP chairman 1976–1981
Hu Yaobang   CCP chairman; after September 1982, general secretary of
the CCP   1981–1987
Zhao Ziyang   CCP general secretary 1987–1989
Jiang Zemin   CCP general secretary 1989–2002
Hu Jintao   CCP general secretary 2002–12
Xi Jinping   CCP general secretary 2012–present

The heads of state of the PRC, under whom they served, were:

---

a nationwide police force; however, counterintelligence and so-called "political security" are its core function.

[142] The Hundred Flowers Campaign proves there was and is no freedom of speech, the press, or assembly. The mass internment of Uyghurs and other Turkic Muslims in the camps has become largest-scale arbitrary detention of ethnic and religious minorities since World War II, ergo there is no religious freedom. Furthermore, in the foregoing discussion there was a discussion of the banning and persecution of religious groups of all sorts.

[143] See footnote 22.

[144] A major tenant of Communism is the eradication of all private industry.

Deng Xiaoping	1979-1989
Hu Yaobang	1981-1989
Jiang Zemin	1989-2002
Hu Jintao	2002-2012
Xi Jinping	2012-present

Holding the positions of chairman of the Central Committee of the Chinese Communist Party (CCP); Premier of the State Council; and Chairman of the Central Military Commission there was no contest who would succeed Mao in 1975. Hua Guofeng did not last long and was ousted by Deng Xiaoping in 1978. His short tenure began with political tumult. There was no consensus among the party elite as to how to proceed. Hua chose a new course rather than continue down the same path. His goal was to bring order out of the chaos of the Cultural Revolution. His movement towards transformation consisted of five components: the purge of the "Gang of Four" (the group most faithful to the ideological principles of the Cultural Revolution) and their followers, the rehabilitation of veteran cadres, institutionalization, relaxation of restraint on thinking, and the transition of the party's key task.

Much like Hitler's purge of the SA, on October 6, 1976, Hua had the ultra-leftists arrested. Hua assume the Party's Chairmanship. When the "Gang of Four" was removed, the Cultural Revolution lost a substantial supporting force, and this gave Hua a freer hand in ideological issues. Since the "Gang of Four" controlled the media, this was a major step in consolidating his control of the state.

Hua then rehabilitated the veteran cadres who had been purged during the Cultural Revolution. In the Eleventh Central Committee their rehabilitation became apparent as of 68 of the newly elected members, 20 were veteran cadres.

Hua also directed relaxation on the controls over thought. Mao was intolerant of it and in his "Hundred Flowers" campaign used a relaxation on free thought to identify and purge his opponents. Hua, however, accepted criticism, even allowing himself to be criticized.

Hua also supported the "Four Modernizations", which had been adopted in 1977 and were strengthening the fields of agriculture, industry, defense, and science and technology in China. To this end, he sent many delegates to Western countries to learn how their economies, etc., worked, and to gather ideas that could be usefully implemented in China to repair the disruptions produced by the Cultural Revolution. Sadly, Hua's program of modernization, called the "Western Leap Forward", was a failure, but the program had a support of the party. It was not an arbitrary decision by Hua.

In September 1976, Deng Xiaoping outmaneuvered Hua Guofeng and became China's de facto paramount leader in December 1978 at the 3rd Plenary Session of the 11th Central Committee.

Hua's major contributions were the rebuilding effective political institutions, encouraging democratic discussion, and switching the party's key task to modernization. He ended the chaos produced by the Cultural Revolution.

It was in early 1978 that the Chinese invaded Vietnam. China launched an offensive in response to Vietnam's actions against the Khmer Rouge in Cambodia in 1978, which ended the rule of the Chinese-backed Khmer Rouge. Both China and Vietnam claimed victory in the last of the Indochina Wars. Though it was claimed that the Chinese attack was to defend their allies, some historians claim that this was an effort similar to the occupation of Tibet to reclaim any and all lands that had once belonged to the Chinese Empire. Militarily, the Vietnamese crushed the Chinese attacks and send them back to China with their tails between their legs.

This was not dissimilar to the 1969 Sino-Soviet border war that lasted for seven months. Once again, the Chinese had moved to occupy territory that had once been part of the Chinese Empire. There were numerous clashes and at least one major battle. Once again, the Chinese were decisively beaten.

In 1981 Hua Guofeng was replaced by Hu Yaobang, a move engineered by Deng Xiaoping and in 1982 Hu Yaobang became Party chairman. Despite that, Hu continued the movement away from Maoism started by Hua Guofeng. The removal of Hua Guofeng, which simply part of a struggle for power within the party, marked the Party leadership's consensus that China should abandon strict Maoist economics in favor of more pragmatic policies, and Hu directed many of Deng Xiaoping's attempts to reform the Chinese economy.

Hu's proposed reforms included reforming China's political system by 1.) requiring candidates to be directly elected in order to enter the Politburo; 2.) holding more elections with more than one candidate; 3.) increasing government transparency; 4.) increasing public consultation before determining Party policy; and, 4.) increasing the degree to which government officials could be held directly responsible for their mistakes.[145]

Hu attempted to rehabilitate and bring back into society the victims persecuted during the Cultural Revolution. He changed the policy towards Tibet Autonomous Region and apologized to the Tibetans for their suffering as a result of previous policies. One of the major issues had been the flooding of Tibet with thousands of Han Chinese with an eye of out populating the Tibetans with ethnic Chinese who would be loyal to the regime. Those that remained were required to learn the Tibetan and Uyghur languages. He also took steps to revive the Tibetan and Uyghur cultures. In addition, he ended the program of the *Bingtuan* (soldier farmers) in Xinjiang Uyghur Autonomous Region.

In an attempt to curb corruption, he initiated a large-scale anti-corruption program that included the investigation of the children of high-ranking Party elders who traded their parent's influence for favorable treatment. It is not surprising that Hu's investigation of Party officials belonging to this "Crown Prince Party" undercut his support among many Party officials

In December 1986 public protests in a dozen cities produced a crisis. Deng Xiaoping disliked the principal leaders of this movement and ordered Hu Yaobang to dismiss them from the party. Hu Yaobang refused. In January 1987 Deng forced Hu to resign because he was too lenient with student protesters and for moving too quickly towards free market-style economic reforms.

This done Deng Xiaoping promoted Zhao Ziyang to replace the liberal Hu as Party General Secretary, putting Zhao in a position to succeed Deng as "paramount leader."

Prior to his promotion, Zhao had sought to establish special economic zones in the provinces in order to attract foreign investment. His reforms led to rapid increases in agriculture and light industry through the 1980s, but this produced inflation which drew some criticism.

Zhao's activities drew the ire of the conservative Marxists, who labeled him as a revisionist. He was a Marxist but defined it differently than the conservatives. He advocated government transparency and a national dialogue that included ordinary citizens in policy making. This earned him great support from the citizenry.

During the 1980s, Zhao had not focused on political reforms. That task belonged to Hu Yaobang. However, Zhao soon began cooperating with Hu in these reforms. Among those reforms were truly contested

---
[145] en.wikipedia.org/wiki/Deng_Xiaoping.

elections to various offices. Zhao also participated in Hu Yaobang's anti-corruption campaign, which earned him the ire of the party's elders.

When Hu Yaobang was dismissed, Deng had Zhao replace Hu as general secretary and placed him in line to succeed Deng as the "paramount leader" of China.

Among his financial reforms Zhao introduced the stock market in China and promoted futures trading there. In 1984 three cities became experimental cities of a joint-stock system. In November 1985, the first share-issuing enterprise was established in Shanghai and publicly issued stock, which attracted investors. Zhao hosted a financial meeting August 2, 1986, calling for the joint stock system to be implemented nationwide in the following year.[146] He had clearly recognized that the anti-capitalist stance of Marxism was not conducive to the economic development of China's struggling economy.

It was in 1989 that students, intellectuals, and other elements of the urban population gathered on Tiananmen in a spontaneous demonstration of public mourning for Hu Yaobang. However, the economic uncertainty and rising inflation soon transformed the crowd into a nationwide protest calling for political reform and an end to the corruption of the CCP. The demands of the demonstrators were:

- Affirmation of Hu Yaobang's views on democracy and freedom as correct.
- Admit that the campaigns against spiritual pollution and bourgeois liberalization had been
  wrong.
- Publish information on the income of state leaders and their family members.
- Allow privately run newspapers and stop press censorship.
- Increase funding for education and raise intellectuals' pay.
- End restrictions on demonstrations in Beijing.
- Provide objective coverage of students in official media.

The first thought of the CCP was that this protest was the result of Zhao's rapid pace of reforms and that the protestors had been encouraged by the fall of the Soviet Union and the liberation of the Warsaw Block nations of Eastern Europe.

---

[146] en.wikipedia.org/wiki/Zhao_Ziyang

Zhao was sympathetic with the protesters. By April 26th, the protests began to die down and Zhao was obliged to make a state visit to North Korea. While he was away, Premier Li Peng organized a meeting between Deng Xiaoping and the Standing Committee, in which Li and his allies convinced Deng that the protests were threatening the Party and that they were motivated with anti-socialist motives. An article was published that inflamed the situation and soon over 10,000 protesters were in Tiananmen and there were more nationwide protests.

In an effort to calm the situation, Zhao attempted to institute several reforms in government, including establishing a special commission to investigate government corruption. The efforts of this commission, however, were blocked by Li Peng and other senior party members.

Finally, Deng declared martial law. The protestors were called on to disperse, but they refused. The army was sent in with tanks and heavily armed soldiers. The protestors fought back in a hopeless struggle and hundreds to thousands of protesters were killed as the square was swept clean on June 4th. The actual number of dead is a state secret and will never be known.

From June 19-21 the Fourth Plenum of the Thirteenth Party Congress was held with the goal of consolidating support for the armed crackdown and removing Zhao from office. The retention of power by the party was obviously more important that the welfare of the nation. Zhao was dismissed and replaced by Jiang Zemin as General Secretary of the CCP and successor to Deng Ziaoping. Many of Zhao's supporters were subsequently purged.

Though after Tiananmen, the economic reforms by Zhu Rongj, with Jaing's support, had stabilized the economy and placed it on an upward trajectory, there were still many social and economic problems. China was still riddled with political corruption and Deng's policies had produced a growing gap in the wealth between the coastal areas and the interior provinces. In addition, the unprecedented economic growth and deregulation in a number of heavy industries resulted in the closing of many state-owned operations. This was referred to as "breaking the people's iron rice bowl."

The "breaking of a rice bowl" is a very old Chinese concept that needs to be explained. In 19th century China and before, beggars were ubiquitous. Since money was scarce, beggars had rice bowls and when they begged their benefactors would simply push some food into the beggar's rice bowl. Thus, the beggar could eat and survive. That said, if you wanted to kill a beggar, you broke his rice bowl, and he could no longer beg for food. Then he would starve to death. Today, the concept has morphed into meaning taking away someone's job. So, when the state heavy industries were closed because of the new economy, those who worked in the old economy lost their jobs and their rice bowl, their means of earning an income, was taken away from them.

Unemployment rose as high as 40% in some urban areas and there was an unprecedented migration from the rural areas to the urban areas. Meanwhile the wealth gap between the rural areas and urban areas continued to widen. As for corruption, it was figured that at least 10% of the GDP was lost due to graft and corruption. To resolve this, Jiang sought to establish a stable economy by means of highly centralized power. To do this Jiang put off political reforms, which exacerbated the problems of the economy. This led Jiang to encourage the rich coastal cities to provide financial, technological, and managerial assistance to those provinces that were struggling.

Amid the many issues and problems facing the Chinese people, there was a resurgence of spiritual and religious beliefs. Falun Gong, (Chinese: "Discipline of the Dharma Wheel") was founded by Li Hongzhi in 1992. Its movement's sudden prominence in the late 1990s became a concern to the Chinese government, which branded it a "heretical cult."

To deal with this heresy, being heretical to the anti-religious beliefs of communism and a potential threat to his hold on power, Jiang established an extralegal department. It is believed that Jiang feared that this popular new religious movement would infiltrate the CCP and the state apparatus and, subsequently, his hold on to power.

The persecution that followed was characterized a nationwide campaign of propaganda, as well as the large-scale arbitrary imprisonment and coercive reeducation of Falun Gong organizers, sometimes resulting in death due to mistreatment in detention. However, it went beyond simple imprisonment and re-education.

According to Ethan Gutmann's survey-based estimation, from 2000 to 2008, an average of 450,000 to a million Falun Gong practitioners were detained in forced labor/re-education camps at any given time.[147] As the detainees were held from 1-3 years in the forced labor camps and for shorter periods in other facilities, it is estimated that from 2,000,000 to 4,000,000 people were detained between 2000 and 2008.

---

[147] Gutmann, E, *The Slaughter: Mass Killings, Organ Harvesting, and China's Secret Solution to Its Dissident Problem,* (New York: Prometheus Books, 2014).

In 2002 Jiang stepped down as general secretary and left the Politburo Standing Committee, but retained the chairmanship of the Central Military Commission, which controlled the army and the nation's foreign policy. He continued advising Hu Jintao, who replaced him, but Hu was not considered a "core" leader like Jiang, Deng and Mao. In 2003 Jaing resigned his position as chairman of the Central Military Commission.

Hu Jintao and premier Wen Jiabao assumed control of a China suffering from internal social, political and environmental problems. The wealth disparity between the rich coastal provinces and the interior provinces continued to produce discontent and anger that was threatening the rule of the CCP. The corruption of the Chinese civil service, the military, educational system, the courts, and medical system steadily tore at the foundation of the country's stability.

To deal with this, in 2006, Hu Jintao launched the "8 Honors and 8 Shames" movement in a bid to promote a more selfless and moral outlook amongst the population. It was promulgated as a moral code for all Chinese, but particularly, it was imposed on the membership of the CCP. This program was a set of moral concepts that contained the following points:

The Eight points were:

- Honor to those who love the motherland, and shame on those who harm the motherland.
- Honor to those who serve the people, and shame on those who betray the people.
- Honor to those who quest for science, and shame on those who refuse to be educated.
- Honor to those who are hardworking, and shame on those who indulge in comfort and hate work.
- Honor to those who help each other, and shame on those who seek gains at the expense of others.
- Honor to those who are trustworthy, and shame on those who trade integrity for profits.
- Honor to those who abide by law and discipline, and shame on those who break laws and discipline.
- Honor to those who uphold plain living and hard struggle, and shame on those who wallow in extravagance and pleasures.

It is difficult to assess the impact of this program, but the internal problems of China continue to this day.

On November 15, 2012, Xi Jinping was elected to the posts of General Secretary of the CCP and Chairman of the CMC by the 18th Central Committee of the CCP. This made him, informally, the paramount leader of China. Since then Xi has been re-elected to his position twice. Upon his third election, in the meeting of the 20th National Congress, he directed the forceful removal of Hu Jintao.

A View from the Streets of China Over the Last 50 Years

In order to understand communism, it is always best to talk about it as much as one can see from the perspective of those who live under it. The reader might recall the earlier account of the siege of Leningrad during WWII by Elena Skrjabina and her struggles both with life and her observations of the corruption of the leadership. The problem is finding such accounts. Fortunately, such an account of life in Communist China can be found in the magazine Foreign Affairs.[148]

In this article, Cai Xia talks about her experiences while living in China and being part of the academic world. As a youth she was a fully indoctrinated communist who thought that communism was wonderful and the only way to run a society. Her experiences, however, very rapidly destroyed her faith in what she'd been taught.

"In June 1989, the government cracked down on pro-democracy protesters in Tiananmen Square, killing hundreds. Privately, I was appalled that the People's Liberation Army had fired on college students, which ran contrary to the indoctrination I had received since my childhood that the army protected the people; only Japanese 'devils' and Nationalist reactionaries killed them. Alarmed by the protests, plus the fall of communism in eastern Europe, the CCP's top leadership decided it had to counteract ideological laxity."

As a result, Cai was sent to the Central Party School to have a refresher course in the party's ideology. She was admitted to the master's program in the theory department. Her ideological commitment to the party line was such that she was given the nickname "Old Mrs. Marx." When she completed her studies, she received a PhD and joined the school's faculty. Apparently, the party trusted no one, even their most dedicated teachers

---

[148] Cai Xai, "The Party that Failed; An Insider Breaks with Beijing" *Foreign Affairs*, Volume 100, No. 1. pp.78-96.

of Marxist ideology, as their lectures were monitored with video cameras. The lectures were later reviewed by supervision. It was not uncommon for the students to have questions about the contradictions within official ideology and other such issues. Amendments were added to the Chinese constitution in 2004 that said that the government protected human rights and private property. The latter point, private property, was in direct contradiction to Marxist theory, so the student's questions were logical. This was at the time when Deng wanted to "let a part of the population get rich first" so as to motivate and stimulate production. This conundrum confused Cai's students, and they wanted to know how this "squared with Marx's promise that communism would provide to each according to his needs." She understood the question and it began slowly cutting into her firm belief in the communist system.

On February 25, 2000, the "Three Represents" of Jiang were released. In the radio broad cast announcing this, Jiang said they had to represent three aspects of China: "the development requirements of advanced productive forces," cultural progress, and the interests of the majority.

Cai goes on to say that she was constantly questioning her beliefs, but despite that, remained loyal. It seems, however, that these same questions had penetrated Chinese academia in general as there were discussions of " 'Marxist humanism,' a strain of Marxist thinking that emphasized the full development of the human personality." It would seem that the Chinese leadership had realized that pure Marxism was not working, but that it was holding China back; that it was necessary to adopt some elements of capitalism in order to compete on the world stage. However, in order to continue to control the Chinese people, the leadership of the CCP had to maintain the façade of being Marxists.

At this point Cai took a daring step. In her PhD dissertation she "challenged the ancient Chinese slogan 'rich country, strong army' by contending that China would be strong only if the party allowed its citizens to prosper." As time progressed, she presented papers and talks in which she "suggested that state enterprises were still too dominant in the Chinese economy and that further reform was needed to allow private companies to compete." She even went on to address that the corruption in the government was not an individual failing, but a systematic problem resulting from governmental control of the economy. Fortunately for her, these comments aligned with Jiang Zemin's thoughts on the economy as he sought to stimulate private enterprise with the "Three Represents."

Watching the "Three Represents" being brought out Cai realized that this was a major shift from the CCP's policies of a planned economy and national self-sufficiency. Indeed, she saw it as an abandonment of the Marxist core belief that capitalists were exploiters of the proletariat.

Cai then collided with the system. She began preparing episodes for Chinese TV (CCTV) to sell the new program and was confronted by four senior vice presidents of CCTV. Her work began undergoing a series of reviews and in her words, she "learned even more about the party's hypocrisy."

Cai was then tasked with preparing content relating to the Three Represents by the Propaganda Department. She was the only woman among 18 male scholars. And as she says, "At dinner the men gossiped and cracked jokes. I found the off-color, alcoholic-fueled conversation vulgar and would always slink out after a few bites of food. Finally, another participant took me aside. Talk of official business would only get us in trouble, he explained; it was safer and more enjoyable to confine the conversation to sex." Obviously, the conversations of the elite academics who prepared material for the consumption by the Chinese public were listened to and China was a police state where the least slip might have undesirable repercussions.

As Cai worked on this project, she cataloged and organized Jiang's thoughts and quotations from various sources that were for the consumption of the party's internal consumption. She says about this that she "couldn't add or subtract text, but I could change a period to a comma and connect one quote to another. I was amazed that the formal explanation of one of the party's most important ideological campaigns (The Three Represents) in the post-Mao era would be little more than a cut-and-paste job." She goes on to say: "My understanding of the Three Represents as an important pivot in the ruling party's ideology had been completely squeezed out of the document and replaced by pablum. Remembering the lewd character around the dinner table every night, I felt for the first time that the system I had long considered sacred was in fact unbearably absurd."

Cai had learned that the ideas party "sanctimoniously promoted" were nothing more than self-serving tools used to deceive the Chinese people. And in a twist of the most ironic hypocrisy, she realized that they were a means of making money. It seemed that publishing books was a way to wealth. The CCP had, at this time, some 3,600,000 organizations, each of which was expected to buy a copy of any new publication. At 10 yuan per copy, this meant 36,000,000 yuan, some $5,000,000 coming from the budgets of the party branches that vanished into the pockets of corrupt individuals. This was a rice bowl that was jealously guarded.

For Cai a turning point came in 2008 when she visited Spain. She saw firsthand how Spain had transformed from the fascist autocracy of Franco into a stable and prosperous democracy in 1975.

She "came to the pessimistic conclusion that the CCP was unlikely to reform politically." She noted that Franco's successor, King Juan Carlos, had looked to the interests of the country, not his personal interests. She realized that the CCP was a permanent monopoly on political power and that the party's record, particularly Tiananmen Square, demonstrated "that it would not give up that monopoly peacefully. And none of the post-Deng leaders had the courage to push for political reform; they simply wanted to pass the buck to future leaders."

Cai goes on to say that she noted that Spain had created an environment suitable for reform, established judicial independence, and the freedom of the press. By contrast, she noted that the CCP saw demands for "social and economic justice as threats to its power, suppressing civil society and restricting people's liberties. The regime and the people had been locked in confrontation for decades, making reconciliation unthinkable."

She now rejected her formerly unshakable faith in Marx and his theories. The evidence was before her eyes. She now saw that the "highly centralized, oppressive version of Marxism promoted by the CCP owed more to Stalin than to Marx himself." She also came to realize that it was "an ideology formed to serve a self-interested dictatorship."

When Cai returned to China, Jiang had been replaced by Hu Jintao and that he was moving away from Jaing's program. Hu had put forward "the Scientific Outlook on Development" to replace Jiang's Three Represents.

The rapid development of China had provoked the seizure of peasants' land that was desired for industrial development and "factories squeezed workers" to produce more profits. The number of people that were concerned with governmental policies grew significantly and nation wide demonstrates exceeded more than 100,000 per year. This demonstrated to Cai that it was becoming more and more difficult for China to develop its economy without "liberalizing its politics."

Hu, according to Cia, had decided that "economic, political, and ideological reforms that the party had made so far should be maintained, but not pushed forward." Apparently, Hu was dealing with attacks from both the right and left. As a result, China "entered a period of political stagnation and decline similar to what the Soviet Union experienced under Leonid Brezhnev."

There was yet hope. Xi Jinping had come to power. The reputation of his father, a former leader of the CCP, who had liberal inclinations, and Xi's more pragmatic approach suggested there was hope that he might be willing to undertake the bold changes China's political system needed. There were two groups of prescient skeptics.

"The first group consisted of princelings – descendants of the party's founders. Xi was a princeling, as was Bo Xilai, the dynamic party chief of Chongquin, Xi and Bo rose to senior provincial and ministerial positions at almost the same time, and both were expected to join the highest body of the CCP, the Politburo Standing Committee, and were considered top contenders to lead China.

Bo lost favor after being implicated in the murder of his wife and was sentenced to life in prison, leaving XI an open path to the throne.

"The second group of skeptics consisted of establishment scholars." Cai, a professor from her school, and a reporter from a Chinese magazine were chatting about Xi. The reporter asked the professor what he thought of him now that he was the party's general secretary. "The professor's lip twitched, and he said with disdain that Xi summered from 'inadequate knowledge.'"

A speech Xi gave in December 2012 suggested Xi was a reformist and had a progressive mentality, while other statements he made suggested a throwback to the pre-reform era. In conversations with her former colleagues, one of them said to her, "It's not a question of whether Xi is going left or right, but rather that he lacks basic judgement and speaks illogically." Hope of him leading a political reform vanished.

In 2013 Xi set forth a comprehensive plan for reform and it was hoped in academia that he would bring about major reforms, but Cai was skeptical about this and thought he would do exactly the opposite. The biggest problem in China had been "corruption, excessive debt, and unprofitable state operations [that were] rooted in party officials' power to meddle in economic decisions without public supervision." Despite this Xi launched an ideological campaign to revive Maoist rule. It called for "intensified societal surveillance and a clampdown on free expression." The discussion of constitutional democracy and universal values were banned shamelessly under the slogan "governance, management, service, and law."

Further legal reforms occurred in 2014 which exposed "the party's intent to use the law as a tool for maintaining totalitarian rule." Xi was now clearly not looking to reform China's longstanding problems, but to establish his hold on absolute power. Politically, China was moving backwards and soon instituted a new Cultural Revolution-like campaign.

The direct result of this new campaign was further suppression of the right of the people to criticize their government, which had been instituted under the Hundred Flowers campaign, and in a like manner was used to draw out those who might challenge the authority of the party. Cai had seen people labeled "anti-party" and were then deprived not only of their rights but subjected to "harsh persecution."

Cai responded to the situation of Ren Zhiqiang, who had been labeled "anti-party" by writing a defense of Ren and sending it to a WeChat group. Her article simply quoted the party's constitution and the code of conduct, but the Central Party's disciplinary committee accused her of "serious errors." She was then subjected to several "intimidating interviews in which [her] interrogators applied psychological pressure and laid word traps [for her] in an effort to induce a false confession of wrongdoing." Shortly later she came to the conclusion that the authorities had tapped her phone, were reading her electronic mail, and following her to see who she was meeting. She had become a victim of the police state.

As a result, Cai's writings were being reviewed and in 2016 it was determined that a speech she had given at Tsinghua University, in which she argued that if ideology violated common sense, it deteriorated into lies attracted the attention of the party. She was called meet with the school's disciplinary committee where she was denounced. Hence, she was blocked from all media moving forward, be it print, online, or television. Her name could not even be published.

Following this she was called before the Central Party School where she was told that she was to keep silent on all political issues and if she uttered one word against the system, she would be subjected to disciplinary action, including reduced retirement benefits. Subsequently she was subjected to regular interrogations by party officials. The school's disciplinary committee repeatedly threatened her with announcing punishment in front of a large public meeting.

The last straw was a case of police brutality. In May 2016, Lei Yang, a scientist, went to the airport to pick up his mother-in-law. For no known reason he was taken into custody and died in the custody of the Beijing police. To cover their actions, the police accused Lei of soliciting a prostitute. His university classmates joined his family in seeking justice and the results reverberated throughout China. To stop the outcries, the CCP ordered an investigation.

What happened was that Lei's parents, his wife, and his children were placed under arrest and the local government offered them $1,000,000. On their refusal the bribe was raised to $3,000,000, but Lei's wife refused, demanding that her husband's name be cleared. The CCP then announced that no one would be charged and forced Lei's family lawyer to end his legal actions.

Cai was now totally disillusioned with her country's system. It had become a one-party dictatorship interested solely on perpetuating itself, no matter what the cost to the Chinese people or morality. Fortunately, she was allowed to travel and went to the US. While there she put her opinions in writing and called for Xi to step down.

In response she was expelled from the party and lost her retirement benefits. Her bank account was frozen, and it was clear that she should not return to China. Formerly she was a devoted and fervent communist, but she had seen with her own eyes how it had become a lie; that the corruption of the party was omnipotent and concerned only with protecting itself and its privileges, and that Xi was solely interested in his power. She defected to save her life.

The Belt and Road

The Belt and Road Initiative is China's expansive program aimed at connecting countries around the globe. It included plans for pipelines and a port in Pakistan, bridges in Bangladesh, railways to Russia and many similar projects. The idea was based on the ancient Silk Road that connected China with the West and it superficially was to promote trade between the East and West as it had in the Middle Ages. It also looks to create a new era of globalization.

It is envisioned to connect at least 68 countries with an investment of up to $8 trillion that would create a network of transportation, energy, and communications infrastructure that will link Europe, Middle East, and Africa. It is also intended, through infrastructure financing a large part of the global economy, to build key economic, foreign policy, and security objectives that will serve the Chinese government. These are its "goals" but there are other, unspoken goals: gaining access to resources to support its own economic growth and to increase energy security.[149] There is yet one other goal and that is weakening the political alliance between African nations and the United States and Russia.

Officially, China provides eight types of foreign aid: complete projects, goods and materials, technical cooperation, human resource development cooperation, medical assistance, emergency humanitarian aid, volunteer programs, and debt relief. It is involved in a wide spectrum of fields, ranging from agriculture, education, transportation, energy, communications and health.[150]

Much of the loans are "concessional loans." It then expands into direct investment, soft loans, and commercial loans. Chinese agencies and commercial entities to "closely mix and combine foreign aid, direct investment, service contracts, labor cooperation, foreign trade, and export.[151]

If, in the future, it follows China's present process of infrastructure financing, of lending money to poor nations, particularly in Africa, and has created and will create a series of states that are deeply in debt to China. In 23 countries there is a significant vulnerability of producing debt distress.

The Chinese claim that this assistance is purely selfless and altruistic, but in its execution, it has another side. This assistance has produced diplomatic recognition with 44 African countries, countries that are in the United Nations and which vote at China's beck and call. It also produces favorable attitudes in those countries towards Chinese companies, including state-owned enterprises. As many of these loans are backed by natural resources, Chinese companies have bought or taken control of mines and other sources of needed resources. In Congo it controls the production of cobalt and copper, taking 50% of its production of cobalt. The Congo also has significant reserves of zinc, oil and gas that Chinese are exploiting. In Angola it is oil, where Chinese oil companies have the exploitation rights to much of Angola's oil reserves. China's interest in Africa is closely tied to oil and it is believed that Africa contains about 8% of the world's oil reserves.[152] In addition, materials such as iron, copper,

---

[149] Mushota, C.E., *China in Africa: Partner or Exploiter? The Case of Zambia*, Cuny Academic Works, https://academicworks.cuny.edu/cgi/viewcontent.cgi?article=1997& context=cc_etds_theses p.9.

[150] Yun Sun, *China's Aid to Africa; Monster or Messiah*, Brookings Institute, Friday, February 7, 2014 https://www.brookings.edu/opinions/chinas-aid-to-africa-monster-or-messiah/

[151] Yun Sun.

[152] Mushota, C.E., *China in Africa: Partner or Exploiter? The Case of Zambia*, Cuny Academic Works, https://academicworks.cuny.edu/cgi/viewcontent.cgi?article=1997& context=cc_etds_theses p.10.

zinc, magnesium, cobalt, uranium, and gold have been of particular interest to the Chinese.[153]

The many loans to poor countries produced a concern in the West that it will create an unfavorable degree of dependency on China, as it has become a major creditor in Africa. This indebtedness has exacerbated internal and bilateral tension in some countries, such as Sri Lanka, where there are frequent clashes with the police over an industrial zone surrounding the port of Hambantota and in Pakistan where Chinese officials have meddled in local politics by appealing to opposition politicians to embrace the construction of the China-Pakistan Economic Corridor.[154]

One impact of the Belt and Road Project has been to cause debtor nations to sacrifice of domestic spending on infrastructure and social services to service the debt. The debtor nations have often resorted to borrowing more money. This was common from the 1970s into the 1990s, where debtor countries compounded their debt at an annual rate of approximately 20%. The total debt has risen, as a result, from $300 billion to $1.5 trillion.[155]

Because of the debt incurred by Djibouti, it has accepted the establishment of China's currently only overseas military base. Djibouti's debt, in 2018, was estimated to be between 50% and 85% of Djibouti's GDP. Much of this debt is owed to the China Exim Bank. The many Chinese projects in Djibouti totaled nearly $1.4 billion, with further projects that include two new airports, a new port at Ghoubet, an oil terminal, and a toll road. There is also the Addis Ababa-Djibouti Railroad.

There are doubts that Laos, one of the poorest countries in Southeast Asia, to service its debt that it has incurred from the construction of the China-Laos railway. This involved a $465 billion loan. This was followed by a $600 million project to build a hydropower system. Laos shares a common border with China. As Djibouti found itself compelled, because of its loan, what can China demand of a country on its border? Indeed, the Lao kingdom of Lan Xang and its successor states were tributaries of Ming and later Qing China. In the late 15th century, the Chinese backed Lan Xang against their common rival, the Vietnamese. This becomes a complex relationship because China has a history of expansion to recover territories that were once part of China, i.e. Tibet, parts of the Indo-Chinese

---

[153] Mushota, C.E., *China in Africa: Partner or Exploiter? The Case of Zambia*, Cuny Academic Works, https://academicworks.cuny.edu/cgi/viewcontent.cgi?article=1997& context=cc_etds_theses p.24.

[154] Hurley, Morris and Portelance,CDG Policy Paper 121, March 2018, p. 2.

[155] Hurley, Morris and Portelance,CDG Policy Paper 121, March 2018, p. 32.

frontier, and even parts of modern Russia north of the Amur River. By establishing a creditor-debt relationship with Laos it has re-established that old tributary relationship. What more can it ask of Laos in relationship to China's historical claim on parts of Vietnam?

China's Belt and Road in Africa has produced a form of neo-colonialism, so hated by Lenin, where imperialist colonial powers occupied all of Africa and used it as a dumping ground for their manufactured goods and a source of raw materials to feed the industrial base back in the homeland. This process destroyed local industry, what little of it existed in the 19th century and certainly depressed the development of it in the 20th century.

With regards to raw materials, this is probably China's number one objective. I've already referenced the oil from Angola and the cobalt and copper from Congo. The process starts with infrastructure. The Chinese construct the roads, railroads, and other infrastructure necessary to reach the resources. Their sole purpose of this type of project is to give them access to the mineral wealth of the target country. There are promises of jobs and cash flow into the country, but control over the resources that are extracted is frequently in the sole hands of the Chinese. China is the principal consumer of the natural resources in their subject African states, which means that the wealth generated there is China's wealth. At the time of the writing of this work, the World Bank estimated that China received 16% of African exports and 14% to 21% of its resource imports.[156] It is a capitalistic equivalent of a parasite and its host that holds the debt of the country over its head to enforce its will.

The increased Chinese presence in Africa is producing much discontent in many countries. One issue is that, by my own observations and experiences in Africa, when the Chinese construct an infrastructure project they bring in Chinese workers and hire very few locals. The contracts between China and the various African states require that 70% of the workers be Chinese.[157] In addition, they bring in all the material and equipment, which leaves when the project is completed. And, of the Chinese who they bring into work on these projects a large number of them stay in the country. In addition, the working conditions in the mines, factories, and other areas are what in the West we would call inhuman. The

---

[156] Mushota, C.E., *China in Africa: Partner or Exploiter? The Case of Zambia*, Cuny Academic Works, https://academicworks.cuny.edu/cgi/viewcontent.cgi?article=1997& context=cc_etds_ theses p.21.

[157] Karlsson, P., *China in Africa: An Act of Neo-Colonialism or a win-win relationship.* Master's Thesis.http://www.diva-portal.org/smash/record.jsf?pid=diva2%3A1437583&dswid=-6283.

use of child labor is common, and the pay is insignificant.

As part of the Chinese penetration of Africa, they dump cheap Chinese goods into the local markets and crowd out local African manufactured goods.

Another source of dissatisfaction is the practice of grabbing land, environmentally unfriendly processes for extracting resources and the collusion of Chinese businessmen with local businessmen.[158]

Furthermore, two further apparent results of this is an actual increase in poverty and political corruption.[159]

All these activities are part of what Lenin called "comprador" and was where the imperialist colonizers extracted raw materials, dumped cheap goods into the colony, and incorporated part of the colony's population into their process of exploitation of the colony. This process gave the colonizing power a strong foothold in the colony and facilitated its exploitation of the resources of the colony.

The worst part of neo-colonialism is when the imperial colonizer deploys its military into the state in question. A stark example of this is the Chinese military base in Djibouti. However, this process also includes the sale of weapons, educating the local police, military and officials, all of which China has done in Africa. The presence of Chinese military forces has given the Chinese greater influence in the region. The People's Liberation Army has conducted military activities, such as joint training exercises throughout the region.

The military presence is highest in the countries where the Belt and Road Project is most active. On the other hand, the Chinese have meddled in the Sudanese civil war. This activity totally focused on China's economic interests, particularly oil and minerals, and it has actually deployed PLA troops to guard the oilfields. China has also considered deploying is military to Nigeria so as to protect its personnel, its economic interests and its oil companies.

To reinforce this China has provided the African Union with equipment and training, specifically aimed at combatting Al-Qa'ida in the Islamic Magreb (AQIM) and other terrorist organizations in the Sahel. Despite this aid, China has also hacked into the servers of the AU in 2018

---

[158] Karlsson, P., *China in Africa: An Act of Neo-Colonialism or a win-win relationship.* Master's Thesis. http://www.diva-portal.org/smash/record.jsf?pid=diva2%3A1437583&dswid=-6283.

[159] Mushota, C.E., *China in Africa: Partner or Exploiter? The Case of Zambia,* Cuny AcademicnWorks, https://academicworks.cuny.edu/cgi/viewcontent.cgi?article=1997& context=cc_etds_theses p.8.

and stole data according to the French newspaper Le Monde.[160]

There is also the process of education and the construction and control of media systems in the colony. Media, otherwise called propaganda, is used to spread Chinese influence throughout the host country.

In Kenya there is a multilingual radio station that is Chinese state owned and an English language newspaper, the China Daily.

China has made a massive investment in educating Africans. They sought to provide 50,000 government fellowships, train 1,000 African leaders, invited 2,000 African students to study in China, and provided 50,000 training opportunities to African government officials, scholars, journalists, and other technical experts. This may sound altruistic, but it has the process of creating a base of support among the local leadership that are totally pro-Chinese in their attitudes and which, as part of the comprador class, will support Chinese objectives.

In South Africa their Department of Education has recently implemented a program of making Chinese the second language of their country by teaching it from 4th to 12th grade to all students. Expanding on this, China offers scholarships for African students and offers places in Chinese universities for self-funding students; it trains professionals in a wide rang of areas; and it builds educational infrastructures in the African countries. It also has established Confucius Institutes in Africa as part of their soft power program.

Another leg of neo-colonialism is in the area of technology, where the imperial power tries to increase the dependency of the colony to its technological know-how and telecommunications.

A significant result of this process is China's ability to influence policy making. It is penetrating civil society, sector and professional organizations with the goal of penetrating deeper into African politics and control, or at least influence, African policy making.

An immediate result of this is that the infected African countries have steadily broken diplomatic relations with Taiwan and have turned to not recognizing its independence, but declaring it to be a rogue province, which is the official PRC stance on Taiwan. All the African nations except for Swaziland have pledged their support to China in its effort to absorb Taiwan. This has a major impact in UN decisions relating to Taiwan.

---

[160] Mushota, C.E., *China in Africa: Partner or Exploiter? The Case of Zambia*, Cuny Academic Works, https://academicworks.cuny.edu/cgi/viewcontent.cgi?article=1997& context=cc_etds_theses p.30.

Twin Evils

Let us look at Zambia as a case study. Its situation is characterized by an elevated level of poverty, which is not unusual as 80% of Africans earn $2 or less a day. It also suffers from unequal income distribution and is highly dependent on commodity exports.

In 1970 Zambia's economy was greatly hurt by the first oil crisis and an economic recession. Three years later, when oil prices rose significantly and the demand for copper fell by 40% in 1975 and again 1979 it took two more major blows.[161] The resultant economic crisis led to Zambia's taking major loans from the IMF and World Bank to make up for the draining of its foreign currency reserves and fall in revenues.

In the 1970's China built the Tanzania-Zambia Railroad. Its goal was to give Zambia another path for the movement of its mineral wealth and ended its economic dependence on the apartheid regimes of South Africa and Zimbabwe. China provided a $400 million interest free loan and shipped a further $1 million in materials for the project. This created a strong diplomatic bond between Zambia and China.

Between the various loans that Zambia took and the nature of the Tanzania-Zambia Railroad it soon found it burdened with high inflation and gross depreciation. Its dept was estimated to have risen to $12 billion or 51% of its 2018 GDP.

The next blow was the appearance of COVID-19, which exacerbated Zambia's critical economic situation, and, in 2020, this resulted in Zambia defaulting on a $42.5 billon Eurobond loan. It had, before this default, suspended debt service payments to private sector creditors. Meanwhile, the government continued taking out massive loans for infrastructure projects, including the Levy Mwanawasa football stadium in Ndola. This forced it to negotiate and sign loan agreements for these projects and to support the running of the country.

Other infrastructure projects funded by Chinese money include hospitals, roads, public buildings and water supply programs. These certainly have a humanitarian element, but they all serve Chinese interests overtly and covertly, particularly the debt bomb.

About this time the Tanzania-Zambia Railroad was completed and with new trade routes, it eliminated Zambia's economic dependence and stimulated its economy. However, the $400 million loan that China had provided Zambia was never serviced, nor was it transformed into a grant.

---

[161] Mushota, C.E., *China in Africa: Partner or Exploiter? The Case of Zambia*, Cuny Academic Works, https://academicworks.cuny.edu/cgi/viewcontent.cgi?article=1997& context=cc_etds_theses p.34.

The railroad was, however, a two-edged sword. Though it helped Zambia's economy, it gave China, the world's largest consumer of copper access to Zambia's copper, Zambia being the second largest copper producer in the world. China's lust for copper is clearly the driving reason for its involvement in Zambia and mining comprises over 88% of China's investment in Zambia.

In the usual "comprador" process the railroad also allowed cheap Chinese goods to flood into Zambia, killing Zambian national industry. Chinese money flowed into Zambia and though seemingly interest-free or soft loans, they were closely tied to Chinese economic interests. China holds 44% of Zambia's national debt, which gives it a powerful position to influence Zambian policies to the point where China has been accused of practicing "debt trap diplomacy."

Large numbers of Chinese nationals have migrated into Zambia as part of the infrastructure development of Zambia. They include laborers, government officials and technical experts, creating a strong economic tie between Zambia and China. The UN estimated that in 2019 there were 80,000 Chinese nationals living in Zambia.

This influx of Chinese immigrants competed with Zambian nationals for low- and mid-level jobs. Zambians have been laid off and Chinese workers hired to replace them and work on Chinese projects. The Chinese companies claim this is because of language issues and cultural differences. As mentioned earlier, the Chinese generally refuse to learn about or be open to Zambian culture, customs and languages.[162] This is, of course, a source of friction among the Zambian population. In essence, a new ruling class of wealthy, compared to the Zambians, Chinese are pushing them aside and supplanting them. Though jobs are created, they are generally given to immigrant Chinese.

There is another issue and that is Human Rights. Like in Congo with the cobalt industry, in the Zambian copper industry the Chinese owners of the mines do not provide working gear that ensures the safety of the workers who work 12–18-hour shifts in the extreme African heat. The workers are not issued face masks, safety shoes, or proper work clothing. Fifty-two Zambian workers died in 2005 as a result of the lack of safety procedures in an explosive factory. The Chinese management opened fire on Zambians in 2010 and again in 2011. The Zambians protested over bad

---

[162] Mushota, C.E., *China in Africa: Partner or Exploiter? The Case of Zambia*, Cuny Academic Works, https://academicworks.cuny.edu/cgi/viewcontent.cgi?article=1997& context=cc_etds_theses pp.44-45.

wages in the Collum Coal Mine at the same time and this resulted in dead Zambian workers and injured Chinese workers. In 2017 and 2018 major disagreements erupted because of the lack of fair compensation, illegal mining, and hazardous working conditions.[163]

The Chinese have invested in three solar plants in Zambia and have diversified Zambia's renewable energy sector. The Chinese have controlling interests in both Zambia's power supply and telecommunications.

Zambia has been subtly and progressively invaded and converted into a Chinese colony. The Chinese have compromised the corrupt Zambian government with their money, they have bought up its natural resources, they have sent an army of Chinese immigrants into the country that has pushed Zambians out of any significant jobs, they have flooded Zambia with cheap Chinese goods, suppressing any Zambian industrial growth, and the treat the Zambian people as slaves.

This is neo-colonialism in its purest form. It is normally a remnant of the colonial system where the colonial power continues to exploit the colony while giving the indigenous people of the colony the illusion of freedom. It is in fact; "killing of two birds with one stone by establishing a colony of exploitation and settlement" and "divide and rule [t]here by artificially creating a bourgeoisie of the colonized."[164] In this case, however, China has slipped like a thief in the night into the countries of Africa, dangling pretty bobbles in the face of corrupt politicians, buying them with seemingly beneficial projects that will allow the development of those countries, but which have strings attached, where Chinese money is an addictive form of crack causing these politicians to beg for more and more until they are like Briar Rabbit and inextricably stuck in the Chinese tar baby.

Though the communists decry this system, the largest communist state in the world currently engages in this practice and they have absolutely established a comprador situation in Zambia and other African states that are puppets that dances to China's tune on the world stage.

There were also Soviet efforts in Africa which have many of these elements. The Soviet Union engaged in some of the military aspects of the Chinese process by selling and giving large quantities of arms. During 1956-1986, the Soviets sent "military advisors" and the South African Border War (1966-1990), the Ogaden War between Ethiopia and Somali

---

[163] Mushota, C.E., *China in Africa: Partner or Exploiter? The Case of Zambia*, Cuny Academic Works, https://academicworks.cuny.edu/cgi/viewcontent.cgi?article=1997& context=cc_etds_theses p. 46.

[164] Sartre, J. Colonialism and Neo-Colonialism. (London: Rutledge, 2001) p. 139.

(1977-1978)., and the Soviets supplied and trained combat units from Namibia (SWAPO) and Angola (MPLA) at the African National Congress (ANC) military training camps in Tanzania.

The goal of Soviet aid in the Ogaden War was to eventually establish a naval base at Berbera, Somalia, which is about 20 miles from Djibouti. It is not just a coincidence that both China and the USSR sought a naval base on the entrance to the Suez Canal.

The total of military hardware delivered to Africa in and before 1976 came to $340 million and there were 2,000 Soviet military advisors and Cuba had 7,900 advisors and troops in Angola. There were also 1,000 advisors in Somalia in 1974[165]

The Soviet Union provided African nations with four types of economic assistance: loans, trade credits, short term credits (swing credits) granted by Soviet foreign trade organizations intended to finance their exports as part of bilateral cleaning agreements and scholarship programs. The loans were generally 50% grants and, like the Chinese grants and loans, involved the construction of production facilities and technical assistance. Trade credits rarely had grant elements that exceeded 20%.

The Soviet Union, too, saw opportunity in the political stance of the first prime minister of the Congo, Patrice Lumumba, and in addition to a proxy war that would last five years, the main concern for both nations was not the well-being of the Congolese people or even financial gain. Rather, it was the rich uranium mines in the southern areas of the Congo that were extremely valuable because of the purity of the deposits. Though the USSR had massive natural resources, this was one that it did not have and wanted desperately because of the nuclear arms race that had existed during the Cold War.

There was a similar effort in Guinea where there are rich deposits of bauxite, the ore of aluminum. This was the USSR's largest project, which came to $92 million. Included in its efforts in Guinea were, since 1960, the presence of 100 military advisors and $38 million in arms.

The Soviets also took many Africans to the USSR to be educated, and Russian is still a second language in many African nations where Soviet had influence. Apart from economy and politics, the Soviets made a big effort raising new, pro-Soviet African elites, inviting students from Africa to study in the USSR. It is not clear if this was an effort to create a comprador class, but had the USSR not fallen, it might well have been

---

[165] DIA Intelligence Appraisal entitled *Soviet Involvement in Sub-Saharan Africa.* (Declassified by Dos on May 4, 2006) Formerly Classified Secret NOFORN.

such a class. From 1949 to 1991, around 60,000 Africans studied in the USSR. The biggest university to welcome them was the UDN (People's Friendship University) in Moscow, named after Patrice Lumumba, the pro-Soviet premier of Congo.

Initially, under Khrushchev, the goal was to sell communism to the Africans. This took some selling, as they were not inclined to it. The Soviets signed cooperation treaties with 37 African countries and were involved with the construction some 600 enterprises, factories and plants. Among them, including the Aswan Dam, which was crucial for Egypt's agriculture and energy system, the Capanda hydroelectric dam, which provided Angola with electricity, plants in Congo and Nigeria and and similar projects throughout Africa.

The efforts of the Soviets to gain the support of the various African nations they were involved with did not give them the influence of those nations in the UN. Here the Chinese were infinitely more successful.

The efforts of the USSR in Africa came to an abrupt stop when the USSR collapsed. Overall, they had minimal success, which according to a DIA document[166], was due to ineptitude and insensitivity. As a result of this the Soviets had projected a negative image that continued for many years among several major African leader that caused them to distrust the Soviet's motives.

The PRC in Tibet

Tibet had been part of Imperial China, and the leaders of the People's Republic of China (PRC) had refused to recognize that it had become an independent nation. It returned to the control of the PRC when the Government of Tibet signed the Seventeen Point Agreement which the 14th Dalai Lama ratified on October 24, 1951.

On March 10, 1959, the Tibetans began a rebellion against the PRC and Chinese troops soon overran Tibet, crushing the rebellion. In response the PRC government closed the monasteries in Tibet and imposed Chinese law and custom in the region. On September 9, 1965, the Chinese government established the Tibetan Autonomous Region.

Many human rights abuses have been documented in Tibet and include the executions, disappearances, torture, poor prison conditions, arbitrary arrest and detention, denial of fair public trial, denial of freedom

---

[166]DIA Intelligence Appraisal entitled *Soviet Involvement in Sub-Saharan Africa.* (Declassified by Dos on May 4, 2006) Formerly Classified Secret NOFORN.

of speech and of press and Internet freedoms. They also include political and religious repression, forced abortions, sterilization[167], and even infanticide.[168]

The PRC security apparatus regularly employed torture and degrading treatment on detainees and prisoners, according to the U.S. State Department's 2009 report. Tibetans repatriated from Nepal have also reportedly suffered torture, including electric shocks, exposure to cold, and severe beatings, and been forced to perform heavy physical labor.

Marxism / Maoism in Cambodia

The Khmer Rouge were the communist party in Cambodia. Their ideology was an unusual mix of Stalinism, Maoism, and the post-colonial theories of Frantz Fanon. And yet there were elements of the purest Marxist thought and xenophobic Khmer nationalism that overlaid all of it. Like Mao, however, they focused on the rural peasantry rather than the urban proletariat, since Cambodia was, in the 1970s, much like China had been when Mao began his revolution. It also placed emphasis on initiatives along the line of Mao's Great Leap Forward. It sought to abolish personal interest in human behavior, promoted communist living and eating, and focused on what it called "common sense" over technical knowledge. As for its "nationalistic" inclination, it was more racism and favored the Khmer tribes and over the other groups that lived in Cambodia at that time.

Other communist nations, particularly North Vietnam, at that time, saw it as deviating from orthodox Marxism. It did focus on Maoism instead of Marxist-Leninist thought. It believed that human willpower could overcome material and historical conditions instead of the orthodox Marxist-Leninist thought which held that historical materialism and the idea of history was a progression towards communism.

In an act of Communist solidarity, when the North Vietnamese launched their assault across the DMZ into South Vietnam, they also launched an offensive into Cambodia against the Cambodian army. After the USSR had collapsed and their archives were opened to the world it was discovered that this had been done in coordination with the Khmer Rouge. The North Vietnamese were soon within 15 miles of Phnom Penh when

---

[167] Ingram,P., "Genocide in Tibet - Children of Despair" www.crin.org/docs/resources/treaties/crc.12/ China_CFT2_NGO_Report.pdf
[168] en.wikipedia.org/wiki/Human_rights_in_Tibet#:~:text=They%20also%20include%20political-cal%20and,U.S.%20 State%20Department's%202009%20report.

their invasion was stopped. Three months after Sihanouk was removed, the northeastern third of Cambodia had been cleared of government troops. These territories were then turned over to the local insurgents. Meanwhile the Khmer Rouge established itself in the areas in the south and southwest where they operated on their own.

In April 1975 the Khmer Rouge had taken power and in January 1976 they established the Democratic Kampuchea. With this, two things occurred: 1.) a period of genocide and 2.) an invasion of 15,000 Chinese "military advisors" supported by substantial aid. Earlier, in 1975, the Cambodian leadership had met with Mao where they received Mao's blessings and advice. Mao also passed on to them his "Theory of Continuing Revolution under the Dictatorship of the Proletariat.

The Democratic Kampuchea did not last long as in January 1979 the now unified Vietnamese overthrew it and the Khmer Rouge fled into Thailand.

In 1981, after the Cambodian-Vietnamese War, the Khmer Rouge attempted to gain foreign support by renouncing communism.

Khmer Rouge on Education and Work

As mentioned earlier, the Khmer Rouge were a unique form of communism. Upon taking power, they immediately undertook a program of isolating the country from all foreign influences, closing hospitals, schools, and some factories. They abolished banking, finance and currency, and collectivized agriculture. They believed that after a period of self-imposed economic isolation and national self-sufficiency would stimulate the rebirth of the crafts and the country's latent industrial capability.

This included another evacuation of the major cities of Cambodia, continuing what had begun in the early 1970s. This time it was Phnom Pen and the other major cities. Initially subterfuges were used to encourage the urban population to evacuate their cities, but soon they turned to violence, threatening to execute those who refused and to burn down their houses. Then became another long march, but this time of the urban population into the country side, a veritable trail of tears in which thousands of children, elderly, and sick died.[169]

When the evacuees arrived in the villages to which they were assigned, they were forced to write essays that focused on their activities

---

[169] Kiernan, B. *How Pol Pot Came to Power: Colonialism, Nationalism, and Communism in Cambodia, 1930–1975*. (New Haven, CT: Yale University Press, 2004) pp. 251–310.

during the Khmer Republic Regime and this was used to determine their fate. Military officers and elite professions were sent for "re-education", which was in fact summary execution or a labor camp.[170] Engineers and others with special technical skills were quickly returned to the cities put to work restarting the factories, but everyone else was sent to agricultural communes to work in the peasants' now collectivized fields. The communist government expected that in this manner they could triple the productivity of the farms.

However, as it turned out, the city dwellers knew nothing about farming and famine was soon in the land. Communist ideology was such that picking wild fruit or berries, in order to survive, was seen as "private enterprise" and those who dared to do so were executed. Long hours and little food produced even more deaths. Execution became the common punishment for attempting to escape the collectivized farms or for minor breaches of rules and even if one was denounced.

Money being eliminated, the economy returned to barter. The economy became unworkable and began to collapse. This clearly shows that Engels theory that money was the source of all evil was wrong.

The Khmer Rouge also intruded into the traditional Cambodian family unit. The government imposed strict morality rules, prohibiting sex outside of marriage. Marriages required permission from the government and marriages were only permitted between people of the same class and the level of education. The party cadres were held to even stricter standards. The extended family concept was also attacked in favor of small units of parents and children.

Education in the Democratic Kampuchea was such that some have concluded that the Khmer Rouge actively sought to impose functional illiteracy on the people of Cambodia. Part of this comes from the fact that the Khmer Rouge sought to eliminate all traces of Cambodia's colonial past. In fact, the Khmer Rouge did provide an inconsistent primary education, but nothing beyond that. There were areas where the educational system was disrupted during the war and never re-established. It was by this means that they sought to gain complete control of the information the Cambodian people received so they could ensure the spreading of revolutionary culture among them.[171]

---

[170] Bergin, S. *The Khmer Rouge and the Cambodian Genocide*, (New York: Rosen, 2008) p. 31.
[171] Chigas, G., Mosyakov, D., Yale University Genocide Studies Program, "Literacy and Education under the Khmer Rouge, https://gsp.yale.edu/literacy-and-education-under-khmer-rouge

Some technical education was provided, but to select people favored by the Khmer Rouge. Indeed, there are recorded instances of people being executed because they boasted of having advanced educations.[172]

Khmer Crimes Against Humanity

The Khmer Rouge engaged in a purge of Cambodian society and arrested, tortured, and executed anyone who belonged to the group that one would best describe as "enemies of the people." Those people were:[173]

"• People with connections to former Cambodian governments, either those of the Khmer Republic or the Sangkum, to the Khmer Republic military, or to foreign governments.
"• Professionals and intellectuals, including almost everyone with an education and people who understood a foreign language. Many artists, including musicians, writers, and filmmakers were executed. In its practical implementation, this meant that if you wore glasses it was assumed that you did so because you could read and, therefore, were educated
"• Ethnic Vietnamese, ethnic Chinese, ethnic Thai and other minorities in the Eastern Highlands, Cambodian Christians (most of whom were Catholic), Muslims and senior Buddhist monks. The Roman Catholic Cathedral of Phnom Penh was razed. The Khmer Rouge forced Muslims to eat pork, which in Islam is forbidden. Many of those who refused were killed. Christian clergy and Muslim imams were executed.
"• 'Economic saboteurs' as many former urban dwellers were deemed guilty of sabotage because of their lack of agricultural ability.
"• Party cadres who had fallen under political suspicion: the regime tortured and executed thousands of party members during its purges.[174]"

Over 150 prisons were established for political opponents.

According to P. Heuveline, the most widely accepted estimates of excess deaths under the Khmer Rouge range from 1,500,000 million

---

[172] Vickery, M. *Cambodia 1975–82* http://michaelvickery.org/vickery1999cambodia.pdf p. 185
[173] Frey, R. J., *Genocide and International Justice*. (New York: Infobase Publishing, 2009) pp. 266–267.
[174] Jackson, K.D (1992). *Cambodia, 1975–1978: Rendezvous with Death*. (Princeton, NJ: Princeton University Press, 1992) p. 3.

to 2,000,000, but the broader scope of estimates range from 1,000,000 to 3,000,000.[175] Another academic source (citing research from 2009) indicates that execution may have accounted for as much as 60% of the total deaths and indicating that there are 23,745 known mass graves containing approximately 1,300,000 million suspected victims of execution.[176] There are many educated estimates, but P. Heuveline estimates that between 1,170,000 and 3.420,000 Cambodians died unnatural deaths between 1970 and 1979. These numbers include starvation, illness resulting from policies, and execution.

Marxism in Vietnam

Ho Chí Minh was born in the French protectorate of Annam. He was also one of the founding members of the French Communist Party. While living in France Ho was exposed to communism and became a dedicated socialist. He was involved with discussions relating to installing Bolshevism in Asia and even attempted to persuade French socialists to join Lenin's Communist International.

In 1930, he founded the Communist Party of Vietnam and in 1941, he returned to Vietnam and founded the Viet Minh independence movement. He led the August Revolution against the Japanese, who had occupied French Indochina in 1940, in an effort to liberate Vietnam. In August 1945 in an effort to gain the independence of the Democratic Republic of Vietnam.

In September the French returned to reclaim their former colony and the Viet Minh collaborated with the colonials to massacre supporters of the Vietnamese nationalist movements in 1945–1946, and of the Trotskyists. Trotskyism existed in Vietnam but did not rival Ho's party outside of the major cities, while particularly in the South, in Saigon and Cochinchina, they had been a challenge.

The Communists eventually suppressed all non-Communist parties, but they failed to secure a peace deal with France. In the final days of 1946, the Democratic Republic of Vietnam government found that war was inevitable. On December 19, 1946, Ho Chi Minh declared war

---

[175] Heuveline, P., (2001). "The Demographic Analysis of Mortality Crises: The Case of Cambodia, 1970–1979". *Forced Migration and Mortality*. (Washington, D.C.: National Academies Press, 2001) p. 105.

[176] Seybolt, T.B.; Aronson, J.D.; & Fischoff, B. *Counting Civilian Casualties: An Introduction to Recording and Estimating Nonmilitary Deaths in Conflict*. (Oxford, UK: Oxford University Press, 2013) p. 238.

against the French Union, beginning the Indochina War. It was a long war that ended in 1954, after the battle of Dien Bien Phu, where more than 10,000 French soldiers surrendered to the Viet Minh. Ho's victory was not complete as the south rebelled against him and subsequent negotiations resulted in the division of Vietnam into the communist North Vietnam and the anti-communist South Vietnam. The border between the two countries was the 17th Parallel and a demilitarized zone (DMZ) was established to keep the two apart.

Arthur Dommen estimates that the Viet Minh assassinated between 100,000 and 150,000 civilians during the war.[177] By comparison to Dommen's calculation, Benjamin Valentino estimates that the French were responsible for 60,000–250,000 civilian deaths. Adding to the issues, between 800,000 and 1,000,000 people migrated to the South, mostly Catholics out of fear for persecution for their religious beliefs.

Ho Chi Minh believed that in order for Vietnam to become a socialist nation, it had to transition through national liberation and then the establishment of a people's democratic regime. The national liberation was the elimination of French colonial rule, but the establishment of the people's democratic regime required the elements of feudalism, colonialism and imperialism that remained. Even though the people's democratic regime was established after that had been done, the private ownership of anything still needed to be addressed. The redistribution of land was an example of people's democracy.

Between 1953 and 1956, the North Vietnamese government instituted various agrarian reforms, including "rent reduction" and "land reform", which were accompanied by political repression. As had been experienced in the Soviet Union and China, there was significant resistance against the seizure of land from the peasants. The North Vietnamese government responded with executions, and it is estimated that about 13,500 peasants were executed because they refused to surrender their land.

Ho Chi Minh said that the basic economic tenets of a people's democratic regime was state ownership of certain segments of production - considered socialist since the state belongs to the people. Cooperatives, which had elements of socialism, were to transition into fully socialist economic organizations, and the economics of individual handicraft and peasantry developed into cooperatives, private capitalism and state

---

[177] Dommen, A. J., *The Indochinese Experience of the French and the Americans.* (Blomington, IN: Indiana University Press, 2001) p. 252.

capitalism. In these cooperatives, etc., the state shared capital with capitalists which would develop the country. There were, as a result, different types of ownership, which meant that the people's democracy could not be considered truly socialist.

From 1954 to 1975 the Vietnamese Communist Party (VCP) began working on socialism in North Vietnam and, as an extension of its Viet Minh heritage, a revolutionary and nationalistic struggle in the South which was aimed reunification.

In 1960 the Vietnamese Communist Party set out the way to socialist revolution in the North by simultaneously carrying out three revolutions: 1.) the revolution of production relationship, 2.) the revolution of science - technology and 3.) the revolution of ideology and culture. The science - technology revolution was key, and socialist industrialization was considered as a central task during the transition period.

It was also in 1960 that the North Vietnamese organized the Viet Cong (VC), whose objective was to foment an insurgency in South Vietnam that would lead to the reunification of the South with the North. The VC began a guerilla war in South Vietnam that would eventually lead to the US involvement in Vietnam. This reunification effort was, in essence, nationalism.

The VC were noted for the brutality of their campaign in the South. In 1961 the US State Department estimated that the VC were killing about 1,500 civilians per month.[178] In October 1964, U.S. officials in Saigon reported that from January to October 1964 the VC killed 429 Vietnamese local officials and kidnapped 482 others.[179] The victims ran from political officials to Catholic priests, to doctors and medical workers, and simple civilians. From 1967 to 1969 the VC and People's Army of North Vietnam, committed 36,000 and 68,000 murders.[180] It is estimated that 80% of these murders were of civilians and only 20% were of government officials, police, members of the self-defense forces or pacification cadres.[181] The methods used ranged from bombings and random shootings, to carefully aimed executions designed to intimidate and spread terror. For the VC terror was a tool to be used to weaken the support of the general population for the government. It was used to demonstrate that the South Vietnamese

---

[178] Pike, D., *The Viet-Cong Strategy of Terror* https://vva.vietnam.ttu.edu/images.php?img=/images/231/2311404008a.pdf p. 94.
[179] Ibid. p. 98.
[180] Bonds, R. *The Vietnam War: The Illustrated History of the Conflict in Southeast Asia.* (Lebanon, PA: Salamander Books Limited, 1979) p. 127.
[181] Ibid. p. 273.

government was incapable of protecting the population and drive a wedge between them.[182] According to D. Pike, it was used "almost exclusively [for the] control of the people." Two thirds of the citizens of Vietnam lived in villages and they were more exposed to the predations of the VC than the city dwellers because of their isolation. "All the [VC] programs contain elements of terror, not as a capricious addition, but as an integral part. In short, the communists operat[ed] a population control system resting in part on terror." He goes on to say that the "average communist in Vietnam thinks of his system not in moral, but in utilitarian terms. He finds terror to be the single greatest advantage he has over the government, one which he credits for making possible most of his successes."[183]

In interrogations of VC who had executed terrorist attacks, D. Pike quotes them as saying, in regard to killing civilians: "We never did it without reason. We advised people who worked with the government to stop. Some of them were very stubborn. We would warn them three times, but some refused to leave the government side. Since they stayed with the government, it meant they supported the government's fascist suppression efforts. So, they deserved to be punished for it."

The terrorist behavior of the VC has many examples. "For example, last month an armed propaganda team stopped a local school bus on a side road one morning and told the driver the children were not to attend school anymore. The driver conveyed this message to the parents who could not believe the communists were serious. The bussing continued until a few days later when the same team stopped the same bus, took off a little girl and cut off her fingers. The school has been closed since."[184]

As for assassination, there were 15 types of South Vietnamese that came within the scope of the assassination program. They were:[185]

1.) Enemy personnel in fields of espionage, police, public security, special forces psywar, including covert organizations.
2.) Members of reactionary political parties and organizations, and parties working behind a religious front (i.e., Dai Viets, VNQDD, Cao Dai, Hoa Hao).
3.) Members of enemy military and para-military organizations.
4.) Puppet government officials, from inter-family level upwards.
5.) Leading and key popular organization leaders, (i.e., village

---

[182] Pike, D., pp. 18-22.
[183] Pike, D. pp. 17-21.
[184] Pike, D. p. 29.
[185] Pike, D., pp. 30-31.

organizations such as farm cooperatives, women's and youth organizations, and trade unions).
6.) Members of the enemy's cultural, art, propaganda, and press establishment.
7.) Leading and key members of religious organizations still deeply superstitious (i.e., Catholics).
8.) Thieves, assassins, gangsters, prostitutes, speculators and fortune tellers.
9.) Defectors who have given information to the enemy, who have taken with them automatic weapons or important documents, or who are suspected of having done the same; or who were cadres or officers.
10.) Members of the exploiter class and their spouses, who have not specifically sided with the workers. (The communists in Vietnam as elsewhere divide society into exploiter and exploited.)
11.) Individuals with backward political tendencies, including those who do dishonest and corrupt deeds, try to justify them.
12.) Relatives of people engaged in enemy espionage, security, special forces or psywar organizations; relatives of important members or leaders of reactionary political parties or religious groups still deeply superstitious, families of military above the rank of private; members of families of government officials from the village level upwards.
13.) Relatives of people who have been punished by the Revolution (i.e., in earlier years) and who subsequently have grumbled about the Revolution; relatives of those jailed by the Revolution for spying.
14.) Deserters or AWOL's who have returned to the Revolution, but without clear explanation (i.e., who may be government penetration agents.)
15.) Individual with suspicious backgrounds or records of previous activity.

As can be seen there was a wide variety of individuals who could be completely innocent of any political activity, pro or con vis-à-vis the communists. They were innocents targeted solely for the purpose of intimidating others. This may seem purely theoretical, but if you examine the number of civilians executed by the VC and NVA at Hue in 1968 one finds it was not. The estimated death toll was between 2,800 and 6,000 **civilians and prisoners of war, or 5–10% of the total population of Hue.** Subsequent to the battle, the South Vietnamese government released a list of 4,062 victims identified as having been either murdered or abducted. Victims were in mass graves found bound, tortured, and sometimes buried alive

In 1970, while the American participation in the Vietnam war was winding down, the effects of the war had caused the Communist Party to start the initial step of the transition to a purely communist state by accumulating capital for industrialization and the transition from small scale production to large scale socialist production.

In 1975 the Vietnam War ended with the North occupying the South and completing the process of unification. On September 29, 1975, the 24th Conference of the Central Executive Committee set out to complete the unification of the country and move the country as quickly as possible to socialism. The situation in the south was still unstable and the North took a firm hand in dealing with the citizenry of the South. To this end the communists set up re-education camps.

The camps imprisoned from 200,000 to 300,000 former military officers, governmental workers, and supporters of the old regime, but the total may be as high as from 500,000 to 1,000,000.[186] The victims of the camps were called "war criminals" to justify their treatment.

The communist Vietnamese process of re-education was, in fact, both revenge and a method of repression and indoctrination. Torture was common and prisoners were held for periods ranging from a few weeks to as much as 18 years.

After occupying South Vietnam, in May 1975 the communist government ordered various groups of South Vietnamese to register. In June, the newly established government ordered those who had registered to go to various locations for re-education. Simple soldiers and non-commissioned officers of the South Vietnamese Army (ARVN) were sent to a three-day "reform study" after which they were sent home.

This was not a new process. In 1966 reform sessions were introduced by Northern cadres and subsequently became a standard institution in areas lightly controlled by the communists. "The magnitude of the effort is indicated by one captured document from the zonal level (roughly 10

---

[186] en.wikipedia.org/wiki/Re-education_camp_(Vietnam)#:~:text=Re%2Deducation%20 camps%20 (Vietnamese%3A,former%20government%20of%20South%20Vietnam.

provinces) in the Mekong Delta in which it was reported that 2,700 people in a three-month period had taken the district-level 'thought reform course.' The system employed with such people [was] as follows: He (or she) is persuaded to go voluntarily for a district level camp established for the specific purpose of thought reform. If he refuses, he is taken under guard. The 'classes" in the camp run from two weeks to a month, after which the individual, if reformed, is allowed to return home. If he indicates he is not 'reformed' he is run through the course again. If he still remains recalcitrant (and one wonders why he would not overtly go along with his captors) he [was] sentenced to jail at the provincial level. A person who is allowed to return home finds that his relatives have been notified ahead of his arrival that they will be held accountable for his behavior. This is the so-called double-hostage system, also employed in the military ranks (if a son serving in the communist forces deserts, his parents will be punished; if they do not support the cause, the son will suffer)."[187]

As for the post war re-education, the ARVN junior officers, 2nd lieutenant to captain, low ranking police officers and intelligence cadres were given orders to go to other locations and to bring with them 10 days of food, clothing, etc. for what would be a 10-day re-education process. Senior officials of the South Vietnamese government were ordered to bring 30 days provisions, etc., with them for their 30-day reeducation.

The terms indicated by these instructions were in fact a ruse. In the beginning of their re-education, which could run from a few weeks to a few months, the inmates were subjected to intensive political indoctrination. They were told that the American Imperials exploited the workers in other countries, they talked about the glory of hard work, and the gloated about their victory over the US.

In addition, the re-education included confessing of alleged misdeeds during the war. All inmates were required to write confessions, no matter how trivial, of those crimes. The former ARVN generals wrote about significant military operations, while mail clerks were told that they were guilting of aiding the "puppet war machinery." Priests were declared guilty of providing spiritual comfort and encouragement to the ARVN troops.

The indoctrination relating to labor was much in line with Lenin's thoughts on the subject and labor was required from all, particularly the rich, who had exploited the poor. The labor in the Vietnamese camps was much like that in Stalin's gulags. It included mine clearing, which killed

---
[187] Pike, D. p. 26.

and wounded many. Of course, there was the usual agricultural work, the digging of wells, clearing of jungle and even constructing the barracks in which they were to live. Work quotas were given and those who filed to meet them were shackled, brutally beaten by the camp guards, and placed in solitary confinement.

As in the gulags, there was little food and no medical care. As would be expected, the death rate was very high. The usual tropical diseases of malaria, beriberi and dysentery took a heavy toll and tuberculosis was not uncommon.

The inmates were prohibited books or magazines. They were forbidden to reminisce on their lives in the prior regime, harboring reactionary thoughts or having "superstitious" believes.

Infractions were brutally punished and punishments included being tied up in contorted positions, shacked in metal Conex boxes or dark cells, working extra hours, reduced rations and even beaten to death.

As for the development of the now unified Vietnam, the Vietnamese Communist Party (VCP) focused on the development of heavy industry and the collectivization of agriculture. Private businesses and private homes were seized by the government and their former owners were often sent to the New Economic Zones to clear land, often to uninhabited forested areas. Members of the VCP, the NVA or the former Viet Cong and their families shared the spoils and were given confiscated properties, often in downtown areas of cities and towns. As mentioned before, farmers were forced into state-controlled cooperatives. All food production was collectivized in the South as it had been in the North. Farmers and fishermen were forced to sell their goods to the government at very low prices that were set by the government. If they did not, they could not purchase farming supplies and fishing equipment. The movement of food and goods between provinces became a state monopoly and it was illegal for individuals to do so. As a result, as it had happened over and over again during the collectivization process in the other communist countries, food shortages soon appeared.

The SRVN government implemented a Stalinist dictatorship of the proletariat in the South as they did in the North. All religions had to be organized into state-controlled churches. Any negative comments about the Party, the government, Ho Chi Minh, or anything else that was critical of Communism could result in being designated as a "reactionary", with consequences ranging from harassment by the police, to expulsion from one's school or workplace, or imprisonment. Despite these controls, the Communist Party black markets flourished for food, consumer goods, and banned literature. In addition, a diaspora began that the SRVN government's security forces were unable to stop. Corruption of party officials appeared, as it had in China and other communist countries, and some security officials not only accepted bribes to turn a blind eye to various activities, but some also actually became involved with the organization of escape schemes.

The diaspora of Vietnamese grew so great that it is estimated that 2,500,000 (approximately 5% of the population of Vietnam) fled. Some went by sea and others through Cambodia.

By the mid-1980s, Vietnam's economy was in crisis. The government took some very pragmatic steps to soften its ideological approach to the economy with a number of economic and political reforms, once again demonstrating that communist economic theories led to failure. Private enterprise and foreign investment was encouraged, which revived the economy. By the late 1980's the party officially adopted the idea of a "market economy with [a] socialist orientation." Change began spreading and the government began making overtures to the United States to lift the embargo.

Behind the scenes, the Vietnamese government sent Washington signals that it was willing to compromise on many issues. It abandoned its claim for $3,500,000,000 in reconstruction aid, compensation for Agent Orange, and war crimes. It even agreed to pay off the old regime's debt of $146,000,000. By 1994 relations between the US and Vietnam had been re-established and Vietnam's economy started growing by up to 8.4% a year, and Vietnam was soon one of the world's biggest exporters of rice.

The old guard communists resisted much of this, but success is a strong argument. The new system greatly reduced poverty, there were primary schools in every community and secondary schools in most of them. A basic free healthcare system was also established. However, during the late 1990s, the World Bank offered Vietnam massive loans if it would sell its state-owned companies and cut its trade tariffs. These offers were rejected.

Despite this, the rate of change accelerated and in the 2000s the political balance shifted. Vietnam finally approved the sale of its state-owned companies. It also struck a trade deal with the US, and finally hit a peak in 2006 when it was given membership of the World Trade Organization, which meant more foreign investment and aid. Though the government is still nominally "communist" in nature, in fact it has abandoned all elements of communist rule and Vietnam has become fully integrated into the globalized capitalist economy. It had become very clear to the Vietnamese that the paradise promised by Marx, Engels, and Lenin was a chimera that delivered nothing but suffering and misery.

Chapter 6
Global Marxism

Fidel Castro's reputed form of Marxism was as a rejection of injustice in any form - political, economic, or social. It is very similar to the liberal democracy and Pan-Americanism of the liberator of the Spanish colonies of Latin America, Simón Bolívar. Castro's early socialism appeared to be similar to that of the French Revolution, but gradually it revealed itself as being fully Marxist, with a few exceptions. Lenin might well have called it a heresy, though it aimed to establish a purer form of Marxism in Cuba and railed against alleged American imperialism, a single-crop economy, and the low initial level of political and economic development. In fact, it followed all other Marxist countries and became a dictatorship for life with Fidel Castro being its leader. However, unlike most other Marxist countries it had a hereditary twist and when Fidel became ill in 2006 his brother Raúl Castro took the helm. Raúl was re-elected president on February 24, 2013. He then announced that he would not run for re-election after his second term. He was replaced by Miguel Díaz-Canel in 2018, but remained the First Secretary of the Communist Party, and was thus the *de facto* leader of the country. In 2021 he withdrew from politics and Miguel Díaz-Canel replaced him.

When Fidel Castro took power, he seized all the American industries, American bank accounts, and American owned agricultural land in Cuba and made them state property. The country's farms were collectivized.

Fidel also subscribed to the concept of international communism as he supported rebellions throughout South American, most notably with Che Guevara who was killed while trying to provoke a communist revolution in Bolivia and the fiasco in Zaire (Congo). Cuba's spreading of international communism was the function of the *Dirección General de Inteligencia* (DGI) in 1961 and was, in 1989, renamed the *Dirección General de Inteligencia* (DGI). It is the main state intelligence agency of the government of Cuba. It is responsible for all foreign intelligence collection and comprises six divisions divided into two categories, which are the Operational Divisions and the Support Divisions. It is responsible for intelligence, counterintelligence, and disinformation activities inside

Cuba and abroad.[188]

Cuban intervention included the 1975 dispatch of combat troops to support the communist People's Movement for the Liberation of Angola (MPLA) as it fought pro-western National Union for the Total Independence of Angola (UNITA) and National Liberation. Up to 55,000 Cuban troops fought in Angola in 1988. South African troops fought them and supported the UNITA forces, bring about a negotiated settlement.

The Military Units to Aid Production (UMAP) camps, the Cuban form of the Gulag, were created in 1964. They were used to hold those who applied for Cuban passports, enemies of Fidel Castro or his communist revolution, homosexuals, political dissidents, and religious minorities. These prisoners were forced to work for below minimum wages and cultivate agricultural fields. The great majority of laborers worked in sugarcane fields to boost sugar production. Prisoners were not only exposed to hard labor but also physical and emotional abuses.[189]

Cuba regularly imprisons activists and obstructs any organization that appeared to be or is in opposition to the government's activities. The range of repressive measures includes short-term arbitrary detention in the UMAP camps, official warnings, removal from jobs and housing, surveillance, harassment, intimidation, and forced exile.

Dissidents who publicly criticize the government risked serious consequences that ranged from wrongful arrests and potential prosecutions to the loss of their homes and sources of income, as well as the significant emotional costs wrought by so-called repudiations, and through forced exile. Repercussions include actions against the activists' family members.

Then there was how Cuba handled AIDS victims. Anyone who was infected with AIDS from 1986 to 1994 about 10,000 Cubans were involuntarily sent to sanatoriums

Even though the Pope was allowed to visit in 1998, and twice subsequently, the activities of religious leaders and their followers are closely monitored. Actions are also taken against members of independent political parties, teachers, medical professionals, artists, and activists of all types who are seen as potential problems. In sum, all "enemies of the people" who are or may be "counterrevolutionaries" are closely monitored.

The extrajudicial executions that have occurred under the

---

[188] en.wikipedia.org/wiki/Direcci%C3%B3n_de_Inteligencia#:~:text=The%20Intelligence%20Directorate%20(Spanish%3A%20Direcci%C3%B3n,of%20the%20government%20of%20Cuba.

189 Institutional Digital Archive: "Cuba's Unresolved UMAP History: Survivors' Struggles to Counter the Official Story", https://ida.mtholyoke.edu/handle/10166/4039.

Communist rule of Cuba are reported to number 10,723.[190]

Communism in Venezuela

Hugo Chavez, the leader of the United Socialist Party (PSUV), was elected president of Venezuela in 1998. Though s communist he ran in the democratic elections held by Venezuela and won the office by a majority of the votes. This is most unusual for a communist takeover, as you can see, since there was no armed insurrection against an "oppressive" capitalist government. He ran on a program that he called the "Bolivarian Revolution" which was named after Simón Bolívar, a Venezuelan revolutionary leader, whose revolution won the independence of most of northern South America from Spanish rule. According to Chávez and other supporters, the Bolivarian Revolution sought to build an inter-American coalition to implement Bolivarianism, nationalism, and a state-led economy. The idea of a state-led economy was very Marxist, but nationalism was an anathema to Lenin though Marx had little to say about it. Indeed, nationalism is a key element of fascism, which truly makes Chauvez's communism a hybrid.

The central points of Bolivarianism as presented by Chávez are the following:[191]

- Latin American economic and political sovereignty (anti-imperialism);
- Grassroots political participation of the population via popular votes and referendums (participative democracy);
- Economic self-sufficiency (in food, consumer durables and so on);
- Instilling in people a national ethic of patriotic service;
- Equitable distribution of (South America's) vast natural resources;
- Eliminating corruption.

Chavez's first step was to introduce a new constitution that called for a socialist economy and socialist policies that were to be funded by Venezuela's oil industry. Not only were the foreign owned oil facilities nationalized, but there was also land reform. In 2001, laws were passed that focused on redistribution of the land and wealth of the rich and from

[190]https://www.aei.org/carpe-diem/counting-victims-of-the-castro-regime-nearly-11000-to-date/
[191]en.wikipedia.org/wiki/Bolivarianism#:~:text=The%20term%22Bolivarianism%22%20is%20often,political%20sovereignty%20(anti%2Dimperialism)

private companies to the Venezuelan poor. His programs included various anti-poverty activities that included the distribution of food, a vaccination campaign, and improvements in the educational system in the country's slums. In addition, Chavez concentrated all political and economic power in the hands of the state. In 2005 he began implementing his land reform program by seizing large estates and dividing the land up among the rural poor.

Chavez's programs were very popular among the mass of the Venezuelan public, and he won his third election to the presidency in 2006 with 63% of the vote.

Feeling that he had a mandate, he then undertook the nationalization of key energy and telecommunication companies with the approval of parliament. Initially Exxon Mobile and Conoco-Philips resisted this, but their facilities were eventually expropriated.

He continued the process of the state takeover of private property, industry, and the banks, when in 2008 he seized the Bank of Venezuela.

After being president for 14 years, Chavez died in March 2013 and was replaced by Nicolas Maduro, who before the Chavez take over had been a bus driver. Having no particular education, running a national economy was far beyond Maduro's intellectual capabilities. The seizure of the oil industry and the assumption that the Venezuelans had the technical skills and managerial skills necessary to operate it, coupled with massive corruption by communist party officials, collapsed the economy. It is true that part of the problem was due to the normal variations in oil prices on the world market did not help the situation, but the fundamental problem was mismanagement, corruption, and theft.

As a result, Venezuela fell into its worst-ever economic crisis that included hyperinflation and a shortage of food and basic necessities.

The stories of suffering in Venezuela under Maduro are numerous. Starvation was rampant as nobody could afford food. The minimum wage is $50 per month, and price controls have caused goods of every sort, and particularly food, to vanish from the shelves of stores. There are stories of the poor turning their children out on the streets because they could not afford to feed them, and they hoped that those who had food would feed them. Sadly, even the orphanages are overflowing with children and the government is not providing them with the supplies they need. All the animals in the zoos were killed and eaten. Thousands fled Venezuela to Columbia where they hoped to find work and be able to feed themselves and their families. Infant mortality has doubled because there is no food to feed them. If you need hospitalization, you need your own medication and medical supplies if you want to be treated. Every sort of drug from antibiotics, insulin, and other medications are extremely scarce. Of course, many also migrated north and entered the United States. It is reported that 7,300,000 Venezuelans have fled in this diaspora.

Torture in Venezuela is nothing new and abuse of political dissidents and opponents had existed before the Maduro presidency, but under him it increased. The SEBIN, the Venezuelan secret police, are headquartered at La Tumba (the Tomb) Prison, which should give an idea of the nature of the activities that occur in it. Indeed, every known form of torture is practiced there.

As a response to this, in December 2014, the United States implemented the Venezuela Defense of Human Rights and Civil Society Act which imposed targeted sanctions on Venezuelan individuals responsible for human rights violations.

The United Nations Committee Against Torture called Venezuela before it to examine cases of torture reported to have happened between 2002 and 2014. The commission expressed its concerns over reports of "beatings, burnings, and electric shock [being used] in an effort to extract confessions. Sadly, only five individuals were charged as a result of these hearings. The Venezuelan Government ignored all requests and as a result, the UN Special Rapporteur on Torture, Juan E. Méndez concluded, on March 11, 2015 "that the government violated the rights of prisoners" and went on to say that the Maduro government failed "with the obligation to investigate, prosecute and punish all acts of torture and cruel, inhuman or degrading treatment".

During the 2017 Venezuelan protests, more than 290 cases of torture and thousands of extrajudicial executions were documented by the Organization of American States. "Venezuelan human rights project Lupa por La Vida documented more than 700 alleged extrajudicial executions between January and November 2022 alone. In September 2022 the FFM warned that patterns of detention, torture and other violations continue 'as part of a plan orchestrated at the highest levels of the government to repress dissent through crimes against humanity.'"[192]

---

[192] Global Centre for the Responsibility to Protect: https://www.globalr2p.org/countries/venezuela/

North Korea

Once again, we find some similarities between the leaders of communist countries and ideology. Kim Il-sung was, according to experts, born into a middle-class Presbyterian family. Though they were not rich, they lived comfortably and were never close to living in dire poverty. His father was a teacher and senior cleric of their church. Kim Il-sung's parents were active in anti-Japanese activities. His mother founded the Anti-Japanese Women's Association, and his father founded the Korean National Association (KNA), an underground brotherhood of anti-imperialist insurgents and guerilla fighters. The KNA was the largest such organization in all of Korea.

Kim Il-sung's father also filled him with stories about Vladimir Lenin and the events of the October Revolution. This was the source of his desire to establish a socialist society modeled after the Soviet Union.[193]

Kim Il-sung was born to the anti-Japanese fight and Japanese Imperialism, which as time pass easily converted into anti-capitalist-Imperialism and then anti-Americanism.

The Communist Party of Korea (CPK) was founded in Seoul in 1925. It became the Korean section of the Communist International at the 6th Congress of the International in August–September 1928. Shortly later it was disbanded by the Comintern because of feuds within its ranks. The CPK scattered and some joined the Chinese Communist Party (CCP) in China in it fight against the Japanese.

When WWII ended, the Communist Party leader Pak Hon-yong, who had been a resistance fighter, became active in Seoul upon his release and organized a Central Committee, of which he was Secretary.

The Soviets had been fighting the Japanese in Manchuria and had a large army there, which after the end of the war, pushed into northern Korean. The Soviets then made use of ethnic Korean communists and one, Kim Il-sung, who had fled to the USSR and become a captain in the Soviet Army, arrived in Pyongyang just as the Soviets were looking for a suitable puppet to assume the leadership of North Korea.

The North Korea Bureau of the Communist Party of Korea (CPK) was established on October 13, 1945. In theory it was under the control of the Seoul based party leadership, but there was little contact between the

---

[193] C. Rivers Editors, *Kil-Il-sung : The Controversial Life and Legacy of North Korea's First Supreme Leader* (Monee, IL: C. Rivers Editors, 2022) This work has no page numbers to reference.

two groups. The North Korean Bureau (MKB) worked closely with the Soviet Civilian Authority and began entrenching itself.

Though membership in the CPK was theoretically available to any Korean, in fact only those with respectable roots, glittering qualifications, standards of reliability, and sufficient political loyalty were accepted. Those that made the cut became the state's elite and their job was linked with a lengthy list of benefits, including prioritized housing, better food rations, education, and healthcare.[194]

Kim Young-born, the first chairman of the NKB had worked closely with the Soviets and in the 1930s had been sent into Korea to conduct guerilla warfare against the Japanese. Kim Il-sung, then a member of the Bureau, replaced him as chairman in December 1945.

Kim Il-sung was a noted admirer of Stalin and this had come to the attention of the Soviets. It made him the ideal leader for them to support as they looked to spread communism throughout the world.[195]

On July 22, 1945, the NKB joined with the New People's Party, the Democratic Party and the Chondoist Chongu Party (supporters of an influential religious movement) to form the North Korean Fatherland United Democratic Front. Though initially separate entities, on July 29, 1946, the New People's Party and the NKB merged and formed the Workers Party of North Korea. Kim Il-sung did not hold a major position in this organization at that time.

The New People's Party was mostly formed of intellectuals while the Communist Party was mainly based amongst workers and peasants. As in the earliest days of communism in Korea, disputes and feuds existed in this newly organized party. Some of this was a result of the discussions on the role of Marxism-Leninism as the ideological foundation of the party. During inaugural congress of the party, Kim Il-sung stated that "...the Workers Party is a combat unit and the vanguard of the working masses. We must fight with our utmost to maintain the Party's purity, unity, and iron discipline. If we were to fight against the enemy without meeting these conditions within our ranks, it would be nothing less than folly", arguing in favor of maintaining a Marxist–Leninist orientation.[196]

The remainder of the Communist Party of Korea, still functioning in the southern areas, worked under the name of Communist Party of South Korea. The party merged with the New People's Party of South Korea and

---

[194] Ibid.
[195] Ibid.
[196] Chong-Sik Lee, *Politics in North Korea: Pre-Korean War Stage,* (UK: Cambridge University Press, 2009) p. 14.

the fraction of the People's Party of Korea to found the Workers Party of South Korea on November 23, 1946. It was outlawed in South Korea, so it formed clandestine cells and gathered a large following.

When the communists took over North Korea they began the usual process of redistribution of the land, taking it from the landlords and distributing it to the landless peasants. This process caused the ex-landlords and another 400,000 "malcontents to flee to the south.

In 1947 the party initiated armed guerrilla war in the south to prevent a separate South Korean state from being formed. The struggle did not go well and much of the leadership was forced to move to Pyongyang. The party was opposed to the formation of a South Korean state and in 1948 it started general strikes in opposition to its formation.

On June 30, 1949, the Workers' Party of North Korea and the Workers' Party of South Korea merged, forming the Workers' Party of Korea, at a congress in Pyongyang. Kim Il-sung became the party Chairman and Pak Hon-yong and Alexei Ivanovich Hegay became vice chairmen.[197]

The next major event was the Korean War, which began on June 25, 1950 and ended on July 27, 1953. Kim Il-sung launched his invasion in the hopes of unifying all of Korea under his rule. Among his first acts when he occupied Soeul was to purge the "class enemies", being any capitalist, banker, etc., that they could find. In addition, of the South Korean soldiers that were trapped north of Soeul, none were ever seen again. To be fair, there were massacres on both sides as the South Koreans began killing known or suspected communists.

The UN organized a force to defend South Korea and as a result of the landings at Incheon the North Koreans were pushed back into North Korea. The UN forces pushed them to the area of the Chinese border and China responded by sending in their army. The Chinese pushed the UN forces south and soon a stalemate evolved. Negotiations began and ended in an armistice. Technically, North Korea is still at war, as no peace treaty has ever been signed. The Korean War dominated the first five years of the WPK's rule.

At this time, Kim Il-sung was the acknowledged leader, but he did not yet have absolute power. Even though the war was raging he resorted to the usual process of purges and initially attacked those individuals who threatened his control. A plethora of trumped up charges and lies about his opponents provided Kim Il-sung with the basis for the removals.

---

[197] Lee, Chong-Sik. "Evolution of the Korean Workers' Party and the Rise of Kim Chŏng-il." *Asian Survey*, Vol 22 (Berkeley, CA: University of California Press, 1982) pp. 434–448.

Shortly after the signing of the armistice ~~12~~ twelve leaders of the domestic faction were subjected to a show trial and executed or sent to forced labor. They were accused of being US agents, sabotage, assassination, and even planning a coup.

Kim Il-sung's 3 Year Plan of 1954-1956 began. It was followed by the 5 Year Plan of 1957-1961 and his 7 Year Plan of 1961-1967 followed. "All three were aimed at rehabilitating the industrial production and the development of city infrastructure in the hope of restoring them to pre-war levels, or at least to bring back some level of order and stability."[198]

In 1953, with the death of Stalin, Kim Il-sung dumped the creeds of communism and socialism and redirected all his efforts on rebuilding the Korean national identity and establishing his cult of personality, which was pushed with a tightly run propaganda program. This process required the North Korean authorities to devote he last years of the 1950's to uprooting the foundation of Soviet influence, while treading carefully to avoid their wrath. Stalin's portrait was removed from all public spaces. Songs that were devoted to the CPSU were modified to pay homage to the party. Kim Il-sung worked to raise the idea of North Korean supremacy and Stalin was reduced to an "honorable figure" who kowtowed to the Great Leader Kim Il-sung.[199]

In 1955 Kim Il-sung introduced the idea of "Juche". In 1965, in another speech, he introduced its three principles of "independence in politics," "self-sustenance in the economy" and "self-defense in national defense." This was followed with more and more Maoist ideas, such as the concept of self-regeneration, appearing in official communications. The first application of Juche was in the 1956-1961 Five-Year Plan, which focused on the economic development of North Korea and focused on heavy industry. In that sense, it followed both the Soviet Union and China in over-emphasizing industry and under-emphasizing agriculture.

In the 1960's Marxist-Internationalism morphed into a radical nationalism riddled with ethnocentric undertones. By 1962 all marriages between foreigners and locals were no longer recognized and any future interracial union was forbidden. North Korea rejected any invitation from international conferences, which exacerbated the concerns among the rest of the world. All information that reached outside was filtered through the carefully controlled government. Indeed, all literature inside North

---

[198] C. Rivers Editors, *Kil-Il-sung : The Controversial Life and Legacy of North Korea's First Supreme Leader* (Monee, IL: C. Rivers Editors, 2022).
[199] Ibid.

Korea was purged and books by Lenin Engels, Marx, and other communist philosophers vanished from the shelves of the libraries. They were replaced solely by the works of Kim Il-sung.

It was at this time that the *songbun* classification system was instituted. It divided the North Koreans into three principal brackets: the "core," the "wavering," and the "hostile classes." These were then broken down into 51 sub-classes. Of course, the most prestigious was the ruling class or the "core.", which consisted of the Kim family, both immediate and extended. It also included veteran freedom fighters who had risked their lives for the cause, party members, loyalists, and other "national treasurers." The majority of the masses, the lowly laborers, farmers, merchants, and other member of the peasantry formed the wavering class.

The lowest class, the "Hostile" class consisted of actual criminals, Japanese apologists, party traitors, malefactors who committed "crimes against the states" and anyone who disobeyed Kim Il-sung. It also included former landowners, aristocrats, esteemed intellectuals, and religious leaders who were to be punished for having enjoyed privileges during the Japanese colonial era.

The *songbun* was an hereditary cast system and all children and future generations of those who belonged to the hostile class were condemned forever to hard lives of farming and mining for no pay.

Another control mechanism instituted by Kim Il-sung was the "Public Distribution System." This established the amount and quality of necessities and, particularly, food. It also extended to material goods. It was an almost Pavlovian system of control over the masses and it motivated a fawning obedience to every whim of the Great Leader.

In 1967 Kim Il-sung instituted the "Monolithic Ideological System." This ended all forums for debate within the party to stamp out the existing discord. This was followed with the removal of Geum-Cheol, Kim's rival, along with his associates from all their posts. They were spared execution, but they were accused of many crimes and spend the rest of their lives working in state-owned factories in remote regions of North Korea.[200]

It now became imperative for Kin Il-sung to expand this Monolithic Ideological System with a new program that he called "10 Principles for the Establishment of the One-Ideology System. It consisted of 10 articles and 65 clauses. The first principle reads: "We must give our all in the struggle to unify the the entire society with the revolutionary ideology of the Great Leader, Kim Il-sung."

---

[200] Ibid.

The second principal ordered everyone to "honor the Great Leader Comrade, Kim Il-sung with all [their] loyalty. Another principle reads: "We must make absolute the authority of the Great Leader Comrade Kim Il-sung." The final principle read: "We must pass down the great achievement of the revolution by the Great Leader Comrade.... from generation to generation, inheriting and completing it to the end." Thus, a nominally communist nation became an hereditary monarchy.

In 1975, when it became necessary to identify a successor to Kim Il-sung, it was determined that Kim Jong-il, who had been blindly obedient to his family and long associated with the party, was the ideal candidate.

At this point is is appropriate to talk about some of Kim Il-sung's personal behavior. He had what was called the "*Kippumjo*" or pleasure brigade. Yes, it was a means for him to satisfy his physical needs, but it also allowed him to exhibit his "supreme and sexual power." The members of this brigade were, in fact, concubines and the country was scoured to find the most beautiful girls to populate. Some of them were noted for their dancing and singing skills and then there was the "satisfaction team." Kim Il-sung was apparently generous with the ladies' favors and allowed his men to indulge. The women were on-call 24 hours a day.[201]

The women who were brought into this organization had no choice and if they refused the pleasure they went to the labor camps. On the other hand, a member of the brigade received better housing, food rations, health care, and other things that they would have never otherwise had access to. Service in this brigade was for 7 years, and the ladies retired from it at age 25.

As death approached Kim Il-sung became desperate. He arranged regular blood transfusions from robust young men, believing that this young blood would reverse the inevitable course of aging. He died in 1994, despite these ludicrous treatments.

The 65 clauses expanded and clarified the 10 principles. Article 3.6 reads: "Portraits, plaster figures, bronze statues, emblems of the respected and beloved Great Leader ... publications that include the Great Leader's portrait, and works of art symbolizing the Great Leader" were now to be treated with the meticulous care and reverence that in the West would be given to priceless works of art. An example of how these portraits are handled is demonstrated by the death of Otto Warmbier after he attempted to steal a North Korean propaganda poster.

---
[201] Ibid.

Twin Evils

Otto Warmbier was a student from Wyoming, Ohio, who was on a trip to North Korea. He was arrested for taking the poster in 2015. He was sentenced to 15 years hard labor. Shortly later he fell into a coma as a result of an undisclosed circumstance. In fact, he was brutally beaten several times. In 2017 the North Koreans released a statement saying that his neurological situation was the result of botulism and a sleeping pill. He returned to the US. Shortly later a US federal court found the North Korean government liable for his torture and death.

The reputation of the North Korean gulag was such that the people submitted rather than object to the new state of affairs.

As is typical, corruption at every level of the government now grew to heretofore unknown levels. Bribery became commonplace, but there was no bribe sufficient to allow someone to escape punishment for mocking the Great Leader.

The 10 Principles became an integral part of the North Korean educational system at every level and everyone was expected to memorize them by heart. To reinforce this, bi-weekly mandatory "evaluation" meetings were required, and no one was exempted.

Kim Il-sung also established what he called "group think." This was intended to eliminate any independent thought and was intended to establish a statewide collective thought. Concurrently, all civic organizations, alumni associations, and public groups in general were now banned. This went so far as to ban the Worker's Party from meeting secretly so that they could not plot against Kim.

The Principles were followed by more and more draconian laws. North Koreans were prohibited from leaving North Korea. It was common for one to spend their entire life in their hometown and to have never gone to another city without a state-issued permit.

All forms of music, excluding patriotic hymns and anthems were dedicated to Kim Il-sung. A ban on interracial relationships and marriages were banned, as they had been in Nazi Germany.

It is worthy of note that Kim Il-sung and Kim Jung Il were involved in a constant struggle to seize and retain absolute control of the government. The latest in the Kim Dynasty, Kim Jung On undertook to secure his control of the North Korean government by removing the threat to his control posed by his half-brother Kim Jong-nam, who he had assassinated, on February 13, 2017, at Kuala Lumpur International Airport in Malaysia.[202] For all its claims of progressiveness and evolution into a modern society focused on

---

[202] https://en.wikipedia.org/wiki/Assassination_of_Kim_Jong-nam.

the needs of the people, this was little more than a medieval elimination of a potential rival for the throne. This is quite similar to the disappearance of the two princes, who were rivals to Edward V for the throne of England in 1483. Rivals to the throne must be eliminated.

Juche Philosophy

Juche is the official state ideology of North Korea and the Worker's Party of Korea. It was conceptualized by Kim Il-sung. It was initially a variant of Marxism-Leninism, but Kim Il-sung's son, Kim Jung-il declared it a distinct ideology in the 1970's and expanded it subsequently by making ideological breaks from Marxism-Leninism. Though it incorporates the historical materialist ideas of Marx, it emphasizes the individual and nationalism. Those who study it call it variously a quasi-religion or a nationalistic ideology.

It finds its roots in the Korean right to throw off Japanese imperialism and it evolved into a cult of personality, focusing on Kim Il-sung as the "Great Leader" or the "Dear Leader."

The concept of Juche is that the North Korean government the master of revolution and reconstruction of North Korea. It entails holding fast to an independent position, rejecting dependence on others, using one's own brains, believing in one's own strength, displaying the revolutionary spirit of self-reliance, and thus solving one's own problems for oneself on one's own responsibility under all circumstances.

It believes that man dominates the world and transforms it and that the world is made of material and ceaselessly changes and develops. "On the basis of man's essential qualities, which distinguish[es] man radically from all other material beings and man's outstanding position and role as the master of the world capable of transforming the world are to be clarified. Only on the basis of man's essential qualities as a social being with independence, creativity and consciousness scientifically clarified by the Juche philosophy has the basic principle that man is the master of the world and plays a decisive role in transforming the world been clarified."

And further on we read: "Marxist philosophy established socio-historical view of dialectical materialism, historical materialism, through the application of the general law of the development of the material world to social history. Of course, we [Kim Jung-il] do not deny the historic merit of historical materialism. Historical materialism made an important contribution to defeating the reactionary and unscientific socio-historical view which was based on idealism and metaphysics. In addition, since man lives in the objective material world and society is inseparably linked with nature, the general law of the development of the material world acts on social phenomena. However, if you overlook the social movement being governed by its own law and apply the general law of the development of the material world mechanically to social phenomena, you cannot avoid acquiring [a] one sided understanding of social history." [203]

"The social movement is the movement of man who dominates and transforms the world. Man transforms nature to dominate and transform the objective material world. By transforming nature man creates material wealth and [the] material conditions for his life. Transforming nature and creating material wealth is the endeavor to satisfy people's social demands and this work can only be one through people's social cooperation. People transform society to improve and perfect the relations of social cooperation. It is man who transforms both nature and society. While transforming nature and society man transforms and develops himself continuously. The domination and transformation of nature, society, and himself, and the popular masses are the motive force of this undertaking. The popular masses are the motive force of this undertaking. The popular masses create all the material and cultural wealth of society and develops social relations." [204]

Then we have this: "The fundamental difference between the Juche philosophy and the preceding philosophy [Marxism] results, in the final analysis, from a different understanding of man.

"The Marxist philosophy defined the essence of man as the ensemble of social relations, but it failed to correctly expound the characteristics of man as a social being. The preceding theory explained the principle of the social movement mainly on the basis of the general law of the development of the material world, because it failed to clarify the essential qualities of social man. For the first time, the Juche philosophy gave a perfect elucidation of the unique qualities of man as a social being." [205] This is the essence of Juche in Kim Hong Il's words.

The goal of Juche is to establish a self-reliant state that independently determines its political, economic, and military affairs. It focuses on

---

[203] Kim jong-il, "The Juche Philosophy is an Original Revolutionary Policy", Discourse published in Kuiloja, *Theoretical Magazine of the Central Committee of the Workers' Party of Korea*, July 26, 1996 taken from *Essential Juche Works*, (Red Flame Press, work lacks all publication data), p.3.
[204] Ibid, p. 4.
[205] Ibid, p. 4.

self-sufficiency and self-defense as a path to consolidating the political independence of North Korea, building a solid independent national economy that will assure reunification of the two Koreas, independence and prosperity. Indeed, is extremely focused on the reunification of South Korea with North Korea. Kim Il Sung made his radical nationalism a principal element of Juche and much time is spent in his various writings on reuniting all Korean people, who have a common heritage and history, under one flag, his flag. Of course, the Korean War was the first effort of Juche to bring about this reunification.

It is appropriate at this time to make a small diversion from the discussion of Juche to point out that the North Korean system was such a failure that beginning in 1995, the United States has provided North Korea with over 1.1 billion in assistance, about 60 of which has paid for food aid.

In theory Juche stresses equality and mutual respect among nations. It asserts that every state has the right to self-determination. However, there was an underlying element is Korean nationalism. In reading Kim Jung-il's *On Preserving the Juche Character and National Character of the Revolution and Construction*, and *National Reunification*[206] there is a tremendous nationalistic element in the Juche philosophy. This is in stark contrast to Marx, Engels, and Lenin's approach to communism. Indeed, nationalism is the central element of fascism. This manifests itself in *National Reunification* and other works by Kim Jung-il, there is a constant tirade about the necessity to incorporate South Korea into North Korea. Indeed, the emotion and nature of this work causes one to believe that there will be yet another invasion of South Korea by the North.

It looks on economic self-sufficiency as a principal eminent necessary to achieve political independence. Kim Il Sung saw excessive foreign aid as a threat to a country's ability to develop its socialist economy and that only a strong economy could do permit socialism to develop. This was followed, logically, with a drive for technological independence and self-sufficiency in resources. As for North Korea's self-sufficiency in resources, it has few resources to support an industrial state. It also as so little arable land that it has, over its existence, suffered from frequent famines.

National survival has been seen as a driving issue in North Koran diplomacy to the point of paranoia. That said, national survival is

---

[206] Kim jong-il, "The Juche Philosophy is an Original Revolutionary Policy", *On Preserving the Juche Character and National Character of the Revolution and Construction, June 19, 1997.* pp. 18-43. And *National Reunification,* pp. 97-175.

inextricably linked with the survival of the rule of the Kim family. As it watched the Warsaw Pact countries fall away from socialism and institute market reforms, the Kim dynasty instituted a re-emphasis on Juche in theory and practice. The collapse of the Eastern Block's communist economies is seen as a threat to the North Korean state and the rule of the Kim family, which is based on the viability of its socialist economy.

"Unlike Marxism-Leninism, whose basic idea is that the development of the material condition of production and the exchange of goods as the driving force of historical progress, Juche looks on the human as the driving force in history, which it summarizes as the "popular masses are placed in the center of everything, and the leader (Kim Il Sung) is the center of the masses." In this "man-centered ideology" man is the master of everything and makes all decisions. In contrast to Marxism-Leninism, which states that man's decisions are the results of their relations to the means of production, it is the position of Juche that the masses may consider their relationship to the means of production but are independent of it. It believes that history is governed by laws, but that it is man who drives history. It goes on to state that in order for the masses to be successful they need a "Great Leader."

Juche stands against individualism and, as a result, it advocates conformity among the masses. Kim Jung-il says, in *Giving Priority to the Ideological Work is Essential for Accomplishing Socialism:* "Bourgeois and all other outmoded reactionary ideas are based on individualism. Exploitive societies were all based on individualism and the people in these societies were tainted with individualism for thousands of years. Individualism is an obstinate, conservative idea which is deeply rooted in people's consciousness, customs, and lives. Even in socialist society, individualism and other outmoded ideas persist to a great deal and, when even small chances present themselves, these ideas will sprout again and spread far and wide.

"Socialist ideology is a new ideology, fundamentally different from all kinds of outmoded ideas, which are based on individualism. The work of contradicting socialist ideology is an ideology revolution to radically change the ideological lives. It can only be done through tireless and positive ideological education and ideological struggle."[207]

This is to say that the individual must sacrifice himself for the greater good and to achieve this the state requires massive and continual

---

[207] Kim jong-il, "The Juche Philosophy is an Original Revolutionary Policy", *Giving priority to the Ideological work is Essential for accomplishing Socialism,* pp. 29-30.

propaganda.

Further on we find in the same document: "However, progressive ideas can never develop freely in capitalist society, where the means of propaganda and education such as mass media are in the hands of monopoly capitalists and reactionary rulers. The reactionary bourgeois ruling class tolerates progressive ideas to some extent, to make capitalist society seem democratic, but when they are considered the slightest threat to its ruling system, it mercilessly suppresses them. Outwardly, different thoughts appear to be tolerated in capitalist society, but all kinds of thought throughout it are, without exception, none other than various forms and expressions of bourgeois ideology. The 'freedom' of ideology talked about by imperialists is a deceptive slogan to dress up under the signpost of 'freedom' their oppression of progressive ideas in capitalist societies and their resorting to every method of propagate reactionary bourgeois ideas. It is a deceptive slogan to justify their ideological and cultural infiltration into other countries.

"Only in socialist society, where exploitation, oppression and antagonisms have been eliminated, can all members of society be equipped with a single ideology, because of their common purpose, aspirations and interests. Only then can a single ideology prevail. Socialist ideology is a scientific ideology which reflects man's intrinsically independent nature and throws light on how to realize the masses' independence. It is only natural that the popular masses accept it as their own ideology. It is only when they are fully equipped with socialist ideology that the popular masses can shape their destiny independently and creatively and accomplish socialism."[208]

It is clear from all this that this "education" that is necessary to purge the natural urges of individualism from the North Korean people is mass brain-washing and acceptance of is made mandatory by the combination of a militarized state and a system of informants ready to relate to the leadership any deviation from the party line. Clearly no different of thought is acceptable and, in fact, this ideology is inculcated into the North Korean people from birth.

This is done by media, art, and literature. "The media and art and literature are powerful ideological weapons for education, organizing, and mobilizing the masses.

---

[208] Kim jong-il, "The Juche Philosophy is an Original Revolutionary Policy", *Giving priority to the Ideological work is Essential for accomplishing Socialism,* p. 52.

Twin Evils

"In socialist society, the media, art, and literature and all other ideological and cultural channels must fully serve the purpose of defending and advancing socialism to meet the masses' desire for independence, under the party's leadership. If ideological and cultural channels depart from the guidance and control of the working-class party in socialist society, they will be used as counter- revolutionary instruments....." "The working-class party must keep the media, art, and literature, and other ideological and cultural channels under tight control. It must steadily enhance their role so that they all creditability fulfil their mission and duty on the socialist ideological front."[209]

Then there is: The socialist state must adopt administrative and legal measures to protect the socialist system and people from the infiltration of imperialist ideology and culture." Again, any individualism is prohibited, and this prohibition is enforced by "administrative and legal measures." This means the North Korean gulag and it is reinforced by the following: "In our country today, a well-regulated system whereby the part, people, and army all study has been set up and is run in a regular way. All members of society regularly take part in study sessions, public lectures, and other collective study sessions *without exception*, and study in earnest. Study has become daily routine for people and a social attitude in our country."[210]

Then we find the concept of the "Great Leader." According to Juche the Great Leader is indispensable, he is the mastermind who will lead the masses in the class struggle and will guide them through the difficult tasks and the necessary revolutionary changes to achieve the socialist dream. It goes on to declare that the Great Leader is flawless and incorruptible and will never commit any mistake; that he is always benevolent and rules for the masses. For this to be successful, the Great Leader must be supported by a unitary ideological system, i.e. Juche.

Kim Il-Sung was treated as an almighty and all-knowing divinity. He was faultless and a perfect being that was the only man capable of leading the entire nation.

In the early days of Juche, it was used to rationalize the state's decision to sever all ties with the outside world. North Korea became totally isolated from any outside influence.

Kim Il-sung preyed on the people's paranoia and his state promoted the idea of "us against them." The North Koreans were kept in a permanent

---
[209] Kim jong-il, "The Juche Philosophy is an Original Revolutionary Policy", *Giving priority to the Ideological work is Essential for accomplishing Socialism,* p. 64.
[210] Kim jong-il, "The Juche Philosophy is an Original Revolutionary Policy", *Giving priority to the Ideological work is Essential for accomplishing Socialism,* p. 69.

state of alarm by the state's propaganda, that warned them of the terrible South Korean and American soldiers waiting to pounce, even though it had been the North Koreans who acted first when they launched the Korean War.

At this time only Communist citizens who had been thoroughly vetted were allowed into North Korea and their every movement was still monitored. Freedom of the press vanished and was replaced by state-run media. Anyone caught listening to Western radio stations or were found with any foreign publications were arrested, pushed through a kangaroo court, and summarily executed.[211]

There is an interesting quote in *National Reunification*[212] relating to the leader's nature. It reads: "Being fond of the others style and imitating it is not the attitude befitting *masters* who are responsible for the destiny of the nation." Master! Masters order, leaders lead. This is an interesting word for Kim Jung-il to use for himself as the one who is "responsible for the destiny of [his] nation." The word "master" appears frequently in *Giving Priority to the Ideological Work is Essential for Accomplishing Socialism.*

There are many interpretations of Juche, but this last quote clearly indicates that it is an ideological system whose principal goal is to maintain the Kim family in power as the *masters* of North Korea by imposing an absolute police state on the people of North Korea that demands absolute loyalty and, despite its claims of supporting individualism, demands thoughtless obedience. It also moves the process of socialism to nationalism, which happens to be a fundamental element of fascism.

So too is the concept of the "leader", which we will explore further in the chapters on fascism. That said, it matters little if the leader is called the hegemon, rex, Caesar, roi, könig, kaiser, czar, Fearless Leader, Great Leader, or the Dear Leader. Absolutism is absolutism, tyranny is tyranny, a dictator is a dictator and, strangely enough, the word for "leader" in German is "Fuhrer."

In an unusual twist, Kim Il Sung is referred to in the present tense, i.e. "The Great Leader Comrade Kim Il Sung *is* the sun of our nation and the lodestar of national reunification."[213] This sentence comes from *Let*

---
[211] C. Rivers Editors, *Kil-Il-sung : The Controversial Life and Legacy of North Korea's First Supreme Leader* (Monee, IL: C. Rivers Editors, 2022).
[212] Kim jong-il, "The Juche Philosophy is an Original Revolutionary Policy", *National Reunification,* pp.31-32.
[213] Kim jong-il, "The Juche Philosophy is an Original Revolutionary Policy", *Let us Carry Out the Great Leader Comrade Kim Il Sung's Instructions for National Reunification,* Juche 86,

Twin Evils

us Carry Out the Great Leader Comrade Kim Il Sung's Instructions for National Reunification and at the time it was written, August 4th, 1997, Kim Il Sung was dead.

Freedom in North Korea

The North Korean constitution allows for many rights, but there are legal loopholes in the constitution that allow the North Korean government to circumvent those rights if, for any reason, it decides to negate that right. A good example is how Christianity is treated. Kim Il-sung and his followers have been accused of persecuting thousands of North Korean Christians. Of course, any gathering for a church service was already addressed by the ban on any meetings where the citizenry might plot against Kim Il-Sung, so a Christian church was already forbidden.

North Korean government documents state that "freedom of religion is allowed and provided by the State law within the limit necessary for securing social order, health, social security, morality and other human rights."[214] The necessary limit is such that any slip-up by a North Korean Christian can send them into prison forced labor, torture, sexual violence, and death.

Christians are considered a "hostile class" in the *songbun* system. In this system the people derive status from loyalty to the state and its leadership. Christianity calls for loyalty to God, which is unacceptable to the North Korean government. As a result, any element of Christianity draws a rapid and brutal response from the government. The U.S. Department of State, in reporting on how the North Korean government response to this they report an instance an entire family, including their two-year-old child were imprisoned following the discovery of their religious practices and for the mere possession of a Bible. In another instance a man was found with a Bible. He was taken by the authorities to an airfield and executed before a crowd of thousands.

To reinforce his control, Kim Il-sung created a system of prison camps, which were in essence the North Korean form of the Soviet gulag system. Thought its purpose was to "reeducate" those who strayed from the rules. There was also the *"kwan-il-so"* which were true concentration camps. Political prisoners who were doomed to life in prison were sent to these facilities where they were worked to death. Satellite images

---

August 4, 1997, p. 111.
[214] https://www.yahoo.com/news/christians-caught-bible-north-korea-203536926.html.

examined by civilians suggest that there are as many as 150,000 to 200,000 prisoners in them at any time, but since some crimes result not only in the criminal, but also his extended family being condemned to those camps for life so the numbers are probably much higher.

This generational condemnation to prison resulted from an edict issued by Kim-Il-sung in 1972. The idea of "guilt by association" was introduced to the process of imprisonment and up to three generations of a political criminal's family and relatives, and even potentially neighbors and friends, were shipped to these camps. The idea was that they knew and did not report it and by sending them off to the camps, others were encouraged to save themselves by reporting to others.

The prisoners were reduced to slaves. They performed 12 hours or more of hard labor a day, such as logging, mining, farming, or factory work. As a minor gesture children were exempted from this hard labor. Food was limited to one meal a day of barely edible food. In the desperation of their starvation, these prisoners actively hunted any animal, be it rats, mice, snakes, and even insects to supplement their diets. They are even known to pick through animal dung for undigested grain.

Genocide in North Korea

We have already talked about the North Korean gulag system as well as what it took to get someone condemned to it. Those camps were much like Hitler's camps in that it was the intention of the government that the inmates would be worked to death. In addition to these camps we have spoken of various purges and summary executions for violations of the draconian laws in effect in North Korea.

Because of the control measures established in North Korea it is very difficult to obtain exact numbers of those that the Kim Regimes have killed. Most of the information available comes from defectors. Estimates range from 710,000 to over 3,500,000 dead as a result of these systems.

R.J. Rummel has studied this and examined various sources. He estimates that from the Korean War there were "probably close to 2,550,000 people were killed on all sides, not counting the war-time democide."[215]

Rummel was unable to identify any overall estimates of executions or deaths resulting from incarceration in the labor or concentration camps, or those who were purged, executed as a result of land reform, or other

---

[215] Rummel, R.J. *STATISTICS OF DEMOCIDE* Chapter 10 *Statistics of North Korean Democide Estimates, Calculations, and Sources.* https://www.hawaii.edu/powerkills/SOD.CHAP10.HTM

causes. Despite this, it is clear that thousands were killed for political reasons, but the number has not been documented.

During the Korean war North Korean troops were followed by communist officials who systematically massacred former South Korean government officials, anti-communists, and others deemed hostile to the communists. As the UN forces drove the North Koreans back the killings intensified.

The North Koreans also executed the South Korean troops that they had captured, and estimates run as high as 70,000. However, it is known that 5,500 were executed and as many as 50,000 may have been dragooned into the North Korean Army. These figures suggest that they did kill as many as 5,000 to 12,000 South Korean troops and another 5,000 to 6,000 American prisoners.

The North Koreans also forced 400,000 South Korean civilians into their army. Being expendable, these men were sent on the most dangerous missions. It is known that the North Korean Army suffered about 350,000 killed during the war, which is 250% of the army's original strength. Rummel estimates that from $1/3^{rd}$ to $2/3^{rds}$ of the impressed South Koreans were killed, which gives North Korea a count of 225,000 killed.

He goes on to estimate that the North Korean communists probably killed about 500,000 Koreans, in the a foregoing processes, and to that must be added an estimate 1,500,000 civilians killed in the war.

Altogether, during the war the North Korean communists probably killed near 500,000 Koreans (excluding at least 6,000 killed by the South, including their own citizens. With a probable 1,500,000 civilians killed in the war, this democide seems, if anything, an underestimate and the true figure may be closer to the high democide calculation of almost 775,000 dead.

As for the camps, again, there are only limited and inaccurate sources from which estimates can be made, so Rummel comes up with a figure of from 71,000 to 707,000 killed in the camps, but the most likely number is 265,000.

To this must be added the numbers of North Koreans who died as a result of forced labor of millions. Periodically the Kim government would order thousands and sometimes tens of thousands of their citizens to go to remote locations to work on projects ranging from dams, irrigation canals, bridges, etc., for months at a time. Little attention was paid to the well-being of these people, and the food was invariably poor, which added to long hours of strenuous work, surely caused many deaths in addition to those executed for laziness or anti-party behavior. Rummel estimates these conditions caused from a 20% to a 30% death rate in the camps. Expanding that over the 39 years of the camps' existence, he estimates almost 1,000,000 died. There were close to 4,000,000 "hostiles" incarcerated in 1989.

His calculations add up to a probable North Korean domestic democide of 1,293,000 men, women, and children.

Rummel summarizes his estimates by saying: "Still, the uncertainties involved in these calculations, the paucity of estimates, and the origin of what few estimates there are being the South Korean government, invites considerable caution about my domestic democide total. And the same holds true for the foreign democide figures, which when added to that of citizens totals given a probable 710,000 to 3,549,000 people killed, or a mid-value of 1,663,000. This appears to make the North Korean regime and in particular Kim Il-sung a mega murderer, but for the reasons given I argue that we can do no more than indict North Korea for these killings."

For all the reasons listed above, plus various natural disasters that have occurred over the period 1990 and 1998, North Korea has experienced an average annual growth rate of -4.1%.

Summary of Features of Communism

It is simplest to summarize the common traits of communism, as it has historically been implemented and is currently practiced, with a list:

1.) They preach the elimination of exploitation and oppression, but do the opposite, setting up totalitarian dictatorships.
2.) Confiscation of personal property.
3.) Mass starvation.
4.) Purges of political opponents.
5.) Government run media, i.e. no freedom of the press.
6.) No freedom of religion.
7.) No freedom of assembly.
8.) A system of gulags i.e. forced labor camps.
9.) Mass murder.
10.) Corruption and abuse of power.
11.) They demand absolute obedience.
12.) No freedom of thought, i.e. everyone must conform to the government's approved thought.

Twin Evils

13.) They replace the old ruling class with a new class of political elites.
14.) Kangaroo courts.
15.) One is presumed guilty if taken to trial. There is no presumption of innocence.
16.) Criticizing the government is a crime.
17.) Elections are shams and not free.
18.) The leadership is either hereditary or kept with a small circle of political elites.
19.) They all preach the elimination of exploitation and oppression but do the exact opposite.

CHAPTER 7

WHAT IS FASCISM, MUSSOLINI'S RISE TO POWER, AND ITALIAN FASCISM.

What is fascism? That is an interesting question. There was not a single philosopher, no Karl Marx, who conceived the idea of fascism and presented his concept of how the world should be run. Indeed, fascism apparently developed emphasizing the ideas of fear of change, anger at the present, and a demand for action. It has no coherent universal philosophy. Fascism evolved as a hydra with as many different faces as it had heads.

Although there are several definitions, fascism is not a single ideology. Fascism was more a spontaneous movement that may have had its roots in the 1880's. It erupted in the post-World War I era, not only in Italy and Germany, but also in every European country to the west of the Russian border. It also existed in Brazil and in the United States. The Rumanian form of fascism was different from those of Belgium and England. So too were other forms of fascism that appeared different from every other form of fascism. Fascism's rise depended upon the soil and where the seeds of fascist discontent fell.

Of course, there is the communist definition. The communists define any political ideology that opposes them as being fascist and they use that pejorative with wild abandon painting their ideological enemies with the sins of Nazi Germany. Communists overuse this definition to such a high degree that it has become as mindless as the present cries of racism. However, there are still fascists in the world

This fascist movement was based on the idea of a revolt against materialism, rationalism, bourgeois society, positivism, and liberal democracy. The people who adhered to the *fin de siècle* concepts believed in emotionalism, irrationalism, subjectivism and vitalism.[216] Fascist, saw civilization as being in a crisis that required a massive and total solution.

There were some very specific situations that existed in 1918 that led to the appearance of fascism. According to Robert O. Paxton,[217] fascism arose because of the following:

---

[216] Sternhell, Zeev. "Crisis of Fin-de-siècle Thought." International Fascism: Theories, Causes and the New Consensus. London and New York (1998): 169.
[217] Paxton, R.O., *The Anatomy of Fascism* (New York: Vintage Books, 2005), p. 43. J.

- A sense of overwhelming crisis beyond the reach of any traditional solutions;
- The primacy of the group, where the individual has duties superior to every right, whether individual or universal, and the subordination of the individual to it;
- The belief that one's group is a victim, a sentiment that justifies any action, without legal or moral limits, against its enemies, both internal and external;
- The dread of the group's decline under the corrosive effects of individualistic liberalism, class conflict, and alien influences;
- The need for closer integration of a purer community, by consent if possible, or by exclusionary violence, if necessary;
- The need for authority by natural leaders (always male), culminating in a national chief who alone can incarnate the group's destiny;
- The superiority of the leader's instincts over abstract and universal reason;
- The beauty of violence and the efficacy of will, when they are devoted to the group's success; and,
- The right of the chosen people to dominate others without restraint from any kind of human or divine law, right being decided by the sole criterion of the group's prowess within a "Darwinian struggle."

Crisis: Though World War I ended and life was attempting to return to the pre-war norm, a massive economic crisis followed. The punitive requirements of the Treaty of Versailles included reparations to be paid by Germany to the Allied nations. The reparations were greater than the German gross national product. At the end of the war Germany had an unemployment rate of 25%. Additionally, Germany had accumulated massive debt. The decision of the Weimar Germany's government to engage in what today is called Keynesian Economics or Modern Monetary Theory. The economic theory contends the government can print all the money it needs to get the economy moving and reduce unemployment. As a result, Germany was on the brink of disaster. Then it happened. France suffered a small economic setback and decided to solve their problem by demanding an immediate payment of the German debt. Germany's economy collapsed into hyperinflation and was one of the worst economic crises of modern time. Although starvation occurred in Germany during the war, it returned with a vengeance in 1923. The inflation was very severe so that farmers refused to sell their food to the market; by the time farmers were paid, the money they received was worthless. The economy was reduced to barter.

In Italy, according to the historian Emilio Gentile, the crisis element resulted from the "dysfunctional aspects of the belated Italian unification known as the Risorgimento, the acute cultural crisis of the turn-of-the-century Italy, and the deep socio-economic and political crisis that followed the First World War."[218]

Primacy of the Group: During World War I, all the participant nations engaged in propagandizing their people, stirring national pride, inspiring their citizenry to support the war effort. This propaganda advocated the righteousness of their cause, the superiority of their nation, and the superiority of their culture, over what the fascists considered the "degenerate nations" they were fighting. It also focused on inspiring individual sacrifices that the fascists further advocated "for the greater good," the greater good being the war effort. The sacrifice by the individual was a key element of fascism. Though there were varying concepts of how much sacrifice should be made once World War I began and greater sacrifices were required by the war effort, this propaganda increased in its intensity.

When World War I ended and Marxist internationalism began appearing in Germany, and among other countries. The Germans, who had been fed a consistent diet of national pride and supremacy, reacted to the Marxists as antithetical to their sense of nation.

Taking advantage of the groundwork laid by this propaganda, Nazism condemned Marxist and liberal internationalists as threats to German national unity. The various other fascist parties, perceiving the same threat, sought to replace the concept of internationalist class solidarity with nationalist class collaboration and the sacrifice of individuality for the greater good.

In ideological terms, scholars believe that ultra-nationalism arises from seeing modern nation-states as living organisms that are directly akin to physical people. Nation states, like individuals, can decay, grow, and die. They can also experience rebirth. The subject of rebirth was addressed by fascists and became a common theme in both German and Italian fascism. Both had specific plans for widespread national renewal.

---

[218] Griffin, R., *Fascism; An Introduction to Comparative Fascist Studies* (Medford, MA: Polity, 2022) p. 51.

Twin Evils

Victimhood: The sense of victimhood varied. The Austro-Hungarian Empire was dismembered. Its Germanic core believed it had been victimized. The Germans, who ruled that empire felt a loss of international status and the loss of an empire that was 1,000 years old. In addition, the Hungarians, who were a part of that empire, lost large portions of their territory that was used to form several new, ethnically based countries. They too believed they were victimized.

Then there was antisemitism. It was considered an element of victimhood. Antisemitism had existed in Europe since the earliest days of the Roman Catholic Church which blamed the Jews for the death of Jesus. In addition, the Jews were proscribed by the Church and states from many professions. Therefore, the Jews adopted the business of money lending, which was prohibited by the Church for Christians and a function that was needed by many kings and emperors in the sea of Medieval politics. No matter what the interest rate, it was looked upon as usury.

J.-F.-A. Peyré, in his account of the 1st Crusade, reports to us an incident that enflamed this hatred.[219] Apparently in 1009 A.D. the Jews of Orléans, jealous of the influence that Christians had gained in the East and especially in Jerusalem, sent a message to Sultan Hakem that the desire to visit the tomb of Christ was becoming so compelling day by day in the West, that one could be assured that the influx of pilgrims would threaten to annihilate the power of the Muslims in Jerusalem for as long as this monument of Christian worship remained standing. This letter even went so far as to say that a formidable army was gathering among the Franks, to cross into the East and wage a war of extermination against the Saracens. On receipt of this notice the Egyptian caliph, whether he was truly frightened by the dangers that this communication foreshadowed, or whether he simply wanted to give his people a striking proof of his hatred against the Christians, a pledge which he could believe necessary because of the Christian religion professed by his mother, hastened to send orders so that the Church of the Holy Sepulcher was razed to its foundations, as well as the Church of Saint George, object of the veneration of Christians in the city of Ramle, ancient Arimathea; and this order was only too faithfully executed by the governor of the latter city, named Hyaroë.

During the early days of the 1st Crusade there were numerous incidents of religiously inspired attacks on Jewish residents of much of Europe. Particularly egregious massacres occurred in Mainz and Cologne, where the entire Jewish communities were slaughtered by Crusaders who

---
[219] Peyré, J.-F.-A. *Histoire de la Première Croisade* (Paris : A. Durand 1859), pp. 18-19.

were preparing to go to Palestine and liberate the Holy Land.

If one studies Russia, we find the word "pogrom" which basically means "everyone run over to the Jewish village, rape, loot, and burn." Under Lenin, even though there were Jews in the Communist Party and the Soviet government, particularly Trotsky, there were many Jews who were involved in the practice of money lending. If one recalls there had been a land redistribution before the Russian Revolution and that many Russian peasants, for many reasons, fell into debt and lost their land to those who had lent them money. Surely many of those lenders were Jews, which focused more hatred against all Jews.

As previously mentioned, antisemitism also existed in Western Europe. There was always a strong vein of antisemitism in Europe. It erupted in late 1894, when French Army Captain Alfred Dreyfus, a graduate of the École Polytechnique and a Jew of Alsatian origin, was accused of handing secret documents to the Imperial German military. The French had been humiliated by the Franco-Prussian War and they needed an excuse. That humiliation demanded a scape goat, which easily mixed with antisemitism. The French government prosecuted Dreyfus, and the subsequent trial was the worst form of a miscarriage of justice. Naturally, he was found guilty. This was followed by street riots in which Jewish shops were looted.

On January 13, 1898, Émile Zola touched off a new dimension in the Dreyfus Affair. Outraged by the French refusal to convict the actual criminals, Zola published the famous article "J'accuse...! [I accuse...] It was a direct attack, explicit and clear, and identified collaborators, denouncing those who had conspired against Dreyfus, including the French Minister of War and the General Staff. This demonstrates the depth of hatred for the Jews by the French.

This attitude was unabated in France after the Germans conquered it in World War II. In the 1960's, I met a Frenchman who, during World War II, had been sent to college by the Germans to earn a degree in engineering so that he could work for the Reich. He had significant contact with the occupying German forces and related to me how the Germans were stunned at the eagerness with which the French gendarmerie swept up the French Jews for shipment to the camps.

I also knew an elderly Belgian woman, who had been a teenager in World War I. She related to me, how before World War I in Belgium, one would occasionally be approached by a "greasy Jew" who would "pull out a filthy rag holding a fortune in diamonds." She also related her terror when a Jewish merchant proposed marriage to her. She may not have hated

Jews, but her attitude towards them was very negative and very typical of the attitude of the Belgians towards the Jews.

We have already mentioned how Marx, while living in England, had been victimized by Jewish money lenders. Surely those money lenders had taken advantage of the English lower classes; the result was the same hatred.

In Germany there were several sources for a sense of victimhood that included antisemitism. Aside from the usual usury issue, there was the "stab in the back" theory. In 1919, a German parliamentary committee of inquiry interviewed General Paul von Hindenburg, the Commander-in-Chief of the German Army. This committee sought the reasons why Germany had lost the war. Von Hindenburg claimed that Germany had lost because the new German government had not supported him and had commenced peace negotiations. In addition, he stated the German army had been weakened by the revolutionary atmosphere within the army, the mutiny of the German naval fleet, and the revolutionary movements among the German citizenry. He quoted an English general, who had allegedly said: 'The German army has been stabbed in the back.'

This theory maintained that the Imperial German Army did not lose World War I on the battlefield, but that it had been betrayed by specific citizens on the home front – especially Jews, revolutionary socialists - who fomented strikes and labor unrest. Also accused as "back stabbers" were republican politicians who had overthrown the House of Hohenzollern in the German Revolution of 1918–1919. Advocates of this theory denounced the German government leaders of the Sozialdemokratische Partei Deutschlands, (SPD, The Social Democratic Party of Germany) and the Centre Party, the socialists Hermann Müller and Johannes Bell, who had signed the Armistice of November 11, 1918, as the "November criminals."

The Jewish connection is Walther Rathenau, who was foreign minister. In 1922, he negotiated Treaty of Rapallo, which normalized relations and strengthened economic ties between Germany and Soviet Russia. The agreement, along with Rathenau's insistence that Germany fulfill its hated obligations under the Treaty of Versailles, led right-wing nationalist groups (including a nascent Nazi Party) to brand him part of a Jewish-communist conspiracy.

The politics of Müller, Bell, and Rathenau, all socialists, also added to "Stab-in-the-Back" theory and the subsequent hatred of all things socialist in Germany.

The Treaty of Versailles had also stripped territories from Germany to reconstitute the nation of Poland. This inflicted another injury to German national pride.

Decline of the Group: This issue is the direct philosophical result of the first concept, the "Primacy of the Group," and is closely linked to the second concept, the "Pure Community." Fascism promised a rebirth of the nation and national society. This involved returning to ancient times and mythology that spoke of the greatness of the nation, while modern society had brought into decline. Almost all the countries that had fascist parties delved into their history, seeking to find an ethnically and spiritually homogenous origin. They viewed themselves as heirs of those ancient tribes who were charged with the mission of purging the nation of this decadence and created a "new man" or even the "Uber mensch."

In addition, in reaction to World War I, much of society threw itself into debauchery, an orgy of frivolity and lax morality and other vices to forget the horrors of the war. The values of the group were declining, and elements of the national societies were prepared to fight against this decline. The decline in morality appalled the conservative elements of societies and drew them into the fascist circles.

Pure Community: The western world was industrializing. People were moving from the countryside into the cities. Society was undergoing massive change and together with migration into the urban world, the sense of community that had existed for centuries was beginning to change. As a result, groups that had previously been homogenous in their nature were breaking up and mixing. This was exacerbated by the influx of Jews, among others, fleeing the Bolsheviks and the Poles. This produced stresses in the social fabric of every European nation. The Jews did not intermix with the local societies. However, they were among the waves of immigrants of various backgrounds that included, but were not limited, to the Gypsies.

Authority by Natural Leaders and Superiority of Leader's Instincts Over Reason: According to J. Barnes "as no society can hold together unless someone be over all, directing all to strive earnestly for the common good, every civilized community must have a ruling authority, and this authority, no less than society itself has its source in nature, and has, consequently, God for its author."[220] Of course God is an issue of faith; but there is always a human being who fills that role on earth. Over the cen-

---

[220] Barnes, J.S., *The Universal Aspects of Fascism* (Location unk: Reconquista Press, 2020), p. 83.

turies, many forms of divine style claimed leadership existed. Leadership was provided by absolute monarchies throughout the world and over the centuries, except in England, until 1789. In 1789, the French Revolution overthrew the Bourbon Monarchy and began the spread of various forms of democracy based upon the ideas of Voltaire and the other philosophers of the Age of Enlightenment

In the Age of Enlightenment reason was valued over faith. It attacked superstitious beliefs, including but not limited to religion, and based philosophical opinions on rational ideas. It also valued individualism, where one developed one's own talents to the highest degree to live life for one's own sake rather than for the general good. We will see that this latter point clashes with the Fascist concept of the primacy of the state and service to the state for the benefit of the group.

According to fascist ideology, the advocacy of individualism including individual reason, necessitated the need for a leader's instincts to replace reason. This was based on his supposed superior understanding of what best served the general good.

Reason and the rejection of faith, as conceived by Voltaire and the other 17th century philosophers, was rejected, and replaced by fascism's emphasis upon spiritualism. There was also a rejection of liberalism principles and classical liberalism, which had evolved from the Enlightenment.

In short, liberalism is a political and moral philosophy based on the rights of the individual, liberty, consent of the governed, political equality, the right to private property, and equality before the law.

Classical liberalism is a political tradition and a branch of liberalism which advocates free market and laissez-faire economics, and civil liberties under the rule of law. Special emphasis is placed upon individual autonomy, limited government, economic freedom, political freedom, and freedom of speech.

Both political theories focus on the individual, while fascism focuses on the group, or in fascist terms, the state. If one examines the two previous conditions necessary for the development of fascism, one will see the concepts of group and community that are a crucial element of the fascist state. Individualism, a fundamental element of all forms of liberalism, is antithetical to the concepts of group, community, and state, which are governing fundamentals of fascism.

In fascism, the individual is subordinate to the state and has freedom only within limits. The individual is subject to the authority of the state, and he is restricted in his liberties within the institutions and laws of the state that emphasize the general good. In theory the individual was not subordinate to the state. However, as the state has no limits upon its authority, this makes the state an end in itself. Fascism regarded the concept of individual happiness indirectly but only as a goal of the state. True individual happiness is dependent upon general well-being, which the state has an obligation to promote. Fascism held that no individual had the right to seek his personal happiness at the expense of the general good.

The result of this was a focus upon the duty of the individual to the state and opposition to unrestrained individualism. It naturally evolved that the leader was the key to the functioning of fascism. This led to the concept of the supremacy of the leader, who by inspiration and intuition, knew what was best for the group.

The concept of the supreme leader evolved into the "Führer Principal," which was the fundamental basis of political authority in Nazi Germany. It meant that the Führer's word is above all written law and that governmental policies, decisions, and offices were to work towards this end. In German history, this concept originates from Nordic sagas and flowed through Frederick the Great and Otto von Bismarck. It was interpreted to emphasize the value of unquestioning obedience to a visionary leader. It also existed in fascist Italy.

Violence and Will: World War I taught a generation of young men that violence was a way of life and a way of resolving problems. This took form in revolutionary violence, initially in socialist and communist violence in the streets as they attacked their class enemies. The response was equal violence by anti-communist elements within the various states. In this regard, there were many differences between Russia and western Europe. As discussed earlier, there were large numbers of landless peasants in Russia who had joined the workers in their revolution. However, in western Europe, there was not a significant population of landless peasants; the small farmers had no incentive to join the communist movement. Indeed, they surely knew of the collectivization concept of communism and, fearing for the loss of their land, encouraged them to join the fascist ranks where they fought to protect their land. In Italy, Mussolini had a very specific situation among the small farmers of the Po Valley, who became strong supporters of the fascist movement in Italy in reaction to the communist threat to their property.

Anti-communist violence was the result. In Germany it was the Brown Shirts who fought the communists in the streets and anyone who they perceived as an enemy. In Italy it was the Black Shirts, the Blue Shirts in England, the Silver Shirts in the United States, and Green Shirts in Ireland. There were similar groups of a semi-military nature in every country where fascism existed. All these groups practiced violence against their political enemies.

Darwinism: By the late 19th century Darwinism had merged with the concept of Social Darwinism. Both theories viewed the human condition as an unceasing struggle in which only the fittest should survive. This merged with the concept of nationalism that arose during the French Revolution, and spread to the rest of Europe, and increased its influence with the propaganda of World War I. Social Darwinism challenged positivism's claim of deliberate and rational choice as the determining behavior of humans. It focused on heredity, race, and the impact of the environment. Social Darwinism's emphasis on ethnicity, and the role of organic relations within societies, reinforced the concept and acceptability of nationalism. Human behavior, it claimed, as justified by rational choice, was rejected by the period theories of social and political psychology.

Under Weimar, "racial science" was given both a central organization and an enhanced legitimacy in 1927 with the foundation of the Kaiser Wilhelm Institute of Anthropology, Human Hereditary, and Eugenics, an institution science-based racial state."[221]

If one adds Darwinism to the various elements of the concept of community and group, one finds a natural home for extreme ethnic or racial nationalism and its fruit - antisemitism and other forms of racism.

The Garden in Which These Seeds Were Planted.

There were many issues that made Europe fertile ground for the appearance of fascist organizations. One of the major elements that allowed and provoked fascism occurred in the late 1880's. In the late 1880's there was a movement advocating mass enfranchisement. The near universal franchise had pushed many of the social elites, the very wealthy and the nobility, out of politics. replacing them with professional politicians. Corruption resulted among plebeians who had moved into politics looking upon it as a source of their living. Scandals occurred. This corruption angered the electorate and caused them to look for a change.

Two major fascist states, Germany, and Italy, were essentially new states, compared to Great Britain, France, Austro-Hungarian Empire, and

---

[221]Griffin, R., *Fascism; An Introduction to Comparative Fascist Studies* (Medford, MA: Polity, 2022) p. 70.

additional long established governed European states. In addition to the relatively new states of Germany and Italy, were the new states formed because of the Treaty of Versailles - Yugoslavia, Poland, Bulgaria, Rumania, Hungary, and Czechoslovakia. There existed an inherent instability in these states as they sought to establish themselves in the world.

Italy had been steadily moving towards unity since the era of the Napoleonic Wars., Italy had been formed as a state on March 17, 1861. Germany, earlier held under the concept of the Holy Roman Empire, which Napoleon had destroyed in 1805, remained a patch work of little principalities and duchies until August 18, 1866. As a result, in these two countries, there was a sense of inferiority and a need to prove oneself. Except for Poland, the states formed by the Treaty of Versailles were collections of mixed ethnic groups that had co-existed under the Austro-Hungarian Empire. They now became hot beds for groups that were struggling for political dominance organized along ethnic lines.

In addition, the World War I veterans of the combat trenches were furious at the war's industrialized murder into which they had been sent and blamed the politicians who had gotten them into that war. Every country involved in the war suffered, which, in addition to provoking anger against the politicians, also created a sense of victimhood.

There also existed a popular movement against the political left and against liberal individualism. The classic liberals interpreted liberty as individual personal freedom, preferring it to being overseen by a limited constitutional government. The classic liberal preferred an economic world of *laissez-faire* economics with minimal, if any, governmental intervention. Liberals understood equality as opportunity being accessible to talent because of education, and accepted inequality of achievement, power, and wealth resulting from the lack of initiative and not oppression. Classical liberalism ran afoul against rising nationalism, where the success of members of one ethnic group was seen to have occurred at the expense of the other ethnic groups.

In addition to the various political and economic crises there was the perception of cultural degeneration as mentioned earlier. There are always elements that oppose change, and the greater the change, the greater the opposition.

World War I and Mussolini's Rise to Power.

At the outbreak of World War I in August 1914, the Italian political left became severely divided over its position on the war. The Italian Socialist Party opposed the war. However, several Italian revolutionary syndicalists supported intervention in the war on the belief that the war could serve to mobilize the masses against the *status quo* and that the national question had to be resolved before the social one. Among the latter was Corradini, who presented the need for Italy as a "proletarian nation" to defeat a reactionary Germany. There was Angelo Oliviero Olivetti who formed the Revolutionary Fascio for International Action, which also supported Italy's entry into the war. At the same time, Benito Mussolini joined the interventionist cause. At first, these interventionist groups were composed of disaffected syndicalists. These groups believed that their attempts to promote social change through a general strike had failed and then looked to use the transformative potential of militarism and war. These latter groups would form the Fascist Party.

This early interventionist movement was very small and lacked coherent policies. It attempted and failed to gather mass meetings, and it was regularly harassed by government authorities and violent groups of socialists. The interventionists responded to socialist violence with their own violence. Attacks on interventionists were very violent and set the ground for equally violent responses.

Among the interventionists was Benito Mussolini, who ran a very popular newspaper, *Il Popolo d'Italia* that had been founded to support the interventionist cause. It received financial support from the governments of various Allied powers that wished to bring Italy into the war on the Allied side. It also received financial support from Italian industrialists and agrarian interests who sought to profit from the war. Mussolini sought to appeal to various readers ranging from dissident socialists who opposed the Socialist Party's anti-war stance; democratic idealists who believed the war would overthrow Europe's autocratic monarchies; imperialists who dreamed of a new Roman Empire; and Italian nationalists, who wanted to recover ethnic Italian territories from Austria including Trieste and other land along the eastern bank of the Adriatic Sea.

As the war progressed, Mussolini turned to the nationalist position and began arguing that Italy could recover Trieste and Fiume and expand its northeastern border to the Alps to secure "Italy's natural frontier," as the French had so often sought to acquire the right bank of the Rhine for the same reason. Mussolini's thoughts then turned towards an Italian Empire, a successor to the Roman Empire, which would include conquests in the Balkans and the Middle East. His supporters began calling themselves *fascisti*, which came from *fascio*, the Italian word for bundle, which in this case represents bundles of people. Its origins are in Ancient Rome, when the fasces were a bundle of wood with an ax head, carried by leaders.

In addition to urging for empire, Mussolini shifted from his earlier socialist leanings and assumed a positive attitude towards capitalism and capitalists. Mussolini's positive attitude toward capitalism was consistent with his transition supporting class collaboration instead of class warfare and an "Italy first" position. Mussolini tried, when Italy entered the war in 1915, to take credit for the government's decision; however, in truth, he had no significant influence upon that decision. As a patriot, he enlisted in the army and fought until 1917, when he was wounded in a training accident. Though not part of the Arditi, Mussolini was drawn to them. They were an elite force of Italian shock troops. They were trained for a life of violence beyond that of the normal soldiers and their elite status was characterized by a black shirt and fez. It should be recognized that elite troops are all volunteers who are motivated, usually, by extreme patriotism. Therefore, they were natural candidates for Mussolini's political plans.

When the war ended this elite force formed the Associazione fra gli Arditi d'Italia. By mid-1919, they numbered approximately 20,000 men. Mussolini appealed to the Arditi, and they became the basis of the Fascist Squadristi movement.

When the Russian Revolution occurred in 1917 the remainder of Europe was pierced with a general fear of similar revolutions. The result was that Fascist movements began forming as an anti-communist reaction. While communism emphasized class warfare and internationalism, fascism took the opposite tact and focused on national interests. Many fascists saw communism as a Jewish invention, which was not surprising since Marx was an ethnic Jew and there were many prominent Jews in the movement, notably Trotsky. This struck the broad sense of antisemitism that existed throughout Europe. In addition, as mentioned earlier, there were not many landless peasants in the west, or particularly in Italy and Germany, at this time. Subsequently, most of their respective populations were not attracted to communism and found fascists a group that would protect their property from state seizure.

Mussolini already had a taste for power and admired Lenin's boldness and forceful seizure of power. However, he was angered by Lenin's

Twin Evils

restriction of free speech and creating a "tyranny worse than that of the tsars." As a result, being a publisher, he presented himself as an ardent opponent of censorship and a champion of free speech.

In 1919 Mussolini achieved control over the fascist movement and formed the *Fasci Italiani di Combattimento* in Milan. He presented the *Fasci Italiani* as a populist movement, an alternative to socialism. He offered his own version of a revolutionary transformation of Italian society. In addition, the Italian *Fasci Italiani* was dedicated to turning war veterans and extreme patriots into a revolutionary force. The use of "*combattimento*" (combat) in its title was a direct illusion to the "*combattentismo*," the heroic fighting spirit of the trenches exemplified by the *Arditi*.[222]

Italian Arditi dressed for trench warfare with armor and grenades.(Wikipedia)

Mussolini presented these ideas of populism and revolution in a speech given in Milan in March 1919. In his speech, he set forth his ideas that included nationalism, Sorelian syndicalism, the idealism of the French philosopher Henri Bergson, and the theories of the Italians Gaetano Mosca and Vilfredo Pareto.

As it was already apparent that communism had destroyed the Russian economy, Mussolini seized on this fact to sell fascism, further declaring that communism was antithetical to Western civilization and nationalism. It was his intent to use a two-branch appeal to the Italians. The first being the patriotism that had been enflamed by wartime propaganda; and emphasizing a different form of the economy. Mussolini addressed the concerns of the working class, while not attacking the creation of wealth as had the Russian communist system. This was an

---
[222] Griffin, R., *Fascism; A quick Immersion* (US: Tibidabo Publishin g, 2020), p. 13.

attempt to create a broad appeal as possible attracting all class and political persuasion. He also presented his concept of a new Roman Empire in the form of Italian expansion overseas participating in the race for colonies.

Later in 1919, Alceste De Ambris and futurist movement leader Filippo Tommaso Marinetti created The Manifesto of the Italian Combat Fasci [*Il manifesto dei fasci italiani di combattimento*] (also known as the Fascist Manifesto). The Manifesto was presented on June 6, 1919, in Mussolini's fascist newspaper *Il Popolo d'Italia*.

The Manifesto[223] was divided into four sections. The Manifesto described the movement's objectives in political, social, military, and financial fields. The elements of the Manifesto were as follows:

- Universal suffrage with a lowered voting age to 18 years and voting and electoral office eligibility for all ages 25 and up.
- Proportional representation on a regional basis;
- Representation at government level of newly created national councils by economic sector.
- The abolition of the Italian Senate (at the time, the Senate, the upper house of Parliament, was elected by the wealthier citizens, but the senators were direct appointments by the King. (It has been described as an extended council of the Crown);
- The formation of a national council of experts for labor, for industry, for transportation, for public health, for communications, etc. Selections were to be made by professionals and tradesmen with legislative powers, and elected directly to a general commission with ministerial powers.

In labor and social policy, the Manifesto called for the following:

- The quick enactment of a law of the state that sanctions an eight-hour workday for all workers;
- A minimum wage;
- The participation of workers' representatives in the functions of industry commissions;
- Demonstrate the same confidence in the labor unions (that prove

---

[223] https://en.wikipedia.org/wiki/Fascist_Manifesto#:~:text=%22The%20Manifesto%20of%20the%20Italian,founded%20in%20Milan%20by%20Benito.

to be technically and morally worthy) as is given to industry executives or public servants;
- Reorganization of the railways and the public transport sector;
- Revision of the draft law concerning invalidity insurance;
- Reduction of the retirement age from 65 to 55.

In military affairs, the Manifesto further advocated the following:

- Creation of a short-service national militia with specifically defensive responsibilities;
- Nationalization of armaments factories;
- A peaceful but competitive foreign policy.

In finance, the Manifesto advocated:

- A strong extraordinary tax on capital of a progressive nature, which took the form of true partial expropriation of all wealth;
- The seizure of all the possessions of the religious congregations and the abolition of all the bishoprics, which constitute an enormous liability on the nation and on the privileges of the poor;
- Revision of all contracts for military provisions; and,
- The revision of all military contracts and the seizure of eighty-five (85) percent of the profits therein.

These early positions reflected in the Manifesto would later be characterized by Mussolini in *The Doctrine of Fascism*[224] as "a series of pointers, forecasts, hints which, when freed from the inevitable matrix of contingencies, were developed in a few years into a series of doctrinal positions entitling Fascism to rank as a political doctrine differing from all others, past or present."

Most of these points are obvious. However, the formation of National Councils is not obvious; it consisted of experts selected from professionals and tradespeople, elected to represent, and hold legislative power over their respective areas. Included were labor, industry, transportation, public health, and communications, etc.

Mussolini also wanted to pull the Italian government out of areas that were not related to the civil and public life of the nation, which meant

---

[224] Mussolini, B., *The Doctrine of Fascism*, (location unknown: Izhingoora Books, date unknown).

turning over such things as the railroads to private enterprises.

The Manifesto also included Mussolini's desire for the creation of a new Roman Empire. He pressed for the annexation of Dalmatia by peaceful means so that Treste and Fiume could be recovered to Italy together with other territories. To this end, he used his military service and newspaper to gain popularity among patriots and veterans. He had joined Gabriele d'Annunzio, the leader of the annexationist faction, which demanded the annexation of Dalmatia and areas along the Adriatic as suitable compensation for the Italian participation in the war. The principal Allies had different ideas and they intended to use it in the formation of Kingdom of Serbs, Croats, and Slovenes (later renamed Yugoslavia). The Allied goal ran afoul of the Italians' growing sense of nationalism and desire to bring all ethnic Italians into the fold of the new Italian nation state.

The *Fasci Italiani di Combattimento* entered the 1919 elections with the Manifesto as its campaign platform. The results of the election were a disaster.[225] No fascists were elected to any office. In response Mussolini shifted his politics to the right and sought an alliance with the conservative elements of Italy.

Socialist agitation soon provoked conflicts in the regions of Emilia and along the Po Valley. This gave Mussolini an opportunity to gain credibility among the conservatives and to establish Fascism as a paramilitary movement instead of a political party.

Disappointed and angered by the failure of the Allies to support Italian claims, the Italians raided Fiume and founded the Charter of Canaro in 1920. The Charter advocated national-syndicalist corporatist productions among other things. Many fascists saw the Charter of Carnaro as an ideal constitution for a Fascist Italy.

In the same year the communist inspired strikes by industrial workers. The strikes reached a crescendo and caused the years 1919 and 1920 to be known as the "Red Years." Though initially supporting the strikes, Mussolini abruptly reversed his position and opposed them, seeking financial support from big business and landowners. This was not the first time Mussolini showed his opportunism and lack of a firm political ideology in his quest for power. Money flowed into his coffers in unusually large quantities because of this shift. Again, visions of the communist Russia and its actions towards industrialists and capitalists caused them to seek a savior. This caused the fascists of Milan to become a national political force.

---

[225] Griffin, R., *Fascism; A quick Immersion* (US: Tibidabo Publishing, 2020), p. 54.

Mussolini's next step was to create his own militia, known as the "Blackshirts," who were inspired by the *Arditi*. Thus armed, Mussolini began a campaign of violence against communists, socialists, trade unions, and cooperatives while claiming to preserve the internal peace of Italy and presenting himself as the champion of Italian national interests. His earlier proposals for territorial expansion added to his nationalistic credentials.

It was in 1921 that the Italian Fascist Party was founded, and it operated both as a legal electoral and as a semi-legal paramilitary force. It was an armed political party. Because it was a legal political party, and its Blackshirts acted violently in the streets, there appeared the phrase "*fascismo manganello e doppiopetto*" [Fascism of the rubber truncheon and of the double-breasted jacket.][226]

Fascism was, at this point, a confused mixture of elements that defied definition. It contained national syndicalists, futurists, technocratic modernizers, and extreme army patriots. Its name, *Fascio*, "suggested *trincerismo*, the only partly mythical spirit of extreme nationalism, heroism, and self-sacrifice, born of the combat community of the trenches. The Italian fascists were forged by three years of fighting in horrendous and lethal conditions of the Italian front-line, high in the forbidding, often freezing, Austro-Italian Alps, "where the enemy was not shrapnel and mud, but shrapnel mixed with shards of mountain granite."[227] These men were the *avant garde* of the elite *Arditi*, that were to form the nucleus transforming Italy into a great nation.

Mussolini sent his Blackshirts into the city of Treste where they fought in the streets against the Slavs and pushed for the annexation of the city into Italy. When he entered the city, he was received with acclamations by the Italian elements of the city. Once there he denounced the Italian government of Giovanni Giolitti, who had withdrawn Italian troops from Albania and had not pushed the Allies to allow the Italian annexation of Dalmatia. This drew more disaffected veterans into the Fascist ranks.

Fascists identified their primary opponents as the socialists who had opposed intervention in World War I. The fascists and the rest of the Italian political right held common ground; both held Marxism in contempt, discounted class consciousness and believed in the rule of elites. The Fascists assisted the anti-socialist campaign by allying with the other political parties and the conservative right in a mutual effort to destroy the Italian Socialist Party and labor organizations committed to class identity

---

[226] Griffin, R., *Fascism; A quick Immersion* (US: Tibidabo Publishing, 2020), p. 55.
[227] Griffin, R., *Fascism; A quick Immersion* (US: Tibidabo Publishing, 2020), p. 56.

above national identity.

Italian politics, always a swirling mass of multiple parties, became more complicated in 1921 when the radical wing of the Italian Socialist Party left the Communist Party of Italy (CPI). The CPI, now the Socialist Party of Italy, though diminished in numbers, was still the largest party in the Italian Parliament. With the departure of the radicals, the Socialist Party became more moderate and became a potential coalition partner for Giolitti's government. Had this happened, the alliance would have held a majority in Parliament and allowed an effective government. Mussolini acted immediately to prevent this. He offered to ally his Fascists with Giolitti. The offer was accepted and Giolitti assumed that the small fascist movement could be held in check more easily than the larger CPI.

This new coalition contained conservatives, nationalists, and liberals who stood against the socialists and communists in the 1921 elections. This resulted in the fascists, who in the past had held some socialist ideals, identifying themselves as the most extreme right-wing element of this new coalition. Though there had been talk of a new Roman Empire, Mussolini expanded this idea of national expansion and called for the modern Italians to re-establish the old Roman concept of *Mare nostrum* [Our Sea] and Italian domination of the Mediterranean Sea basin. This was an appeal to Italian pride, as when the Roman Empire ruled the world – a greatness that had been lost.

The Blackshirts then went to work in the streets fighting their opponents and intimidating the weak to prevent them from voting. As they were part of the new coalition, the police, and courts, which were controlled by Giolitti's government, turned a blind eye, and allowed the violence to continue. The Blackshirts killed many and parts of Italy fell completely under their control and prevented socialist supporters from voting and meeting.

Despite this, the Socialist Party still held the largest number of parliamentary seats, and the fascists were a small minority with only 35 seats. Having done far better than in the previous election, Mussolini believed his strategy of declaring the fascists as extreme rightists using the tactics like street violence was working. To reinforce this idea of being rightists, he had his membership sit on the extreme right of the amphitheater of the parliament. In his first speech, Mussolini attacked the fundamental elements of socialism and argued against collectivism. He also continued to argue that the post office and railroads should be privatized.

Fascist violence continued and expanded to the extent that the Communist Deputy Misiano was attacked and thrown from a building window based on the claim that he had been a deserter during the war. Indeed, they openly threatened socialist members in the chamber of Parliament with guns. This threat was, again, protected by the Giolitti government.

The concept of *squadrismo* was embraced by the Fascist Party and para-military squads, based on the *Arditi*, were formed throughout Italy. Giolitti had taken the serpent to his breast, and it would eventually bite him as it used military force to seize the reins of government.

Meanwhile the fascists began attacking the trade unions, which were the foundation of the Socialist Party. To do this, the fascists organized their own trade unions, called "syndicates" among strategic groups, such as the postal workers, taxi drivers, and the railroad workers. The objective was to increase their strength and to control labor. Though the fascist unions had not penetrated the organized working class, they did have some support among the lower middle class and small landowners.

Having the support of the middle class, the police, and the army, Mussolini then set about destroying the socialist trade unions. Mussolini became indispensable in Rome. The Blackshirt squads gradually took over more and more cities in the provinces. In 1922, only Parma and Bari were able to resist the Blackshirts. The efforts of the left to organize their own para-military squads proved to be a complete failure.

In August 1922, the Socialist-led Confederation of Labor called for a major anti-fascist protest strike; it collapsed quickly. This greatly strengthened Mussolini's bargaining position, and he profited from this situation to inflict further damage on the left and union institutions. The offices of *L'Avanti* were attacked and destroyed. In October Mussolini organized the famous March on Rome. On October 26, 1922, greater than 25,000 Fascist supporters converged on Rome, coming from all over Italy. They seized control of railroad stations and governmental offices. The prime minister responded by asking the king to declare martial law. However, Victor Emmanuel III refused, fearing that the army might revolt and a civil war erupted. Instead, he asked Mussolini to form a government on October 29, 1922, hoping to placate him by using constitutional means.

Mussolini, despite all expectations, had taken control of Italy by constitutional means. With the king's blessing, Mussolini formed a coalition government that included nationalists, two fascist ministers, liberals, and, until April 1923, two Roman Catholic ministers from the Popular Party. For the next eighteen months the government functioned in its normal manner. However, Mussolini spent his time consolidating his power incorporating the fascist squads into an official Voluntary Militia for National Security. Having the power to distribute government jobs, he filled government positions with a flood of job seekers that became newly baptized fascists in a process of providing government jobs in turn for political loyalty. The new membership expanded the base of the party and made it more respectable.

The election laws were changed in 1923 by the Acerbo Law. It stated that any political alliance of various groups that received 25% or more of the votes, would be awarded an absolute majority of the seats in Parliament, so that a government could be formed by a coalition that had as little as 25% of the overall vote. This brought many of the former liberal deputies into a new national alliance. The elections of April 1924 were held under this new system.

In preparation for the election, the fascists sent the Blackshirts into the streets where they employed their usual threats and violence to manipulate the vote. The fascists block took 64% of the vote, but the socialists and other parties won a majority of the vote in Northern Italy. The result was that the parties that opposed the fascists fell into chaos, criticizing each other and proved ineffective.

Democratic Italy was now dead. Giacomo Matteotti, who led the socialists, denounced the elections as a sham and claimed that there had been widespread intimidation of his supporters. The result was his murder by Blackshirts. This new crisis produced much distrust of Mussolini and the Fascist Party. Mussolini was accused of personal involvement in Matteotti's murder. He was denounced in the papers and the opposition parties walked out of Parliament.

The coalition partners of the Fascist Party began falling away. The current situation angered the fascist extremists, who were threatened with dismissal by the new militia commander. A showdown was demanded and Mussolini, too weak to rule by constitutional means, agreed.

In a speech given on January 3, 1925, in the Chamber of Deputies, Mussolini accepted responsibility for fascist rule and Matteotti's death. He promised a crackdown on dissenters. The king took no action. Mussolini then proclaimed himself dictator of Italy, assuming full responsibility over the government and announcing the dismissal of parliament. From 1925 to 1929, fascism steadily became entrenched in power; opposition deputies were denied access to parliament, censorship was introduced. In December 1925 royal decree, Mussolini was made solely responsible to the king.

The day after this speech orders were given to all prefects to take control of all suspect political organizations. This was followed by searches, arrests, and the elimination of many political offices and organizations.

Not having been removed from power, over the next two years, Mussolini disbanded most of the constitutional and conventional safeguards that protected the Italian democracy. Elections were abolished. The freedom of speech and assembly eliminated, and opposition parties and unions were dissolved. Freemasonry was outlawed, which struck a tremendous blow against the non-Catholic anti-fascists. A Special Tribunal for the Defense of the State was established. It was run by militia and army officers that focused its efforts on the elimination of anti-fascist subversives. Thousands of anti-fascist politicians were imprisoned or exiled. A few were even executed.

In 1927, Mussolini established a network of informants and spies called the *Organizzazione di Vigilanza Repressione dell'Antifascismo* (Organization for the Vigilant Repression of Anti-Fascism; OVRA), to counter anti-fascist subversives. It even engaged in assassinations within other countries prior to the outbreak of World War II.

To establish firm control over the population, the press was censored, and motion picture newsreels were generally fascist propaganda. All radio was tightly controlled by the government. Once the movements were established, new textbooks were imposed on the educational system. The government also provided mass leisure activities, such as sports, concerts, and seaside holidays. Not surprisingly, these activities were very popular. One could reasonably compare them to the Roman Emperor Caligula's program of bread and circuses, which was focused on gaining for him the support of the Roman population and allowed him to retain power.

This carrot went hand in hand with the stick of the OVRA. The fear of arrest, imprisonment, or economic marginalization intimidated thousands of anti-fascists and former oppositionists; silence replaced the propaganda of the *biennio rosso*. Fascist control of daily Italian life extended to the most basic levels. In 1938 the government imposed the use of *Voi* as the formal pronoun instead of *Lei* and banned handshakes in all places of public work. Foreign words and names were purged from the language. The walls of offices, schools, and public buildings were covered with slogans and murals paying homage to Mussolini and fascism, such as "Mussolini is always right" or "Better to live one day as a lion than 100 years as a sheep." This is a strange parallel to what was imposed by the Kim Regime in North Korea after World War II.

George Nafziger

What is Fascism?

We have already addressed the communist definition of fascism – anything that opposes communism. Unfortunately, with the many different forms of fascism during the post-World War I period, giving a single definition of it is impossible. Therefore, we should confine our study to definitions provided by the two most significant fascist leaders – Mussolini and Hitler.

In his own words, drawn from *The Doctrine of Fascism,* Mussolini tells us that fascism contains the following fundamental principles:[228]

1.) Philosophical Conception

>Like every concrete political conception, fascism is thought and action. It is action with an inherent doctrine, that, arising out of a given system of historical forces, is inserted in its doctrine and works on it from within. It has, therefore, a form co-related to the contingencies of time and place; but it has at the same time an ideal content which elevates it into a formula of truth in the higher region of the history of thought.
>
>There is no way of exercising a spiritual influence by means of a human will-power commanding the wills of others, without first having a clear conception of the particular and transient reality in which the will-power must act, and without having a clear conception of the universal and permanent reality in which the particular and transient reality has its life and being. To know men, we must have the knowledge of man, and to have a knowledge of man we must know the reality of things and their laws.
>
>There can be no conception of a state which is not fundamentally a conception of life. It is a philosophy or intuition, a system of ideas which evolves into a system of logical contraction, or which concentrates itself in a vision or in a faith, but which is always, at least virtually, an organic conception of the world.

---

[228] Mussolini, *The Doctrine of Fascism.* The edition of this work consulted has no page numbers. This quotation is drawn from the very beginning of the work.

2.) Spiritualized Conception.

Fascists would therefore not be understood in many of its manifestations (for example, in the organization of the Party, its system of education, its discipline) were it not considered in the light of its general view of life; a spiritualized view.

Fascism holds that the world is not this material world which appears on the surface, where man is an individual separated from all other men, standing by himself and subject to a natural law which instinctively impels him to lead a life of monetary and egoistic pleasure. Fascism maintains man is an individual who is the nation and the country. He is this by a moral law which embraces and binds together individuals and generations into an established tradition and mission; a moral law which suppresses the instinct to lead a life confined to a brief cycle of pleasure in order instead a life dedicated to the orbit of duty in a superior conception of life, free from the limits of time and space; a life where the individual, by self-abnegation and by the sacrifice of his particular interests, even death, realizes the entirely spiritual existence in which his value as a man consists.

3.) Positive Conception of Life as a Struggle.

Fascism is a spiritual conception, a result of the general reaction of the century against the languid and materialistic positivism of the Enlightenment Century. Anti-positivism yet positive, neither skeptical nor agnostic, neither pessimistic nor passively optimistic, as are in general the doctrines (all of them negative) which place the center of life outside of man, who by his free will can and should create his own world for himself.

Fascism wants a man to be active and to be absorbed in action with all his energies., It wants him to have a manly consciousness of the difficulties that exist and to be ready to face them. It conceives life as a struggle, holding that it is the duty of man to conquer the life within himself (the physical, moral, intellectual life). The instruments with which to build life worthy of him,

As for the individual, so for the nation, so for mankind. Hence the high value of culture in all its forms (art, religion, science) and the supreme importance of education. Labor is the essential value by which man conquers nature and creates the human world (economic, political, moral, intellectual).

4.) Ethical Conception.

This positive conception of life is evidently an ethical conception. It comprises the whole reality and the human activity which dominates it. No action is to be removed from the moral sense; nothing is to be in the world that is divested of the importance which belongs to it in respect of moral aims. Life, therefore, as the Fascist conceives it, is serious, austere, religious, entirely balanced in a world sustained by the moral and responsible forces of the spirit. The fascist disdains the "easy" life.

5.) Religious Conception.

Fascism is a religious conception in which man is considered the powerful grip of a superior law, the objective which transcends the individual, elevating him into a fully conscious member of a spiritual society. Anyone who has stopped short at the mere consideration of opportunism in the religious policy of the fascist regime has failed to understand that fascism, besides being a system of government, is also a system of thought.

6.) Historical and Realist Conception.

Fascism is a historical conception in which man could not be what he is without being a factor in the spiritual process to which he contributes. This contribution is either in the family or in the social sphere, in the nation or in history in general, to which all nations contribute. The great importance of tradition in the records, language, customs, and rules of human society is subsequently derived. Man without a part in history is nothing.

For this reason, fascism is opposed to all the abstractions of an individualistic character based upon materialism typical of the eighteenth century. Fascism is opposed to all the Jacobin innovations and utopias. It does not believe in the possibility of happiness on earth as conceived by seventeenth century economists' literature; it spurns all the ideological conceptions of final causes through which, at the great period of history, a final systematization of humanity would take place. Such theories only mean placing oneself outside real history and life, that is a continual ebb and flow and process of realizations.

Politically speaking, Fascism aims at being a realistic doctrine. In its practice, fascism aspired to solve only the problems that present themselves of their own accord in the process of history, and that find or suggest their own solution. To have the effect of action among men, it is necessary to enter the process of reality and to master the forces at work.

7.) The Individual and Liberty.

The fascist conception of the state is anti-individualistic. It was for the individual only insofar as he coincides with the state. It is opposed to the classic liberalism which arose from the need for reaction against absolutism. Classic Liberalism had accomplished its mission in history when the State had become transformed by the popular will (the will of the group, not the individual) and the group's consciousness.

Liberalism denied the state in the interests of the individual. Fascism reaffirms the state as the only true expression of the individual.

And if liberty is to be the attribute of the real man, and not of the scarecrow invented by the individualistic Liberalism, then fascism is for liberty. Fascism is for the true liberty that is serious – the liberty of the state and of the individual within the limits established by the state. For the fascist, all is comprised in the state and nothing spiritual or human exists – much lass has any value – outside the state. Fascism is a totalizing concept, and the fascist state – the unification and synthesis of every value – interprets, develops, and potentiates the entire life of the people.

8.) Conception of a Corporate State.

There are no individuals nor groups (political parties, associations, labor unions, classes) outside the state. For this reason, fascism is opposed to socialism. Socialism clings rigidly to class warfare in the historical evolution and ignores the unity of the state, which molds the classes into a single, moral, and economic reality. In the same manner, fascism is opposed to the unionizing of the laboring classes. But within the orbit of the state with coordinative functions, the real needs, which give rise to the socialist movement and to the forming of labor unions, are emphatically recognized by fascism. They are given their full expression in the corporative system, which conciliates every interest in the unity of the state.

9.) Democracy.

Individuals form classes according to categories of interests. They are associated according to the differentiated economical activities, which have a common interest; but first and foremost, they form the state. The state is not merely the numbers, or the sum of individuals, composing most of the people. Fascism, for this reason, is opposed to democracy because democracy, as viewed by fascists, identifies people with the greatest number of individuals and reduces them to a majority level. Fascists believe that if people are conceived, as they should be, qualitatively and not quantitatively, then fascism is democracy in its purest form. The qualitative conception is the most coherent and truest form and is, therefore, the most moral; it sees a people realized in the consciousness and will of the few or even of one only; an ideal which moves into realization in the consciousness and will of all. By "all" is meant those who derive their justification as a nation ethnically, from their nature and history, and who follow the same line of spiritual formation and development, possessing one single will and consciousness. This justification is not a race, nor a geographically determined region; it is as a progeny resulting from history which perpetuates itself - a multitude unified by an idea embodied in the will for power and to exist, conscious of itself and of its personality.

10.) Conception of the State.

This higher personality is truly the nation, because it is the state. The nation does not beget the state, according to the decrepit nationalistic concept which was used as a basis for the publicist of the national states in the nineteenth century. On the contrary, the nation is created by the state, which gives the people, conscious of their own moral unity, the will, and subsequently an effective existence. The right of a nation to its independence is derived not from a literary and ideal consciousness of its own existence - and much less from a *de facto* situation inert and unconscious - but from an active consciousness, from an active political will disposed to demonstrate as its right - a kind of state already in its pride (*in fieri*). The state as a universal ethical will, is the creator of right.

11.) Dynamic Reality.

The nation as a state is an ethical reality which exists and lives in measure as it develops. A standstill is its death. Therefore, the state is not only the authority which governs, and gives the forms of law and the worth of the spiritual life to the individual's will, but it is also the power which gives effect to its will in foreign matters. The nation is subsequently recognized and respected. It demonstrates, through facts, the universality of all the manifestations necessary for its development. Therefore, the nation is an organization and is also an expansion. The nation may be considered, at least virtually, equal to the very nature of the human will, that in its evolution recognizes no barriers, and realizes itself by proving its infinity.

12.) The Role of the State.

The fascist state, the highest and most powerful form of personality is a spiritual force. It reassures all the forms of man's moral and intellectual life. It cannot, therefore, be limited to a simple function of order and safeguarding, as contended by liberalism. It is not a simple mechanism that limits the sphere of the presumed individual liberties. It is an internal form and rule, a discipline of the entire person; it penetrates the individual's will and intelligence. Its principle, a central inspiration of the living human personality in the civil community, descends into the depths and settles in the heart of the man of action and the thinker, the artist, and the scientist. The state is "the soul of our soul."

13.) Discipline and Authority.

Fascism, in short, is not only a lawgiver and the founder of institutions, but an educator and a promoter of the spiritual life. It aims to rebuild not the forms of human life, but its content, the man, the character, the faith. For this end it exacts discipline and an authority which descend into and dominates the interior of the human spirit without opposition. Its emblem, therefore, is the historian *fasces*, symbol of unity, of force, and of justice.

The Italian Fascist Concept of the State

The most important concept of fascism is the state. It was seen as not simply a national, racial, religious or morale group though it may coincide with these groups. The fascists did recognize from history it may develop from such a group or from several different groups and that it could even result in the creation of such groups. However, as these groups can exist independently of the state, they do not necessarily constitute a state. They saw the state as a political organization that contained laws and a system for the enforcement of those laws. That political organization necessarily required some form of leadership that created and enforced that system of laws.[229]

"The State, whose only interest and duty is to promote the general good, is the only power capable of taking an impartial view in the interests of the whole between individuals or individual groups, whose interests come into conflict. Hence, if any such conflicts fail to be settled in the first instance by a friendly discussion between the parties it is the duty of the State by means of a constitutionally appointed court, to settle the dispute an enforce the settlement (*cf.* Article 5 of the Labor Charter, Section VI)."[230]

Fascists saw the state as both a natural and voluntary organization, whose organization was the product of natural forces and of man being a social animal. As such man requires a supreme ruling authority which makes a society a state and to make a society function in an organized manner. This authority tends to homogenize its elements under a moral code that allows it to create an environment capable of social and economic process.

As the state is a political organization that establishes judicial institutions and police. The concepts of state and authority naturally became closely linked. As time passes, these elements evolve and develop like the elements of any living organism. "And like any living organism it fights to assure its existence. This is a natural law, but Moral Law transcends it, even though it can never be in an essential conflict with it. This is where the law of life and the way the Moral Law transcends it is by the sanctioning of the sacrifice of the individual life, whenever a richer, more vigorous life and a generally higher (more moral) life is rightly judged to be the consequence"[231] of that sacrifice. It follows that because the life of the state is greater than the life of the individual, the family is logically the true unit of the state.

This concept's result is that the state has the right to promote, or even demand, self-sacrifice among its members for the common good. This is probably the major rule of fascism. This demand could extend to calling its members to risk, or even risk and end their lives, in the service of

---

[229] Barnes, J.S. *The Universal Aspects of Fascism*, p. 84-85
[230] Barnes, J.S. *The Universal Aspects of Fascism*, p. 166.
[231] Ibid, p. 87.

the greater good. This is, however, not a concept unique to fascism. Every state regularly calls upon its young men to join the armed forces and go to war defending the state. The difference is, however, the fascist concept - the reaction to the Enlightenment concept of individuals working solely for their personal benefit - that demands individual sacrifice for the betterment for the common good of the group. This idea is very close to the socialist concept of "from each according to his ability, to each according to his need."

  Fascists saw authority as consisting of the right of government and a moral power that was a reasonable, unifying, and beneficial principle requiring conscious responsibility from those exercising authority upon the citizens of the state. The concept of morality appears repeatedly in the discussion of the state. The unspoken issue, however, is "whose moral code?"

  The fascists further defined the national state as the highest form of the state because the most perfect harmony occurs when the national unity, based on a community of traditions, coincides with political unity. This community with common traditions is a constant element that winds through the factors that Robert O. Paxton[232] provides in his list of situations existing post-World War I. Paxton's list of situations, existing prior to World War I, created the environment that fostered the appearance of fascism.

  Italian fascists believed that the state could not tolerate the propagation of ideas that might undermine religion, the family, or the state. Italian fascists believed it was the duty of the state to censure any propaganda of such ideas and to prosecute, for contempt, any individual who through disrespectful words or actions, against religion, the institution of the family, and the main institutions of the state (e.g., king, the prime minister, or others who may serve as the head of the executive, parliament, or the law courts).

  Furthermore, the Italian fascists believed, that it was the duty of the state to construct a society where it became easy for the individual, in the pursuit of his private interests, to make his interests coincide with those of the community; and, that the state had a duty to raise the moral standards of the people and encourage their sense of communal responsibility and self-discipline.[233] Nowhere do Marx, Engels, or Lenin address morality.

[232] Paxton, R.O., *The Anatomy of Fascism* (New York: Vintage Books, 2005), p. 43.
[233] Barnes, J.S. *The Universal Aspects of Fascism*, p. 165. Barnes is an unusual source. He was born in India and raised in Italy and England. He was Secretary General of the International Centre of Fascist Studies in Lausanne, Switzerland, and a friend of Benito Mussolini in this work he set out to define the philosophy, the world view, and

Authority

The fascists believed that authority arose spontaneously as an element of society. The fascists believed authority was necessary to ensure the general welfare of the community. They also believed that that the state was a continually evolving living entity. The fascists believed that authority resided in the community and if there was no community there was no authority. They further believed that authority was only to be exercised for the sake of the community. Fascists also believed that authority was not derived from the community, "because the community is incapable of either creating it or abolishing it."[234] Again, the fascists maintained that real authority arose spontaneously and if it did not, society would dissolve into chaos.

Morality

When private moral judgement is not founded upon true doctrine, or a moral philosophy, there is moral chaos. In the Italian version of fascism, the state had to conform to a moral philosophy and judged according to it. It is, therefore, the moral philosophy which is acknowledged, protected, and spread throughout the community and nation. The fascists also believed that the state has no right to appropriate the right to judge itself; nor that the individual has the right to make capricious standards. Accordingly, the state must conform to that moral philosophy. It is important that this philosophy be acknowledged, protected, and spread through the state.

To this end, Italian fascism, but not Nazism, formally recognized the Roman Catholic religion as the state religion and the source of all morality.

Italian fascism sought to establish an ethical State that rested upon the following principles:

a.) Man, besides being an individual, has a corporate existence and

---

the principles that underlay Fascism.

[234] Barnes, J.S., *The Universal Aspects of Fascism* (Location unk: Reconquista Press; 2020), p. 109.

disciplinary authority is a natural component of this existence.
b.) Human actions are subject to the moral law, which is based on the eternal law of God, and obedience to that law is the source of societal harmony.
c.) Every group of humans, the nation state being the most perfect, is an organic system that encompasses the series of generations of individuals that form it and possessed a sense of community, and is subject to natural laws that give the community and the individual shape and form, but which are transcended by moral law.

The General Will

All living organisms have the self-preservation instinct. It is also the first duty of the government to act within the moral law to preserve society from dissolution, so man can attain his highest development and satisfy his needs. Unfortunately, there are no means to determine the general will. Reason, therefore, must be the final criterion government must use to determine the general will.

Italian fascists believed that the organized public opinion was seldom anything more than the "organized opinion of a sectional interests, the sum of individual wills of the members of a community is never the same thing, even if unanimous, as the general will."[235]

The Executive

It was believed that the executive should be vigorous and his bureaucracy expeditious and efficient. In addition, those that administer government should be from an aristocracy of intelligent and moral men. The bureaucracy should not be too rigid or too fluid. It should contain a mechanism for constructive and effective criticism that addresses and provides constructive influence upon the acts and proposed acts by the government to assure the general good, as opposed to any good. Though Italian fascists believed that power should be strong and capable of acting swiftly, they also believed that power should be, in many respects, independent of the legislature.

Governance

---
[235] Barnes, J.S., *The Universal Aspects of Fascism*, p. 160.

"The business of the State is to govern."[236] Fascists believed that a weak state was a decadent state. They believed that it was the business of the government to assure that the activities of the individual and the groups within the state were directed to the general good. This is because the proper business of the state is to assure the general good since the state will outlast the individuals that compose it. The state's purpose, thus, is to harmonize the needs and wishes of the individual with that general good.

In return it is the duty of the individual to recognize that he is not isolated, but that he is a member of a community and he is responsible in all his actions to the members of that group. It is his duty to direct his actions towards the general good. In consideration, it is the duty of the state to help him accomplish this by arranging society so that his individual interests are, as much as possible, coincident with the general interest. This is to be accomplished by using the law to provide the necessary sanctions against all activities that do not coincide with the general interest of the community.

Fascists believed that the individual possessed some natural rights, which do not conflict with his obligations to the community. The fascists believed man's natural rights were the foundation of society and if the state were to infringe on those rights, it would defeat its own purpose.

It was also believed that the state's duty was to make the individual's interests coincide with the general welfare and that the individual be made one with that of the state.

Thus, the individual was subordinated to the state. He was subject to the authority of the state. His liberties were restricted within the institutions and the laws of the state, and thus directed at the general good.

Though subordinated in that "sense," the individual was not the subordinate of the state in the sense that the state has no limits to its authority over him or that it made individual subordination the state's objective. The happiness of the individual could be described as indirectly dependent upon the general well-being, which is the direct concern of the state. Therefore, no individual had the right to seek happiness by acting against the general well-being.

In summary, though it would be improper to say that within the laws and institutions of the state, the "State uses the individual for its own purposes and subordinates him to the social organism, [T]his would be true if interpreted only as meaning that all laws and institutions are di-

---
[236]Ibid. p. 114.

rected to promote individual action along lines coincident with the general interests of society and so require that the individual submit to the authority of the State, except [that] the State betray its trust."

From a judicial perspective, i.e., the state's point of view, it may be accurately said that the individual was a subordinate factor, not because he was a less considerable factor than the community, but because he lived by the community, and the protection of the community from dissolution is the first practical duty of the state; for without authority, without laws or customs having the force of law, society cease to be."[237]

The fascists believed that government was not a popularity contest. They believed that a popular government was not necessarily a good government. Fascists believed that government could make mistakes, but that it should make as few as possible regarding public interests. The purpose of government was to provide exact enforcement of the laws and laws were not legitimate based on the numbers of people that supported them, but on their reasonableness and justice.

The Italian fascists believed that government should develop the means to enable the central government to keep in touch with the needs of the community.[238]

The Individual and Liberalism.

Individualism is the heart of liberalism. From the fascist perspective, the liberals saw the individual as the center of the universe and that the supreme object of the individual's life was "self-realization" or the maximization of happiness for the individual; that the individual alone determines what permits, and what defines his self-realization. However, if the world was focused on self-realization, it would be a world of chaos, that only a few could achieve self-realization and would do so at the expense of others. Liberals believed that the purpose of government should be limited, securing a compromise, as much as it is possible, allowing the maximum opportunity for everyone to achieve self-realization – i.e., "the highest realizable means of opportunity for self-realization of everyone (the formula "the greatest happiness of the greatest number" was an effort to express this ideal.)"[239]

---

[237] Ibid. p. 115.
[238] Barnes, J.S., *The Universal Aspects of Fascism* (Location unk: Reconquista Press; 2020), p. 167.
[239] Ibid. pp 116-117.

Twin Evils

The fascists perceive in this perfect liberal state merely a situation where the mass of the people live in fear of exploitation by those few who possess energy and ambition. Socialism and communism agree with fascism on this point.

In liberal state, as various classes competed to maximize their self-realization, class warfare would erupt as everyone recognized that they could maximize their self-realization by gaining control over the state. Control over the state would enable individuals to further exploit their neighbors. Under this situation, the individual would be justified in doing so, as there is no universal moral code and all is left to the judgment of the self-serving individual.

Liberalism was the philosophy that overthrew the rule of the nobility and tyrants; but it also prepared the way for a new dictatorship by class (i.e., communism) or a socialist slave state.

Another element of liberalism was the concept of *laissez-faire*, which fascism was committed to end. What may seem strange to today's modern liberals is that fascists agreed with John Maynard Keynes, a prominent liberal and noted economist. His book *The End of Laissez-faire*, published in 1926, was seen as a useful introduction to the fascist concept of economics. Keynes believed that "enlightened self-interest [does not] always operate in the public interest.... We cannot, therefore, settle on abstract grounds, but must handle on its merits in detail what Burke termed *one of the finest problems in legislation, namely, to determine what the State ought to take upon itself to direct by the public wisdom, and what it ought to leave, with as little interference as possible, to individual exertion.*" Finally, he concluded very convincingly that Socialism and Individualism are reactions to the same intellectual atmosphere."

The *laissez-faire* approach sees government's role as taking a "hands-off approach" to economics. This would allow capitalism to operate uncontrolled and unanswerable to the state and community. This resulted in the socialist approach to economics, which directed the nationalization of the means of production and distribution, an option that fascism rejected.

Keynes saw that the coming political struggle would not be based on economic issues, but on issues that "may be called psychological or, perhaps moral." It was on this moral issue that fascism took a stance in its political struggle. Fascists maintained that the desire for wealth was a powerful motivating force benefitting the economy; but fascists rejected that the desire for wealth would always be the main driving force. Fascism chose to make its appeal to limit the individual desire for wealth based on patriotism and religion in a nation where the artisan was encouraged. The fascists held that industry should be organized on a corporative basis with definite social and political functions defined for each corporation. In the Italian form of fascism, under Mussolini, it was expected that appropriate legislation would eliminate the "curse of usury" and penetrate society with a moral code that would prohibit the majority of the population to become wage-slaves of the state, as they are under communism, or allow continued productive power of the community to operate unhampered or unrestrained.

In speaking of the individual and the state, Barnes says: "Fascism regards it as the duty of the individuals to contrive his life that the pursuit of of his interests coincides with those of the community. The State is and can be the only impartial judge as to whether the individual is doing this or not. If he is not, the State has the right and the duty to interfere."

Barnes further adds, "Private initiative in the field of production is considered as a general rule the most efficacious and most useful instrument in the interest of the community (*cf.* Article 7 of the Labor Charter, Section VI); and thus, the institution of private property is sanctioned as a natural right, whereby the family tie, the most important and fundamental of all ties, is strengthened; which makes, more than anything else, when widely distributed, for true Liberty."

"Private property, however, is a public trust. If man's subjective rights to private property are abused, if he fails to exercise his rights in a manner which corresponds with a sense of responsibility to the community at large, he becomes liable to having his rights curtailed or even abrogated altogether – that is; not in general but in a particular department where his sense of duty has failed him."

"We may say, indeed, that Fascism sanctions an objective 'functional' theory of rights. Similarly, this sense of responsibility, which a true sense of Religion, which family affection, which patriotism and a consciousness of nationality provide, is the only true basis of citizenship, that is, the eligibility to assume responsibilities in the Government of the country. In other words, only those persons with a public conscious are fit to exercise public responsibilities and are therefore entitled to political rights."[240]

This idea of property and property rights stands in marked conflict with those of socialism and communism. Under communism, all property

---
[240] Ibid p. 164.

was state property and its utilization or exploitation left to the decision of the government, i.e., the Communist Party and its minions. Individual or corporate risk taking was to be avoided because of the potential of punishment under a communist system. The result was a lack of motivation on the part of the workers to take risks that might contribute to the public good. Fascism, in contrast, clearly recognized that personal gain, received from the individual taking risks, benefited the entire society.

Italian fascism also believed that the individual could not owe allegiance or serve a political body outside of the national state, i.e., the *International*. They believed that the individual must chose; and if they chose the *International* they were to be treated as foreigners.[241] This a clear distinction from Lenin's form of communism, which called for international concept of the world view.

Yet Italian fascism also held that the cooperation, for the benefit of the community, was the "order of the day." To this end, local government and various autonomous public institutions were not permitted to be at variance with the aims of the central government. In contrast to communism, where the central government had appropriated and nationalized all property and made all the decisions regarding the utilization of all property, Fascism took the approach of setting broad outlines defining how an individual was to use his private property and permitted him free rein in its utilization until he stepped outside those broad outlines.

Liberty

It is the fascist concept of liberty that the "individual possesses by nature certain personal rights, rights which belong to him, because though he cannot live except as a member of society and under the authority of the State, they are not subject to State interference as having authority to do so with his position *qua* member of society, but as having solely to do with him as an individual and as a member of a family."[242] This evolves from the fascist concept of moral law. As a result, the fascists believed that the state has no right to impose on the individual any more than is necessary to achieve the general good; that excesses beyond that are to be condemned. Of course, in practice, this was generally ignored, particularly by the Nazis.

Paxton goes on to say that some rights, such as the rights of a father over his family - the family being the foundation upon which the state is

---
[241] Ibid. p. 165.
[242] Ibid. p. 121.

built - must be respected by the state; that the state cannot forcibly remove children from their parents "without urgent and grave reasons touching the general well-being." This element is one fundamental differences between communism and fascism. Communism seeks to destroy the family so that the government can control the education of children and train them in communist ideology without the interference of the parents, who might hold ideas that are antithetical to communism. In practice, however, both Italian fascism and German Nazism took control of the schools to train children in their philosophy and established groups to further that indoctrination.

Another point of conflict with communism, fascism believed that no state had the right to persecute an individual because of their private opinions unless those opinions are made public. Paxton notes that the fascist state cannot permit a member to die lacking the means of subsistence and that the individual has the right to acquire property for himself and his heirs; that the individual cannot be placed in a condition of slavery or semi-slavery; and the individual cannot endure interference in his home and in his personal affairs. The fascists held the individual's home cannot be invaded without the issuance of a legal warrant; nor can the individual be condemned without a fair trial in accordance with the laws of the land.

In the course of their history, both communism and fascism violated every one of these rights. Communism absolutely prohibited any individual from acquiring property, let alone passing it on to his heirs. Indeed, Engels railed against the ability to pass on one's estate to one's heirs as one cause of all the world's evils.

Paxton qualifies these rights saying that "The liberties which such laws would safeguard are concrete liberties, inherent in the moral notion of an individual's natural rights. But no man possesses the natural right to propagate any personal views he likes, to destroy wealth, or to attempt to disrupt society. Any liberties beyond those which pertain to his natural rights and which may be granted to the individual in excess of such rights are as the State, in legislating, calculates what will prove beneficial to the community as a whole, invigorates it, vitalizes it, and so gives individuals the opportunity for a better and higher life. Such liberties are definite and concrete, as all liberties should be. There is no such thing as freeing man in the abstract."[243]

Paxton continues to say that all an individual's liberties must be in the interest of the collective. This sounds very much in agreement with

---
[243] Ibid. p. 122.

the attitude of the communists. Paxton also quotes Mussolini who said: "Liberty is not a right; it is a duty. It is not a concession granted to us; it is a conquest. It is not a matter of equality; it is a privilege. The notion of liberty changes in time. There is a liberty for times of peace and another liberty in times of war. There is a liberty for prosperous times, another for lean times."[244]

Paxton believed that the fascist state had the right to intervene when the individual's private interests do not coincide with the general interests. He gives an example of an individual buying property but says that the individual systematically destroys the value of his property by impoverishing the soil or by cutting down the timber unduly to make a profit; or, if he neglects to develop it as the state deems desirable, the state has the right to interfere. One must wonder, therefore, if one can truly own property in a fascist state and how much the decision to interfere can be swayed by the personal opinions of an individual bureaucrat, versus what may be stated in the law concerning a specific subject.

Paxton goes on to say that moral law steps in and regulates the limits of the rights of the individual. Again, whose morality? Or is it so codified that the individual knows what are his obligations to the state? The repeated use of the term "moral law" seems to be an "open door" established by a vague, wonderful sounding term to justify oppression similarly imposed by communism upon its victims.

Democracy

In citing Aristotle, Barnes says that one can "conclude that in a government where authority is exercised by many, but in accordance with a system of checks and balances, wherein the more responsible offices are held by an aristocracy of intelligent and morality, wherein there exists one office of outstanding or unifying authority, is likely to prove, in practice, the best form of government."[245] He continues to say that fascism completely agrees with this concept. This concept is clearly seen in the execution of fascism in Italy and Germany. In both nations there was a single, charismatic leader, who was perceived by the people as meeting those standards, and was given absolute power.

Barnes says that such a government meets, in some sense, the modern term of democracy; that it claims to be as democratic as any other polit-

---
[244] Ibid. p. 125.
[245] Ibid. p. 132-133.

ical creed because it is broadly based on the will of the people.

There is a second meaning of the word democracy that the fascists also accepted; a meaning that involves the concept of equal opportunity. This meaning is that every man has an equal opportunity to rise to the highest degree of self-realization. Fascists also recognized that if all men are equal before the law and have equal opportunity to rise, all men are not endowed with the same gifts by nature, that the circumstances of their upbringing are not equally conducive to rising to the same level of success, and that cultural and various social conditions can detrimentally affect their potential to maximize their self-realization.

Considering this, the concept of equal opportunity was viewed by fascists as an unreachable goal. They believed equal opportunity was undesirable; it would mean sacrificing the family, which fascism saw as the most sacred institution of the state. Fascists viewed the family, as among other things, producing responsibility and variety, that the fascists did see as desirable.

Since equal opportunity is unobtainable, fascists saw that it was undesirable and contrary to nature; however, in the ordinary practical sense of the term "equal opportunity," they had no objections to the idea. As described by Aristotle, the fascists wanted the best and most capable individuals, those who demonstrated the greatest intelligence and morality, to assume the responsibility of the most important offices of the state.

The concept of democracy is often confounded with what Aristotle called "mob rule." Fascism, according to Barnes, accepted a popular and elective government, but they believed that where a supreme parliament is elected, that it tends to move towards mob rule. That is, it evolves into what is called the dictatorship of the majority and the rights and liberties of the minority are not only ignored, but also crushed. This is why the fascists wanted checks and balances in the form of a governing class. They believed that no great harm could result if there existed a governing aristocracy that was firmly entrenched within the state bureaucracy.[246]

Empire and War.

Barnes sees that war is inevitable between states since they struggle for existence in a world of comparative anarchy, as they look for resources. However, according to Barnes, it was not so under the idea of empire as fascism interpreted it. He believed that those empires of the 1920's, that

[246] Ibid. 136.

controlled all the world's resources and regions suitable for colonization, did not allow other nations to expand and gain resources to support their industry and feed their populations. Therefore, because of their covetousness for territory and enlarged empire, these empires were responsible for wars that might occur.

Mussolini saw the establishment of empire as a method of merging the colonized lands with the homeland and spreading the homeland's culture to those backward lands and bring law and peace to unsettled, backward lands. When ancient Greece had been conquered by Rome, Rome absorbed the Greek culture and Greece absorbed Roman culture. The resultant merger of those two cultures was spread across the world to the benefit of all humanity. In a similar sense, the Roman Catholic Church was part of Italian culture that had a beneficial effect to the world as Christianity spread through-out the world. This was followed by the way that the Italian Renaissance formed yet a third culture wave. This third cultural wave also improved the world. Barnes saw the spreading of Italian fascism as a fourth such wave.

One can also see this same idea spreading from England in Kipling's comments on an ideal imperialism that spread "all that is best in the English public-school spirit."

Then there is pacifism. Mussolini wrote in *The Doctrine of Fascism*, "As far as the general future and development of humanity is concerned, and apart from any mere consideration of current politics, Fascism above all does not believe either in the possibility or utility of universal peace. It, therefore, rejects the pacifism, which masks surrender and cowardice. War alone brings all human energies to their highest tension and sets a seal of nobility on the peoples who have the virtue to face it. All other tests are, but substitutes which never make a man face himself in the alternative of life or death. A doctrine which has its starting-point in the prejudicial postulate of peace is, therefore, extraneous to Fascism."

Mussolini continues to say, "Fascism also transports this ant-pacifist spirit into the life of individuals. The proud *squadrista*, motto of '*me ne frego*' [I don't give a damn][247] scrawled on the bandages of the wounded is an act of philosophy – not only stoic. In summary of a doctrine not only political, it is an education in strife and an acceptance of the risks which it carried: it is a new style of Italian life. It is thus that the Fascists loves and accepts life, ignores, and disdains suicide; understands life as a duty,

---

[247]This is a very old term in Italian military history and dates at least back to the Napoleonic Wars.

a lifting up, a conquest, something to be filled in and sustained on a high plane; a thing that has to be lived through for its own sake, but above all for the sake of theirs near and far, present and future."[248]

Class Warfare.

Italian fascism recognized that there was class warfare. However, Italian fascists believed it was not necessary. This communist concept was seen by the fascists as a wedge intended to divide society, while the fascists sought to strengthen the bonds of the people within society. The fascist response was to deprive those who sought to promote class warfare of their political rights. They did, however, see that class warfare should not be confused with individual competition, considering the dynamic conditions of life, where individuals competed for better economic conditions or social status. This conflict between those who sought to rise and those who resisted individual versus group advancement as the "struggle of capacities." The fascist did not define this struggle as class warfare, but a fact of the human existence.[249]

In *The Doctrine of Fascism*, Mussolini states, "Fascism having denied historical materialism, by which men are only puppets in history, appearing and disappearing on the surface of the tides while in the depths the real directive forces act and labor, it also denies the immutable and irreparable class warfare, which is the natural filiation of such an economic conception of history; and it denies above all that class warfare is the preponderating agent of social transformation."[250]

Corporations Under Italian Fascism.

The Italian fascism looked to organize the industrial forces of the country "within the orbit of the State."[251] This was so that private interests might better coincide with the general good and eliminate any chance for class warfare. By this means the fascists sought to increase the cooperation between the various factors of production, substituting the state's justice for destructive labor strikes and lock-outs that plagued industrial disputes.

---

[248] Mussolini, *The Doctrine of Fascism*, pages not numbered. Point 3.
[249] Barnes, J.S. *The Universal Aspects of Fascism*, p. 166.
[250] Mussolini, *The Doctrine of Fascism*, pages are not numbered, point 5.
[251] Barnes, J.S., *The Universal Aspects of Fascism* p. 183.

This increased cooperation between production factors increasing the productivity of labor and producing a sense of responsibility to the nation - a basic of requirement of citizenship.

Fascism sought to organize industries and worker groups into "professional associations" that adhered to the following requisites:

> a.) Each professional association was to represent one category and one category only of employers or workers so that they shared common interests and would protect the interests of that class.
>
> b.) That there should be only one association of the members of any category in any one district.
>
> c.) That no employer's association could be recognized unless the members represented and employed at least 10% of the workers engaged in that category within a district.
>
> d.) No association whatever may be recognized unless their articles of the association, their objectives, are directed to improving the moral and economic interests of their members, and participate in in their technical instruction. This included the religious, moral, and national education of their members

These associations were to be able to collect dues and, among other purposes, to address the welfare of its members.

The government's courts were to decide the interpretation of contracts and decided on the conditions of new collective contracts based on the principle of equity. Strikes and lock-outs were forbidden and liable to heavy penalties if they occurred. They believed that it was appropriate for the state to intervene, but only when private initiative was lacking or insufficient, or when political interests of the state were involved; and then, the state could only assume the form of supervision, assistance, or direct management.

CHAPTER 8
Nazism and Hitler

Where Mussolini was a prolific writer and presented a document that specifically and uniquely discusses his political philosophy, Hitler took the path of writing a biographical political work, *Mein Kampf,* in which he not only presented the development of his political thought, but much of his biography. Intermixed with this is the history of the development of the Nazi Party or, more properly, the NSDAP [*Nationalsozialistische Deutsche Arbeiterpartei* – National Socialist German Worker's Party].

Let's begin with a short examination of Hitler's rise to power. It may seen strange, but there is evidence that in 1918, after the end of WWI that Hitler was associated with the People's State of Bavaria.[252] This state was established on November 8, 1918, as an attempt at a socialist state to replace the Kingdom of Bavaria.

In September 1919 when Hitler joined the Deutsche Arbeiterpartei (DAP; German Workers' Party). His oratory talent and charisma allowed him to rise to prominence in the party and he eventually became the party's leader.

It was in 1920 that the DAP renamed itself to the *Nationalsozialistische Deutsche Arbeiterpartei NSDAP.* This name was chosen so as to be attractive to the various left-wing German workers, but it always had a streak of socialism in it, which we will discuss a bit later. There were, as a result many anti-capitalists and anti-bourgeois elements, which were eventually purged because they could not support the pro-business stance of the NSDAP.

On November 8, 1923, Hitler and General Ludendorff, supported by several hundred Brownshirts (*Sturmabteilung* or SA) seized a *Bürgerbräukeller* (beer cellar) where they seized several members of the Munich and Bavarian government. Hitler proclaimed a national revolution and attempted to repeat Mussolini's March on Rome. The putsch failed

---
[252] https://www.youtube.com/watch?v=UpuGRO72GbA

and Hitler and his accomplices were prosecuted and imprisoned. It was in prison that Hitler wrote *Mein Kampf*. He was sentenced to five-year term but only served eight months.

The Great Depression struck Germany in 1929 and produced tremendous political instability. Hitler had resumed his leadership of the Nazi Party and continued his political activities with new notoriety. In 1930 he negotiated an alliance with the Nationalist Alfred Hugenberg to campaign against the Young Plan, which was a renegotiation of Germany's war reparation payments. Hugenberg controlled several newspapers, and it was by this means that Hitler reached a national audience. Their alliance also gave Hitler access to many business and industrial leaders, who were anxious to establish a strong right-wing response to the communists. They provided the money necessary to begin a national campaign for the Nazi Party. This support by industrialists is probably another source of Hitler's unwillingness to full blown socialism.

In 1932 Hitler ran against Hindenburg in the presidential election and the Nazi Party took 36.8% of the votes on a second ballot. This gave Hitler a strong negotiating position. He engaged in a series of intrigues with conservatives, which gained the Nazi Party their support. Though the Nazi Party's votes in November 1932 election declined, Hitler insisted that he be made chancellor. On January 30, 1933, Hindenburg offered him the chancellorship of Germany, and he was within striking range of absolute power. The opportunity was not long in coming.

On February 27th, 1933, a few weeks after Adolf Hitler became Chancellor of Germany. Marinus van der Lubbe, a Dutch communist, was alleged to have set the Reichstag on fire. As Rahm Emmanuel famously said, "Never let a good crisis go to waste," Hitler blamed communist agitators for the fire and claimed communists were plotting against the German government. He then persuaded President Paul von Hindenburg to issue the Reichstag Fire Decree which suspended civil liberties and began a ruthless war on the communists. There is a significant debate over the truth that Marinus van der Lubbe set the fire, or because he was mentally challenged. It has been suggested that he was induced into the act or even set up so he would be caught and charged with act by members of the Nazi Party. Nonetheless, this gave Hitler the *casus belli* to seize absolute power. In essence he had followed Mussolini's March on Rome.

Hitler's Early Life.

In the beginning, *Mein Kampf* closely follows Hitler's early life. It furthermore gives us the basis for the evolution of thought as it ties to his personal experiences. There is, however, much that is unsaid. It is necessary, therefore, to "read between the lines" of his frequent tirades and try to determine their origin.

Born on 20 April 1889, near Linz, Austria, Hitler's mother was a housewife and dearly loved by him. His father was a minor bureaucrat in the government of the Austro-Hungarian Empire, which gave him some status in Austrian society. He believed that it was extremely important, based on his having escaped life on the farm and its harshness. He wanted this for his son, but Hitler revolted against it. He wanted to be an artist and later an architect.

When he completed his schooling, Hitler went to Vienna, the cultural center of the Austro-Hungarian Empire. Hitler failed in his application to art school and was told he should consider becoming an architect. Though upset, he decided to pursue architecture and began studying it, but money was a major issue, so he took up work as a menial laborer.

It is during this period of menial labor when most of Hitler's politics developed. First, the reader must understand that Hitler was a narcissus, an egomaniac, and an elitist. He was also a radical nationalist, and this nationalism arose from his sense of self identity. His narcissism meant he thought he was superior to all others. This easily produced his idea that his ethnicity was superior to all others. This is the simplest form of nationalism, that I and my ethnic fellows are superior to all others - their culture, their language, etc. are superior to all others. This easily led Hitler to the fascist philosophy.

Ideological Developments in Vienna.

In *Mein Kampf,* Hitler explains that it was in Vienna that his sense of nationalism solidified. By nationalism, however, he did not mean the "state" or a piece of ground, but an ethnic nation, a homogeneous group of people joined by a common language and culture.

In Hitler's view, the Czechs were taking a dominant role in the government and culture of the Austro-Hungarian Empire. Hitler, being an ethnic German, resented this. He revolted against the Slavification of his homeland. He said,

"What history taught us about the politics followed by the

House of Habsburg was corroborated by our own everyday experiences. In the north and in the south the poison of foreign races was eating into the body of our [the German] people and even Vienna was steadily becoming more and more a non-German city. The Imperial House favored the Czechs on every possible occasion….."[253]

Hitler explains,

> "What I know of Social Democracy in my youth was precious little and that little was for the most part wrong. The fact that it led the struggle for universal suffrage and the secret ballot gave me an inner satisfaction; for my reason then told me that this would weaken the Hapsburg regime, which I so thoroughly detested. I was convinced that even if it should sacrifice the German element the Danubian State would not continue to exist. Even at the price of a long and slow Slaviz-ation of the Austrian Germans, the State would secure no guarantee of a really durable empire. Therefore, I welcomed every movement that might lead towards the final disruption of that impossible state which had decreed that it would stamp out the German character in 10,000,000 people. The more this babble of tongues wrought discord and disruption, even in Parliament, the nearer the hour approached for the dissolution of this Babylonian Empire. That would mean the liberation of my German Austrian people, and only then would it become possible for them to be reunited with the motherland."[254]

Later, talking about Social Democracy, we find this comment about his sense of nationalism:

> "This probing into books and newspapers and studying the teachings of Social Democracy reawakened my love for my own people. And thus, what at first seemed an impassable chasm became the occasion of a closer affection."[255]

Why should Hitler have issues with Social Democracy? He explains as

---

[253] Hitler, A., *Mein Kampf My Struggle*, (USA, Midgaard, 2014) p. 18.
[254] *Mein Kampf*, p. 27.
[255] *Mein Kampf*, p. 28.

follows:

> "In the literary effusions which dealt with the theory of Social Democracy there was a display of high-sounding phraseology about liberty and human dignity and beauty, all promulgated with an air of profound wisdom and serene prophetic assurance; a meticulously woven glitter of words to dazzle and mislead the reader. On the other hand, the daily Press inculcated this new doctrine of human redemption in the most brutal fashion. No means were too base, provided they could be exploited in the campaign of slander. These journalists were real virtuosos in the art of twisting facts and presenting them in a deceptive form. The theoretical literature was intended for these simpletons of the *soi-disant* intellectual belonging to the middle and, naturally, the upper classes. The newspaper propaganda was intended for the masses."[256]

Hitler had little regard for the Social Democrats. He said,

> "The Social Democrats know how to create the impression that they alone are the protectors of peace. In this way, acting very circumspectly, but ever losing sight of their ultimate goal, they conquer one position after another, at once time by methods of quiet intimidation and at another time by sheer daylight robbery, employing these latter tactics at those moments when the public attention is turned towards other matters from which it does not wish to be diverted, or when the public considers an incident too trivial to create a scandal about it and thus provoke the anger of a malignant opponent........"
>
> "......I also came to understand that physical intimidation has its significance for the mass as well as for the individual. Here again the Socialists had calculated accurately on the psychological effect."
>
> "Intimidation in workshops and in factories, in assembly halls and at mass demonstrations, will always meet with success as long as it does not have to encounter the same kind of terror in a stronger form."[257]

---

[256] *Mein Kampf*, p. 28.
[257] *Mein Kampf*, p 29.

Twin Evils

As Hitler saw it the bourgeois were not considering the justifiable demands of the workers in their factories and the "bourgeoise parties can never repair the damage that resulted from the mistake they then made. For they sowed the seeds of hatred when they opposed all efforts at social reform."[258] Like the Socialists and Marxists, he was concerned about the working class; particularly during his stay in Vienna, Hitler was one of them. He went on to say, "And thus they gave, at least, apparent grounds to justify the claim put forward by the Social Democrats – namely, that they alone stand up for the interest of the working class." Hitler adds the following:

> "While thus studying the social conditions around me, I was forced, whether I liked it or not, to decide on the attitude I should take towards the Trades Unions. Because I looked upon them as inseparable from the Social Democratic Party, my decision was hasty – and mistaken. I repudiated them as a matter of course. But on this essential question also Fate intervened ad gave me a lesson, with the result that I changed the opinion, which I had first formed."
>
> "When I was twenty years old, I had learned to distinguish between the Trades Unions as a means of defending the social rights of the employees and fighting for better living conditions for them and, on the other hand, the Trades Unions as a political instrument used by the [Social Democratic] Party in the class struggle."[259]

The concept of "class struggle" is fundamental to Marxism. So, it is apparent that though talking here about Social Democrats, their behavior, their motives, and their actions were quite within the scope of Marxist philosophy.

To expand on the concept of Trades Unions standing for the workers as "juxtaposed against them being a political group," Hitler goes on to say,

> The Social Democrats understood the enormous importance of the Trades Union movement. They appropriated it as an instrument and used it with success, while the bourgeois parties failed to understand it and, thus, lost their political prestige.

---
[258] *Mein Kampf*, p. 30.
[259] Ibid.

They thought that their own arrogant veto would arrest the logical development of the movement and force it into an illogical position. But it is absurd and also untrue to say that the Trades Union movement is in itself hostile to the nation. The opposite is the more correct view. If the activities of the Trades Union are directed towards improving the condition of a class, and succeeded in doing so, such activities are not against the Fatherland or the State, but are, in the truest sense of the word, national. In that way the trades union organization helps to create the social conditions which are indispensable in a general system of national education. It deserves high recognition when it destroys the psychological and physical germs of social disease and thus fosters the general welfare of the nation.[260]

In this passage we see Hitler beginning to blend his concept of nationalism, the improvement of the condition of the working class, and the hijacking of the trade union movement for political purposes by the Social Democrats.

In justifying the trade union movement, Hitler goes on to say, "Is it, or is it not, in the interest of the nation to remove the causes of social unrest?"[261] How different is this from the Marxist concept of removing the act of employment from the hands of the individual and putting it into the hand of the collective? Hitler uses the term "nation" and Marxism speaks of the "collective." What difference is there between these two philosophies? Therefore, the genuine purpose of the movement [trades unions] gradually fell into oblivion and was replaced by new objectives. The Social Democrats never troubled themselves to respect and uphold the original purpose upon which the trade unionists' movement was founded. They simply took over the Movement, in its entirety, to serve their own political ends. Within a few decades the Trades Union Movement was transformed, by the expert hand of Social Democracy, from an instrument which had been originally fashioned for the defense of human rights into an instrument of the destruction of the national economic structure.[262]

It is at this point that Hitler turns to his next issue, the Jews. "Knowledge of the Jews is the only key whereby one may understand the

---

[260] Ibid.
[261] *Mein Kampf*, p. 31
[262] Ibid.

inner nature and therefore the real aims of Social Democracy."

When it comes to Hitler's position on the Jews, one needs to "read between the lines." Yes, he was a fervent racist and anti-Semite. And, certainly, this is linked to his sense of German superiority, i.e., his nationalistic ideas. Hitler was also a Catholic and the Catholic Church did not officially repudiate the idea of collective Jewish guilt for Christ's death until the Second Vatican Council in 1965. This idea had led to strong anti-Semitic feelings throughout Europe for centuries. That said, there is an issue why Hitler specifically targeted the Jews with so much hatred, when early in *Mein Kampf* he specifically spoke-out against the Slavs in general and the Czechs in particular.

He clearly says in *Mein Kampf* that he knew a Jewish boy in his school and that he had no animus towards him. However, when Hitler arrived in Vienna something happened that he does not discuss. As one reads on, Hitler's comments on politics, specifically Marxism and even the Social Democrats, he frequently conflates those two political parties with the Jews in his rantings. It derives from the analysis of his various comments about Marxism in conjunction with his rants against the Jews that in his mind Marxism and Judaism were synonymous. One can read passage after passage, substituting "Jew" with "Marxist" and in the context of the whole document there is no difference. It appears that in Hitler's mind, there was no difference.

Why is this? In his discussion of his life in Vienna Hitler begins his discussions of the press, which he hated fervently because it was anti-Nationalist and because it advocated the internationalist philosophy. Throughout *Mien Kampf* Hitler repeatedly speaks of the "Jewish Press." Of course, Karl Marx was a Jew, so when Hitler encountered Marxism, he associated Marx's religion with his philosophy. Therefore, when Marxism attacked Hitler's fervent nationalistic theories, he saw it as the "Jewish Press" attacking his narcissistic love of his nationality.

The second argument that inclines one towards believing that Hitler's anti-Semitism, was Semitic association with trade unions, which he strongly believed were under their control.

Though this is purely speculation, his treatment as a manual laborer lends credence to this speculation. While he lived in Vienna, Hitler worked for pennies, struggled to live, and frequently suffered from hunger resulting from the low wages he was paid. He does not mention anything about his employer, not even his name. This leaves one to wonder why, because he frequently mentions the names of newspapers he felt were Jewish, politicians he thought were stupid or corrupt, and other individuals. So, let us speculate that his employer was a Jew and that in his mix of hatred and self-love, he could not admit that he had actually worked for a Jew.

Again, he'd known a Jewish boy in school and felt nothing particular about that child or his race; but after Vienna he is a rabid anti-Semite. Pure politics, the rantings of so-called "Jewish Press" certainly would not have provoked this hatred. It must have been a personal experience that he believed to be utterly shameful.

In speaking of the Jews, and building on his attitude towards the Social Democrats, Hitler says,

> I gradually discovered that the Social Democratic Press was predominately controlled by Jews. But I did not attach special importance to this circumstance, for the same state of affairs existed in other newspapers. But there was one striking fact in this connection. It was there was not a single newspaper with which Jews were connected that could be spoken of as [being] National, in the meaning that my education and convictions attached to that word.
> "Making an effort to overcome my natural reluctance, I tried to read articles of this nature published in the Marxist Press; but in doing so my aversion increased all the more. And then I set about learning something of the people who wrote and published this mischievous stuff. From the publisher downwards, all of them were Jews. I recalled to mind the names of the public leaders of Marxism, and then I realized that most of them belonged to the Chosen Race - The Social Democratic representatives in the Imperial Cabinet as well as the secretaries of the Trades Unions and the street agitators. Everywhere the same sinister picture presented itself. I shall never forget the row of names – Austerlitz, David, Adler, Ellenbogen, and others. One fact became quite evident to me. It was that this alien race held in its hands the leadership of that Social Democratic Party with those minor representatives I had been disputing for months past. I was happy at last to know for certain that the Jew is not a German.[263]

As can be seen in this paragraph, the press is Marxist, the people

---
[263] *Mein Kampf,* p. 36.

running the press are Jews., Therefore, my contention is that, in his mind, Hitler drew little or no distinction between Marxist philosophy and the Jews. The fact that Karl Marx was a Jew, surely reinforced this in his mind. Yet, he becomes even more clear in his conviction that the Jews and the Marxists were inseparable. Hitler adds the following:

> And so, I began to gather information about the authors of this teaching [Marxism] with a view to studying the principles of the movement. The fact that I attained my object sooner than I could have anticipated was due to the deeper insight into the Jewish question, which I then gained, my knowledge of this question being hitherto rather superficial. This newly acquired knowledge alone enabled me to make a practical comparison between the real content and the theoretical pretentiousness of the teaching laid down by the apostolic founders of Social Democracy, because I now understood the language of the Jews. I realized that the Jew uses language for the purpose of dissimulating his thought or at least veiling it, so that his real aim cannot be discovered by what he says, but rather by reading between the lines. This knowledge was the occasion of the greatest inner revolution that I had yet experienced. From being a soft-hearted cosmopolitan, I became an out-and-out anti-Semite.[264]

At this point I would like to speculate further about Hitler's motives for hating the Jews so fervently. I have speculated that Hitler had a Jewish boss. If that was the case, then it would seem reasonable to assume that he became quite familiar with that man and possibly his family. Hitler was clearly a very emotional man. Imagine if his Jewish boss had a daughter and Hitler became infatuated with her only to have her rebuff his advances or her father, his boss, oppose Hitler's romantic interests in her. Could this crushed romantic longing not have turned into a burning hatred to a point where murdering not only the men, but also the women and children was acceptable to him? One might argue that his Jewish boss had abused him financially or in some other way, but it seems unlikely that such would have created in anyone such hatred that murder women, children, and the elderly was an all-absorbing necessity.

I travel down this path because at one point Hitler said he had

---
[264] *Mein Kampf,* p. 37.

"many issues" with the Jewish people.[265] One of those issues was their involvement with Marxism. It must be remembered that Marxism is a form of socialism and the Nazi Party was the National *Socialist* German Worker's Party. They are both forms of socialism so something else provoked this hatred, even though, in Hitler's eyes, Marxism was just another characteristic of the Jews, who he hated. Another possible reason was the Jews being part of the bourgeois, the employer class, which he saw as oppressive. Then there is his belief that Germany had been "stabbed in the back" by the Jews, which had caused Germany and its Austrian ally to lose World War I. One should add that the hated Treaty of Versailles was signed by Hermann Müller, a Social Democrat. Some of these reasons post-date Hitler's Vienna experiences, but others were at its heart. So, what would turn the later "national socialist" against Marxism, which Hitler directly linked to the Jews and is also very socialist? I propose that it was a crushed romantic infatuation that lit the fuse of Hitler's hatred and that many subsequent events that brought about his blazing hatred of Jews. Following are the 26 Points or Positions of the National Socialist Deutsches Arbiten Partie (National Socialist German Workers' Party), the Nazis:

The 26 Points or Positions of the Nazi Party

1. We demand the union of all Germans in a Greater Germany on the basis of the principle of self-determination of all peoples.
2. We demand that the German people have rights equal to those of other nations; and that the Peace Treaties of Versailles and St. Germain shall be abrogated.
3. We demand land and territory (colonies) for the maintenance of our people and the settlement of our surplus population.
4. Only those who are our fellow countrymen can become citizens. Only those who have German blood, regardless of creed, can be our countrymen. Hence no Jew can be a countryman.
5. Those who are not citizens must live in Germany as foreigners and must be subject to the law of aliens.
6. The right to choose the government and determine the laws of the State shall belong only to citizens. We therefore demand that no public office, of whatever nature, whether in the central government, the province, or the municipality, shall be held by anyone who is not a citizen.

---

[265] Toland, J. *Adolph Hitler,* Vol II, p. 608.

7. We wage war against the corrupt parliamentary administration whereby men are appointed to posts by favor of the party without regard to character and fitness.

8. We demand that the State shall above all undertake to ensure that every citizen shall have the possibility of living decently and earning a livelihood. If it should not be possible to feed the whole population, then aliens (non-citizens) must be expelled from the Reich.

9. Any further immigration of non-Germans must be prevented. We demand that all non-Germans who have entered Germany since August 2, 1914, shall be compelled to leave the Reich immediately.

10. All citizens must possess equal rights and duties.

11. The first duty of every citizen must be to work mentally or physically. No individual shall do any work that offends against the interest of the community to the benefit of all.

Therefore, we demand:

12. That all unearned income, and all income that does not arise from work, be abolished.

13. Since every war imposes on the people fearful sacrifices in blood and treasure, all personal profit arising from the war must be regarded as treason to the people. We therefore demand the total confiscation of all war profits.

14. We demand the nationalization of all trusts.

15. We demand profit-sharing in large industries.

16. We demand a generous increase in old-age pensions.

17. We demand the creation and maintenance of a sound middle-class, the immediate communalization of large stores which will be rented cheaply to small tradespeople, and the strongest consideration must be given to ensure that small traders shall deliver the supplies needed by the State, the provinces and municipalities.

18. We demand an agrarian reform in accordance with our national requirements, and the enactment of a law to expropriate the owners without compensation of any land needed for the common purpose. The abolition of ground rents, and the prohibition of all speculation in land.

19. We demand that ruthless war be waged against those who work to the injury of the common welfare. Traitors, usurers, profiteers, etc., are to be punished with death, regardless of creed or race.

20. We demand that Roman law, which serves a materialist ordering of the world, be replaced by German common law.

21. In order to make it possible for every capable and industrious German to obtain higher education, and thus the opportunity to reach into positions of leadership, the State must assume the responsibility of organizing thoroughly the entire cultural system of the people. The curricula of all educational establishments shall be adapted to practical life. The conception of the State Idea (science of citizenship) must be taught in the schools from the very beginning. We demand that especially talented children of poor parents, whatever their station or occupation, be educated at the expense of the State.

22. The State has the duty to help raise the standard of national health by providing maternity welfare centers, by prohibiting juvenile labor, by increasing physical fitness through the introduction of compulsory games and gymnastics, and by the greatest possible encouragement of associations concerned with the physical education of the young.

23. We demand the abolition of the regular army and the creation of a national (folk) army.

24. We demand that there be a legal campaign against those who propagate deliberate political lies and disseminate them through the press. In order to make possible the creation of a German press, we demand:

(a) All editors and their assistants on newspapers published in the German language shall be German citizens;

(b) Non-German newspapers shall only be published with the express permission of the State. They must not be published in the German language;

(c) All financial interests in or in any way affecting German newspapers shall be forbidden to non-Germans by law, and we demand that the punishment for transgressing this law be the immediate suppression of the newspaper and the expulsion of the non-Germans from the Reich.

Newspapers transgressing against the common welfare shall be suppressed. We demand legal action against those tendencies in art and literature that have a disruptive influence upon the life of our folk, and that any organizations that offend against the foregoing demands shall be dissolved.

25. We demand freedom for all religious faiths in the state, insofar as they do not endanger its existence or offend the moral and ethical sense of the Germanic race.

The party as such represents the point of view of a positive Christianity without binding itself to any one particular confession. It fights against the Jewish materialist spirit within and without, and is convinced that a lasting recovery of our folk can only come about from within on the principle:

COMMON GOOD BEFORE INDIVIDUAL GOOD

26. In order to carry out this program we demand: the creation of a strong central authority in the State, the unconditional authority by the political central parliament of the whole State and all its organizations.

The formation of professional committees and of committees representing the several estates of the realm, to ensure that the laws promulgated by the central authority shall be carried out by the federal states.

The leaders of the party undertake to promote the execution of the foregoing points at all costs, if necessary, at the sacrifice of their own lives.[266]

Many of these issues were unique to Germany at the time and have no significance to the concept of the political agenda of Fascism in general i.e., that they have no relevance to the definition of Fascism in general. Therefore, let us look at only those issues that are the core of ideological Fascism. Those issues are the following:

> "We demand that the State shall above all undertake to ensure that every citizen shall have the possibility of living decently and earning a livelihood. If it should not be possible to feed the whole population, then aliens (non-citizens) must be expelled from the Reich."

In terms of todays politics, this is a minimum wage that is a "livable wage." This is a concept that is clearly found in all Socialist and Communist literature. There is absolutely no divergence between Fascism, Socialism, and Communism on this point and it surely comes from the same source.

1. All citizens must possess equal rights and duties.

---
[266] http://www.historyplace.com/worldwar2/riseofhitler/25points.htm

2. The first duty of every citizen must be to work mentally or physically. No individual shall do any work that offends against the interest of the community to the benefit of all.

Points 1 and 20 are, in other words, a command economy, where the "community" or, more properly, the government, decides what is to be produced. It also sets "community" standards. The question is what are those "community" standards and that is to be determined by the government.

11. That all unearned income, and all income that does not arise from work, be abolished.
12. Since every war imposes on the people fearful sacrifices in blood and treasure, all personal profit arising from the war must be regarded as treason to the people. We therefore demand the total confiscation of all war profits.
13. We demand the nationalization of all trusts.
14. We demand profit-sharing in large industries.
15. We demand a generous increase in old-age pensions.
16. We demand the creation and maintenance of a sound middle-class, the immediate communalization of large stores which will be rented cheaply to small tradespeople, and the strongest consideration must be given to ensure that small traders shall deliver the supplies needed by the State, the provinces and municipalities.

Points 11 to 16 are clearly the seizing of assets of the rich and the redistribution of them to the poor. It is an effort to produce an egalitarian society. Point 12 is a reference to the big corporations that made a profit as a result of Germany's involvement in World War I. It is possible that Hitler is referring to Krupp, which had a patent on the primer used in the bullets of the Maxim machine gun, which the British Vickers machine gun used. After the war, Krupp sued Vickers for patent infringement and actually won the civil law suit, which resulted in a large payment to Krupp. So, it can reasonably be inferred that Krupp literally profited from the killing of German soldiers during the war.

This attitude towards the armaments industry continued. During the Vietnam War it was not uncommon for anti-war protestors to attack industries because they made napalm particularly, and other munitions in general.

> 17. We demand an agrarian reform in accordance with our national requirements, and the enactment of a law to expropriate the owners without compensation of any land needed for the common purpose. We further demand the abolition of ground rents, and the prohibition of all speculation in land.

Again, Point 17 is a redistribution of wealth from the rich to the poor. It is unusual in Germany at this time since there were no corporate farms as there are through-out the world today. But instead, it was most likely an attack against large property owners, the ci-devant nobility who held large tracts of land and rented it to peasants.

> 18. We demand that ruthless war be waged against those who work to the injury of the common welfare. Traitors, usurers, profiteers, etc., are to be punished with death, regardless of creed or race.

Point 18 is more difficult to put into modern terms, but the words "profiteers" and "usurers" do reflect the concept of the capitalist who use their money to work for them. It can be considered analogous to those on Wall Street who use the stock exchange, buying and selling, to make a profit. This clearly arises from Hitler's attitude towards capitalism, which he considered part of the international Jewish conspiracy. (There are passages in Mein Kampf that speak to this).

> 20. In order to make it possible for every capable and industrious German to obtain higher education, and thus the opportunity to reach into positions of leadership, the State must assume the responsibility of organizing thoroughly the entire cultural system of the people. The curricula of all educational establishments shall be adapted to practical life. The conception of the State Idea (science of citizenship) must be taught in the schools from the very beginning. We demand that especially talented children of poor parents, whatever their station or occupation, be educated at the expense of the State.

Point 20 recognizes the importance of controlling the educational system and using it from the child's first day in school to inculcate in them the ideas of fascism. Under the Third Reich this included such organizations and the Hitler Youth. In Russia this was the Young Pioneers.

21. The State has the duty to help raise the standard of national health by providing maternity welfare centers, by prohibiting juvenile labor, by increasing physical fitness through the introduction of compulsory games and gymnastics, and by the greatest possible encouragement of associations concerned with the physical education of the young.

Point 21 should sound very familiar. It is nationalized health care, single payer health care, a system where the state controls the type and amount of healthcare provided to everyone. There is, however, a difference. Hitler wanted as many children to be born as possible; so, he included maternity welfare centers here. Though in the USSR such facilities were also established; it approved and supported the creation of more workers (and soldiers). But in modern socialism, this has switched and been replaced by abortion centers. This shift is not a major philosophical shift, however. Margaret Sanger, who started Planned Parenthood, looked upon abortion as a way of eliminating unwanted minorities. In essence, where Hitler took adults to concentration camps and eliminated them, the modern socialists have chosen to remove them one at a time while in the womb.

23. We demand that there be a legal campaign against those who propagate deliberate political lies and disseminate them through the press. In order to make possible the creation of a German press, we demand:
(a) All editors and their assistants on newspapers published in the German language shall be German citizens.
(b) Non-German newspapers shall only be published with the express permission of the State. They must not be published in the German language.
(c) All financial interests in or in any way affecting German

newspapers shall be forbidden to non-Germans by law, and we demand that the punishment for transgressing this law be the immediate suppression of the newspaper and the expulsion of the non-Germans from the Reich. Newspapers transgressing against the common welfare shall be suppressed. We demand legal action against those tendencies in art and literature that have a disruptive influence upon the life of our folk, and that any organizations that offend against the foregoing demands shall be dissolved.

Point 24 is closely associated with Point 20 – education, but in this case, it is also propaganda. In order to bring the population under control, it was necessary to control the flow of information. This actually was not a German idea, but came from Edward Louis Bernays, an American, who wrote the books *Crystallizing Public Opinion* (1923) and *Propaganda* (1928) from which the word propaganda came into common use. Hitler's propaganda minister, Goebbels, was inspired by this work and used it as the basis for developing his theories and practices of propaganda.

In the USSR and all other communist nations, propaganda has played a major role. In the USSR there were only approved newspapers, which were heavily censored and always carried the party line. Maoist China did the same, as did every communist and most socialist countries. Control of the media was always considered critical.

Early on, Hitler understood the importance of other media - radio and film - using them to spread his message. The *Triumph of the Will* was released in 1935 and directed, produced, edited, and co-written by Leni Riefenstahl. It documents the the 1934 Nazi Party Congress in Nuremberg, where 700,000 Nazi supporters gathered. It presents excerpts from speeches given by Adolf Hitler, Rudolf Hess, and Julius Streicher. In order to give it greater majesty, it contains footage of the Sturmabteilung and Schutzstaffel marching and the adoring reaction of the public. It was commissioned by Hitler and used to show the German people the power of their nation.

It is a major example of film used as propaganda and is recognized as one of the greatest propaganda films in history. It earned it several awards, not only in Germany but also in the United States, France, Sweden and other countries.

Triumph of the Will is the premier example of Nazi propaganda, but in an earlier film, *The Victory of Faith* (*Der Sieg des Glaubens*) Riefenstahl showed Hitler and SA leader Ernst Röhm together at the 1933 Nazi party congress. However, after Röhm was eliminated, all but one copy was destroyed and that copy was in Britain. The direction and sequencing of images is almost the same as that Riefenstahl used in *Triumph of the Will*.

Today, film has been surpassed by television as a medium of mass propaganda; but it still operates within the realm of television and regularly transmits socialist and communist ideas, just as it did during the Third Reich.

> 25. In order to carry out this program we demand the following: the creation of a strong central authority in the State, the unconditional authority by the political central parliament of the whole State and all its organizations.

The formation of professional committees and of committees representing the several estates of the realm ensure that the laws promulgated by the central authority shall be carried out by the federal states. The leaders of the party undertake to promote the execution of the foregoing points at all costs, if necessary, at the sacrifice of their own lives. Point 25 is the most significant common thread found in fascism, socialism, and communism. It is based on the concept that if individuals are left to their own devices, if their efforts are not controlled and directed by a superior organization that purportedly looks to the common good, the individual is only interested in their particular good and advancement and does so to the detriment of the others.

Among the many ideas of socialism and communism was the concepts of private property and the free enterprise system. The communists looked to abolish both, while the fascist Hitler believed in the "inviolability of private property and the retention of free enterprise."[267]

---

[267] Toland, J. *Adolph Hitler*, Vol II, p. 895.

CHAPTER 9.
COMPARISON OF COMMUNISM AND FASCISM

Some might argue that the Nazis were a right-wing organization, and it is certainly true that they fought with and eradicated the German communist parties, but this was not so much as an ideological, right-left dispute, but a simple struggle for political power. That being said, the true name of Nazi Party was the *Nationalsozialistische Deutsche Arbeiterpartei* or the National Socialist German Worker's Party.

In describing the differences in the Nazi and Communist philosophies, a scholar once said that the principal difference was that the Communists said that the "People are the State," while the Nazis said that "The State is the People." That difference is purely a semantic difference. A better distinction between the two political philosophies is that the Communists focused on an international philosophy of world rule by the world's proletariat, while the Nazis looked at a socialist and nationalistic government. The Nazis or Fascists were nationalists where the Communists were internationalists. That is not to say that there weren't disputes between communist states. One should particularly note the tensions that frequently arose between Communist China and the USSR and the Communist Chinese invasion of North Vietnam after the Vietnam War ended.

It would be a worthwhile exercise to look at a number of the major principals of the Nazis and the Communists to get an understanding of the similarities and differences between these two political theories.

In the first table we will compare the 10 points of Marx's Communist Manifesto to the related issues of Hitler's 26 points from *Mein Kampf* as well as actual practices of the Nazi regime that are related to Marx's 10 points.

George Nafziger
Marx's 10 Points Compared to Hitler's 26 Points[268]

Marx's 10 Points	Hitler's 26 Points
Abolition of private property in land and application of all rents of land to public purpose.	We demand the creation and maintenance of a sound middle-class, the immediate communalization of large stores which will be rented cheaply to small tradespeople, and the strongest consideration must be given to ensure that small traders shall deliver the supplies needed by the State, the provinces and municipalities.
A heavy progressive (graduated) income tax.	That all unearned income, and all income that does not arise from work, be abolished.
Abolition of all rights of inheritance.	We demand an agrarian reform in accordance with our national requirements, and the enactment of a law to expropriate the owners without compensation of any land needed for the common purpose. We further demand the abolition of ground rents, and the prohibition of all speculation in land.
Confiscation of the property of all those who emigrate and rebels.	Note: Those who fled Germany upon and after Hitler's rise to power had their abandoned property seized by the Nazi State.
Centralization of credit in the hands of the state, by means of a national bank with state capital and an exclusive monopoly.	We demand the nationalization of all trusts.
	Note: There existed State owned banks in Germany prior to Hitler. The Nazis favored public-sector banks, as a less "capitalistic" way of managing money and investment. The Nazi attitude toward privately owned joint-stock banks was infected with anti-Semitism. They were seen as "Jewish," and some banks were subjected to anti-Jewish boycotts in 1933.

---

[268] All of Marx's points have been listed, but only those of Hitler's 25 points that are related to or of similar thought are included. Many of Hitler's 25 points were related to specific political issues, etc., that existed only in Germany.

Twin Evils

Centralization of the means of communication and transportation in the hands of the state.	We demand that there be a legal campaign against those who propagate deliberate political lies and disseminate them through the press. In order to make possible the creation of a German press, we demand:
	(a) All editors and their assistants on newspapers published in the German language shall be German citizens.
	(b) Non-German newspapers shall only be published with the express permission of the State. They must not be published in the German language.
	(c) All financial interests in or in any way affecting German newspapers shall be forbidden to non-Germans by law, and we demand that the punishment for transgressing this law be the immediate suppression of the newspaper and the expulsion of the non-Germans from the Reich. Newspapers transgressing against the common welfare shall be suppressed. We demand legal action against those tendencies in art and literature that have a disruptive influence upon the life of our folk, and that any organizations that offend against the foregoing demands shall be dissolved.
Extension of factories and instruments of production owned by the state; the bringing into cultivation of waste lands, and the improvement of the soil generally in accordance with a common plan.	Note: In Nazi Germany private companies were protected and allowed to remain in private hands so long as they supported the economic goals of the government, but they could face significant penalties if they did not comply with national objectives and programs.
Equal obligation of all to work. Establishment of industrial armies, especially for agriculture	The first duty of every citizen must be to work mentally or physically. No individual shall do any work that offends against the interest of the community to the benefit of all.

Combination of agriculture with manufacturing industries; gradual abolition of the distinction between town and country by a more equable distribution of the population over the country	Note: Not an issue in Nazi Germany.
Free education for all children in government schools. Abolition of children's factory labor in its present form. Combination of education with industrial production, etc. etc.	In order to make it possible for every capable and industrious German to obtain higher education, and thus the opportunity to reach into positions of leadership, the State must assume the responsibility of organizing thoroughly the entire cultural system of the people. The curricula of all educational establishments shall be adapted to practical life. The conception of the State Idea (science of citizenship) must be taught in the schools from the very beginning. We demand that especially talented children of poor parents, whatever their station or occupation, be educated at the expense of the State.
	All citizens must possess equal rights and duties.
	Since every war imposes on the people fearful sacrifices in blood and treasure, all personal profit arising from the war must be regarded as treason to the people. We therefore demand the total confiscation of all war profits.
	We demand profit-sharing in large industries.
	We demand a generous increase in old-age pensions.
	We demand that ruthless war be waged against those who work to the injury of the common welfare. Traitors, usurers, profiteers, etc., are to be punished with death, regardless of creed or race.
	The State has the duty to help raise the standard of national health by providing maternity welfare centers, by prohibiting juvenile labor, by increasing physical fitness through the introduction of compulsory games and gymnastics, and by the greatest possible encouragement of associations concerned with the physical education of the young.

	In order to carry out this program we demand the following: the creation of a strong central authority in the State, the unconditional authority by the political central parliament of the whole State and all its organizations.
[1] All of Marx's points have been listed, but only those of Hitler's 25 points that are related to or of similar thought are included. Many of Hitler's 25 points were related to specific political issues, etc., that existed only in Germany.	

As can be seen by this table, there are very strong relations between Marx's 10 points and Hitler's 25 points and Nazi economic practices. In fact, there is not one of Marx's points that does not have a Nazi equivalent. This produces an interesting conundrum in that it clearly demonstrates that there are few significant differences between Communism and Nazism. The differences occur only in minor details.

Now, let us summarize those issues and actual economic practices in a more concise manner:

Comparison of Major Elements of Nazism and Communism

	Part of Nazi Philosophy	Part of Socialist /Communist Philosophy
Land Reform.	No	Yes
Everyone must work.	Yes	Yes
Abolition of unearned income - "no rent-slavery", i.e. rent control	Yes	Yes
Nationalization of industry.	Yes	Yes
Sharing of profits.	Yes	Yes
Extension of old age welfare.	Yes	Yes

Education to teach "the German Way", Education of gifted children, i.e. Centralized State Control of education and political indoctrination.	Yes	Yes
Duty of the state to provide for its people.	Yes	Yes
Duty of individuals to the state	Yes	Yes
Against Free Market Capitalism	Yes	Yes

It is now appropriate to look at other issues in common between Communist States and Fascist States. To this end we will look at elements of state structure and state operations.

Comparison of Nazi and Communist Governmental Structures

Governmental Element	Nazis/Fascists	Communists
Dictators	Germany-Hitler Italy – Mussolini Spain - Franco	USSR- Lenin, Stalin, Khrushchev, etc. China – Mao Tse Tung Cambodia – Pol Pot Vietnam – Ho Chi Min, etc. Venezuela – Chavez & Maduro Cuba – Castro, etc. Romania – Nicolae Ceausescu Bulgaria – Todor Zhivkov E. Germany – Erich Honecker Poland - Władysław Gomułka

Twin Evils

Secret Police	Germany (Gestapo) Fascist Italy (OVRA) Fascist Spain (BPS)	USSR- Cheka/GPU/)GPU-NKVD/GUGB/NKGB/NGB/KGB China – 610 Office Bulgaria – CDS Albania – KHAD Cambodia – Santebal Hungary – AVO & AVH Poland – BP & SB N.Korea – State Security Dept. Romania – SCR Venezuela – BIS/DIM/DISIP Yugoslavia – UDBA/KOS
Concentration/ Re-education Camps	Germany (yes) Italy (no) Spain (no)	USSR - gulags China N.Korea Vietnam
Used National Army against Citizens	Germany (no) Italy (no) Spain (no)	USSR – Yes (& in Hungary 1956, E. Germany 1953) N. Vietnam – Yes Cambodia - Yes China – Yes Venezuela – Yes
Freedom of speech	Dissidents killed or imprisoned	Dissidents killed or imprisoned
Citizens allowed to have firearms	No, death penalty	No, death penalty
Freedom of Religion	Yes, but not Jews	Only State Controlled Religions, all others others are forbidden.

Freedom of press	State Censorship	State Censorship, Radio and Press Organs of the State
Right to Assemble	No	No
Right to be Secure in Persons, Properties and Papers against unreasonable search and seizure	No need for search warrants. Police can seize anything at will.	No Need for search warrants. Police can seize anything at will.
Right to speedy trial	Trials optional, State can go directly to imprisonment or execution without trial.	Trials optional, State can go directly to imprisonment or execution without trial.
No cruel or unusual punishment	Torture common	Torture common
Seek geographical expansion	Germany Yes Italy Yes Spain No	Russia/USSR – Yes China – Yes N. Vietnam – Yes N. Korea – Yes Cuba – Yes Romania, Hungary, Czechoslovakia, E Germany, Venezuela, Cambodia – No.

Mass Murder and Genocide

DATES	NAME AND/ OR LOCATION	NUMBER MURDERED	PARTY RESPONSIBLE
1958-63	*Great Leap Forward* Communist China	18,000,000-55.600,000	Chinese Communist Party Political genocide

1941-45	*Holocaust* Nazi Germany	15,000,000 +/-	Nazi Party Combination racial/political
1932-33	*Holodomor* in Ukraine USSR	1,800,000-7,500,000	Soviet Communist Party Purely political/class hatred
1974-79	Cambodia	1,386,734-3,000,000	Cambodian Communist Party Purely political/class hatred
1965-66	Indonesian Genocide	2,000,000-3,000,000	Religious/Racial hatred
1971	Bangladesh Genocide	300,000-3,000,000	Religious/Racial hatred
1915-22	Armenian Genocide	700,000-1,800,000	Ottoman Turkish Government Religious Hatred
1932-33	Kazakh Genocide	1,300,000-1,750,000	Soviet Communist Party Purely political/class hatred
1994	Rwandan Genocide	500,000-1,701,000	Tribal hatred
1941-45	Ustase & Serbian Genocide	357,000-600,000	Religious/Tribal Hatred Croatian Fascist Ustase Party

Restriction of Owning Weapons in Communist and Socialist Countries

Despotic governments are afraid of an uprising of the citizenry and so quickly take steps to remove firearms from the public. The reasons presented for this varied greatly, but they all had the same underling reason: socialist and communist governments impose misery on their citizenry, and they fear an uprising of the people. It is one of the measures they use to ensure that they have absolute control over their citizens. The Warsaw Ghetto uprising of 1944 clearly indicates the type of reaction that can result from an oppressed people and the Nazis had every reason to fear that if they did not disarm the Jewish population of Germany before they launched the Kristalnacht in 1936 that they might well be met with armed opposition.

In the case of Nazi Germany there were two reasons. The first was the usual control of the public, but the second was to protect their minions from any possibility of a Jewish uprising while the Nazis pursued their "final solution."

"Newspapers all over Germany published an article on November 9 declaring the need to disarm the Jews due to the Paris shooting.[269] Yet, this pretext was a sham; the confiscation of arms in Berlin had already been going on for several weeks, netting 2,589 swords, knives, and clubs, 1,702 firearms, and about 20,000 rounds of ammunition. A Berlin publication stated: 'The provisional results clearly show what a large amount of weapons have been found with Berlin's Jews and are still to be found with them.' The names of Jews with firearms licenses were available to the police under the Nazi *Waffengesetz* (Weapons Law) signed by Hitler and SS Reichsführer (Interior Minister) Wilhelm Frick earlier that year and previous laws. On November 10, newspapers in both Germany and Switzerland reported a document entitled 'Weapons Ban for Jews' in which SS Chief Heinrich HImmer decreed: 'Persons who, according to the Nürnberg law are regarded as Jew, are forbidden to possess any weapons. Violators will be transferred to a concentration camp and imprisoned for a period of up to 20 years.'

"The seizure of firearms from Jews gave the Nazis assurance that their attacks would not be resisted. The Nazis then proceeded to smash, loot and burn Jewish shops and temples. Throughout Germany, thousands of Jewish men were taken from their homes and arrested. The property destruction was carried out by wrecking crews under the protection of uniformed Nazis or police. The Swiss press took note of the widespread disarming of the Jews and the anti-Semitic attacks.

---

[269] This is a reference to the 1936 shooting of Swiss Nazi Wilhelm Gustloft by a Jewish medical student in Paris.

Twin Evils

The Regulations against Jews' Possession of Weapons (*Verordnung gegen den Waffenbesitz der Juden*) were promulgated by Interior Minister Frick on November 11, the day after *Kirstallnacht*. The regulations stated that 'Jews ... are prohibited from acquiring, possessing, and carrying firearms and ammunition, as well as truncheons or stabbing weapons. Those now possessing weapons and ammunition are required at once to turn them over to the local police authority,'"[270]

The nature of firearms held by civilians in the Soviet Union was different. Russia had collapsed in 1917, and its army literally walked off the battlefield. This was followed by a civil war between the Reds and the Whites, as well as various Allied contingents that came to defend Western interests. Guns were everywhere. The December 1918 decree of the CPC entitled: "On the surrender of weapons", ordered people to surrender any firearms, swords, bayonets and bombs, regardless of the degree of serviceability. The penalty for not doing so was ten years' imprisonment.

On 12 December 1924 the Central Executive Committee of the USSR issued a degree "On the procedure of production, trade, storage, use, keeping and carrying firearms, firearm ammunition, explosive projectiles and explosives." By it all weapons were classified and divided into categories. As a result of it ordinary citizens could only legally own smoothbore hunting shotguns. Rifled firearms were restricted to people put on duty by the Soviet State, police, army, etc. The possession of an illegal weapon was severely punished. After March 1933, the manufacture, possession, purchase, sale of firearms (except for smoothbore) hunting weapons without proper authorization was punishable for up to five years in prison. In 1935, the same penalty was imposed for possession of knives. When the Germans invaded in 1941 all weapons held by the civilian population had to be turned over to the Red Army, including weapons abandoned by the Germans as they withdrew. They were to be handed over within 24 hours.

The Russians had used firearms to overthrow the Czar and did not want their citizenry to rise up and overthrow them. In Ukraine there was an armed anti-Soviet insurrection until about 1952. This was a mix of men with political and economic issues with the Soviet system and of men who had lost family as a result of the collectivization of the farms of the *Kulaks* in the Ukraine in 1936. That collectivization and the confiscation of food stuffs to feed the cities resulted in the starvation and death of up to

---

[270] Halbrook, S.P. *Target Switzerland, Swiss Armed Neutrlaity in World War II*(Rockville Center, NY: Sarpedon, 1998 p. 56)

7,500,000 Ukrainians. Surely the example of the Warsaw Ghetto uprising gave reason for the Soviets to fear a similar response.

In China the presence of guns dates back to their invention. There were controls on ownership of firearms in the 19th century and they continue to today. Prior to WWII there was a civil war in China between the Kuomintang and the Communists, but it ended because a greater threat, the Japanese, had appeared in China. Though illegal in private hands, firearms were everywhere. When the Japanese left the Communists ant Kuomintang fought a civil war and the Communists finally won it. When the Communists took over private gun ownership was prohibited.

In the *Selected Works of Mao Tse-Tung*, we find: "Communists do not fight for personal military power (they must in no circumstances do that and let no one ever again follow the example of Chang Kuo-tao), but they must fight for military power for the Party, for military power for the people. As a national war of resistance is going on, we must also fight for military power for the nation. Where there is naivety on the question of military power, nothing whatsoever can be achieved. It is very difficult for the laboring people, who have been deceived and intimidated by the reactionary ruling classes for thousands of years, to awaken to the importance of having guns in their own hands. Now that Japanese imperialist oppression and the nation-wide resistance to it have pushed our laboring people into the arena of war, Communists should prove themselves the most politically conscious leaders in this war. Every Communist must grasp the truth, *'Political power grows out of the barrel of a gun.' Our principle is that the Party commands the gun, and the gun must never be allowed to command the Party*. Yet, having guns, we can create Party organizations, as witness the powerful Party organizations which the Eighth Route Army has created in northern China. We can also create cadres, create schools, create culture, and create mass movements. Everything in Yenan has been created by having guns. All things grow out of the barrel of a gun. According to the Marxist theory of the state, *the army is the chief component of state power*. Whoever wants to seize and retain state power must have a strong army. Some people ridicule us as advocates of the 'omnipotence of war' Yes, we are advocates of the omnipotence of revolutionary war; that is good, not bad, it is Marxist. The guns of the Russian Communist Party created socialism. We shall create a democratic republic. Experience in the class struggle in the era of imperialism teaches us that it is only by the power of the gun that the working class and the laboring masses can defeat the armed bourgeoisie and landlords; in this sense we may say that only with guns can the whole world be transformed. We are advocates of the abolition of war, we do not want war; but war can only be abolished through war, and in order to get rid of the gun it is necessary to take up the gun."[271]

A can be seen, Mao recognized the power of the gun. Though this famous quotation does not speak specifically to civilian ownership of guns, when one looks at the phrase *"the gun must never be allowed to command the Party"* it is clear that Mao recognized that guns in the wrong hands, wrong hands being defined as anyone looking to overthrow the party's control, were not to be tolerated. When he said *"the army is the chief component of state power,"* it is clear that he intended to control the population by means of the army and its guns.

This absence of guns among the civilian population allowed the massacre known as the Great Leap Forward or the Cultural Revolution. Though not as bloody, the absence of guns among the civilian population prevented the 1989 Tiananmen uprising from becoming more serious. Nonetheless, there too 1,022 civilians were murdered.

Today in China laws are strong against private ownership of guns, they being prohibited, except under limited and special conditions. The penalty is not as draconian as Nazi Germany, but range of from three to seven years imprisonment, depending on the nature of the offense. Nonetheless, the intent is to ensure party control and the continued oppression of the civilian population.

There is a relationship between gun control and genocide. It was nicely summarized by a letter to the Chicago Daily Herald, dated 28 January 2013:

- 1929: The Soviet Union established gun control. From 1929-1953, 20,000,000 dissidents rounded up and murdered.
- 1911: Turkey established gun control. From 1915-1917, up to 1,800,000 Christian Armenians rounded up and exterminated.
- 1938: Germany established gun control. From 1939-1945, 13,000,000 Jews and others rounded up and exterminated.
- 1935: China established gun control. From 1948-1952, 20,000,000 political dissidents rounded up and executed.
- 1956: Cambodia established gun control. From 1975-1977, 1 million educated people rounded up and executed.

---

[271] *Selected Works of Mao Tse-tung*: Vol. II. Marxists Internet Archive (transcription by the Maoist Documentation Project). Retrieved 27 May 2013., Vol. II, pp. 224-225

1964: Guatemala established gun control. From 1981-1984, 100,000 Mayan Indians rounded up and executed.

1970: Uganda established gun control. From 1971-1979, 300,000 Christians rounded up and exterminated.

In the 20th century more than 56,000,000 unarmed people were rounded up and exterminated because the victims had been disarmed and could not defend themselves against the armed State.

In sum, there is only one significant difference between communism and fascism as they have been implemented. Both engage in mass murder, both have secret police, both control the media and deny free speech, both deny their citizens the right to own firearms, and both use concentration camps to control dissidents.

The one and only major difference is that in communist societies nobody owns any property, i.e. land or factories or buildings. In communist countries all production is determined and controlled by State agencies, not individuals. As a result, incompetence, mismanagement, and corruption within state agencies caused the standard of living to collapse to such a low level that you needed coupons to get coupons.

In contrast fascism allows private individuals to own property, but they must do with their property what the state directs them to do with it. In the case of both Nazi Germany and Fascist Italy this state direction of property and the means of production was the result of an agreement between the barons of industry and the state, by which both profited at the expense of the common man.

So even with this small difference, the common man suffered.

In our introduction we spoke about how communism and fascism were branches of the same philosophical root. If you look at the King James version of the Bible, Matthew 7:15-20 you will see the following: {15} "Beware of false prophets, who come to you in sheep's clothing, but inwardly they are ravenous wolves. {16} You will know them by their fruits. Do men gather grapes from thornbushes or figs from thistles? {17} Even so, every good tree bears good fruit, but a bad tree bears bad fruit. [18] A good tree cannot bear bad fruit, nor can a bad tree bear good fruit. [19] Every tree that does not bear good fruit is cut down and thrown into the fire. [20] Therefore by their fruits you will know them."

Does this not describe both fascism and communism? They are false prophets who promised a worker's paradise, and we surely know them by their fruits. We have only to open our eyes and look at what has been documented in this chapter. The fruits they deliver deliver mass murder, oppression, and misery. They promise equality, fairness, and justice, but at best these promises are selectively given and only to the preferred individuals. The only promise they keep is the elimination of the those who they call the oppressor class, be they the Jews or the capitalists. They cycle the political system back to a modified form of feudalism where there is an elite class of new dukes, counts, earls, and barons with a divinely inspired, all knowing tyrant who rules by a new form of the divine right of kings.

      Neither system, no matter where it has been attempted, nor who ruled it, has lived up to its promise. Both are rife with corruption in all levels of the party membership. Do you recall the story of Elena Skrjabina during the siege of Leningrad in Chapter 3? Even the lowest party officials used their positions of power to feed their family sumptuous meals, while the rest of the city of Leningrad starved. Look at Kim Jung Un. He is morbidly obese, while the North Koreans starve to death. As recently as 2024 Xi Jinping of China used corruption as a reason to purge many members of the communist party.

      As for corruption in Fascist Italy or Nazi Germany it existed and vanished with the destruction of those two states in 1945.

CHAPTER 10.
THE HISTORIC AND PSYCHOLOGICAL BASIS OF COMMUNISM AND FASCISM.

To understand the psychology of the individual attracted to and embracing communism and fascism one must examine his nation's history and culture in which both philosophies took root. A nation's history and culture not only explain an individual's acceptance of totalitarianism but also his personal mind-set. One always tends to gravitate to what is familiar and comfortable. When societies, therefore, change, when revolutions flood into the streets and destroy the old system, there is a tendency among persons to return to the old, the familiar, the comfortable.

Russia has, throughout its history, been an authoritarian state characterized by an absolute ruler. Russia followed Western Europe into establishing a feudal society complete with serfdom, a form of slavery. Serfdom continued in Russia until 1861. Although formally abolished, feudalism continued because most of the peasantry did not own land. As discussed earlier, before the 1917 Russian Revolution there was only very limited redistributions of the land. In addition, one needs to recognize that famines were not uncommon in Czarist Russia.

The Communist Revolution succeeded in Russia because most of the Russian population was confronted with the choice between an oppressive Czarist system, where they lived on the edge of starvation, and any governing system that promised less oppression and a prosperous future. As a result of the Communist Revolution, Russai became the Union of Soviet Socialistic Republics (USSR, Soviet Union). Sadly, the Soviet Union evolved into an equally oppressive system as Czardom. Like Czarist Russia, the Soviet Russian citizen continued to suffer famines. This continued until 1991. The Soviet Union then collapsed for the same reason as Czarist Russia – massive discontent with the existing system resulting from a near economic collapse, the lack of consumer goods, and the diversion of the vast majority of the nation's gross domestic product (GDP) to the military.

Following the fall of the Soviet Union, there initially were gleamers of true democracy. However, they were soon eradicated by the establishment of the Putin dictatorship. The reason for this return to authoritarian government was the Russian people who historically experienced, and knew no other system, than authoritarian government. They were willing to submit to totalitarianism when it was imposed upon them. It was the system the Russian people knew by historical tradition and were comfortable, at least in the beginning. A repetitive cycle occurs where an authoritarian or totalitarian state is overthrown, slowly re-emerges, and assumes power only to be again overthrown.

China is different. A budding "democracy" under Sun Yet Sen, had overthrew the emperor. Ancient China lacked democratic experience and prominence of the individual. In the early twentieth century, an attempt was made to institute democracy. Unfortunately, old habits are endemic in Chinese culture; corruption was rampant in this democratic effort and the suffering of the peasantry was not mitigated. Though not serfs by the European definition, the Chinese peasant was tied to the land and subject to the whims of the land owner. The Chinese peasant owned nothing, only what he was given by the landlord. There was no significant merchant class or middle class, tradesmen in China as existed in Europe or even Russia in 1860. Another condition should be noted – starvation. Starvation was a constant threat to the average Chinese. There is an old Chinese greeting that translates, "Have you eaten today?"

When the Chinese peasants heard the communists promising land and full bellies, the peasants were willingly swept into the communist, totalitarian system. The peasants believed they had nothing to lose and everything to gain. Once in the system where communism had sunk its roots deep into the Chinese government system, communism proceeded to destroy the history of the old system and eradicated any resistance. Communism re-established a new empire and a new emperor – Mao Tse Tung and his successor Xi Jinping.

Vietnam is different in some ways. It had an emperor, but he had been later replaced by French colonial power. In this situation, the absolute ruler was a foreigner; therefore, there was a natural antipathy towards French colonial rule. The average peasant's life was miserable and offered little other than endless labor and living hand-to-mouth. The Vietnam mercantile middle class was small and under developed. There was the ruler, a ruling class, and there were the peasants. However, added to this were the historical events that broke the once independent and single nation of Vietnam into two competing countries. A strong urge arose for reunification of both Vietnamese nations.

Korea, like Vietnam, had been once a single nation under an Emperor. In 1910 Japan annexed Korea. The Japanese treated the Koreans as serfs. Korea was liberated in 1945. Through manipulation by the Soviet Union, Korea was divided into two separate countries. Like Vietnam, there was a nationalistic urge to reunite into one nation. However, there were two emperors - Kim Il Sung in North Korea and Syngman Rhee in South Korea. Communism was imposed on the North. Under the occupation and direction of the United States, South Korea evolved into a capitalistic democracy.

Now, let us examine Germany and Italy. Germany had been a cluster of independent states, some large and many very small. They were all ruled by nobility, be it a King, as in Prussia and Bavaria, or Dukes as in Wurttemberg. Serfdom existed in the Middle Ages and ended between 1770 and 1830. Germany had a long tradition of tradesmen and merchants in its cities; therefore, the growth of the middle class grew rapidly as serfdom ended. Simultaneously, the peasantry quickly became a land-owning peasantry. Of course, famines were not unknown, but they were not as common as in Russia or China. The pressure that drove the Russian peasants to revolution had existed earlier in Germany resulting in the Peasant War of 1524. The Peasant War resulted from oppressive taxes and duties imposed on the peasants. In 1848 a major revolution erupted in Germany and Austria caused by a severe economic depression. This depression halted industrial expansion and aggravated urban unemployment. In addition, there was a series of crop failures and famine. The people revolted, but the revolution failed and many of the revolutionaries fled to the United States.

In 1870 German united into a single country under the leadership and rule of Prussia, the northern German state ruled by its King. The Prussian King now became the Kaiser of Germany. His rule was as absolute as that of the oriental and Russian czars; however, in the case of Germany, there was more freedom of movement. The ideas of liberty, equality and fraternity had been spread across Germany by the French Revolutionary and Napoleonic armies between 1792 and 1813. Nonetheless there was a strong and brutal class structure. The German nobility was socially and governmentally on the "top of the heap." There was also the concept of "Befehl ist Befhel" (Orders are orders.) Everyone knew his place, but within the bounds of one's social position, there was a fair degree of freedom. Although Marx was German and his theories took some root in Germany, his advocates found themselves opposed by the fascists. There was no popular fascist resistance in Russia, China, Vietnam, or Korea. In these nations communism prevailed.

Italy followed the German model. It too had been a collection of states with a couple of kings and a mass of nobility, plus a pope, who was a secular, and a religious ruler. Italy became a unified state in 1861. Serfdom ended in Italy in 1789. Serfdom existed, however, in a society where merchants grew excessively wealthy in independent city states. Many of these states, most particularly Venice, were republics. Although there was a sense of authoritarianism, there was also a very high degree of individual liberty. Like Germany, there was a communist movement, but the Italian people's condition was not desperate. Many saw that they had more to lose from the process of collectivization than they had to gain. Again, there was a large percentage of the arable land that was owned by the working class and they did not want to surrender it to a central government that would confiscate their land and make them work for the benefit of the state, not for the benefit of the individual land-owning peasant. A degree of individual choice existed in Italy and Germany that did not exist in Russia, China, or North Korea.

France is arguably the birth place of socialism. This argument was referenced in Chapter 2's discussion about Gracius Babeuf. Serfdom had been a declining institution in France from the mid-fifteenth century; it formally ended in 1789 with the French Revolution. Along with the decline of feudalism and serfdom, there was a consistent transfer of land to the peasants, together with a growth of a merchant and artisan classes in the cities. There was also growth in individual freedom of choice and the ability of individuals to make decisions for themselves affecting their lives. The French Revolution occurred because of a long series of crop failures leading to massive starvation. Starvation was so bad that, in early 1789, men drove wagons through the streets of Paris picking up the bodies of those who had died of starvation. Famine was not uncommon in France and war was equally common.

There was also a series of wars involving France. The War of the League of Augsburg's, from 1688 to 1697, was followed by the War of the Spanish Succession - 1701 to 1714; the War of the Austrian Succession - 1740 to 1748; and, the Seven Years War - 1756 to 1763. The French then became involved in the American Revolution. These wars drained the finances of France and led to heavy taxation. In addition, the king's growing financial demands to finance and maintain the nobility in his court continued to grow. As a result, unlike the famine that occurred in the early 18th century, where Louis XIV was able to reduce military expenses and divert funds to import wheat to feed the starving French peasants, Louis XVI lacked those resources. The French people looked at the French nobility in their fancy carriages and extravagant life-style, while the French people's children died of starvation. As in Russia in 1905 and 1917, the French people had nothing to lose and they rose up in rebellion.

Unlike Russia and China, many Frenchmen held property and possessed a fair degree of freedom in their personal decision-making processes vis-à-vis their financial activity. Initially France had a democracy; however, it dissolved into an oligarchy and finally an empire under Napoleon Buonaparte. With the end of Napoleon's rule, the French royal family, the Bourbons, attempted to re-establish their absolute rule of government. It ended with the 1830 revolution. A democracy arose that continues to this day. This is another example of the cycle from authoritarianism to revolution, and a return to authoritarian or totalitarian government. We have the revolution of 1789, the Convention, which was a democratic institution, replaced by a dictatorial oligarchy, which was then replaced by Napoleon's dictatorship. The Bourbon restoration was a passing re-imposition of the older dictatorship. When the Bourbons were overthrown in 1830, a new democracy began that slowly evolved into a new Emperor, Napoleon III, followed again by another revolution, and a new surge of democratic institutions.

The Normans instituted serfdom in England beginning in 1066 A.D. English serfdom started ending with the Peasants' Revolt in 1381. Absolute monarchial rule began to end with the signing of the Magna Carta in 1215. Serfdom had largely died in England by 1500 and totally ended when Elizabeth I freed the last remaining serfs in 1574. At the same time, England began developing a massive mercantile and middle class composed of tradesmen. With the decline of serfdom, the common man began to own land. Later in history, when the ideology of socialism arrived on English shores, there already existed many English citizens who resist the idea of collectivization which would end their ownership of private property, be it land or factories. There were both communists and fascists in England. However, as in France, they were unable to overwhelm and destroy the democratic institutions that existed in those two countries.

Examining the history of these nations indicates three distinct environments. The first, in both England and France, was a long and steady decline of absolutism, a growth of the ownership of private property, and a high degree by each person's ability to make major personal life decisions. The growth of personal decision making gave both Englishmen and the Frenchmen the opportunities for maximum personal growth and improvement of their social and financial situations.

The second environment is a long history of absolute authoritarian rulers with no movement away from a rigid class structure that enslaved the lower classes and placed all property ownership in the hands of the upper classes – the nobility. In this situation the peasantry, in its desperation, saw nothing to lose and revolted against the existing system. However, the peasantry was so conditioned to the idea of an absolute ruler, experiencing and knowing no other governing arrangement, they lacked any capability or opportunity to make any significant decisions for themselves.

The third example is a "half way" situation between these two ends of the spectrum. This is represented by Germany and Italy. Germany and Italy began their transition from feudalism after France and England, but long before Russia and China. Both Germans and Italians had some experience with individual personal decision making and limited influence upon their governments; however, it was not a long history and there were survivors from previous generations who experienced, and understood, the world of absolutism.

The last two environments discussed above were conducive socialism, communism, and fascism ideologies. If one returns to earlier chapters, one can see that socialism, in its extreme form communism, is a totalitarian political system. A totalitarian government is "a highly centralized government under the control of a political group which allows no recognition of or no recognition to other political parties."[272] It represses individuals, subordinating the individual to the needs and desires of the state as expressed by the desires of the government officials. These government officials constitute the totalitarian government.

A nation's history and culture are not the exclusive cause and bases for totalitarian governments. In traditional democratic and capitalist nations, persons who advocate and work to create a totalitarian government, possess specific psychological characteristics. Why do individuals embrace, or at least tolerate, communist repression and totalitarian repression in general? Research has been conducted by clinical

---

[272] *Webster's* Collegiate Dictionary (Springfield, Mass.: G&C Meriam Co., Publishers:1960), p. 897.

psychologists and psychiatrists to answer this question. Sociologist and psychoanalyst Dr. Erich Fromm, documents his findings in his celebrated book, *Escape From Freedom.* Fromm discovered that a person attracted to totalitarianism is "the expression of the inability of the individual self to stand alone and live."[273] Persons embracing totalitarianism desire to suppress their individuality by submitting to the power and direction of someone in authority. Persons who desire authorities to make the decisions affecting their personal lives, lack maturity and are avoiding personal responsibility. Subsequently, they submit themselves to another's authority. These persons fear making decisions and choices, fearing they will make the wrong and personally harmful choice. They believe the safety and security they seek takes priority over their rights, and the right of their fellow citizens, to make their own choices affecting and directing their personal lives. Sometimes, however they are blind to the possibility that it is their rights and freedoms that will be lost.

An individual who embraces socialism, communism, or fascism, and rejects capitalism, seeks to escape the results of their actual or potential poor decision-making skills. Persons attracted to totalitarian government systems believe they are "a victim." Because they are not willing to take risks, they find it easier to claim they are victims to excuse their lack of courage and the responsibility for their choices and actions. Believing they are incapable of escaping the persons or organizations that victimize them (i.e. the victimizer) by their own initiative, they desire government authority to remove, or to a lesser degree, control the victimizer. American psychiatrist, Dr. Scott Peck, in his book The Road Less Traveled, explains that persons avoiding responsibility for their decisions see themselves as "victimized by these forces" and by doing so are relinquishing their freedom.[274] Dr. Scott Peck, based upon clinical experience, agrees with Dr. Fromm. In his book, The Road Less Traveled, Dr. Peck states the following:

> The difficulty we have in accepting responsibility for our behavior lies in the desire to avoid the pain of the consequences of that behavior.......
> Whenever we seek to avoid the responsibility for

---

[273] Fromm, Erich, Escape From Freedom, (New York: Avon Books, 1941, copyright renewed 1969), p.184.
[274] Peck, Scott, M.D., The Road Less Traveled, (New York: A Touchstone Book, 1978), p. 43.

our own behavior, we do so by attempting to give that responsibility to some other individual or organization, or entity. But this means we then give away our power to that entity, be it "fate" or "society," or the government, or the corporation or our boss.[275]

One's desire not to make one's own personal decisions, fearing the possible consequences, demonstrates a lack of courage. The ancient Greek philosopher, Thucydides, stated "The secret to happiness is freedom, and the secret to freedom is courage."[276] When one has courage one assumes risks based upon rationale thinking. One's courage enables one to take a different action that may improve one's condition but, perhaps, also forego comforts in the process.

We have frequently addressed the idea of victimization in this work. The appeal of communism in Russia and China was the promise to give land to the landless peasants, who were victimized by the nobility, and relief to the factory workers who were victimized by the factory owners. We addressed this again in Chapter 6 where the sense of the group being victimized led to the emergence of fascism. We will again address victimization in Chapter 10.

The opinions of political scientist, Dr. William Ebenstein, coincide with Dr. Fromm's conclusions. Ebenstein notes that a primary psychologic factor creating a personal attraction to totalitarianism is a lack of personal security. Ebenstein refers to this desire for submission to authority as a desire to maintain the "father-child relationship for security in dependence." [277] Ebenstein describes the parent-child relationship as follows:

> Rational democrats may not understand why anyone should prefer to obey rather than take the responsibility of making decisions for himself; they take it for granted that men should make their own decisions rather than have their actions dictated by others. But this democratic stereotype overlooks what are the comforts of irresponsibility to many persons. Children love the feeling of being

---

[275] Loc. cit., p. 42.
[276] Hewitt, Hugh, Happiest Life (Nashville, Tennessee, Nelson Books, Dominion Productions, 2013), p. xiii.
[277] Ebenstein, William, Today's ISMS, Fourth Edition., (Englewood Cliffs, N.J.: Prentice Hall, Inc., 1964), p. 107.

sheltered and secure behind the benevolent power and authority of their parents. The mark of the mature adult is his willingness and capacity to stand on his own feet, to take responsibility, and be independent of others.[278]

Persons attracted and embracing totalitarian government systems feel a lack of personal security and believe they will gain security under totalitarian authority.[279] The result, as Erich Fromm explains, is a masochistic and sadistic striving.[280] Erich Fromm Explains that persons attracted to and embracing totalitarianism, both communism and fascism, possess feelings of "isolation and powerlessness" resulting from their individuality. This causes some individuals "to escape from aloneness and powerlessness."[281] Fromm explains this results in a masochistic-sadistic character and interrelationship. The masochist person, feeling alone and threatened by his environment, believes he finds safety, security, and strength by submitting himself to another human being's authority. When one strives to submit to the authority and perceived protection of another, one compromises one's independence and individuality to acquire the strength and security they believe they lack and unable to provide for themselves. The masochist strives for submission and domination by another for security. However, when one places himself under the authority of another, one relinquishes one's individual independence. Another human being is directing another human being's life. The person "directed" becomes a tool for those in authority.[282]

Another response to the feelings of aloneness and isolation is a desire to acquire safety and security by possessing power and control over other human beings. This is the sadistic response. Sadism, as with masochism according to Fromm, derives also from "the individual wanting to escape his unbearable feelings of aloneness and powerlessness."[283] Sadism exists, to varying degrees, within the same person displaying masochist traits. The sadist, to compensate for his fear, aloneness, and feelings of powerlessness, seeks to control and impose his authority over others.[284] These sadistic traits, according to Fromm,

[278] Loc. cit. p.106.
[279] Loc. cit. p. 107 and p.148.
[280] Fromm, Erich, Escape From Freedom, (New York: Avon Books, 1941, copyright renewed 1969), p.163.
[281] Loc. cit. p.156.
[282] Loc. cit. pp. 161-162.
[283] Loc. cit. p. 173.
[284] Loc. cit. pp. 178-179.

make others dependent on oneself and "have absolute and unrestricted power over them;" sadists exploit other persons and manipulate them; and, sadists make others physically or mentally suffer while the sadist, in a position of authority, witnesses their suffering.[285] Fromm explains the sadist as follows:

> Only instead of seeking security by being swallowed, he gains it by swallowing somebody else. In both cases [masochism and sadism] the integrity of the individual self is lost. In one case I dissolve myself in an outside power; I lose myself. In the other case I enlarge myself by making another being part of myself and thereby I gain the strength I lack as an in dependent self.[286]

The sadist's desires and abilities also include inflicting pain upon another. Inflicting suffering upon the controlled person represents the maximum power over another person. Forcing another person to undergo suffering and unable to defend himself, is the extreme extent of the sadistic drive.[287]

The ability to reason and make choices enables the individual to define and direct his life. The individual makes choices governing his personal life – himself and not another human being - controls his own personal life. Ayn Rand, in her book <u>Capitalism: The Unknown Ideal</u>, explains that the key defining human characteristic is the "rational faculty" - the ability to reason.[288] A choice results from reasoning - choosing one's actions and beliefs. The ability to engage one's mind and reason and make choices defines one as human. Furthermore, the ability to reason, and the individual freedom to choose one's actions and beliefs, is the basis for personal self-development and individual dignity.[289] One may make the wrong choice. Not all choices are personally beneficial or successful; however, one can learn from one's mistakes and correct the situation by making another decision based upon the lessons learned from the previous decision. If it is impossible to correct

---

[285] Loc. cit. 165.
[286] Loc. cit. p. 180.
[287] Loc. Cit. p. 179.
[288] Rand, Ayn, "What is Capitalism," <u>Capitalism: The Unknown Idea,</u> (N.Y.: New American Library, Penguin Grp., 1966), p. 7.
[289] Ebenstein, William, <u>Today's ISMS</u>, Fourth Edition, (Englewood Cliffs, New Jersey: Prentice-Hall, Inc., 1964), p. 156.

a previous erroneous choice, then one must have the courage to accept the consequences.

Freedom of choice permits the individual to experiment, to learn, and to achieve. Personal development results from the individual's reasoning and choices. This leads to innovation, creativity, and mental development. Persons who only follow traditions, and the directions of "higher" government authorities, permitting others to make choices for them, make no choice; they do not engage in any rational thinking which stimulates innovation.[290] Innovative individuals affect their society and nation. A society and nation, where all individuals are permitted to make choices and learn from their mistakes, creates group development and learning. One's decision may prove to be very successful and others are not. When a national population adjusts quickly to proven successful actions, a nation's population will advance and societal happiness occurs. This is a condition not existing in totalitarian nations. Nations that permit and encourage personal development and responsibility, for example France, England, and the United States, have a history of societal, economic, and technological development exceeding any totalitarian or authoritarian nation. This results in various approaches to problem solving. The population experiences how one decision leads to success and others to little success or failure. It is a culturally based decision-making process with the input from potentially millions of people, not the single imposed choice of a governing autocrat, oligarchy. or dictator.

Under totalitarian governments, only one person, or a defined small group of persons (e.g. the Communist Party Central Committee), choose the directed action for the citizenry. Totalitarian government control suppresses any individual thought and innovation that the governing authorities perceive remotely disagree with government policy and ideology. The result is limited social advancement. In a totalitarian state, fascist or communist, under dictatorial or oligarchic control, where only the dictator knows "what is best," individual human and national advancement is repressed. One person, or groups of persons, cannot possibly possess all the knowledge necessary to solve the problems confronting a nation. One person or group cannot perceive and define the actions and products necessary to generate national prosperity and development.

In a totalitarian state, many choices are made affecting each individual citizen by the state. Under communism and fascism, the individ-

---
[290] Ibid.

ual is denied or is permitted only limited self-expression and personal action. However, the need for self-assertion is a strong desire in human nature. The loss of self-assertion results in hostility and aggression. Totalitarian governments compensate for this growing hostility by directing this hostility at an internal enemy (e.g. in Nazi Germany to Jews and communism to the bankers and landowners) or an external enemy, for example the capitalist nations.[291]

Capitalism, by contrast, is an economic system that is democratic. Capitalism incentivizes individuals to make choices based upon their personal mental rational thought processes. The buyers select the products and services that fulfill their individual needs. Producers react accordingly to fulfill the buyers' needs thus maintaining their business's financial stability and survival. A process of experimentation occurs resulting from diverse choices; the optimal choice is permitted to rise and improve a society's, or a nation's, condition. Producers and suppliers who fail to consistently devise new ways to meet buyers' needs and demands eventually cease to exist as a business organization. Capitalism is characterized by competition within the market place. Competition is constructive. It causes producers and suppliers to increase production efficiency and the quality of products and services thus increasing the producers and seller's success addressing buyers' demands within the market place and ultimately his survival as a business. With all suppliers within the market place consistently striving for efficiency and products that surpass their competitors, improvements in products, services, and ultimately the quality of life within a nation and its society occurs.[292]

Historically there was victimization of the masses by the elite, the money lenders, and the landowners. Marx himself is an example of this, but with a twist. He believed himself too good to do physical labor to provide for his family. Instead, he saw himself as victimized by the publishers who rejected his poor writing. He did not see himself at fault for this because he had a PhD. He was the son of a rich lawyer and believed he deserved better. In fact, he was a spoiled brat who thought he was above everyone else and he blamed them, not himself, for his bad choices that led to failure. From his hovel in the alleys of London, he expressed his infantile dream of a paradise where he would be successful and live in comfort. He made bad choices. He refused to apply

---
[291] Loc. cit. pp. 107-108.
292 Loc. cit. p. 166.

himself in law school, where he could have followed in the footsteps of his father and lived comfortably. He chose to be a writer and a philosopher. Yes, we are writers, but we are not trying to feed our wives and children by our writing and we leave it to the market to accept or reject our scribbles. We chose careers in industry and elsewhere that provided. It was only after successful careers that we put pen to paper. We had the freedom to make choices that laid forth the course of our lives.

In a communist regime, instead of having this choice, with children in school, the system would have made the choice, labeling us as suitable for this or that function within society and determining where our lives would lead us. We would not have had the opportunity to venture into the world of literature, philosophy, or politics. Instead of a great experiment where one could start one's career deciding that it was not suitable, one would then make a personal choice - leave it and try another, and another, and another as whim and opportunity presented itself. Communism, far more so than fascism, leaves the adventurous and the creative individual no opportunity to bloom and "spread his wings." It chains the worker, without or despite his wishes, to a machine and ties his future to the assembly line. The timid, the fearful, those who chose to wrap themselves in the cloak of victimhood may find it comfortable not to make any decision that might affect their lives as communism offers them. Without foundation, they put their futures in the hands of a series of government bureaucrats who have historically proven themselves to be poor decision makers. They fear to depart from the party line and attempt something new or different. Innovative thought becomes the path to the gulag.

A particular note needs to be made regarding bureaucrats. They are given a set of rules to follow; those rules are to be followed dogmatically, no matter how ill-considered, inappropriate to a given situation, or stupid. I once saw a governmental auditor confronted with a situation where there were five actions being taken by a contractor that were addressed by two separate governmental orders. The five actions were in complete conformance with the one order, but deviated from the second order, which was completely contradictory to the first order. The auditor reported the contractor for not conforming with the second order. However, if the contractor had complied with the second order, he would have violated the first order.

That same auditor demanded that a specialized study be made of the last lot of a product. To conduct this study, the entire production would have had to be destructively tested, further units made and destroyed in the testing process, and then the lot completely made anew. All this even though several thousand units had been made before and had all passed the specifications established by the governmental design agency. Conformance to an ill-considered and inappropriate order would have cost the government millions of dollars.

As a result of this mind set, workers and bureaucrats are dehumanized. Their individual reasoning is limited or nonexistent. They become automatons, "zombies," placing their minds in neutral, void of thinking and reasoning, and march to the orders and direction of a single decision maker or an oligarchy of decision makers. Government authorities enrich themselves while the workers live in squalor. An example is Kim Jung Un, the ruler of North Korea. His people frequently suffer from famines, but Kim Jung Un has obviously never missed a meal in his chubby little life. Only the weak find comfort in escaping the necessity of making decisions and accepting domination by government authorities.

That said, once the situation becomes too intolerable, the masses revolt and the guillotine or firing squads repeat their bloody business. The cycle once started is difficult to break. It always leads to the same result.

George Nafziger

CHAPTER 11.
Where do we Stand Today

As one looks across the spectrum of world events, and particularly those in the United States, one can see many similarities with the world as it existed in 1923. Let us examine those elements in the issues existing in 1923, that led to the rise of fascism, and how they compare to today's events.

Crisis

The major crisis in both Germany and Italy was the economy. The 1929 crash of the New York Stock Exchange resulted in the Great Depression. This economic event adversely affected the entire world. In Germany and Italy both economic events led to a successful establishment of fascist governments. As we have noted in chapter XXX's discussion of fascism, there were fascist political groups in all the European countries west of the Soviet Union, and in the United States (U.S.), and even Brazil.

The Great Depression economic crisis destroyed the accumulated wealth of many. Indeed, it destroyed the middle class in many countries; however, these economic crises increased the wealth of the very rich. As the middle class sold their possessions to feed themselves, the rich purchased those assets at a bargain basement price. The 1929 New York Stock Exchange crash wiped out millions in wealth and the fortunes of many individuals. However, somebody bought those stock certificates that were being dumped on the market and as they waited out the economic decline. Those stocks eventually returned to pre-crash prices and old fortunes that were not based on stocks rose to new levels. As the depression spread through the U.S. economy, there were food kitchens and lines of providing food to formerly employed Americans looking to get a meal. In 1929 the United States' unemployment rate was 3.2%; by 1933, it rose to a maximum of 24.9%.

In Germany there were also food lines. However, because the inflation of the socialist government using Keynesian economic theories of printing money to stimulate the economy hyperinflation occurred that destroyed the middle class. Hyperinflation had many consequences. One consequence was that farmers started refusing to send their products to market. By the time they were paid, the money they were given was worthless. As a result, they refused to sell and held on to their harvests, eating it themselves and bartering it in small quantities. At the end of 1929 the unemployment in Germany rose from 1,400,000 to over 2,000,000 (approximately 11%). By 1933 there were 6,100,000 unemployed, or one in every three Germans were unemployed.

In Italy, between 1929 and 1932, the unemployment rate ballooned from 3% to 23%. Though real wages remained high until the eruption of World War II, unemployment never fell below 9%.

In England the economic repercussions were also significant. As 1930 came to an end, unemployment rose from 1,000,000 to 2,500,000 (12% to 20%) and exports fell by 50%.

Today it appears that the world is on the edge of another economic crisis. The deficit spending of the United States (U.S.) Government has produced inflation at a magnitude not experienced since the 1970's. This is exacerbated by consistent cries of Climate Change and the impending world doom. On top of the Climate Change crisis there are the efforts by the Climate Change advocates to eliminate all fossil fuels with renewable, non-carbon-based energy forces. At the same time federal government policy rejects the only power source that would allow the United Staes to shift to a non-carbon-based economy – nuclear energy.

Climate change advocates, mandating abandonment of fossil fuels, long before the replacement of existing fossil fuel-based energy systems, are driving the developed world into an underpowered situation where an energy crisis will develop. An energy crisis will have disastrous effects not only on the economy, when industry cannot function because of the lack of power, but where people will be unable to heat and cool their homes.

The U.S. deficit is over $34 trillion. The money presses have not stopped printing more money. The potential of the U.S. finding itself in the same situation that Germany did in the Great Depression are very great. There were four issues that caused Germany to spiral into hyperinflation:

1.) High unemployment. German unemployment was approximately 11% in 1929;

2.) A massive debt. The Treaty of Versailles had imposed on Germany a reparation of 132 billion gold marks ($33 billion at the time or $668 billion adjusted for inflation to 2023). The German GDP in 1919 was 226 billion gold marks;

3.) The use of Keynesian economic theories; and,

4.) A tripping incident. In 1923 the French economy was experiencing a downturn. The French, therefore, sent Germany a demand for the payment of the reparations due because of the Treaty of Versailles.

When France called for the payment of the reparations due it, Germany was unable to meet its treaty obligation. Therefore, France occupied the Ruhr, the heart of German industry. Though a plan was made to pay those reparations, the German economy went into a financial crisis and hyperinflation erupted.

The inflation got so bad that the Germans had over 100 printing presses printing money day and night. The cost of printing currency soon became so bad that the cost of printing both sides of the bills was more than the bills were worth. By October 26, 1939, a 100,000,000 mark note, smaller than a $1 U.S. bill, was being printed on only one side, because it cost more than 100,000,000 marks to print both sides of the bill.

October 25, 1923 – 100,000,000,000 Mark note.

Today there is a very similar situation existing in the U.S. Though the reported unemployment in December 2023 was 3.7%, in April 2020 it had reached 14.7%. The 2020 number occurred because of the Covid pandemic, which was an unusual historical incident. This shows the possibility for massive unemployment like that of the Great Depression. The issue of massive debt exists in the U.S. The U.S. National Debt at the beginning of 2023 was $33 trillion and growing. The U.S. GDP in 2023 was $26.5 trillion. The Weimar German ratio of debt to GDP was 0.584. The U.S. ratio of debt at the end of 2023 to GDB was 1.245. If the GDP debt of Weimar Germany was a key element in the economic crisis of 1923, one must wonder why the U.S. debt to GDP ratio in 2023, which is 2.15 times higher than that of Weimar Germany, is not a far greater threat to the U.S. economy.

Keynesian economics is being applied in 2024. It is now, however, called Modern Monetary Theory. The left side of the U.S. political spectrum believes that it can print all the money it needs to pay its debts. Historically debasing of currency was used before the existence of paper currency and effectively destroyed ancient Rome. Its equivalent, simply printing more money by modern governments, has been the cause of inflation since 1922. When it was used by the U.S. Government from 2020 to 2023 it produced a reported inflation rate of 119% according to the U.S. Bureau of Labor Statistics.[293]

There is the potential of a tripping incident that hangs over the U.S. economy. The People's Republic of China holds about $850 billion of U.S. debt and Japan holds slightly over $1 trillion of U.S. debt. A total of over $7.4 trillion of U.S. debt is held by foreign countries. Most of these countries are not a problem, but China is a potential problem. China is hostile to the U.S. and the Chinese economy is also very weak. There is a very real chance that, to solve its own economic problems, China might, as France did in 1923, call on the U.S. to pay its debt and thus produce hyperinflation in the U.S. Indeed, China might take this step to collapse the U.S. economy to coincide with its constantly threatened military aggression against Taiwan.

We have already mentioned the 1929 New York Stock Market crash that initiated the Great Depression. The crash occurred because of two issues: (1) many investors buying stocks on the margin, i.e. 10% down, and (2) a "bank run" on a small bank near Wall Street, New York, New York.

At this time, banks collapsed for various reasons. This was not uncommon and runs on those banks were a regular occurrence as panicked depositors rushed to withdraw their money before it was all gone. The bank that provoked the 1929 crash was a small, rather insignificant bank, but it was within a few miles of Wall Street. The panic of the depositors somehow spread into the trading floor on the New York Stock Exchange and a selling panic occurred. Since so many of the investors had bought stocks "on the margin," the fall in the stock prices resulted in stock's margin calls thus forcing stock sales. This produced a synergy where each sale produced another sale as margin buyers rushed to cover their bets. The economy proceeded to collapse resulting in the Great Depression.

Today a similar situation exists. Instead of margin buying we have a collapse of the commercial property market. After Covid hit the US and

---

[293] https://www.bls.gov/data/inflation_calculator.htm

offices sent their workers to work remotely, corporations found their rental property empty and began to question why they were spending millions of dollars to rent property or even hold it. In addition, there arose an insignificant increase in crime in various major cities. This increase in crime threatened the safety of those workers as they came to perform their daily occupations and destroyed many of the businesses that supported commercial life in the center of the big cities, e.g. restaurants.

As businesses always try to cut costs, renting high priced office buildings now seemed unnecessary and they began not renewing their leases. The real estate companies that owned those buildings now found that in the market for office space, supply exceeded demand; they were forced, therefore, to lower their lease rates. Lower lease rates reduced the real estate companies' cash flow and could eventually force them into abandoning their properties to the mortgage holders - the banks. Since banks are required to maintain a specific liquidity, their balance sheets will become imbalanced. The banks will begin collapsing because they cannot maintain the required cash balances.

If dozens or hundreds of local banks begin collapsing, not only will there be runs on them, but the Federal Deposit Insurance Corporation (FDIC) will quickly be exhausted, and the government will be forced to print the money necessary to meet their statutory obligations. This would initiate the engines of inflation. Subsequently, the US could face inflation like the level experienced in Weimar Germany.

In summary, there is a very credible possibility of a major economic crisis in the future of the U.S. If the second scenario of bank collapses occur, it would not be a good time to be a politician holding office.

Primacy and Decline of the Group; Pure Community

Previously discussed was the flood of immigrants into Europe following World War I and how their presence in large numbers prevented their integration into European culture and particularly of their host nations. This failure to culturally integrate provoked tensions among the natives of that country, who saw these foreigners as a threat to the purity and the primacy of their national cultures. This was a change that was seen as a threat by the native Europeans, and the community. It provoked a nationalistic response.

If one looks back to the 1960's, it was rare to hear a foreign language being spoken in the U.S. outside of New York City or the other major U.S. cities. It is now commonplace to hear Spanish spoken everywhere. One even finds signs in various stores in both Spanish and English. At pharmacy counters, finding signs in 20 or more different languages that will allow the pharmacist work with his diverse customers is common in the contemporary United States. The Post Office has its hazardous materials questionnaire in both English and Spanish. There are large enclaves of Sudanese in Minnesota and Arabs in Michigan in addition to the old Chinatowns of California, Illinois, and New York. President Biden has even spoken of the time when Caucasians will represent less than 50% of the population of the U.S. Our nation's ethnic mixture is changing very rapidly. The old Caucasian group is declining by the appearance of a large numbers of immigrants who are not integrating into its society. These recent immigrants prefer to stand off and form enclaves that are often "no go zones" where outsiders are not welcome.

These "no go zones" already exist in Europe and may exist in the U.S. There are parts of Paris where non-Muslims are in physical jeopardy if they enter a Muslim area. Sweden ranks sixth in the world for rapes because of the massive influx of Muslims who do not mix with the Swedish community. The Muslims remain in enclaves and do not assimilate into the Swedish culture. Sweden has approximately 5,960 rape incidents per 100,000 people, or approximately 5% of Swedish women have been raped.[294] The rapes occur because, in the Muslim culture, Muslims look upon women who do not wear veils or cover their hair, as prostitutes. They have rejected the Swedish culture and retain their own. Thus, when a Muslim see an uncovered Swedish woman, their culture tells them that it is acceptable to forcibly take her. No such figures exist for the U.S. relating rape to any group.

In the State of Michigan, the cities of Dearborn and Hamtramck are examples of cities with ethnic enclaves. These two cities were once the home of a variety of working-class people of European descent. They no longer reflect European cultures, but have markedly changed as the growing Muslim population has displaced much of these cities previous ethnic populations and now have majority Muslim populations. These cities observe Muslim holy days as city endorsed celebrations. As for "no-go zones" there is a mixture of stories regarding whether theses Michigan cities have become no-go zones for non-Muslims. It is apparent that this group has two features: first, when Muslims move into an area, soon the non-Muslim population will begin leaving and more Muslims tend to replace them; sec-

---

[294] National Library of Medicine - https://www.ncbi.nlm.nih.gov/pmc/articles/PMC8330751/

ond, because of their traditional dress code, i.e. head scarves and bourkas, Muslims stand out when in public; in the post-9/11 world, Muslims are seen with suspicion. One or two individuals dressed in traditional Muslim garb are seen as an exotic curiosity, but large numbers of them could easily be seen as a threat to the existing American culture.

Since 2020, the U.S. southern border has been wide open and there are reports of from 7,000,000 to 10,000,000 illegal immigrants having entered the U.S. by the end of 2023. Composing these are several million "got aways" about whom nothing is known, but who have, most assuredly undesirable intentions for entering the U.S. There are constant reports of rapists and child molesters found among these immigrants, who receive the most cursory background check. Among these illegal immigrants there are people from every nation on earth. It is no longer limited to South and Central Americans. These recent immigrants bring with them a wide variety of customs and an equally broad number of languages. Because their numbers are so great they will congregate in ethnic groups forming more and more enclaves in the U.S., refusing to integrate into the American culture. They will have the means to remain in the U. S. and reinforce their cultural groups. The historical process of integration of immigrants into the U.S. and inculturation has vanished.

America is unusual in that for most of its history it was rare to find a group of people that did not speak English, and as a result after a one or two generations, they had completely integrated. As a result, Americans were notoriously monoglots. Immigrants were constantly coming into the U.S., but they strove to become Americans, to learn the English language, and disappear into the ranks of those pursuing the American dream. This has changed. The question is how much the realization of this is causing the multi-generational Americans to feel that their world, their country, their community, their group is being threatened by external elements. This concern surely arises every day when they encounter people in their schools, in the stores, and on the streets with whom they cannot communicate or who dress in unusual garb.

In post-World War I Germany, Germany experienced an invasion of Slavs and Jews from Eastern Europe. The changes they saw in their society were nowhere as great as what the U.S. experienced from 2020 to 2023. If the correct number of immigrants is 10,000,000, that is a 3% increase in its total population and a larger number than the population of 40 of the states of the United States.

Twin Evils

This is a problem beyond the mere presence of foreigners wandering the streets attempting to deal with the American culture. This will absolutely create great pressure on its culture by competing for jobs. These are not highly skilled immigrants (e.g. PhD, degrees) though there may be a few among them. The vast majority are uneducated and unskilled workers. They will take jobs from U.S. citizens. The reason for this is that they will be clandestinely paid in cash. Unskilled citizens cannot compete against them because the illegal immigrant does not have social security withheld from his pay check and the employer does not pay the matching social security. In addition, the employer does not pay workman's compensation taxes for them either. Hiring a citizen is immediately significantly more expensive; so unscrupulous employers will therefore hire, by preference, the illegal immigrant.

This uncontrolled immigration into the U.S. that has existed from 2020 to 2023 is the introduction of 10,000,000 unemployed immigrants into the population of the U.S. As they become part of the U.S. economy, they will either remain unemployed or displace American workers. Ten million immigrants have, therefore, produced an additional 3% increase in the U.S. unemployment figures.

The substantial sizeable increase of immigrates will create a crisis of unemployment, which was discussed earlier addressing a possible economic crisis. This increased unemployment of American citizens will result in higher governmental expenses. Immigrants and newly unemployed citizens, because immigrants have taken their jobs, received unemployment compensation, or received public welfare. This will increase U.S. government spending, increase taxes, and result in the U. S. government borrowing more money and increasing the government deficit. In addition, more and more of the U.S. citizens, who are on the lower end of the economic scale, will believe that they are being victimized. It is therefore certain that many of them will recognize that they are victimized because of the flood of foreigners into the country. This is a very similar situation to the 1920 and 1930's when Germany experienced a flood of immigrants. Indeed, Black residents of the south side of Chicago in early 2024, were complaining about the immigration problem and how immigrants are taking jobs away from them.

Decline in Morality

Earlier we spoke of how post-World War I there was an explosion of frivolity and lax morality during the Roaring 20's which led to forgetting the horrors of the trench warfare. Today western society is being pushed to accept behaviors that were considered abhorrent and immoral 50 years ago. The normalization of the practices of the LGBQT community of our society is one example. This process is being pushed by the political Left in its crude exploitation by the presumed victimization of these societal groups. There are several elements. They include, but are not limited to, the Left's insistence to expose minor children to the transsexual members of our society, i.e. drag queen reading hour and drag shows for minors and even encouraging minor children to transition from one sex to the other in our schools and then concealing this from their parents. This is a part of the Marxist desire and strategy, to destroy the nuclear family and take the rearing and education of children completely from the parents and place child rearing into the hands of government. Under government control, children can be indoctrinated, controlled, and manipulated by the extreme Marxist Left.

Additionally, the Left makes direct attacks on Christianity which traditionally declares transsexual actions as sinful. There are reports of the FBI investigating Catholic Churches, under the direction of the political left, as being bastions of White Supremacy – again the victimization card. To this one must add that the percentage of the U.S. population that attends church regularly has declined steadily over the last 50 years. That said, individuals who have deeply held religious beliefs are being attacked generally do not accept those attacks well.

Abortion is a related issue, but as it is self-inflicted, those who might be provoked to a physical response by the unrestricted availability of abortion are relatively small. Yes, there are demonstrations by both sides of this issue and there is occasional related violence, vandalism, and fire-bombing; but the violence is overwhelmingly from the pro-abortion elements of the U.S. society, not from those who believe it is immoral.

Overall, however, a large percentage of the U.S. population will see abortion as an example of the decline of the general population's moral standards and will feel threatened by it.

Victimhood

Victimhood is the battle cry of the Left. They exploit it in a manner that would make Lenin smile. However, it is creating a sense of victimhood on both sides of the political spectrum - the Left and the Right. The laws in California and its legal system, excuse shoplifting of products priced at less than $1,000. California has permitted the minorities – indoctrinated with the idea that they are victims of White Supremacists, capitalist exploitation, have resulted in thousands of incidents where crowds rush stores to appease their sense of victimhood and their right to reparations, because they believe they, or their ancestors, were oppressed. On the other side, it creates another class of victims whose stores have been pillaged and driving the shop owners out of business and into bankruptcy. The livelihood of these people is directly threatened. When various local governments do not protect them, they will look for someone to save them, a politician who promises law and order.

Another victim, one which has the potential of reacting to this lawlessness, are the honest citizens who find the cost of what they buy increasing because businesses are being pillaged by thieves. These thieves have two options: (1) go out of business, or (2) raise the prices of the goods they sell. It is passing on of costs to the honest citizens. This has the potential of producing a reaction. These victims will also turn to politicians who promise them law and order.

Another element of the victimhood is the presence and the growth of various foreign criminal gangs in the US. Among them are Barrio Azteca, Angelino Heights Sureno 13, Tren de Aragua, or the "Aragua Train," and the Mexican drug cartels - Beltrán-Leyva Cartel, La Familia Michoacana or Knights Templar Cartel, Gulf Cartel. Juárez Cartel, Sinaloa Cartel, Tijuana Cartel, and Los Zetas. This is a very short list of these gangs. These groups engage in everything from illegal drugs to street crime and burglary. The cartels are also involved in human smuggling, which includes sex slavery of both women and children. They have even made Phoenix, Arizona, the kidnapping capital of the United States. For example, there is the brutal murder of Suren the 22-year-old college student Laken Riley in Athens, Georgia, in March 2024 by an illegal alien. Rampant criminal crime, despite the denials of the Biden administration, are visible daily on the news, creating both outrage and fear. In a word, more and more people are either actual victims of crime or have an increased fear of becoming victims.

In addition to the thievery, there exists the general lack of prosecution of those classes that the Left has declared victims by the local judicial systems. The prosecutors and judicial system are controlled by the Left. When the "victim class" commits a crime against the "victimizer class" in some jurisdictions, the judicial systems plead the sentence down to nothing or prosecutors literally decline to prosecute the criminal. This also creates victims among the retail and property owners when they have suffered pain, injury, or loss, and they cannot receive justice from the justice system. They too will begin looking for a politician who offers them law and order.

A two-tier legal system has developed in the US because of various Leftist prosecuting attorneys being elected to office in various left leaning states and in the major cities where the Left dominates politics. In New York City there is the case of Daniel Penny, who while riding in the New York City subway system on May 1, 2023, found himself confronted by Jordan Neely, who was violently threatening Penny and other passengers. Penny and two other passengers attempted to subdue Neely. In the resulting scuffle, Neely was placed in a strangle hold by Penny and subsequently died. Penny is a Caucasian and Neely was Black. Penny is being prosecuted for manslaughter.

Meanwhile on March 15, 2024, in a situation very similar to the Penny case, a Black man defended himself with a pistol, shooting another Black armed with a knife and a pistol, who was threatening the riders of the subway. The shooter claimed self-defense and was not arrested nor was he charged with anything[295], even though firearms are prohibited on the subway.[296]

As a result of these two incidents, it is apparent that people who are declared to be victims by the Left, i.e. racial minorities, receive different and preferential treatment, but when a Caucasian acts in the same manner against a minority he is hit with the full force of the law. This will also create a sense of victimhood among those who are prosecuted while others, because of their ethnicity, are released for nearly identical crimes.

Violence and Will

Beginning shortly after World War I in Germany and Italy the communists had armed gangs that served them as the muscle to threaten and silence those who politically opposed them. The right responded with armed groups of their own that were filled with patriotic veterans of the Great War. Violence ran in the streets. In Germany there were numerous bloody street fights between machine gun armed Frei Korps engaging in

---

[295] https://abcnews.go.com/US/1-shot-new-york-city-subway-scuffle-man/story?id=108134540
[296] https://new.mta.info/document/36821

political violence. In Germany the right responded to the violence of the left in the form of the Sturmabteilung or SA of the Nazi Party. In Italy it was the Black Shirts that filled this role.

The George Floyd riots in 2020 erupted in at least 140 cities across the United States, and the National Guard has been activated in at least 21 states. There was significant violence by the political left and significant gun fire. Approximately between $1,000,000 and $2,000,000 in property losses because of arson or looting occurred because of those riots. (FN)

ANTIFA is the constant source of demonstrations and riots. U.S. Attorney General William Barr once described ANTIFA's tactics as a "new form of urban guerilla warfare" similar to the guerilla warfare used by Mao Zedong in his cultural revolution, or by the German Communist Party (KPD) in 1918 in the Spartacist uprising. In post-World War I Germany, the presence of these armed groups was a persistent issue. As mentioned earlier, the Right, in both Germany and Italy, confronted them with their own armed militias.

In the U.S. the violence has only been on the part of the leftist and openly communist ANTIFA and BLM groups. ANTIFA is an interesting group. ANTIFA stands for "Anti-Fascist." It is odd that they call themselves "anti-fascists" as there are no true fascists running the streets of the U.S. or Europe, though there are neo-fascist groups in both Europe and the U.S. So far those European neo-fascist groups are acting as purely political parties and have not yet sent armed bands into the streets. Those in the U.S. are so small and insignificant they they are limited to very small groups ranting their anger in back rooms. The question is how long will it be before the victims of the left's activities, the burning of businesses, the riots in the streets, the attacks on the police, and unprosecuted criminal activities react violently and deploy their own armed groups? How long before they start looking for a politician who will promise them law, peace, and order in the streets?

As can be seen in this list of the events that led to the appearance of fascism, history is again repeating itself. It is apparent that those who have failed to learn from history are on the brink of repeating it again.

Every element that scholars have identified as leading to the rise of fascism can be seen evolving in the U.S. today. If our government remains blind to this or torn into impotence by the left as it pursues its goals as the communists did in post-WWI Germany and Italy, the greater the likelihood is that there will be a political reaction by the right. We cannot predict if it will be a new appearance of politicians who were lumped, in the 1930s, under the imprecise and nebular term fascists or if it will be something else. One thing is certain, the left will use their favorite invective and decry them as fascists as they call any group that opposes their politics.

Is There a Fascist/Communist State Coming to the U.S.?

Whether there is a fascist or communist state coming to the U. S. is an interesting question. Certainly, the circumstances that existed in the 1920's are present in the US in the 2020's. It has taken only 100 years for the wheel to turn one cycle repeating what the world faced in 1920.

Let us, therefore, examine what is happening in United States politics today and see if we can find any elements that are common to or unique to one or the other of these systems.

The United States' political system is fundamentally bi-polar. There are two major parties and several insignificant other parties. In one corner we have the nominally conservatives and in the other the progressives. Within both groups there is a spectrum of political thought.

Among the political right-wing conservatives, there are those who are firm believers in the U.S. Constitution and all its elements; they believe in such principles as a balanced budget, a strong military, and personal advancement through merit, hard work, and self-reliance. We describe these as the Constitutionalists, there focus being adhering to the principles of the Constitution.

These beliefs, therefore, very and diminish in their intensity as one examines the other end of the conservative spectrum. Also, this is an undisciplined group where individuals will stand apart from the group and vote against most of their fellow conservatives.

Among the "progressive" branch of American politics there are some elements that touch on the more progressive end of the conservative wing of American politics. This political wing grows increasingly towards socialism and communism, where it espouses the very Marxist idea of equality of outcome, guaranteed minimum income, and state direction and control of the economy, including the activities of industry. In contrast to the Constitutionalists, these "progressives" tend to vote as a disciplined block under the direction of a strict internal power structure. Defections from the group vote are very rare. We will refer to these as the Socialist wing of American politics.

However, there is a twist. Rather than evolving into a purely Communist idea of the state, the "progressive" branch seems to be mor-

Twin Evils

phing into a hybrid between the two political philosophies. To justify this belief, we examine some of the features of both the communist and fascist states and find examples of them in the modern U. S.

Marx's 10 Points	What is Comparable in American Today.
Abolition of private property in land and application of all rents of land to public purpose.	There have not yet been any significant calls for the abolition of private property, because the extremely rich, the multi-billionaires in the US have formed an allegiance with those who might otherwise call for this by supporting their cause with contributions to their causes and political campaigns. This is more reflective of a fascist system where private property was allowed, but the state directed how it was used.
A heavy progressive (graduated) income tax.	The U.S. progressive tax system was passed by Congress on July 2, 1909, and ratified February 3, 1913. The 16th Amendment established Congress's right to impose a federal income tax. For the last several decades, the "progressives" in the U.S. have consistently called for higher and higher taxes upon the rich.
Abolition of all rights of inheritance.	This is mixed. There have been inheritance taxes in many US states, but only 6 still had one in 2024. However, there is a national inheritance tax. As of 2023, the federal estate tax was to be paid if the taxable estate exceeded $12.92 million and increased to $13,610,000 for 2024. In 2024 the federal estate tax rate was 40% and at times has been as high as 50%.

Confiscation of the property of all those who emigrate and rebel.	California has been considering taxing the income of people who leave California to escape its high level of taxes. The proposed law would, for taxable years from 2024 onward, impose a tax of 1.5% on a net worth exceeding $1 billion, and starting from 2026, the proposed tax rate would be 1% on a net worth exceeding $50 million.
Centralization of credit in the hands of the state, by means of a national bank with state capital and an exclusive monopoly.	The US Federal Reserve is moving towards becoming a national bank and instituting a digital currency which would accelerate the creation of a national bank by allowing the Federal government to track all purchases, defunding those who spend in manners contrary to the state's acceptable ways. This was done in Canada during the COVID epidemic to truckers who objected to the government's COVID mandates. In addition, the 2008 bail out of failing banks and the subsequent absorption of failed banks is moving in this direction.
Centralization of the means of communication and transportation in the hands of the state.	Communications are still in private hands, but it is divided into two parts. Each of them is nominally affiliated with one of the two respective political wings. That of the progressives is the dominant and acts as a propaganda ministry spreading progressive story line. The smaller system acts in the same manner towards conservatives, though it appears to be less dogmatic. As for transportation, the Biden administration is taking steps to control transportation and restrict the freedom of movement of Americans by means of electric vehicle mandates.

Twin Evils

Extension of factories and instruments of production owned by the state; the bringing into cultivation of waste lands, and the improvement of the soil generally in accordance with a common plan.	In the progressive program the attacks on industry and agriculture are being driven by the ideology of Climate Change. The regulations being imposed on industry are driving it overseas. The regulations on agriculture are driving down its productivity. The result of this is that both industries and agriculture are being taken over by either foreign countries or individuals of the elite class, particularly Bill Gates, who has bought 242,000 land acres in recent years.
Equal obligation of all to work. Establishment of industrial armies, especially for agriculture	There is no movement in this direction. Instead, the progressives' programs are encouraging many to go on welfare and not work, but to become totally dependent upon government.
Combination of agriculture with manufacturing industries; gradual abolition of the distinction between town and country by a more equable distribution of the population over the country.	There is nothing like this currently in the US and is totally a situation that existed in Marx's time.

Free education for all children in government schools. Abolition of children's factory labor in its present form. Combination of education with industrial production, etc. etc.	The US has had free education for many years and child labor has long been abolished. No one will argue that child labor is bad; but the free public educational system has been taken over by the teachers' unions, who are strong supporters of the progressive program and engage in indoctrinating the youth in that ideology. The Conservative Right is working in many states to allow tax funds designated for education to follow the student if they go to parochial or private schools, and even if they are home schooled. The Left is threatened by this and is working to prevent their monopoly from being broken.

The greatest difference between these communist goals and those of the American socialists is the possession of private property, which was allowed under fascism, but only on the condition that industry act in accordance with the direction of the state. There is a small group of extremely rich industrialists and businessmen who, by their joint operation with the progressives, have brought about this situation in the United States during the last decade. Bill Gates, Mark Zuckerberg, Jeff Bezos, and George Soros, have brought this situation about by openly supporting progressive programs, donating to the favored progressive nongovernment organizations (NGOs) and to the political campaigns of the members of the "progressive" movement. George Soros, especially, has several political action groups that have spent billions of dollars on progressive campaigns. These political campaigns are not confined to national level progressive candidates, but most notoriously support prosecuting attorney election races in major metropolitan areas. The direct result of these latter donations has been several progressives becoming prosecuting attorneys where they have reduced the prosecutions of a multitude of criminals, and in major cities, such as New York, Philadelphia, and Chicago, downgrading felonies to misdemeanors or simply refusing to prosecute criminals who are members of minority groups.

The reason for allowing this non-prosecution of criminals and releasing them back into society makes no sense, until one analyzes it from the Marxist perspective. From this perspective, there is some logic and the purpose is possibly to create a lawless situation that is so intolerable that the average citizen will call for the imposition of martial law to control the crime problem. Then, once this is instituted, martial law will not end until the Left has established itself in permanent control of the government in a silent coup.

Beyond the elements of Marx's 10 points that can be found the contemporary U. S., there are other elements of the United States's political system that are evolving towards activities that are common to both communism and fascism. One is the way the law is employed in both communism and fascism - the use of the law to oppress political opposition.

Hitler's Germany was noted for kangaroo political courts that swiftly led to executions. A prime example is the fate of the German generals and other officers who were involved in the July 20, 1944, coup against Adolph Hitler. "More than 7,000 people were arrested and 4,980 were executed. Not all of them related to the plot, since the Gestapo used the occasion to settle scores with many other people suspected of opposition sympathies."[297]

Using the legal system against political opponents was also common in the Soviet Union. This was epitomized by the statement: "Show me the man and I'll show you the crime." Though popularized in Soviet era Poland, it is attributed to Soviet secret police chief Lavrentiy Beria. This process was used to send any number of individuals who protest the Soviet system or were perceived as a threat to it. Among the many political prisoners of note was the author, Alexander Solzhenitsyn. We have already spoken of the Gulag system which was purely for eliminating political opposition.

Though no longer the old Soviet Union, Russia continues the communist use of the legal system to suppress any opposition. On 13 December 2016, the leader of Russian opposition to Vladimir Putin, Alexei Navalny, announced his intention to run for President of Russia in the 2018 election. He began campaigning for the presidency despite court proceedings against him in a fabricated fraud case, which could bar him from running since the Russian election legislation deprives certain criminals of eligibility. In February 2017, a district court in Kirov upheld his suspended sentence. In May it was announced that Navalny would not be allowed to run. Navalny prepared to appeal to the European Court of Human Rights and continued campaigning to give the government no choice but to accept his candidacy. On December 24, 2017, he registered

---

[297] https://en.wikipedia.org/wiki/20_July_plot

as a candidate for the presidency of the Russian Federation and lost the election. [298]

In October 2017, Navalny was arrested again. In August 2020, Navalny collapsed on a flight from Siberia to Moscow. He was flown to Germany in a coma for treatment. The German doctors found traces of the Soviet-era nerve agent Novichok in his blood. One of the assassins was confronted by Navalny and he confessed that he had been approached by the Russian security services and had put the nerve agent in Navalny's underwear. The Russian government denied any responsibility or involvement.

The Russian government renewed an old fraud conviction against Navalny, alleging he had violated his parole by going to Germany for treatment. Despite this, Navalny returned to Russia in January 2021. He was arrested again and was sentenced to two and one-half years for parole violations. In 2022 he was sentenced to another 9 years. Charges and trials continued and he was eventually given a 19-year sentence and sent to an arctic penal colony where he mysteriously and suddenly died on 16 February 2024. Regardless of Putin's denials, it is obvious that Putin was simply eliminating any political opponents and engaging in a reign of terror to keep any other leader from to opposing him.

It would be logical to compare this with the criminal indictments issued against Donald Trump. However, this is subject to the problems of misinformation, disinformation, and emotion that permeates contemporary United States society today. Instead, let us examine the low-level opposition to the Biden Administration and the U.S. citizens who were involved in the occupation of the Capitol Building on January 6, 2021. However, we must first look at two issues: Brady Violations and the socialists' attitude towards solitary confinement.

In general, a "Brady violation" occurs when a prosecutor fails to provide a defendant, or criminal defense attorneys, with any "exculpatory evidence" – evidence that <u>is favorable or helpful</u> to a defendant's case.

Solitary confinement is frequently attacked as a violation of the 8th Amendment of the US Constitution, which reads: "Excessive bail shall not be required, nor excessive fines imposed, nor cruel and unusual punishments inflicted."

Amnesty International and other nominally socialist groups have protested its use for many years. "While there may be instances where

---

[298] https://www.theguardian.com/world/2017/dec/25/russian-opposition-leader-alexei-navalny-barred-from-running-for-president

holding prisoners in isolation is appropriate and humane, the use of prolonged, indefinite solitary confinement is a violation of the prohibition against torture and other cruel, inhuman, or degrading treatment or punishment opens in a new tab found in international human rights law. By violating this prohibition, U.S. authorities not only abuse the rights of prisoners, they undermine the human rights that protect all of us from abuse." [299]

The American Civil Liberties Union document, entitled *Abuse of the Human Rights of Prisoners in the United States: Solitary Confinement*, reads: "Prisons in the United States have always had solitary confinement cells where prisoners were sent for violating prison rules. However, the use of solitary confinement as a long-term management strategy rather than short-term punishment for misconduct is a relatively recent development." [300] This document further states: "A considerable number of the prisoners fell, after even a short confinement, into a semi-fatuous condition, from which it was next to impossible to arouse them, and others became violently insane; others still, committed suicide; while those who stood the ordeal better were generally not reformed, and in most cases did not recover sufficient mental activity to be of any subsequent service to the community."

This American Civil Liberties Union document summarizes its discussion of solitary confinement with the following: "The Human Rights Council should call on the United States to adopt policies and practices for the use of solitary confinement consistent with the following principles:

"• Solitary confinement should be used only in very exceptional cases, for as short a time as possible and only as a last resort.
"• Segregation of prisoners for their own protection should take place in the least restrictive setting possible.
"• Decrease extreme isolation by allowing for in-cell programming, supervised out-of-cell exercise, face-to-face interaction with staff, and access to television, radio, telephone calls, correspondence, and reading material.
"• Decrease sensory deprivation by limiting the use of auditory isolation, deprivation of light and reasonable darkness, and

---

[299] https://www.amnestyusa.org/updates/the-shocking-abuse-of-solitary-confinement-in-u-s-prisons/#:~:text=While%20there%20may%20be%20instances,in%20international%20human%20rights%20law.
[300] https://www.aclu.org/documents/abuse-human-rights-prisoners-united-states-solitary-confinement

punitive diets.
"• Allow prisoners to gradually earn more privileges and be subjected to fewer restrictions, even if they continue to require physical separation from others.
"• Prohibit solitary confinement of prisoners with mental illness, children under age 18, and death row and life-sentenced prisoners by virtue of their sentence.
"• Prohibit the intentional use of solitary confinement to apply psychological pressure to prisoners.
"• Carefully monitor prisoners in solitary confinement for signs of mental illness and promptly remove them from solitary confinement if such signs appear.
"• Invite United Nations special rapporteur on torture to conduct a fact-finding mission and facilitate access to prisons and inmate victims of prolonged solitary confinement."

In summary, the opinion of these socialist groups, solitary confinement is a violation of human rights for convicted prisoners. Therefore, why is it is used in the confinement of un-convicted January 6th prisoners who have been denied bail and have not yet even had a court date set?

Now, why do we discuss these two issues? The answer is simple; hundreds of American citizens were arrested for entering the Capitol Building on January 6th. They were tracked down, arrested, and many were held in solitary confinement for up to a year before they were taken to trial.

In a Politico article dated April 19, 2021, we find the following: [301] "Most of the 300-plus people charged with participating in the Jan. 6 Capitol riot have been released while they await trial, but dozens of those deemed to be dangerous, flight risks or at high risk of obstructing justice were ordered held without bond. D.C. jail officials later determined that all Capitol detainees would be placed in so-called restrictive housing - a move billed as necessary to keep the defendants safe, as well as guards and other inmates. This means twenty-three hour-a-day isolation for the accused, even before their trials begin.

"And such treatment does not sit well with Warren or Senate Majority Whip Dick Durbin[302] (D-IL), two of the chamber's fiercest critics

---
[301] https://www.politico.com/news/2021/04/19/capitol-riot-defendants-warren-483125
[302] Senator Dick Durban was re-elected to the US Senate as a democrat in 2020 and will serve

of solitary confinement.

"'Solitary confinement is a form of punishment that is cruel and psychologically damaging,'" Warren said in an interview. "'And we are talking about people who have not been convicted of anything yet."

There are numerous articles of this kind to be found and there are numerous individuals arrested because of their involvement in the January 6th protest. The ACLU and Amnesty International, both liberal organizations, declare that solitary confinement is cruel and unusual punishment Therefore, what is it when solitary confinement is inflicted on people who have not been convicted and have been denied bail prior to their trial date? The answer is simple; it is punishment for potentially having political opinions contrary to those of the ruling party. In this case the ruling party are the socialists in power in Washington, D.C.

There is more. It is sufficiently severe when someone is arrested and put into an American gulag and held in solitary confinement, while awaiting trial. There is also the issue of convicting them in politically biased courts, where the prosecution deliberately and successfully withholds potentially exculpatory evidence, i.e. the Brady Violations.

The Capitol Building is under constant video surveillance. According to Barron's[303] there were "More than 40,000 hours of security video from the January 6, 2021 attack on the US Capitol is to be released to the public, the new Republican speaker of the House of Representatives said Friday." That Friday was in November 2023, nearly three years after the occupation. Though participants in the occupation of the Capitol Building were being tried and convicted of crimes since the occupation the prosecutors knowingly and deliberately withheld from the defendant's court appointed defense attorneys' access to these videos which could have easily shown if they had or had not committed any prosecutable crime. The Brady Violation does not relate to guilt; it relates to the government's deliberate refusal to provide the accused defense with "potentially exculpatory evidence." This is a violation of the basic civil rights of the accused and would normally result in the overturning of any conviction. However, those who have been convicted still languish in prison as of 2024, despite the deliberate and willful violation of their rights.

---

until 2026. It is strange that this fierce opponent of solitary confinement has yet to say anything about the confinement of the January 6 protestors three years after the protest.

[303] https://www.barrons.com/news/over-40-000-hours-of-us-capitol-riot-video-to-be-released-a027e4ba

George Nafziger

This is a clear example of the ruling political party using the legal system to punish those who have opinions contrary to those of the ruling party.

That said, the story continues. Stephen Horn was one of thousands who entered the U.S. Capitol on January 6, 2021 and he is one of 1,061 defendants that have been so far charged with entering or remaining in a restricted federal building or grounds on January 6th. Yes, he scaled a statue; but if one bothers to look at the photograph of him there, he is using his cell phone to take pictures of the crowd. Horn is an independent journalist who entered the Capitol so he could accurately document what happened. He was not wearing clothing that showed support for President Donald Trump. He did not join in the chants. He did not assault law enforcement officers. He even warned against breaking any objects in House Speaker Nancy Pelosi's office.

Horn was arrested and tried. He was convicted of four misdemeanors. His sentence, a year in prison. His real crime – being an independent journalist who did not carry the ruling party's story line, but showed that what happened on January 6, 2021 differed from what the ruling party declared it to be.

In an almost identical situation, another independent journalist, Steve Baker, was arrested on March 1, 2024, and began his punishment for not conforming to the ruling party's story line on January 6, 2021. As of February 29, 2024, he did not know what the charges were against him The FBI told him that he should report for processing in flipflops and shorts because it made it easier for him to be put in an orange jump suit and have chains put on his ankles. We say, "punishment" because there were 60 journalists who entered the Capitol building on January 6, 2021; however, only two independent journalists, who were not part of the captive media, were arrested and prosecuted.

Another area where our current system is morphing into a hybrid communist-fascist totalitarian state, is the media.

In Nazi Germany, Paul Joseph Goebbels was the propaganda minister. He had total control over the media – radio and newspapers. Nobody publicized any information that had not been approved by Goebbels' ministry. Everything was censored to conform with the party line. He centralized Nazi control of all aspects of German cultural and intellectual life. Everything was focused on molding the minds of each German citizen to assure that each citizen's total support and subjugation to the will of the Führer. All members of the film industry were required to join the Reich Film Chamber. Through this ministry Goebbels promoted the development of films with a Nazi slant, and ones that contained subliminal or overt propaganda messages. The movie, *Triumph of the Will,* is a major example. A major focus of Nazi propaganda was Hitler himself. The Nazi's purpose was to glorify Hitler as a hero and an infallible leader. The result was that Hitler became the focus of a cult of personality.

In the Soviet Union, propaganda was controlled by the Communist Party's Central Committee. It shared all the elements of Nazi Germany when it came to control the news media, art, culture, and even the cult of personality. In Communist China the "Publicity Department of the Central Committee of the Communist Party of China, also known as the Propaganda Department or Central Propaganda Department, is an internal division of the Central Committee of the Chinese Communist Party (CCP) in charge of spreading its ideology, media regulation, as well as creation and dissemination of propaganda. The department is also one of the main entities that enforces media censorship and control in the People's Republic of China."[304] In Communist China, for the duration of Mao's rule, there was also a cult of personality that focused on Mao's infallibility.

In the United States, there is no Ministry of Propaganda, but there are official and unofficial ministries that control what is now called "misinformation" and "disinformation."

In 2023 the Department of Homeland Security attempted to form a second Disinformation Governance Board after the panel was shuttered last year amid censorship concerns among the opposition to the ruling party in Congress. This attempt to create an overt and established governmental bureau to control political discussions in the various media. Is this not exactly like what the Nazi's, the Soviets, and the Communist Chinese had in their governments to control the political discussion?

During the Covid pandemic all stories that challenged the official party line on Covid and the vaccine were attacked, but not directly by the government, but through their influence over the various social media platforms. Twitter was exposed. Twitter had been influenced to eliminate any postings that disagreed with the party line. As a result, 11.72M accounts were challenged, 11,230 accounts were suspended, and 97,674 had their content removed.[305] Even National Public Radio, the government financed and leftist media outlet, on November 29, 2022, said "Twitter will no

---

[304] https://en.wikipedia.org/wiki/Publicity_Department_of_the_Chinese_Communist_Party
[305] https://transparency.twitter.com/en/reports/covid19.html#2021-jul-dec

longer enforce its policy against COVID-19 misinformation...."[306]

The Biden administration also approached Facebook and YouTube with the same demand. The Biden administration engaged in censoring anyone who held a different position on Covid, including physicians and research scientists. Among the various controls was "defunding" various media platforms and blocking their various posts.

Catherine Herridge is a journalist who was a senior investigative correspondent for CBS News in Washington D.C. from 2019 to 2024.[307] CBS fired her in 2024 and seized her computer and all research related to her investigation of President Biden and his son Hunter. This story has yet to be fully exposed. However, it appears that her research was getting close to disclosing information that would be particularly embarrassing to the Biden administration and had to be stopped. Therefore, CBS was "encouraged" to stop her.

Earlier Cahterine Herridge had been held in contempt by a federal judge for refusing to divulge her source for a series of Fox News stories about a Chinese American scientist who was investigated by the FBI but never charged. "U.S. District Judge Christopher Cooper in Washington imposed a fine of $800 per day until Herridge reveals her source, but the fine will not go into effect immediately to give her time to appeal."[308]

"Cooper wrote that he 'recognizes the paramount importance of a free press in our society' and the critical role of confidential sources in investigative journalism. But the judge said the court 'also has its own role to play in upholding the law and safeguarding judicial authority.'"[309]

It had long been held that a journalist's sources were sacrosanct and could not be handed over to the government, no matter how compelling the government's interest in that information. This was all considered to be part of the concept of a free press as established by the 1st Amendment to the United States Constitution.

Now we have the unusual situation of a law suit brought against the Biden Administration for censoring free speech on various social media outlets. When Elon Musk took over Twitter, he released a mass

[306] https://www.npr.org/2022/11/29/1139822833/twitter-covid-misinformation-policy-not-enforced
[307] https://en.wikipedia.org/wiki/Catherine_Herridge
[308] https://www.cnn.com/2024/02/29/media/catherine-herridge-contempt-refusing-to-reveal-sources/index.html
[309] https://abcnews.go.com/US/wireStory/judge-holds-veteran-journalist-catherine-herridge-civil-contempt-107699511 and https://www.yahoo.com/finance/news/judge-holds-veteran-journalist-catherine-002945116.html

of documentation that showed that the Biden Administration had pressed Twitter to cancel the posts and comments of various individuals who disagreed with the Administration's position on Covid. Similar incidents occurred with Face Book and other social media.

The Biden Administration established the Disinformation Governance Board whose purpose was to eliminate speech that was in opposition to the Administration's position on Covid. Its stated goal to "coordinate countering misinformation related to homeland security." Nina Jankowicz, a well-known figure in the field of "fighting disinformation and extremism," is the board's executive director. Her function was very similar as Joseph Goebbels and his Soviet peers.

All these incidents relating to the media and the control of speech make it clear that there is an effort to suppress free speech and free thought. It is clear that there is an on-going effort to establish total control of the media by the government.

It is appropriate to examine the federal government's efforts to control transportation - the imposition of electric vehicles. This process will have several impacts. The freedom of movement that Americans have enjoyed, particularly since the time of the Model T, is in jeopardy. With gasoline propelled vehicles, one can drive coast to coast in three days of hard driving; but with electric vehicles (EV), hours will be lost at the charging station because the range of an EV is quite short.

Furthermore, the Biden Administration is mandating that by 2032, only 20% of new car sales be gasoline driven. Implementation of this policy will restrict the mobility of the American population and further increase government control over American citizens. Here are the details: first, the average cost of a gasoline powered vehicle in 2024 $33,797 while that of an EV is $66,997 before tax incentives and rebates.[310]

The result will clearly be that Americans will no longer be able to come and go as they please, but can only go as far as their extension cord will stretch. Second, the distance that a gasoline power car can drive on a twenty-gallon tank based on on 2021 standards is 500 miles. That of an EV

---

[310] https://www.google.com/search?q=average+price+of+a+gas+powered+car&sca_es-v=91d34ab46baf2683&ei=Kh0A   ZvHaA9Lp84PsbmqgAc&oq=average+price+of+a+-gas+powered+car&gs_lp=Egxnd3Mtd2l6LXNlcnAiImF2ZXJhZ2UgcHJpY2Ugb2YgYSB-nYXMgcG93ZXJlZCBjYXIqAggAMgsQABiABBiKBRiRAjILEAAYgAQYigUYhgMy-CxAAGIAEGIoFGIYDMgsQABiABBiKBRiGAzILEAAYgAQYigUYhgNIoS9Q7QdYgA-9wAXgBkAEAmAFgoAGWA6oBATW4AQHIAQD4AQGYAgagAsoDwgIKEAAYRxjWB-BiwA8ICBhAAGAcYHsICBxAAGIAEGA2YAwCIBgGQBgiSBwM1LjGgB8Ya&sclient-=gws-wiz-serp

is 250.[311] Gasoline can be found everywhere, but EV charging stations are very rare and it can cost up to $500,000 to install one high speed charger.

The current mandates have had a deleterious effect on the auto industry. Not only are EVs not popular and not selling, their manufacture requires less labor, which will result in layoffs in the automobile industry. This will increase unemployment, which is already being exacerbated by other Administration policies. All this conspires to make mobility less available to the American public. When citizens are less mobile, they are easier to control. So, it appears that Marx's seventh point is being implemented.

Both fascist dictators Hitler and Mussolini, took advantages of crises to seize power and establish themselves as dictators. Mussolini used a political crisis to have the King of Italy declare martial law and he then seized the reins of power. In the case of Hitler, it was the Reichstag fire. On February 27th, 1933, a few weeks after Adolf Hitler became Chancellor of Germany. Marinus van der Lubbe, a Dutch communist, was alleged to have set the Reichstag on fire. As Rahm Emmanuel famously said, "Never let a good crisis go to waste," Hitler blamed communist agitators for the fire and claimed communists were plotting against the German government. He then persuaded President Paul von Hindenburg to issue the Reichstag Fire Decree which suspended civil liberties, and began a ruthless war on the communists. There is a significant debate over the truth that Marinus van der Lubbe set the fire, or because he was mentally challenged. It has been suggested that he was induced into the act or even set up so he would be caught and charged with act by members of the Nazi Party.

The current situation in the United States, vis-à-vis potential crises where some individuals act, or take a series of actions, could provoke a demand by the public for the establishment of martial law. We have the rampant crime in the streets of the major US cities discussed above. Then we have the mass immigration into the US where the screening of the entrants is very limited. Of the estimated 10,000,000 immigrants that have come into the U.S., approximately 2,000,000 are referred to as "got aways." These are people the government has no information concerning

[311] https://www.google.com/search?q=average+mileage+of+a+ev&sca_esv=91d34ab-46baf2683&ei=vB4AZuiTGfvgp84____Pj_iC8A4&ved=0ahUKEwjo4fmn9YyFAxV78MkDH-Q8AO4Q4dUDCBA&uact=5&oq=average+mileage+of+a+ev&gs_lp=Egxnd3Mtd2l6LX-NlcnAiF2F2ZXJhZ2UgbWlsZWFnZSBvZiBhIGV2MgYQABgWGB4yBhAAGBYYH-jIGEAAYFhgeMgYQABgWGB4yBhAAGBYYHjIGEAAYFhgeMgYQABgWGB4yBhAAG-BYYHjIIEAAYFhgeGA8yBhAAGBYYHkjOYlDKVFjfV3ACeAGQAQCYAYwBoAH-dAaoBAzEuMbgBA8gBAPgBAZgCBKACrALCAgoQABhHGNYEGLADmAMAiAYBkA-YIkgcDMy4xoAf0EA&sclient=gws-wiz-serp

their background or location.

In a CNN article dated December 6, 2023 "FBI Director Christopher Wray said Tuesday December 5, 2023 that he has never seen a time during his decades-long career when so many threats against the US were all as elevated as they are now, warning senators he sees "blinking lights everywhere."[312]

"During a hearing before the Senate Judiciary Committee, ranking Republican member of the committee, Senator Lindsey Graham of South Carolina, asked Director Wray if he saw 'blinking red lights' — referring to warning signs the US missed before the attack of 9/11.

"'I see blinking lights everywhere I turn,' Wray said.

Wray also said that the bureau is working "around the clock" to "identify and disrupt" potential attacks by individuals inspired by the Hamas attacks on October 7.[313]

"'Given the steady drumbeat of calls for attacks by foreign terrorist organizations since October 7th, we are working around the clock to identify and disrupt <u>potential attacks by those inspired by Hamas's horrific terrorist attacks in Israel</u>. Wray said in his opening remarks before the committee.

"There is currently no information to indicate that Hamas 'has the intent or capability to conduct operations inside the US," Wray said in a written statement separate from his opening remarks, "though we cannot, and do not, discount that possibility.'"

On October 31, 2023, it was reported that "So far this year, 169 individuals with positive terrorism watchlist matches tried to cross the southern border into the United States. That's according to U.S. Senator Shelley Moore Capito, R-W.Va., who says she is alarmed by the statistics."[314] In 2020, President Biden essentially opened the borders of the United States. One cannot dispute that terrorists are exploiting the massive onslaught of illegal immigrants entering the United States since 2020, to cloak their entry into the United States.

The possibility of the US equivalent of a Reichstag fire is highly possible, be it another 9/11 or some other terrorist inspired incident, and it will be the direct result of Biden's immigration policy. The question is did Biden deliberately establish a situation where he would have plausible deniability for another 9/11 terrorist attack. Establishing this situation <u>would provide</u> the opportunity for Biden, or a successor, to declare martial

---

[312] https://www.cnn.com/2023/12/05/politics/fbi-director-senate-hearing/index.html
[313] https://www.cnn.com/2023/12/05/politics/fbi-director-senate-hearing/index.html
[314] https://www.capito.senate.gov/news/in-the-news/capito-says-169-migrants-on-terrorist-watch-list-tried-to-cross-southern-border

law and seize absolute power?

In summary, every issue that scholars believe provoked the rise of fascism are present in the United States of 2024 and the vast majority of Marx's 10 points are being implemented. However, it does not seem that either a pure Marxist system or a pure fascist system is likely to occur. It is more probable that the U.S. is moving towards a hybrid mixture of the two systems and we will have our own Reichstag fire that will allow a hybrid-communist-fascist government established in the United States.

BIBLIOGRAPHY

Allen, R.C., & Khaustova, E., *Russian Real Wages Before and After 1917: in Global Perspective* (Abu Dhabi, UAE: New York University Abu Dhabi, May 2017)

Anonymous, *Mao Zedong* (Internet: Captivatinghistory.com/ebook, 2018)

Anonymous, *Memoraial alphabetique des choses concernant la Justice, la Police, et les Finances de France, 1st Part, Des Tailles* (Paris: Cochart, 1697).

Anonymous, *Memoire pour l'Entirere Abolition de la Servitude en France* (Paris: Chenault, 1765).

Asveille, V., *Histoire de Gracchus Babeuf et du Babouvism* (Paris : Self Pulilshed, 1884).

Babeauf, G. *Journal de la liberté de la presse. 1. Editions n ° 1 à 22 of « Journal de la liberté de la presse» (17 fructidor an II-10 vendémiaire an III)*, n ° 23 à 32 *(14 vendémiaire-13 pluviôse an III) du «Tribun du peuple ou Le défenseur des droits de l'homme», en continuation du « Journal de la liberté de la presse. »*

Bahnsen, D.L., *Crisis of Responsibility*, (New York: Post Hill Press, 2018).

Barby, H.B. The Advantages and Disadvantages of the Feudal System, (Oxford, UK: Sheldonian Theater, 1848)

Barnes, J.S., *The Universal Aspects of Fascism* (Unknown: Reconquista Press, 2020).

Bergin, S. *The Khmer Rouge and the Cambodian Genocide*, (New York: Rosen, 2008).

von Böhm-Bawerk, Eugen, Translated by Macdonald, A.M., *Karl Marx and the Close of His System* (New York: MacMillan, 1898).

Bonds, R. *The Vietnam War: The Illustrated History of the Conflict in Southeast Asia.* (Lebanon, PA: Salamander Books Limited, 1979).

Buonarroti, P., *Graccus Babeuf et la Conjuration des Ėgaux* (Paris:

Chevalier, 1869).

Cai, Xia (December 4, 2020). "The Party That Failed: An Insider Breaks With Beijing". Foreign Affairs. Archived from the original on December 7, 2020. Retrieved December 4, 2020.

Changyu, Li., Mao's "Killing Quotas" https://web.archive.org/web/20090729194758/http://www.hrichina.org/public/PDFs/CRF.4.2005/CRF-2005-4_Quota.pdf

Chan, A.L, Mao's Crusade: Politics and Policy Implementation in China's Great Leap Forward. (UK: Oxford University Press, 2001).

Chen, Theodore Hsi-En; Chen, Wen-Hui C. (March 1953). "The 'Three-Anti' and 'Five-Anti' Movements in Communist China". *Pacific Affairs*. 26.

Chigas, G., Mosyakov, D., Yale University Genocide Studies Program, "Literacy and Education under the Khmer Rouge, https://gsp.yale.edu/literacy-and-education-under-khmer-rouge

Chinese 3rd Five-Year Plan: http://www.china.org.cn/english/MATERIAL/157608.htm

Chong-Sik Lee, Politics in North Korea: Pre-Korean War Stage, (UK: Cambridge University Press, 2009).

Daline, V.M., *L'Histoiregraphe de Babeuf, (La Pense, Revue du Rationalism Moderne* No. 128, August 1966).

Demante, G. *Etude historique sur les Gens de Condition Mainmortable en France au XVIII Siecle* (Paris: Picard, 1804).

DIA Intelligence Appraisal entitled *Soviet Involvement in Sub-Saharan Africa.* (Declassified by Dos on May 4, 2006) Formerly Classified Secret NOFORN.

Dommen, A. J., *The Indochinese Experience of the French and the Americans*. (Blomington, IN: Indiana University Press, 2001).

Ellman, M. Soviet Repression Statistics: Some Comments. *Europe-Asia Studies,* Vol. 54, No. 7 (Nov. 2002).

Engels. F., Revolution and Counter-Revolution in Germany, *New York Daily Tribune;* October 1851 – October 1852, New York Daily Tribune;

Engels, F., *Socialism: Utopian and Scientific*, http://www.marxists.org/archive/marx/ works/1880/socutop/index.html.

Engels, F., *The Origin of the Family, Private Property and the State*, (Chicago: Kerr, 1902).

Fachan, J.M., *Finances Féodales* (Paris : Félix Alcan et Guillaumin Rénis, 1909).

Frey, R. J., *Genocide and International Justice*. (New York: Infobase Publishing, 2009).

From, E., *Escape from Freedom* (USA: Avon Books, 1969)

Essential Juche Works, (Red Flame Press, work lacks all publication data)

Getty, J.H.; Rittersporn, G.; Zemskov, V., (October 1993). "Victims of the Soviet penal system in the pre-war years: a first approach on the basis of archival evidence." American Historical Review. 98.

Gao, Mobo. *The Battle for China's Past: Mao and the Cultural Revolution*. (London: Pluto Press, 2008)

Gorbunova, Viktoriia; Klymchuk, Vitalii (2020). "The Psychological Consequences of the Holodomor in Ukraine". East/West: *Journal of Ukrainian Studies*. 7 (2).

Griffin, R., *Fascism: An Introduction to Comparative Fascist Studies*, (Cambridge, UK: Poltry Press, 2018).

Griffin, R., *Fascism: A Quick Immersion* (USA: Tibidabo Publishing,m 2020)

Gutmann, E, *The Slaughter: Mass Killings, Organ Harvesting, and China's Secret Solution to Its Dissident Problem*, (New York: Prometheus Books, 2014).

Harding, N., *Leninism* (Durham, N.C.: Duke University Press, 1996)

Heuveline, P., (2001). "The Demographic Analysis of Mortality Crises: The Case of Cambodia, 1970–1979". Forced Migration and Mortality. (Washington, D.C.: National Academies Press, 2001)

Hitler, A., *Mein Kampf – My Struggle*, (USA, Midgaard, 2014).

Hurley, J., Morris S., & Portelance, G., Center for Global Development, CDG Policy Paper 121, March 2018. "Examining the Debt Implicatons of the Belt and Road Initiative from a Policy Perspective."

Institutional Digital Archive: "Cuba's Unresolved UMAP History:

Survivors' Struggles to Counter the Official Story", https://ida.mtholyoke.edu/handle/10166/4039.

Janet, P., *Les origines du socialism contemporaine* (Paris: Ballière, 1883).

Jossa, B., "Marx, Lenin, and the Cooperative Movement", *Review of Political Economy*, Volume 29, Issue 1, January 2005

Jullian, C., *Histoire des Institutions Politiques de l'Ancienne France* (Paris: Hachette, 1890)

Karlsson, P., *China in Africa: An Act of Neo-Colonialism or a win-win relationship.* Master's Thesis. http://www.diva-portal.org/smash/record.jsf?pid=diva2%3A1437583&dswid=-6283

Kiernan, B. *How Pol Pot Came to Power: Colonialism, Nationalism, and Communism in Cambodia, 1930–1975.* (New Haven, CT: Yale University Press, 2004).

Kim Il Sung, *The Selected Works of Kim Il Sung* (Manee, Il: publisher unknown, 2023).

Kung, J.K., Ma, D.; von Glahn, R. (eds.), "The Political Economy of China's Great Leap Famine", The Cambridge Economic History of China: 1800 to the Present (UK, Cambridge University Press, 2002).

Lee, Chong-Sik. "Evolution of the Korean Workers' Party and the Rise of Kim Chŏng-il." Asian Survey, Vol 22 (Berkeley, CA: University of California Press, 1982).

Lenin, V.I., *State and Revolution* (Mansfield Center, CT: Martino Publishing, 2011).

Lenin, V.I., *A letter to American Workingmen* (New York:Socialist Publication Society, 1918).

Lenin, V.I. Collected Works, Vol. 31, "*The Tasks of the Youth Leagues*" first published Pravda Nos. 221, 222, and 223, October 5, 6, and 7, 1920.

Lenin, *Essential Texts of Marxism-Leninism* (Springfield, MO: Pravda Media, 3027), Vol. 1.

Lenin, V.I., *On Utopian and Scientific Socialism: Articles and Speeches* (Amsterdam: Fredonia Books, 2002).

Lih, L. T. *Lenin* (Great Britain: Reaktion Books, 2011).

Lin, J. Y. & Yang, D.. "Food Availability, Entitlements and the Chinese Famine of 1959-61". The Economic Journal. 110 (2000

Loyseau, J.R. *Réflections sur la loi du Maximum et sur les Réquisitions* (Paris : Vialard, 1794-1795).

Kim Il-sung *Essential Juche Works*, Collected and reworked by Red Flame Press.

Kim Il-sung, *The Selected Works of Kim Il-Sung,* ISBN 978-1-6671=1448=81

Mallock, W.H., *A Critical Examination of Socialism*, (New York: Harper & Brothers, 1907).

Mao Tse Tung, *The Little Red Book, Quotations from Chairman Mao,* (UK : Parvus Magna Press, date unknown).

Mao Tse Tung Speeches and Reports

    "On Tactics Against Japanese Imperialism", December 27, 1935.

    "Our Economic Policy", January 23, 1934.

    "Problems of Strategy in China's Revolutionary War:, December 1936

    "The Identity of Interests Between the Soviet Union and All Mankind" ,September 28, 1938.

"Stalin, Friend of the Chinese People", December 20, 1939.

"On New Democracy", January 1940.

"On Coalition Government," April 24, 1945.

"The Work of Land Reform and of Party Consolidation in 1948", May 25, 1948.

"On the People's Democratic Dictatorship", June 30, 1949.

"Request for Opinions on the Tactics for dealing with Rich Peasants," March 12, 1950

"The Party's Mass Line Must be Followed In Suppressing Counter-Revolutionaries", May 1951.

    "On the Ten Major Relationshipis" April 25, 1956.

Marx, K. & Engels, F., *The Communist Manifesto*, (Amazon, 2021).

Marx, K., *Capital (Das Kapital),* (India: Finerprint Classics, 2020).

Marx, K. *The Poverty of Philosophy* (Chicago: Kerr, 1920).

Morel, *La commune de Compiègne 1153-1319* (Compiègne: Lefebvre, 1901).

Mushota, C.E., , *China in Africa: Partner or Exploiter? The Case of Zambia*, Cuny Academic

Works, https://academicworks.cuny.edu/cgi/viewcontent.cgi?article=1997&

context=cc_etds_theses

Mussolini, B., *The Doctrine of Fascism*, (Zhingoora Books, date unknown).

Mussolini, B., *Essays on Fascism* (London : Sanctuary Press, 2019).

Patton, R., *The Anatomy of Fascism* (New York: Vintage Books, 2004)

Peterson, J. *12 Rules for Life,* (Canada, Random House, 2018)

Phillips, T., The Guardian, https://www.theguardian.com/world/2016/may/11/the-cultural-revolution-50-years-on-all-you-need-to-know-about-chinas-political-convulsion

Pike, D., The Viet-Cong Strategy of Terror https://vva.vietnam.ttu.edu/images.php?img=/ images/231/2311404008a.pdf

Pothier, R.-J. *Traite du contract Bail a Rente* (Paris: Debure, 1764).

Quesnay, F. *Tableau Oeconomique* (London, McMillan, 1894).

C. Rivers Editors, *Kil-Il-sung: The Controversial Life and Legacy of North Korea's First Supreme Leader* (Monee, IL: C. Rivers Editors, 2022)

Rochester, A., *Lenin on the Agrarian Question* (New York: International Publishers, `1942).

Rummel, R.J. *STATISTICS OF DEMOCIDE* Chapter 10 *Statistics of North Korean Democide Estimates, Calculations, and Sources.* https://www.hawaii.edu/powerkills/SOD.CHAP10.HTM

Sartre, J. *Colonialism and Neo-Colonialism* (London: Rutledge, 2001)

Secretan, E., *Essai sur la Féodalité* (Lausanne, Switzerland : Bridel,

1858).

Seignohos, C., *The Feudal Regime* (New York: Hold, 1907).

Seybolt, T.B.; Aronson, J.D.; & Fischoff, B. *Counting Civilian Casualties: An Introduction to Recording and Estimating Nonmilitary Deaths in Conflict.* (Oxford, UK: Oxford University Press, 2013).

Spargo, J. *Karl Marx : His Life and Work* (New York: Huebsch, 1912).

Stalin, J., *Foundations of Leninism* (Honolulu, HI: University Press of the Pacific, 2001).

Stalin, J. *Trotskyism or Leninsm?* (Dickinson, ND: SAI Press, 2021).

Stalin, J., *Works, Vol. 12, April 1929-June 1930,* (Moscow: Foreign Languages Publishing House, 1954) pp. 147-178.

Strauss, V., & Southeri, D., Washington Post "How Many Died? New Evidence Suggests Far Higher Numbers for the Victims of Mao Zedong's Era" July 17, 1994.

Swidersky, A.T., Agricultural policy over a period of 10 years. "Puti Sieskogo Khozislstva," official periodical of the Commissariat of Agriculture, 1927, N 10.

Thomassin, *Essai sur les rentes foncières* (Strasbourg: Levrault, 1800) .

Toland, J., *Adolf Hitler* (Garden City, NY: Doubleday, 1976).

Trotsky, *On Lenin* (Chicago, Haymarket Books, 2017)

University of Colorado, *Readings on Fascism and National Socialism* (Denver, A. Swallow, Unknown)

U.S. Commission on the Ukraine Famine (1988). Mace, James Earnest; Samilenko, Olga; Pechenuk, Walter (eds.). *Investigation of the Ukrainian Famine 1932–1933* Vol.1: Report to Congress. Vol. 1 of 3. Washington, D.C.: United States Government Printing Office. p. 67. Archived from the original on 7 January 2007. Retrieved 27 July 2012.

Vickery, M. *Cambodia 1975–82* http://michaelvickery.org/vickery1999cambodia.pdf

Viola, L., *Peasant Rebels Under Stalin* (New York: Oxford University Press: 1996).

Werth, N., Courtois, S., Panne, J.-L., Pzkowski, A., Bartosek, K, Margolin, J.-L. (Kramer, M, Ed) (1999). The Black Book of

Communism, Crimes, Terror, Repression, (Cambridge, Massachusetts: Harvard University Press, 1999) p. 164.

Wolowyna, Oleh (2 October 2021). "A Demographic Framework for the 1932–1934 Famine in the Soviet Union". *Journal of Genocide Research*. 23 (4): pp. 501–526.

Yun *Sun, China's Aid to Africa; Monster or Messiah,* Brookings Institute, Friday, February 7, 2014 https://www.brookings.edu/opinions/chinas-aid-to-africa-monster-or-messiah/

Internet Sources Consulted:

en.wikipedia.org/wiki/Bolivarianism#:~:text=The%20term%20%22Bolivarianism%22%20is%20often,political %20sovereignty%20(anti%2Dimperialism)

en.wikipedia.org/wiki/Deng_Xiaoping

en.wikipedia.org/wiki/Human_rights_in_Tibet#:~:text=They%20also%20include%20political%20and, U.S.%20 State%20 Department's%202009%20report.

en.wikipedia.org/wiki/Direcci%C3%B3n_de_Inteligencia#:~:text=The%20Intelligence%20 Directorate%20(Spanish%3A%20Direcci%C3%B3n,of%20the%20government%20of%20Cuba.

en.wikipedia.org/wiki/Zhao_Ziyang

en.wikipedia.org/wiki/Re-education_camp_(Vietnam)#:~:text=Re%2Deducation%20camps%20(Vietnamese%3A,former%20government%20of%20South%20Vietnam.

Global Centre for the Responsibility to Protect: https://www.globalr2p.org/countries/venezuela/

Twin Evils

George Nafziger

INDEX

A

absolute power, 173, 189, 222, 278, 284, 359

accomplishing Socialism, 230–33

Africa, 32, 190–95, 198–200

African countries, 191, 195, 200

African National Congress (ANC), 199

African nations, 191, 195, 199–200

Africans, 32–33, 196, 199–200

African states, 193, 198

agriculture, 13, 45, 94, 100, 122, 126, 135–37, 144, 150, 168, 179, 200, 202, 223, 346

   collectivization of, 90, 212

American Civil Liberties Union, 350

American culture, 337–38

American Historical Review, 148, 362

Amnesty International, 349, 352

The Anatomy of Fascism, 239, 269, 365

ANC (African National Congress), 199

Angola, 191, 193, 199–200, 216

antagonism, class, 65–67, 112

anti-fascist subversives, 260

antisemitism, 242–44, 248, 251

anti-Semitism, 27, 290, 303

armed forces, 114–15, 269

army, 8, 16, 50, 105, 113–15, 123, 131, 139, 146, 159, 161–62, 173, 181, 183–84, 198, 220, 222, 232, 236, 244, 251, 258, 295, 308, 312–14

Austro-Hungarian Empire, 242, 248–49, 285

authority, 21–22, 41–43, 45–46, 106, 133, 152, 189, 223, 225, 234, 245–47, 266–70, 272–73, 276, 278, 323–27

B

Babeuf, 17–21, 24–25

   world of, 18–19

Babeuf's communism, 19

Barnes, J.S., 66, 245, 268–71, 273, 275, 278–81, 360

Blackshirts, 256–59

Bolivarian Revolution, 217

bourgeoisie, 49, 66–69, 71, 80, 86, 126, 130, 164, 171, 198

bourgeois society, 49, 56, 67, 239

Bukharin, Nikolai, 126, 134–35, 138, 146

businesses, private, 165, 212

C

Cambodia, 50, 178, 201–5, 213, 307–10, 314, 362, 366

Cambridge University Press, 170, 221, 361, 363

capital, accumulation of, 29, 85, 101

capital investments, 46–47, 97

capitalism, 10, 29, 31, 47–50, 57, 67–68, 74, 82, 100–102, 109, 111–12, 117, 131, 150, 175, 207, 251, 274, 298, 323, 326, 328

   development of, 48, 101, 109

   elements of, 152, 185

   evolution of, 66, 100

   product of, 57, 100

capitalist class, 127, 130, 155, 164, 166

capitalist economy, 117, 214

capitalist elements, 139

capitalist nations, 322, 328

capitalist production, 48, 68, 84, 140

capitalist society, 36, 38, 43, 45, 47, 69, 231

capitalist states, 45, 99, 117

capitalist system, 41, 67, 79, 88, 109, 149

Captivatinghistory.com/ebook, 154, 164–66, 169–70, 172, 175, 360

The Case of Zambia, 191–98, 365

Castro, Fidel, 215–16

Catholic Church, 7, 26, 81, 290, 339

CCP. *See* Chinese Communist Party

CCP general secretary, 176

CEC (Central Executive Committee), 158, 210, 312

central authority, strong, 296, 301, 306

Central Committee, 138–39, 172, 177–78, 184, 220, 228, 354

Central Executive Committee (CEC), 158, 210, 312

Central Military Commission, 177, 183

Central Party School, 184, 189

Chaing, 158, 160–61

champart seigneurial, 12–13

chief component of state power, 313–14

children, 11, 15, 34, 47, 57, 68, 70, 72–79, 88, 134, 142, 166, 179, 190, 201–3, 208, 218, 224, 237, 277, 292, 299, 305, 329, 339–40, 347, 351

China's Aid to Africa, 191, 367

China's Secret Solution to Its Dissident Problem, 182, 362

Chinese, ethnic, 179, 204

Chinese capitalists, 164–65

Chinese Communist Party (CCP), 155–60, 162–67, 169, 171–77, 180–88, 190, 220, 354

Chinese communists, 155–56, 160–62, 175, 309

Chinese companies, 191

Chinese economy, 172, 178, 185, 334

Chinese Empire, 163, 178

Chinese government, 155, 182, 190, 200

Chinese immigrants, 197–98

Chinese money, 196–98

Chinese nationals, 197

Chinese peasants, 318

Chinese people, 157, 175–76, 182, 185–86, 190, 364

Chinese workers, 193, 197–98

church, 7–8, 16, 81, 172, 220, 242, 339

citizens, 25, 89, 122, 146, 152, 185, 208, 236, 244, 269, 293–94, 296–97, 304–5, 308, 311, 315, 327, 338, 353, 357

civilians, 113, 206–7, 210, 235–36, 312, 314

civil liberties, 102, 246

    suspended, 284, 357

civil war, 129, 132, 137–38, 150, 258, 312–13

class consciousness, 156, 158

class enemies, 123, 222, 247

classes, 7, 15, 23, 28, 31, 38, 40, 49–50, 65–67, 71, 82, 84–86, 114, 124, 127, 133, 139–40, 144–45, 150, 154–55, 200, 203, 211, 224, 253, 265, 274, 279, 282, 289, 322, 340, 346

    established new, 65–66

    hostile, 224, 234

class struggle, 49, 66, 100, 127, 139, 156, 232, 288, 313

    history of, 49, 65

class warfare, 251, 265, 274, 281

collective farms, 124–25, 136, 139–43

collectivization, 45, 122, 140–41, 151, 165–67, 175, 312, 321

    process of, 141, 167, 212, 320

colonies, 92, 101, 109, 131, 194–95, 198, 205, 253, 293

combination of agriculture, 70, 305, 346

Commissariat of Agriculture, 125, 366

commodities, 27, 34, 39, 42, 47, 53, 55, 59, 63–65, 89

communism, 7, 19, 32, 35, 51, 69, 71, 73, 82, 92, 99, 112, 120, 131, 136, 154–55, 159–60, 176, 182, 184–85, 200–202, 205, 212, 217, 221, 223, 229, 237, 247, 251–52, 261, 274–78, 296, 301–2, 306, 315, 318–19, 322–24, 328–29, 343, 367

    international, 215

communism and fascism, 1, 3, 5, 7, 277, 315, 317, 325, 327, 348

Communism in Cambodia, 202, 363

Communist Central Committee, 134, 159

Communist China, 184, 302, 354

communist countries, 48, 212–13, 220, 315

communist governments, 51, 82, 110, 203, 210, 311

communist ideas, 18–19, 301, 343

communist ideology, 25, 203, 277

Communist International, 156, 220

The Communist Manifesto, 27–28, 36–37, 49–51, 65, 82, 88, 91, 96, 149–50, 364

communist nations, 43, 45, 156, 201, 225, 300

communist party, 18, 35, 50, 67, 69, 72, 100, 102, 122–23, 125, 127, 134, 142, 144, 157, 160, 162, 174, 201, 205, 210, 212, 215, 220–21, 243, 257, 276, 310, 316, 354

Communist Party of Italy (CPI), 257

Communist Party of Korea (CPK), 220–21

communist philosophies, 20, 302

communist revolution, 50, 171, 215–16, 317

communist rule, 110, 163, 213, 217

communists, 18, 25, 50–51, 67–68, 79, 109, 120, 132, 138, 143, 151, 157–62, 164, 175, 184, 198, 201, 205, 208–10, 213, 216–17, 222, 236, 239, 247, 255–57, 278, 284, 300–302, 307, 309, 313, 318, 321, 327, 341–42, 344, 348, 357

communist society, 43–45, 79, 82, 118, 315

communist states, 45, 109, 128, 198, 210, 302, 307, 343

communist system, 46, 169, 185, 276

competition, free, 41, 45

concentration, 67, 77, 94, 100, 308

concentration camps, 175, 234–35, 299, 311, 315

Congo, 191, 193, 197, 199–200, 215

Controversial Life and Legacy of North Korea's First Supreme Leader, 220, 223, 233, 365

CPI (Communist Party of Italy), 257

CPK. *See* Communist Party of Korea

A Critical Examination of Socialism, 43, 364

Critique of Political Economy, 36, 51

Cuba, 43, 51, 199, 215–17, 309

Cuba's Unresolved UMAP History, 216, 362

cult of personality, 147, 223, 227, 354

culture, 74, 82, 122, 162, 171–72, 207, 232, 241, 263, 280, 285, 317, 322, 336, 338, 354

Czarist government, 105, 110, 135, 147

Czarist Russia, 50, 145, 317

D

Daline, V.M., 16–20, 361

Das Kapital, 23, 27–29, 36–38, 40, 46, 48, 50–52, 55, 59, 100–102, 107, 133, 365

death penalty, 17, 308

death rates, 142, 212, 237

debt, national, 197, 333

demilitarized zone (DMZ), 201, 206

democracy, 20, 45, 101, 152, 155, 157, 174, 180, 206–7, 246, 265, 278–79, 317–18, 321

new, 175, 321, 364

Democratic Kampuchea, 202–3

Deng, 179–81, 183, 185

Deng Xiaoping, 177–79, 181

DGI (Dirección General de Inteligencia), 215

dictatorship of the proletariat, 108, 110, 117–18, 120, 130, 139, 156, 172, 202

Dirección General de Inteligencia (DGI), 215

Discourse upon Free Trade, 84

DMZ (demilitarized zone), 201, 206

The Doctrine of Fascism, 254, 261, 280–81, 365

Dutch communist, 284, 357

duty, 13, 25, 76, 115, 232, 240, 247, 262, 268–69, 272–73, 275, 278, 280, 294–96, 299, 305, 307, 312, 319

E

Eastern United States, 60

economic crises, 101, 196, 218, 240, 249, 331–33, 335, 338

economic development, 168–69, 180, 215, 223

economic growth, 163, 181, 191

economy, 10, 23, 28, 39–40, 46, 56, 70, 85, 94, 97, 104, 109, 125, 134–36, 150, 164–66, 171, 175, 177, 180–82, 185, 187, 190, 196, 199, 203, 213, 217–18, 229, 240–41, 252, 274, 331–32, 334, 343

  planned, 136, 186

education, 24–26, 44–45, 68, 71–72, 88, 110, 145, 166, 171, 180, 191, 195, 203–4, 218, 221, 231, 249, 262–63, 280, 291, 295, 298, 300, 305, 307, 347, 361

educational system, 88, 183, 203, 218, 260, 299, 347

enemies of the people, 160, 204, 216

Engels, 39, 51, 55, 67, 73–76, 78, 82–84, 93–94, 98–99, 111–13, 119, 150, 203, 214, 229, 269, 277, 361

  Frederick, 18, 66, 73, 75, 361–62, 364

Essai sur la Féodalité, 10–11, 13–15, 365

established gun control, 314–15

establishment of industrial armies, 70, 304, 346

Etude historique, 14–15, 361

Europe, 8, 26–29, 42–43, 56–58, 62, 101, 130–31, 135, 242–43, 248, 250–51, 290, 318, 335–36, 342

exchange values, 59

exile, forced, 216

F

factories, 29–30, 32, 41–42, 44–47, 51, 63–66, 68, 93–94, 96–97, 108, 110–11, 193, 202–3, 287–88, 321

  modern, 41

factory labor, 70, 347

factory owners, 66, 324

factory workers, 30, 48, 63, 103–4, 108, 138, 156, 324

failure, crop, 28, 137, 151, 319–20

farmers, small, 143, 247

fasci italiani, 252–53

Fasci Italiani di Combattimento, 252, 255

fascism, 5, 7, 92, 229, 233, 239, 241, 245–48, 251–52, 255–56, 259–65, 267–70, 274–82, 296, 299, 301–2, 315, 323–24, 329, 331, 342, 347, 359, 362

  fundamental element of, 8, 233

  key element of, 217, 241

fascist concept, 246, 269, 274, 276

fascist Italy, 247, 255, 308, 315–16

fascist movement, 239, 247, 251–52, 257

fascist parties, 241, 245, 250, 258–59

fascists, 239, 241, 247, 251, 255–59, 262–63, 265, 267–70, 272–77, 279–81, 302, 310, 320–21, 327, 331, 342–43

fascist states, 246, 248, 265, 267, 277–78, 307, 344

fascist system, 344, 359

feudal complexum, 22

feudalism, 5, 10, 23–24, 71, 109, 112, 206, 316–17, 320, 322

The Feudal Regime, 11–12, 15, 366

feudal system, 10, 360

feudal traditions, 172

financial support, 157, 250, 255

firearms, 308, 310–13, 315, 341

Five-Antis Campaign, 164–65

food, surplus of, 74, 170

food production, 74, 91, 212

food shortages, 170, 212

food supplies, 50, 91, 138, 151

forced labor, 23, 147, 223, 234, 236

Foreign Languages Publishing House, 141, 366

France, 7–8, 10, 12, 14–15, 16, 20–21, 23, 25, 81, 90, 205, 240, 243, 248, 300, 320–22, 327, 333–34, 361

French, 8, 24, 102, 132, 205–6, 243, 250, 320, 333

French colonial rule, 206, 318

French government, 16–17, 243

French nobility, 8, 90, 321

French people, 20–21, 321

French Revolution, 7–8, 16, 20–21, 66, 81, 90, 102–3, 114, 145, 215, 246, 248, 320

French revolutionaries, 8, 319

French socialism, 18

French socialists, 18, 205

Friedrich Engels, 54

Fromm, Erich, 323–26

G

general secretary, 157, 176, 180–81, 183–84, 188

genocide, 201–2, 310, 314

Genocide and International Justice, 204, 362

Gens de Condition Mainmortable, 14–15, 361

German army, 51, 244

German citizens, 295, 299, 304, 353

German communist parties, 302, 342

German government, 244, 284, 357

The German Ideology, 37, 40, 51

German industry, 56, 333

German newspapers, 295, 304

German nobility, 54, 319

German people, 293, 300

German press, 295, 299, 304

German Revolution, 102, 244

Germany, 23, 51, 56, 84, 101–2, 135, 239–41, 244–45, 247–49, 251, 278, 284, 293, 296–98, 300, 303, 306–9, 311, 314, 319–20, 322, 331–33, 337–38, 341–42, 349, 361

Nazi, 239, 247, 304–5, 310–11, 314–16, 328, 353–54

Weimar, 240, 333–35

Giolitti's government, 257

Global Marxism, 5, 215

government, 8, 16, 21, 44–45, 64, 88, 96, 102, 110–12, 118, 124–25, 127, 136, 147, 160, 162, 164–65, 172, 181, 184–85, 189, 196, 200, 203, 206–8, 210–13, 215–16, 218–19, 226–27, 234–35, 237–38, 240, 250–51, 257–60, 263, 269, 271–78, 282, 285, 293, 297, 304, 310, 321–22, 324, 330, 334–35, 339, 342, 345–46, 348, 352, 354–57

authoritarian, 318

government authorities, 250, 323, 327, 330

government control, 82, 141, 339, 356

government officials, 160, 179, 197, 207, 209, 236, 322

government schools, 70, 305, 347

government transparency, 178–79

grain, 13, 45, 57–58, 89, 119–20, 123–25, 131, 137–38, 141–43, 151, 166, 169–70

reserves of, 138, 143

tons of, 91, 142, 151

grain exports, 126, 138

grain supplies, 137–38, 142

grain trade, 123, 125

Great Depression, 284, 331–34

great leader, 145, 224–25, 227, 230, 232–33

Great Leader Comrade, 225

Great Leader Comrade Kim Il Sung's Instructions, 233–34

Great Leap Forward, 168, 170–71, 173, 314

gross domestic product (GDP), 182, 196,

317, 333

42, 357

H

Han Chinese, 83, 179
  resettling, 83
Harvard University Press, 143, 367
heavy industry, 136, 165, 167, 181–82, 212, 223
His Life and Work, 26, 63, 366
Hitler, 35, 177, 235, 261, 283–93, 297–303, 306, 311, 354, 357
Hitler's early life, 284–85
Ho Chi Minh, 205–6, 212
The Holy Family, 50–51, 107
Hua Guofeng, 177–78
Hu Jintao, 176–77, 183–84, 187
Hundred Flowers Campaign, 167–68, 174, 176–77, 189
Hu Yaobang, 176–80

I

Il-sung, Kim, 220–27, 232, 234, 237, 364
immigrants, 47, 245, 336–38, 357
  illegal, 337–38, 358
Indians, Mayan, 28, 75, 315
industrial base, 97, 193
industrialization, 23, 126, 150, 165, 168, 210
industrialization program, 138–39
infrastructure projects, 193, 196
institutions, democratic, 321
An Introduction to Comparative Fascist Studies, 241, 248, 362
investments, foreign, 179, 213
Israeli Defense Force, 114
Italian fascism, 239, 241, 270, 276–77, 280–81
Italian government, 254, 256
Italians, 252, 255, 257, 322
Italy, 8, 16, 239, 241, 247–51, 255–59, 269, 278, 307–9, 319–20, 322, 331–32, 341–

J

Jewish boss, 292
Jewish money lenders, 27, 244
Jewish Press, 290–91
Jews, 26–27, 242–45, 251, 289–93, 308, 311–12, 314, 316, 328, 337
Jiang, 182–83, 185–87
journal de la liberté de la presse, 21, 360
Juche, 223, 227–30, 232–33
Juche Character, 229
Juche philosophy, 227–33
judicial systems, 340–41
Jung-il, Kim, 227, 229–30, 233

K

Kampf, Mein, 284–92, 298, 302, 362
Kautsky, Karl, 99–100
Keynesian economics, 240, 334
Keynesian economic theories, 331–32
Khmer Republic, 204
Khmer Rouge, 178, 201–4, 361
Kim family, 224, 230, 233
Kim Il Sung, 229–30, 233–34, 319, 363
Kim jong-il, 225, 228–33
Kim Jung Un, 330
KMT, 156–60, 162, 166, 174
KMT soldiers, 159–61
KNA (Korean National Association), 220
Korea, N., 220–22, 224, 227, 229, 309, 319–20
Korean National Association (KNA), 220
Korean War, 222, 229, 233, 235
kulaks, 123–24, 136–37, 139–42, 154, 312
Kuomintang Government, 50

L

labor, 22, 27, 29–30, 32, 34, 36–39, 41, 46–48, 56, 59–61, 63, 66–67, 78, 85, 88, 94–96, 100, 118, 121, 123, 127, 136, 166, 168, 170, 211, 235, 253–54, 258, 263, 281–82, 305, 318, 357

   child, 28, 194, 347

   division of, 30, 38, 41–42, 45–46, 76, 85, 94

labor camps, 142, 165, 203, 225

   forced, 147, 182, 237

labor unions, 136, 144, 253, 265

land, agricultural, 125, 137, 215

landless peasants, 123, 154, 222, 247, 251, 324

landlord, 10–12, 14–15, 222, 313, 318

landowners, 27, 103, 118, 120, 126–27, 158, 224, 255, 258, 328

land possession, 122, 124

land reform, 163, 206, 217, 235, 306, 364

large estates, 107, 123–25, 218

legal system, 147, 340, 348, 353

Lenin, 93, 99–102, 105–13, 116–20, 122–24, 126–32, 134–36, 141, 144, 147–48, 150–51, 154, 156, 162–63, 174, 193–94, 211, 214–15, 217, 229, 243, 251, 276, 339, 363, 366

   V.I., 113, 119–20, 126, 363

   Vladimir, 35, 46, 105, 144, 220

Lenin and Stalin, 5, 99, 136

Leningrad, 89, 316

Leninism, 107, 109, 111, 130–31, 152, 362

L'Histoiregraphe de Babeuf, 361

liberal democracy, 215, 239

liberalism, 240, 246, 264, 267, 273–74

   classic, 264

   classical, 246, 249

liberate Vietnam, 50, 205

Liberia, 31–32

liberties, 38, 81–82, 102–3, 246, 249, 264, 267, 272, 275–79, 287, 319–20

Liebknecht, Karl, 100

The Little Red Book, 172, 364

M

manifesto, 66–67, 71–72, 79, 150, 253–55

Mao, 35, 154–77, 183, 201–2, 314, 354, 361

Mao and Maoism, 5, 154

Mao and the Cultural Revolution, 172, 362

Mao's leadership, 161

Mao Zedong, 154, 162, 164–67, 169–70, 172, 175, 342, 360

Marx, 7–8, 16–17, 23, 26–43, 45–61, 63, 65, 67–69, 71, 73–74, 76, 81–86, 88, 90–102, 105–8, 110, 112, 118, 122, 126, 130, 133, 144, 147, 149–50, 156, 162–63, 174, 184–85, 187, 214, 217, 224, 227, 229, 244, 251, 269, 290, 302–3, 306, 319, 328, 344, 346, 348, 357, 359, 363

   Karl, 26–27, 30, 52–53, 55, 63, 66, 81, 92–93, 99, 149, 239, 290, 292, 364–66

   paragraph, 42

Marx and Engels, 5, 26, 66–69, 71–72, 75, 83, 90, 96, 98–99, 117, 145

Marx claims, 38, 47–48, 59

Marxism, 7, 21, 33–35, 40, 43, 61, 73, 82, 93–95, 100, 102, 107–8, 148, 162, 174, 180, 185, 187, 201, 215, 228, 256, 288–93

   interpretation of, 107, 132

   orthodox, 107, 132, 201

Marxism-Leninism, 35, 148, 150, 221, 227, 230

Marxist countries, 215

Marxist ideas, 129, 343

Marxist ideology, 40, 106, 136, 185

Marxist-Leninist, 149, 152, 201

Marxist party, 101–2, 107, 133

Marxist philosophy, 32, 34, 227–28, 288, 292

Marxists, 26, 33, 45, 95–97, 99–101, 109, 133, 179, 185, 215, 217, 241, 288, 290–92, 313, 339

Marxist societies, 40, 82

Marxist theoreticians, 34, 95

Marxist theory, 61, 82, 112, 117, 145, 185, 313

Marx's theories, 26, 33–34, 36, 61, 93, 95–96, 99–100, 112

Medieval Europe, 28, 71, 97

Memoire pour l'Entirere Abolition de la Servitude en France, 14–15, 360

military, 81, 105, 114, 116–17, 183, 194, 204, 209, 211, 253, 317, 343

military advisors, 198–99, 202

military force, 102, 159–60, 258

Ministry of Public Security (MPS), 175

money lenders, 27, 244, 328

money lending, 26, 29, 71, 191, 242–43

Monolithic Ideological System, 224

movement
  freedom of, 319, 345, 356
  revolutionary, 72, 117, 244

Movement for the Liberation of Angola (MPLA), 199, 216

MPLA (Movement for the Liberation of Angola), 199, 216

MPS (Ministry of Public Security), 175

murders, mass, 237, 315–16

Muslim populations, 336

Muslims, 204, 242, 336–37

Mussolini, 35, 247, 250–61, 275, 278, 280–81, 283, 307, 357
  Benito, 250, 254, 269, 365

Mussolini's March on Rome, 283–84

Mussolini's Rise to Power, 239, 250

N

Nafziger, George F., 1, 3, 8, 10, 12, 14, 17–367

National Academies Press, 205, 362

national bank, 70, 96, 110, 303, 345

National Character, 229

National Reunification, 229, 233–34

National Revolutionary Army (NRA), 158

National Socialist German Worker's Party, 283, 302

Native Americans, 28

Navalny, Alexei, 348–49

Nazi Party, 283–84, 293, 302, 310, 342, 357

Nazi party congress, 300–301

Nazi propaganda, 300, 354

Nazis, 276, 293, 302–3, 306, 311, 354

Nazism and Hitler, 5, 283

N.C.: Duke University Press, 107, 111, 130, 362

neo-colonialism, 193–95, 198, 363

New Economic Policy (NEP), 125, 138

New People's Party, 221

New World, 8, 92

New York, 11–12, 15, 26, 39, 43, 52, 66, 122, 139, 182, 203–4, 239, 269, 323, 325, 334, 336, 347, 360, 362, 364–66

New York City, 335, 341

New York Daily Tribune, 361

New York Stock Exchange, 331, 334

NGOs (nongovernment organizations), 347

Non-German newspapers, 295, 299, 304

non-Germans, 294–95, 300, 304

nongovernment organizations (NGOs), 347

North America, 60, 92

North American Indians, 74–75

North Caucasus, 144

Northern Italy, 62, 259

North Korean Army, 236

North Korean Christians, 234

North Koreans, 79, 222–24, 226–27, 229–37, 316

North Vietnam, 201, 207, 302

North Vietnamese, 201, 206–7

NRA (National Revolutionary Army), 158

O

October Revolution, 156, 220

Ogaden War, 198–99

On Utopia and Scientific Socialism, 119–20, 126

Original Revolutionary Policy, 228–33

The Origin of the Family, 73, 75, 93, 362

Oxford University Press, 122, 139, 169, 205, 361, 366

P

Paris, 7, 12–15, 16, 19, 21, 24, 66, 81, 83, 109, 242, 311, 336, 360–65

parliament, political central, 296, 301, 306

Partner or Exploiter, 191–98, 365

party members, 144, 164, 181, 204, 224

Paxton, R.O., 239, 269, 276–78

Peasant Rebels Under Stalin, 122–23, 139, 366

peasantry, 81, 99, 101, 118, 120, 123, 125–26, 138–39, 141, 161, 201, 206, 224, 317–19, 322

peasants, 19, 22–23, 28, 48–49, 57, 81–82, 101, 103, 106, 108, 110, 112, 118–20, 122–27, 131–32, 136–39, 141–43, 145, 155, 157–60, 163, 170, 174, 203, 206, 221, 298, 318–20, 364

Peasant War, 319

People's Liberation Army, 184, 194

People's Republic, 162, 172, 175, 200, 334, 354

People's Republic of China (PRC), 162, 175–76, 200, 334, 354

The People's Will, 103

personal property, 16, 69–70, 237

Philosophic Manuscripts, 37

philosophy, internationalist, 92, 102, 290

Philosophy of Poverty, 41

Pike, D., 207–8, 211, 365

Poland, 51, 131–32, 245, 249, 307–8

police, secret, 146, 308, 315

police officers, 116, 211

police state, 186, 189

Policy Paper, 192

Political Economy of China's Great Leap Famine, 170, 363

political elites, 238

political enemies, 147, 248

political independence, 229

political indoctrination, 115, 307

political organization, 259, 268

political parties, 68–69, 176, 208–9, 216, 255–56, 265, 290, 322, 342

political philosophies, 26, 246, 302, 344

political prisoners, 148, 176, 234, 348

Politics and Policy Implementation in China's Great Leap, 169, 361

Politics in North Korea, 221, 361

post-World War I, 269, 339

The Poverty of Philosophy, 28, 30, 53, 55–56, 59, 85, 87, 92, 365

PRC. *See* People's Republic of China

Pre-Korean War Stage, 221, 361

press, free, 355

prices, selling, 62–64

private interests, 269, 278, 281

private property, 38, 40, 68–69, 73, 75–76, 93, 127, 152, 175, 185, 218, 246, 275–76, 301, 344, 347

   abolition of, 69, 303, 344

   ownership of, 321–22

Private Property and the State, 73, 362

production, industrial, 70, 170, 223, 305, 347

proletariat, 49–50, 58, 66–69, 71–73, 78, 106, 122–23, 127, 150, 155, 157, 186, 201, 302

Propaganda Department, 186, 354

property owners, 298, 341

property ownership, 36, 322
Proudhon, M., 30, 55, 85–87, 93
Prussia, 8, 131–32, 319

R

Red army, 138, 146, 150, 160–62, 312
re-education, 147, 173, 182, 203, 210–11, 308
Regimes, Kim, 235, 260
religion, 7–8, 40–41, 81–83, 94, 212, 246, 263, 269, 275, 290, 308
religious freedom, 83, 176
rente foncière, 12
rente foncière seigneurial, 10, 12
republics, democratic, 205, 313
revolutionary bourgeoisie, 50, 150
revolutionary government, 16, 81
rice bowl, 181–82, 187
rights
 civil, 147, 352
 feudal, 21–23
 natural, 272, 275, 277
Rivers Editors, 220, 223, 233, 365
Robespierre, Maximilian, 17–18, 20, 81
Roman Empire, new, 250, 253, 255, 257
Roman law, 12, 294
RSDLP (Russian Social Democratic Labor Party), 133–34
Russia, 8, 42–43, 50, 89, 91, 102–5, 107–9, 113, 118, 120, 122, 131–32, 145, 152, 155, 190–91, 193, 243, 247, 299, 312, 317–22, 324, 348–49
Russian army, 104–5, 113–14, 134
Russian Civil War, 50, 126, 146
Russian communist party, 102, 134, 313
Russian economy, 110, 252
Russian government, 106, 349
Russian peasants, 103, 243, 319
Russian people, 105, 318

Russian population, 122, 317
Russian Revolution, 35, 103, 108, 118, 150, 243, 251, 317
Russian revolutionary movement, 107, 130
Russians, 89, 102, 105, 119, 131–32, 153–55, 199, 312
Russian Social Democratic Labor Party (RSDLP), 133–34
Russian socialists, 102, 108
Russian society, 104, 108
Russian word, 108
Russian Young Communist League, 119, 126

S

school for Socialism, 68–69, 95
Secretan, E., 10–11, 13–15, 365
Selected Works of Mao Tse-tung, 313–14
serfs, 10, 14–15, 23, 49, 65, 318–19, 321
slavery, 23, 76, 92–93, 115, 131, 277, 317
slaves, 24, 49, 65, 95, 103, 119, 198, 235
Social Darwinism, 248
Social Democracy, 155, 286–87, 289–90, 292
Social Democratic, 100, 291
Social Democratic Party, 101, 244, 288, 291
social democrats, 101, 131, 287–91, 293
socialism, 7, 56, 68, 81, 94–95, 99, 103, 107, 109, 111–12, 131, 134–35, 142, 152, 155, 157, 207, 210, 215, 223, 230–33, 252, 265, 274–75, 283–84, 293, 296, 299, 301, 313, 320–23, 343, 361
 school for, 68–69, 95
socialist economy, 217, 229–30
socialist groups, 81, 250, 349, 351
socialist ideology, 230–31
socialist movement, 35, 83, 99, 265
Socialist Party, 250, 257–58
socialist revolution, 114, 135, 152, 207

socialist society, 94, 111, 134–35, 162, 220, 230–32

society, 10, 24, 27–28, 36–42, 45–46, 56, 58, 65–66, 68–69, 75, 78–79, 84–86, 93–94, 96–98, 109, 112–13, 119–20, 122, 127, 135, 144, 149, 152, 156, 162, 166, 172, 175, 179, 184, 209, 224, 228, 230, 245, 248, 268–73, 276–77, 281, 317, 320, 324, 327–29, 336–37, 339, 347, 349, 355

  feudal, 29, 65–66, 150, 317

solitary confinement, 212, 349–52

Soros, George, 71, 347

South Africa, 195–96

South Korea, 221–22, 229, 319

South Korean, 222, 236–37

South Vietnam, 201, 207, 210

South Vietnamese, 207–8, 210–11

Soviet Army, 152, 220

Soviet authorities, 143–44, 152

Soviet citizens, 91, 147

Soviet Communist, 310

Soviet economy, 136, 151

soviet government, 123–24, 137, 139, 141, 143–44, 147, 160, 243

Soviet gulags, 132, 168

Soviet invasion, 131, 151

Soviet Involvement in Sub-Saharan Africa, 199–200, 361

Soviet military advisors, 158, 199

Soviet officials, 143

Soviet of Workers' Deputies, 110, 112

Soviet penal system, 148, 362

Soviet power, 138, 143

Soviet Repression Statistics, 147, 361

Soviet Russia, 125, 138, 244

soviets, 51, 91, 105–6, 112, 132, 135, 139, 142, 147–48, 151, 157, 165, 169, 198–200, 220–21, 312–13, 354

Soviet society, 147

Soviet state, 124, 126, 132, 144, 147

Soviet system, 45, 147, 151, 155, 312, 348

Soviet Union, 18, 83, 88–89, 91, 94, 114, 126, 134–36, 138, 141–43, 145–48, 151–52, 154–55, 157, 165–68, 180, 188, 198–99, 206, 220, 223, 312, 314, 317, 319, 331, 348, 354, 364, 367

  former, 44–45, 150

Spain, 8, 187, 307–9

Spargo, J., 26–27, 51, 63, 66, 68–69, 73, 81–83, 92, 366

SPD, 101–2, 244

speech

  free, 252, 315, 355–56

  freedom of, 168, 176, 246, 260, 308

SRVN government, 212–13

Stalin, Joseph, 35, 45–46, 83, 99, 110, 127, 132–36, 138–39, 141–51, 154, 158, 165–67, 169, 187, 211, 221, 223, 307, 364, 366

starvation, mass, 142, 168, 237

State and Revolution, 112–13, 117, 363

Statistics of North Korean Democide Estimates, 235, 365

steel production, 169

Swedish culture, 336

Switzerland, 10–11, 13–15, 105, 109, 269, 311, 365

system, centralized planning, 91

T

Tanzania-Zambia Railroad, 196

The Tasks of the Youth Leagues, 119, 126–27, 363

teaching Marxist theory, 46, 59

The Theoretical System of Karl Marx, 33

Third All-Russian Congress, 119, 126

Three-Anti and Five-Anti Movements in Communist China, 164, 361

Three-Antis Campaign, 164

Tibet, 83, 163, 178–79, 192, 200–201

Tibidabo Publishing, 255–56

totalitarian governments, 321–22, 327–28

totalitarian government systems, 323, 325

totalitarianism, 317–18, 323–25

trade credits, 199

tradespeople, 142, 254, 294, 297, 303

Trades Union movement, 288–89

trade unions, 68–69, 95, 154, 156–57, 209, 256, 258, 288–91

Treaty of Versailles, 132, 240, 244–45, 249, 293, 332–33

Trotsky, Leon, 35, 105–6, 127, 129, 134–35, 146, 150–51, 163, 243, 251, 366

U

Ukraine, 45, 141–44, 169, 310, 312, 362

Ukrainians, 45, 141, 144, 313

UMAP (Units to Aid Production), 216

UN forces, 163, 222, 236

unions, 11, 67–69, 95, 138, 145, 260, 289, 293, 317

United Nations, 141, 191, 351

United States, 32, 49, 57, 88, 115, 191, 213, 219, 229, 239, 248, 300, 319, 327, 331–32, 337, 340, 342–43, 347–48, 350, 354, 357–59

The Universal Aspects of Fascism, 245, 268–71, 273, 281, 360

U.S. citizens, 338, 349

U.S. debt, 333–34

U.S. economy, 331, 334, 338

U.S. population, 339

USSR, 44, 51, 91, 112, 148, 151–52, 168, 199–201, 220, 299–300, 302, 308, 310, 312, 317

V

VC. *See* Viet Cong

VCP. *See* Vietnamese communist party

Venezuela, 43, 51, 217–19, 307–9

Victims of Mao Zedong's Era, 173, 366

Vienna, 285–86, 288, 290–91

Viet Cong (VC), 207–8, 210, 212

The Viet-Cong Strategy of Terror, 207, 365

Viet Minh, 205–7

Vietnam, 50, 178, 193, 205–9, 213, 307–8, 318, 320, 367

N., 308–9

Vietnamese communist party (VCP), 50, 207, 212

Vietnam's economy, 213

Vietnam War, 171, 207, 210, 297, 302, 360

W

War I Germany, 337, 342

western Europe, 102, 108, 135, 243, 247

Workers Party, 221–22

Workers' Party, 222

Workers' Party of Korea, 222, 228

World Bank, 193, 196, 213

World War I, 101, 104, 240–41, 243–45, 247–48, 250, 256, 269, 293, 297, 335, 341

outbreak of, 100, 250

World War II, 176, 243, 260, 332

Y

Yale University Genocide Studies Program, 203, 361

Young Communist League, 119, 126

Z

Zambia, 196–98

Zambians, 197–98

Zambia's economy, 196–97

[Created with **TExtract** / www.TExtract.com]

George Nafziger

www.ingramcontent.com/pod-product-compliance
Lightning Source LLC
Chambersburg PA
CBHW061248230426
43663CB00022B/2948